The Search for Environmental Justice

THE IUCN ACADEMY OF ENVIRONMENTAL LAW SERIES

Series Editors: Kurt Deketelaere, *University of Leuven, Leuven, Belgium* and Zen Makuch, *Imperial College, London, UK*

As environmental law increases in importance as an area of legal research, this series brings together some of the most current research carried out by the IUCN Academy of Environmental Law, a global network of environmental law scholars. Each volume in the series addresses an important issue in the field and presents original research analysis and assessment, along with a much-needed synthesis of the state of environmental law. Directions as to the positive role that environmental law can play at a global level are also emphasized. This series provides essential reading for scholars throughout the world with an interest in cutting edge environment-related issues, and will no doubt play an important role in shaping future debate.

Titles in this series include:

Environmental Governance and Sustainability
Edited by Paul Martin, Li Zhiping, Qin Tianbao, Anel Du Plessis, Yves Le Bouthillier and Angela Williams

Poverty Alleviation and Environmental Law
Edited by Yves Le Bouthillier, Miriam Alfie Cohen, Jose Juan Gonzalez Marquez, Albert Mumma and Susan Smith

Local Climate Change Law
Environmental Regulation in Cities and Other Localities
Edited by Benjamin J. Richardson

Biodiversity and Climate Change
Linkages at International, National and Local Levels
Edited by Frank Maes, An Cliquet, Willemien du Plessis and Heather McLeod-Kilmurray

Global Environmental Law at a Crossroads
Edited by Robert V. Percival, Jolene Lin and William Piermattei

Water and the Law
Towards Sustainability
Edited by Michael Kidd, Loretta Feris, Tumai Murombo and Alejandro Iza

The Search for Environmental Justice
Edited by Paul Martin, Sadeq Z. Bigdeli, Trevor Daya-Winterbottom, Willemien du Plessis and Amanda Kennedy

The Search for Environmental Justice

Edited by

Paul Martin

Professor, University of New England, Armidale NSW, Australia

Sadeq Z. Bigdeli

Senior Lecturer, University of Waikato, New Zealand

Trevor Daya-Winterbottom

Senior Lecturer, University of Waikato, New Zealand

Willemien du Plessis

Professor, North-West University, South Africa

Amanda Kennedy

Associate Professor, University of New England, Armidale NSW, Australia

With the support of New Zealand Law Foundation

THE IUCN ACADEMY OF ENVIRONMENTAL LAW SERIES

Edward Elgar
PUBLISHING

Cheltenham, UK • Northampton, MA, USA

Published by
Edward Elgar Publishing Limited
The Lypiatts
15 Lansdown Road
Cheltenham
Glos GL50 2JA
UK

Edward Elgar Publishing, Inc.
William Pratt House
9 Dewey Court
Northampton
Massachusetts 01060
USA

A catalogue record for this book
is available from the British Library

Library of Congress Control Number: 2015935870

This book is available electronically in the **Elgar**online
Law subject collection
DOI 10.4337/9781784719425

FSC www.fsc.org MIX Paper from responsible sources FSC® C013056

ISBN 978 1 78471 941 8 (cased)
ISBN 978 1 78471 942 5 (eBook)

Typeset by Servis Filmsetting Ltd, Stockport, Cheshire
Printed and bound in Great Britain by T.J. International Ltd, Padstow

Contents

PART III IMPLEMENTATION CHALLENGES OF ENVIRONMENTAL JUSTICE

PART IV RECOGNITION OF INDIGENOUS PEOPLES' INTERESTS

Contributors

Johnnie Aseron has had 25 years' experience of research, writing and working in and with First Nations communities in education, community development and wellness initiatives. He is currently the International Indigenous Research Liaison, Oorala Aboriginal Centre, University of New England, Australia.

Dr Sadeq Z. Bigdeli is a Senior Lecturer at the Te Piringa–Faculty of Law, University of Waikato, New Zealand. His area of research is the intersection of trade, development and environmental law and policy.

Professor Klaus Bosselmann is the Director of the New Zealand Centre for Environmental Law at the University of Auckland, New Zealand. His areas of specialisation are international environmental law, sustainability governance and environmental constitutionalism.

Christopher Chaulk began studying law after conducting English education and environmental awareness projects in Albania with the United States Peace Corps. He has also worked for the NGO Sierra Club and the chemical trade association American Chemistry Council.

Dr Joel I. Colón-Ríos is Senior Lecturer at the Faculty of Law, Victoria University of Wellington, New Zealand. His areas of research are constitutional and democratic theory, comparative constitutional law, and Latin American constitutionalism.

Professor Donna Craig is Professor of International, Comparative and National Environmental Law and Policy at the University of Western Sydney, Australia. Previously she was the co-director at the Macquarie University Centre for Environmental law.

Trevor Daya-Winterbottom is Senior Lecturer in the Faculty of Law at the University of Waikato, New Zealand.

Professor Willemien du Plessis is Director of the Research Unit of the Faculty of Law, North-West University, Potchefstroom Campus, South Africa. Her areas of specialisation are environmental law and governance, land law and African customary law.

Ben France-Hudson is a lecturer at the University of Canterbury, New Zealand and is completing a PhD through the University of Otago. His research focuses on the law of private property, with a particular focus on natural resources and land law.

Dr Elizabeth Gachenga is a lecturer at Strathmore Law School and Associate Dean of the School of Management and Commerce at Strathmore University, Kenya. Her research areas of interest include: natural resource governance, climate change, legal ethics, biosafety and business law.

Justice Susan Glazebrook is a judge of the Supreme Court of New Zealand.

Lee Godden is a Professor at the Centre for Resources, Energy and Environmental law at Melbourne Law School, Melbourne University, Australia. Her foci are environmental law, water law and climate change. She has undertaken international comparative research on climate change and its biodiversity impacts.

Neyooxet Greymorning is Professor of Anthropology and Native American Studies at the University of Montana, USA and has been named three times (1999, 2004, 2005) to Who's Who Among America's College and University Teachers. Trained in the fields of linguistic and political anthropology, he earned his PhD from the University of Oklahoma in 1992 and began his academic career at the University of Alberta. Since joining the faculty at Montana in 1994, he has also lectured as a visiting scholar at Southern Cross University, Australia (in 1997, 1998, 1999, 2003, 2007, 2009, 2010, 2011) and served as the Acting Director of the Indigenous Governance Programs at the University of Victoria in British Columbia, Canada in 2001–2002.

Ramesh Karky holds an SJD from Golden Gate USA and LLM from VUB, Belgium. He was a Postdoctoral Fellow (2010–13), Visiting Professor of Int'l Trade Regulation (2013) and intellectual property teacher (2012) at Western University, Canada; International Expert Consultant (2006–09); and has expertise in biotech law, intellectual property law, international trade (WTO) law and international law.

Amelia Keene graduated with an LLM from Columbia University in 2013 on the New Zealand Law Foundation Ethel Benjamin Scholarship. She specialises in international law and environmental law. She currently clerks at the International Court of Justice, the Netherlands.

Dr Amanda Kennedy is the Deputy Director of the Australian Centre for Agriculture and Law at the University of New England, Australia. Her research interests are in the areas of environmental justice and land use governance.

Josi Khatarina is a senior legal specialist in the Indonesia Reducing Emissions from Deforestation and Forest Degradation (REDD+) Agency. Her areas of specialisation are environmental law and legal aspect of forest and peat land governance.

Professor Paul Martin is the Director of the Australian Centre for Agriculture and Law at the University of New England, Australia. His areas of specialisation are natural resource governance and rural social justice.

Emily O'Connell is an environmental lawyer and was previously Principal Lawyer and Executive Officer of the Environmental Defender's Office, Northern Territory, Australia. Emily is passionate about community education and knowledge, Indigenous land rights and earth justice.

Mark Perry is Professor of Law at the University of New England, Australia and Emeritus Professor of Computer Science, and of Law, at Western University, Canada. His research focuses on the nexus of law and science, bringing him a global reputation from his speaking and writing in both disciplines.

Wanida Phromlah has extensive experience in taxation law and forest governance system. She has lectured at the Faculty of Law, Mahasarakham University, Thailand for almost ten years.

The Hon. Justice Brian J. Preston SC is the Chief Judge of the Land and Environment Court of New South Wales, Australia; Adjunct Professor at the University of Sydney, Australia; Chair of LAWASIA's Environmental Law Committee. He is the author of 80 articles and book chapters on environmental law.

Vernon Rive is a Senior Lecturer in Law at AUT Law School, Auckland, New Zealand. He teaches and researches public law, environmental law and international environmental law, specialising in climate change mitigation and adaptation.

Dr Justin Gregory Rose is an environmental law researcher and practitioner whose contributions to government, civil society and academia have spanned numerous jurisdictions and areas of environmental concern. He has, since 1998, specialised in Pacific island law.

Mas Achmad Santosa is the Deputy Head of the President Delivery Unit for Development Monitoring and Oversight (UKP4), Indonesia. His areas of specialisation are environmental law, forest and peat land governance and law enforcement.

Aldilla Stephanie Suwana is a legal specialist in the Indonesia Reducing Emissions from Deforestation and Forest Degradation (REDD+) Agency. Her area of specialisation is legal aspect of forest and peat land governance.

Professor Anastasia Telesetsky teaches international environmental law at the College of Law in the Natural Resources and Environmental Law Program, University of Idaho, USA. She focuses on ecological restoration and climate adaptation.

Dr Jacqueline Williams is a senior researcher of the Australian Centre for Agriculture and Law at the University of New England, Australia. Her research interests include natural resource management, governance, social justice and sustainable agriculture.

Preface

Environmental justice is a massive topic. Justice itself means different things to different scholars, and the 'environmental' descriptor adds new dimensions. Notably considering the environmental dimension adds the possibility that non-humans may have rights that should be given legal status, and that human interests in the natural world may give rise to unique jurisprudential considerations. Our aim with this book has been to provide a window into treatments of this topic that are of interest to scholars within the environmental law academy of the IUCN. We do not pretend that this group of academics have a unified perception of the scope of environmental justice or the evolving jurisprudence within it. Virtually any sub-topic of environmental justice covered in this edition can easily justify a complete book. Our ambition with this book is to introduce the reader to the diversity and richness of scholarship in this fascinating and strengthening field of investigation. Even given this limited aim, we know that there are dimensions of the topic that we have not touched upon.

The book is divided into four parts, though such subdivision is artificial because many themes and issues are interwoven through the chapters.

1. Part I (Framing the search for environmental justice) considers perspectives of scholars and judges upon the fundamental nature of environmental justice.
2. Part II (Rights-based conceptualisations) takes a pragmatic perspective on the ways in which human interests are being pursued through legal rights, and the implications of this for environmental justice.
3. Part III (Implementation challenges of environmental justice) considers the ways in which approaches to environment governance are (or are not) embracing the concept of environmental justice.
4. The final Part (Recognition of indigenous peoples' interests) is focused upon indigenous issues and approaches.

1. The search for environmental justice

Paul Martin, Sadeq Z. Bigdeli, Trevor Daya-Winterbottom, Willemien du Plessis and Amanda Kennedy

INTRODUCTION

Environmental law in the 20th century emerged from a growing awareness of the increasing harms to the physical world, and thus to the interests of human beings, from the impacts of technology, industry and growing populations. The legal instruments used were principally regulatory, relying upon the powers exercised by states over corporations and citizens within their jurisdictions. Many developments have altered the nature of the challenges and thus the focus and methods of environmental law. This has generated many instruments and strategies, starting with the explosion of environmental regulation last century, and then the use of market instruments and industry and civil society initiatives.

Part of the process has been a realisation that accumulating environmental harms can prejudice ecosystems, and jeopardise the health and welfare of people. There has been a growing awareness that those directly dependent upon natural systems, particularly Indigenous peoples, are often those most threatened. There is an increasing recognition that nation-state governance systems are often insufficiently effective, particularly in recognition of and respect for the interests of the less powerful. As a result the ideal of environmental justice has become an important concern. Gradually justice concepts are becoming part of the political narrative of international and national environmental law.

Frequently in the early stages of development of social innovation there are competing paradigms.[1] The political banner 'environmental justice' denotes many different ideas, generally pursuing an ideal of improving fairness in how natural resources are used and shared, and how the costs

1 Kuhn's 'preparadigmatic' initial stage of innovation revolutions. Kuhn (1996).

of doing so (including the costs of preserving these resources) are allocated. Characteristic of the different versions of environmental justice is a political belief in the necessity of protecting the vulnerable, whether that vulnerability is of nature itself in the face of industrial power, or of people who have a special dependency upon nature.

Different 'voices' – judicial, philosophical, jurisprudential and community oriented – speak of these issues, but focus upon different aspects and use different arguments. Some focus upon esoteric concerns of jurisprudence and philosophies of social justice and environmentalism; others are concerned with issues of national and international legal doctrine; others are occupied with the practical and conceptual challenges of implementation; and still others focus upon the capacity of the community and governments, policymakers and environmental law scholars to effectively address the fundamental challenges within the search for environmental justice. The chapters in this book support a view that the term 'environmental justice' is, in the famous categorisation of Professor Stone, 'a category of concealed multiple reference': the term embraces many different, often competing, meanings that co-exist in the same scholarly 'space'. Resolution of the difference is a priority only when a specific situation is to be adjudicated or an applied policy decision to be made.[2] There are at least three basic approaches to environmental injustice: a humanistic one based upon recognition of specific human interests in the environment; a more radical advocacy of rights of the environment *per se*; and composites where the recognition of human rights implies protecting natural systems. Whilst such distinctions may appear esoteric, how these discourses are resolved has implications for laws and constitutions, court processes and judicial interpretation, community capacity and the operation of the complete environment governance system.

The broad and evolving concept of environmental justice was the theme for the 11th Annual Colloquium of the International Union for Conservation of Nature (IUCN) Academy of Environmental Law, hosted by the University of Waikato and the University of New England in Hamilton, New Zealand, from 24–28 June 2013. This book presents selected papers from the Colloquium, representing the diversity and richness of the environment and justice scholarship and practice.

We intend that this book advance the shared ideals, without creating a

---

[2] A category of concealed multiple reference exists when a legal term can simultaneously denote or connote different meanings for different uses. In environmental law, terms like 'sustainability', 'precaution' or 'environmental justice' are illustrative. See Stone (1964) 246–8.

misleading sense that the pursuit of environmental justice draws upon a unified field of knowledge, or even unified values about the environment or human interests. The search for environmental justice is characterised by significant differences in what the searchers are aiming to discover through the quest. These differences are partly due to different perspectives from the developed and the developing world, and between authors with different world views or from different jurisdictional backgrounds. This will result in them following different pathways that sometimes will cross, but often will not. The extent to which this heterogeneity of goals and strategies is counter-productive is something for the readers of this book to judge.

The book is structured under four themes: framing the search for environmental justice, rights-based approaches, assessing current approaches to environmental governance, and Indigenous issues and approaches to environmental justice. However, many chapters span different themes.

FRAMING THE SEARCH FOR ENVIRONMENTAL JUSTICE

In the first Part perspectives on the fundamental nature of environmental justice are explored. The volume begins with a dissection of the legal elements required for environmental justice in Justice Preston's chapter 'The effectiveness of the law in providing access to environmental justice'. This chapter proposes that only by achieving distributional justice, procedural justice and justice as recognition together can true environmental justice be achieved. This structure helps to frame many of the chapters that follow. He highlights how existing statutory arrangements privilege consumption and consumption interests over non-human nature and future generations. This chapter links concepts of justice developed through administrative and environmental law, to concepts of 'the rights of nature', and 'rights to nature' that are core concepts of environmental justice.

Many readers will be familiar with distributive justice, which is concerned with fair sharing of environmental benefits and burdens.[3] Justice Preston discusses three fundamental constituents of environmental distributive justice: membership of the 'community of justice', the nature of the benefits and burdens to be distributed and the principles and criteria for distribution. He highlights that both environmental benefits and burdens are subject to distribution through law, and points to the

---

[3] Adopting the Rawlsian concept of justice as fairness. See Rawls (2001).

law's failure to include nature and future generations within the relevant community to be considered.

Procedural justice is concerned with how decisions are made and by whom, and who has power or influence over such decisions. The need for procedural fairness and public participation is increasingly reflected in international instruments; however, he highlights that few jurisdictions go beyond minimum standards. Justice Preston explains that procedural reforms, alongside recognition of broader interests, are essential to distributive justice in practice.

Justice Preston discusses the social and political 'non-recognition' and 'mis-recognition' of interest groups that intersects with legal concerns. Both recognition failures involve ignoring or discounting groups whose interests are non-consumptive. Issues of non-recognition, mal-recognition and rights, when considered together, suggest a link between human rights and environmental sustainability, but he points out that recognition of the rights of current humans can conflict with the interests of the environment itself. This raises a challenging concern of potential conflicts between 'rights of nature' and 'rights to nature', particularly the interests of less privileged and indigenous peoples.

Bosselmann's chapter, 'The rule of law in the Anthropocene', draws from ecology, history and philosophy to argue for radically different fundamental principles of law from those that currently prevail, enabling humanity to respond to the Anthropocene epoch. This term highlights that we have entered a period where the natural world is fundamentally shaped by humans, rather than by natural or geological forces.[4] The chapter points to the necessity of a strong 'rule of law' for sustainability (specifically prioritising the integrity of ecosystems). Bosselmann argues that this requires acceptance within the law of collective self-restraint as essential to human survival. His approach integrates competing principles that are woven into the other chapters of this book. Some authors consider principles of environmental justice based upon human 'rights to nature' (framing environmental justice as a form of social justice), and others, such as Justice Preston, propose the recognition of the 'rights of nature' (investing nature with legal personality). Bosselmann prioritises human values but makes the protection of nature a central principle in protecting those values. He suggests that 'ecological sustainability' is a reason-based Kantian 'Grundnorm' which must qualify any legal norm, including the rule of law.

Framing the discourse of environmental justice is the likelihood that

4 Coined by Crutzen and Stoermer (2000) 17–18; Crutzen (2002) 23.

environmental justice issues become relevant when adjudicating competing claims to use or govern nature. Two fundamental questions emerge from the dialectic: what is the status of the interests of nature relative to the interests of humans; and within the human community what is the relative status of different categories of humans? In relation to this second question, it is important to recognise that there is also competition between the interests of industrial humans, 'traditional' users of primary resources such as farmers and fishers, between current and future generations and between Indigenous persons with their special claims and relationships, and other human members of the community.

Godden and O'Connell's chapter 'Biodiversity justice in a climate change world: offsetting the future', links the doctrinal and philosophical frameworks of the first two chapters to one instrumental approach, the use of environmental offsets. This chapter outlines the philosophical basis of offsetting, and its practical operation with native vegetation offsets in Victoria, Australia. The authors analyse offsets and climate change adaptation, exploring how offsetting might facilitate development without stemming biodiversity loss. There is limited evidence-based assessment of these tools, and a number of distributive justice issues are implicit in the approach. The authors suggest that schemes that allow current losses to be offset by future restoration raise issues of intergenerational equity. The argument reinforces the non-recognition and distributional justice concerns discussed in the two preceding chapters.

The chapter highlights the scientific and value judgement complexities, the risks of which seem not to be reflected in current processes. The authors argue that management of trade-offs over the life of the offset is insufficiently considered. The assumption of fungibility that underpins market mechanisms ignores differences in human values, and, within a 'rights of nature' conceptualisation of environmental justice, that species themselves can have different imputed values. Assumptions of equivalence between ecosystems thus need to be reconsidered, taking into account diverse values and future conditions, and the unpredictability of responses to climate change.

All these issues lead the authors to suggest that offsetting instruments result in an inter-temporal injustice. Whereas Preston highlights spatial distribution issues, Godden and O'Connell highlight inter-temporal distribution as the pivotal concern. They suggest that insufficient incorporation of climate change adaptation requirements further privileges current users over future generations and nature.

RIGHTS-BASED CONCEPTUALISATIONS

Environmental justice exists at the intersection between environmental law and the pursuit of social justice. Central to the pursuit of social justice is the development and implementation of legal rights, particularly of the vulnerable to be protected and to share in the opportunities of society. Overall, the chapters by Glazebrook, France-Hudson and Colón-Ríos bring together the various themes articulated by rights-based approaches to environmental law: human rights, Indigenous rights, and property rights.[5]

Justice Glazebrook argues for a specific human right to the environment in the chapter 'Human rights and the environment'. Whilst some rights related to the environment exist in some constitutions, a general human right to a quality environment has not been widely adopted. If there is a coincidence between a pre-existing human right and the environment, courts have been more likely to protect environmental qualities, but in practice such opportunities are limited. Justice Glazebrook suggests that the failure to widely adopt rights to a quality environment is because procedural rights are politically more acceptable. She suggests that participation rights, particularly based on customary international law, may be a more promising avenue for reform. She argues that rights to participate and substantive rights must be tightly linked for an effective approach. The arguments in favour of an explicit human right to a quality environment include: giving greater prominence to the environment; directly addressing the needs of people who are vulnerable to environmental degradation; and explicitly requiring consideration of trade-offs between human and environmental considerations in public decision making. In part the argument for a human right to the environment is found in considerations of environmental human health, and Indigenous people's rights and interests. She discusses the benefits of such a human right for environmentally displaced persons, with these issues being discussed in later chapters.

Justice Glazebrook considers the counter arguments, to help frame a viable human right to a quality environment. She highlights that the right should reflect a notion of guardianship for future generations, to counter the argument that present frameworks emphasise the present generation with little intergenerational recognition. Decoupling a right to the environment from sustainable development will ensure that the balance

---

[5] See also: Shelton (2009) 91; Whata (2013); and Sian Elias 'Righting Environmental Justice' 12th Salmon Lecture, 25 July 2014.

between protection and development will be contested. The design she proposes suggests a vision of the right close to Bosselmann's formulation, where a human right to the environment incorporates the environment as having an indirect 'quasi-right'. This approach is founded on the Maori concept of 'kaitiakitanga' or guardianship incorporated into New Zealand environmental law as a principle for policy and plan preparation, and resource allocation and use decisions.[6]

In their discussion of the use of market instruments (specifically offsets) Preston, Godden and O'Connell reflect scepticism about market instruments, notwithstanding their support in economic theory, their attractiveness to policy-makers and evidence of their effectiveness in some situations.[7] France-Hudson considers a particular version of emissions trading, 'no private property rights in the atmosphere', and arrives at a positive view of that scheme. He argues that the New Zealand Emissions Trading Scheme (NZETS), whilst relying upon tradeable entitlements, creates neither a private property right nor a right to pollute. Emission remains *prima facie* unlawful. It attracts substantial economic or possibly criminal penalties, unless the emitter surrenders a (tradeable) emissions unit equivalent to that pollution and that this avoids negative effects of offsetting through tradeable entitlements. Reading this chapter alongside the earlier critiques of environmental offsets suggests that it may be naïve to arrive at broad conclusions about the social justice consequences of market instruments as a broad category. Technical details and implementation arrangements within the social and economic context of particular jurisdictions will largely determine effectiveness in environmental terms and fairness in social terms.

Colón-Ríos provides insights into the practical operation of a substantive right to nature in 'On the theory and practice of the rights of nature'. This links abstract consideration about possible rights of nature to the implementation of such rights frameworks. The chapter points out that more than 100 national constitutions have versions of human rights to the environment. Ecuador was the first country to formally embed rights to nature itself in its 2008 Constitution. This framework provides legal mechanisms for those rights to be enforced. Nature is given equal legal status to humans. The regime was tested in the case of the Vilcambamba River. Whilst widening the road a government agency deposited rocks, sand, gravel, and trees into the river. Legal action was taken to require

---

6 See: Resource Management Act 1991 (New Zealand), s 7(a).

7 This evidence is far from definitive. Many market-based interventions, like many regulatory interventions, have not been effective; e.g. Shortle (2012).

remediation, on the basis of the interest of the river. The action exposed many legal complexities. Ultimately the court found on behalf of nature (the river) and required remediation and a public apology. The remedy has only been partly implemented, suggesting practical problems associated with a legal right. This chapter takes a perspective on the extension of rights to non-human creatures different to both Bosselmann and Preston. There is a complex issue of ethnocentrism versus nature-centrism or eco-centrism involved in this discussion. The Vilcambamba case highlights that most cases concerning the rights of nature involve the balancing of the rights of nature and the rights of humans, and determining within these categories which particular human or non-human interests will be recognised and how. Referring to earlier chapters this suggests that resolution of apparently esoteric arguments will be ultimately important in determining real-world environmental justice outcomes. A critical insight from Colón-Ríos in relation to this issue is the need for clearly articulated (procedural, recognitional) rules about standing to give effect to rights for nature.

Ecuador highlights the complicated balancing and trade-offs likely to arise if rights of nature are legally incorporated, as suggested by a number of authors. As the class of rights holders expands, and the rights they hold become more diverse, there is a practical problem of effectiveness and efficiency for the legal system. This problem is likely to become more pronounced. A question this raises is whether this may ultimately undermine public confidence in the legal system, or at least in this aspect of environmental justice. Could our pursuit of abstract social justice goals result in an intellectually elegant but dysfunctional system? Clearly, in the search for environmental justice it is essential to marry esoteric and pragmatic considerations. Even successfully advancing the political case for environmental rights will be insufficient to ensuring genuine beneficial impacts are achieved if implementation gives rise to high transaction costs, confusion, and erratic implementation. This is a significant, and probably under-appreciated, challenge to the academic community.

IMPLEMENTATION CHALLENGES OF ENVIRONMENTAL JUSTICE

The third theme explores how environmental governance is (or is not) embracing environmental justice. Chapters under this theme consider policy innovation responses to (often contentious) environmental issues including the institutional structures to give effect to legal principles and philosophical values. Mirroring the first theme, the chapters highlight implementation difficulties, but also opportunities, in attempting to pursue any version of environmental justice, and the inevitability of political dynamics in the pursuit of environmental justice.

The first two chapters consider a challenge shared by two jurisdictions within the same region, highlighting common governance challenges in the pursuit of environment of justice in Southeast Asia. In 'REDD+ implementation in Thailand: legal and institutional challenges', Phromlah and Martin diagnose the reforms needed in Thailand, whilst Santosa, Khatarina and Suwana describe the reform strategy being undertaken in Indonesia in their chapter, 'Indonesia REDD+: beyond carbon, more than just forest'. REDD+ is an international carbon market initiative, seeking biodiversity and social justice outcomes whilst promoting carbon sequestration by incorporating protection for biodiversity and the interests of forest-dependent communities into the supply conditions of internationally traded carbon units. The role of national governments is to ensure that institutional safeguards have integrity and that the social and environmental justice arrangements are reliably implemented.

Both chapters suggest that whilst REDD+ is a starting point for reducing emissions and strengthening environmental justice, it will not achieve these goals without major institutional reform. Risks in both jurisdictions include insufficient incentives; corruption, mistrust and political tensions; limited citizen participation and ownership; unclear or inappropriate land rights; institutional incapacity, weak agency/organisational coordination and program coherence. The authors demonstrate that in practice achieving environmental justice requires sophisticated property rights that align private and public interests, a high quality public service, effective controls against corruption, empowerment of the less economically or politically powerful and an effective system of checks and balances with independent oversight. These investigations were unrelated, in separate jurisdictions, so the commonalities are startling. Both highlight the depth of the challenge, the need for reform to many laws and procedures (which may not at first sight seem to be relevant), and the significant on-ground effort and investment to convert aspirations and legal instruments into outcomes.

In the next chapter, 'Consensus federalism and freshwater regulation', Keene discusses an innovation in public participation, which aims to place negotiated decision-making authority in the hands of the affected community. The New Zealand approach to 'consensus federalism' has been applied in the management of water resources. It prioritises expertise from the affected region and consensus decision-making by the affected communities. The key feature is that the affected stakeholders are negotiating directly with one another, aiming to reach agreements that will be endorsed and thence binding. The author notes the potential for this approach to increase Indigenous involvement in decision-making. The approach is compared to cooperative federalism in the USA. The comparative evaluation of the two approaches suggests that the New Zealand approach provides for more local consensus than the standards-based approach in the USA. The author argues that this will make the New Zealand regulatory system more effective and more robust. The chapter highlights the importance of procedural reforms and effective community participation in the pursuit of environmental justice. This reflects the arguments by Preston, and the observations by Phromlah and Martin and by Santosa, *et al.* that mechanisms of recognition and participation are fundamentally important.

The two chapters by Rose and Rive, consider the impact of climate change and other environmental pressures in the South Pacific. They identify how actions by developed industrial nations generate fundamental environmental and social impacts upon people whose lives are closely dependent upon natural resources. These challenges highlight the 'big picture' of environmental risks and the very limited response of Western industrialised nations to the existential threats to many Pacific island communities.

Rose and Rive highlight the pervasive nature of doctrinal and procedural failings which translate into continuing and worsening environmental injustice outcomes. It is widely known that human-induced climate change will impact low-lying islands, and that many are in the South Pacific. Because the adverse effects affect the viability of Pacific Island communities, the justice problem is about either the interests of the people or of the environment – both are threatened. The Pacific Islanders' relationship with their islands and waters are both functional and cultural, and these relationships stretch back for millennia. Threats to the environmental underpinnings of island life therefore involve an attack upon cultural traditions. Pacific island communities have striven to be heard on these matters, and to invest substantial effort in this.

Rose's chapter 'International environmental governance in the Pacific island region' discusses the importance of PICs (Pacific Island Countries) and small island states in global governance, given their climate vulnerability. He explores their participation in environmental governance initiatives at a regional and an international (MEA) level, and how fledgling regional arrangements have been 'swamped' by multilateral agreements. This highlights the lack of an effective rights approach and the failure to convert the rhetoric of climate justice and Indigenous empowerment into meaningful outcomes for the people concerned. In common with the REDD+ chapters, Rose's observations suggest that even well-intentioned initiatives can entrench inequities and erode the capacity of Indigenous and vulnerable communities. He implies that pursuing 'soft law' and negotiated MEAs, with their complex negotiations and uncertain paths to implementation, may in practice be detrimental to pragmatic local action.

The critical focus upon the role of wealthier industrialised states, including South Pacific regional powers like Australia and New Zealand is reflected in Rive's chapter 'Safe harbours, closed borders? New Zealand legal and policy responses to climate displacement in the South Pacific'. This chapter highlights the need for environmental justice frameworks to respond to the effects of climate change on low-lying island communities. Whilst relocation may not be the preferred option for inhabitants of threatened Pacific island nations, it may be a necessity as some countries become effectively uninhabitable, or where poverty becomes far worse. The chapter details the issue of climate change refugees in the Pacific, and the lack of a principled response to this issue from New Zealand. It traces the history of regional and broader agreements, and cases involving climate refugees. The issue has been acknowledged as significant but there is as yet no judicial or political determination that would give security to potential refugees. The message of the chapter is that despite rhetorical support for its Pacific neighbours, the New Zealand government has not adequately engaged with the implications of potentially significant flows of climate change-related migration. The chapter speaks of issues of climate justice, adaptation and, specifically, climate-displaced persons.

Telesetsky advocates for greater attention to carbon reduction schemes at the national level in 'Overcoming climate inertia with unilateral action on black carbon'. The author suggests that multilateral attempts to achieve global action on climate policy have succumbed to inertia, with few substantive gains from negotiations to date. She proposes that nations focus their attention onto national policies to combat 'short-lived climate forcers', such as black carbon to achieve what is 'politically possible' in the short term. China and India black carbon emissions are mainly the result of energy and brick production. In both these countries emissions from transport are also significant (as is the case in many countries). Domestic stoves, particularly in industrialising countries, produce a significant part of the world's black carbon. The author details the control approaches in both of these countries, and highlights the need to accelerate these plans. Implementation of effective control requires many actions including capital investment, regulation, potential changes to fuel mixes and other interventions.

The issue of national versus international approaches is picked up by Telesetsky who suggests that the pursuit of an international regime, even if successful, may impede black carbon emission control rather than advance it. She outlines international initiatives and points out that some states have taken tentative steps towards controlling black carbon emissions. She suggests that multinational initiatives lack urgency, and may be being 'swamped' by heavily politicised debates about climate change. Telesetsky stresses the need for state-based action, but highlights that civil action is an important component of environmental governance. This is particularly true when the harmful actions result in human health or welfare consequences, when both public and private law remedies may be available.

The relationship between national and international law, and the search for environmental justice, is not only a matter of substantive law. As highlighted by Preston in the first chapter of this book, procedural matters are the 'third leg' of the legal tripod of effective environmental justice. The following chapter reflects this argument as, Chaulk asks 'Is there relief for transnational harm?' caused by multinational corporations in jurisdictions where legal systems are unlikely to provide effective redress. This chapter explores how decisions in the USA have limited the capacity of foreigners to sue US corporations. He considers the Alien Tort Statute and the doctrine of *forum non conveniens* since the *Kiobel* case. He discusses the Union Carbide Bhopal catastrophe in India, and the violent suppression of local opposition in Nigeria to the effects of petroleum extraction (Royal Dutch Shell). Where the opportunity for effective redress in the home jurisdiction is limited (viz. by undue influence, or ineffective governance), the potential to take action in US courts is important to social justice. The author explores the decisions which have limited the potential for foreign tort actions in the USA jurisdiction. These cases generally involve actions against corporations, and the courts have been explicit in limiting such litigation.

This chapter highlights justice-as-recognition issues, at two levels: within the original jurisdiction, and limited or non-recognition in the foreign (US) courts. Distributional justice concerns are also raised. First is the *inter partes* distribution within the original jurisdiction, resulting in an arguably unjust distribution of the costs to the affected people, to the benefit of the harm-doer. Second is the inequitable distribution of costs and benefits between industrialised and the less-developed states. Third is the allocation of disbenefits and profit between industry as a sector, the agricultural sector, and private citizens. Finally, in some instances there is also an issue of distributional injustice being wrought upon Indigenous peoples as a class with distinct interests.

The author points out that there may be situations where corporate governance fails, and it is in the interests of justice that the corporation be held accountable. Given that the precedents discussed limit this potential, the author considers other options. He points out that whilst the prior cases have limited action against corporations, this does not prevent actions against executives who may have direct involvement. He suggests that this approach may circumvent the restriction imposed through the *Kiobel* case. He points to instances where action against executives has been a catalyst for corporations to settle international legal actions, though without an admission of liability. The combination of legal tactics and protection of the social licence or reputation of the corporation has proven to be a mechanism to redress injustice. This chapter once again highlights that in the pursuit of environmental justice there is a close, perhaps inextricable, link between law and politics.

In the final chapter in this section, 'The Australian biotechnology regulatory framework: issues concerning adventitious presence (AP), co-existence, liability and coherence', Karky and Perry take the discussion of environmental justice in a slightly different direction. They focus upon the environmental justice issues triggered by scientific/industrial innovation, particularly in agriculture. In other chapters we have considered the power imbalances between developed countries and industries, and developing countries and their communities. This chapter draws our attention to the trade-offs between food security and risks of genetic pollution; between 'scientism' and 'communitarianism' in the value-laden but technologically complex issues of biotechnology regulation. It questions how well the distribution of the risks of scientific error or mismanagement is managed through the law.

Biotechnology, as the source of new crops, improved productivity and reduced crop losses, has a critical role to play in food security. Arguments 'for' or 'against' are freighted with values and scientific complexity. Perceptions of the risks differ depending upon the interests of those involved (genetic scientists, environmental scientists, industrial agriculture, organic agriculture and so forth), and the debates are heavily politicised. In jurisdictions like Australia, USA and Brazil policy makers have accepted science as the touchstone for the permitting of these crops. Notably in Europe, a communitarian approach to risk and values has led to stronger restrictions. The facts reported show a trend towards increasing international acceptance of the presence of genetically modified material ('low-level presence' or LLP). The authors highlight the technical details in this chapter, providing details of measurement and thresholds for LLP.

Even within a 'science-based' risk regulatory framework such as in Australia, the opportunity for genes to spread and lead to adventitious presence (AP) is present. Thus legal arrangements embed a risk distribution that has justice implications. This risk impacts upon the coexistence and trade of transgenic, organic and conventional crops, resulting in an allocation of risk and economic loss or gain between growers of transgenic crops, and other farmers for whom the unintended presence of genetically modified organisms will be disadvantageous. Legislation or case law has not responded to these risks with specific liability or other arrangements. The authors suggest that measures to minimise AP levels and specific liability arrangements for damage caused by drifted genes are needed in the interests of environmental justice.

The chapter highlights a little-considered dimension of environmental justice, the implications of 'scientism'[8] in determining distribution and process arrangements under the law. The concept of science-based decision-making, and its incorporation within legal arrangements for issues like the management of genetically modified organisms, is seen as a positive development. However, the approach carries with it an intrinsic prioritisation of the values of an elite group, and the discounting of others. In fields such as community engagement and participative democracy, overcoming the power imbalances that disadvantage non-scientists has been seen as a matter of concern. This points to a problem of non-recognition or mis-recognition of the interests of those antagonistic to this type of transformation of nature, or of nature as part of the community of justice. This issue raises practical and philosophical questions about the status of modified, compared to non-modified, nature. It highlights the many challenges of non-recognition within the legal system. These are taken up in the final three chapters concerning environmental justice and Indigenous peoples.

RECOGNITION OF INDIGENOUS PEOPLES' INTERESTS

The final theme is Indigenous environmental justice. The questions raised in this section bring into sharp focus the ambiguities and complexities of environmental justice, from the perspective of vulnerability, or from the perspective of rights. The chapters all suggest that the frontier of environmental justice is the issue of Indigenous peoples' interests. Responding effectively to these challenges is a fundamental concern both for environmental and social justice advocates.

In the first chapter under this theme, 'Customary law systems for water governance in Kenya', Gachenga highlights non-recognition of customary

---

[8] Reliance upon scientific knowledge with its implicit values, generally to the exclusion of other perspectives.

law in water governance in Kenya. This sets the scene for consideration of what might be required to effectively recognise and respect Indigenous peoples' systems of norms and rules within the dominant legal system of the nation state. A customary water governance system that predates colonial rule operates on the Marakwet Escarpment. The Kenyan national water governance framework is based on the Water Act 2002, which does not explicitly recognise customary rights. However, Kenya's Constitution recognises the existence of customary law, which is given limited application through the Judicature Act. The content and application of customary law is a mechanism for establishing the existence of private rights, to the extent that these are not inconsistent with the formal law.

Under the Marakwet cultural traditions water is sacred. Water rights are associated with land ownership, which is undocumented. The community considers its ability to govern water under its own law as a fundamental matter, and in practice does not recognise state law. There appears to have been no specific conflict of state and traditional laws and in the absence of competition between the Water Act and the customary law, there is no practical reason for state actors or Indigenous people to be aware of their separate governance systems. Indeed, provided that the arrangements are not inconsistent, no functional difficulty may ever arise. Thus the issue of non-recognition might be considered as moot. However, the author mirrors Craig's view (expressed in the following chapter) that non-recognition is intrinsically a violation of a right, hearkening back to the framework for environmental justice outlined by Preston and the rights based approach articulated by Glazebrook. The chapter also contrasts the 'top-down' structure of the Water Act and related administrative structures with the 'bottom-up' and consultative mechanisms of traditional law. This is mirrored in the final chapter by Aseron, Greymorning and Williams.

Gachenga argues it may be possible to use the human right to water[9] or the rights of Indigenous peoples[10] as a basis for legal recognition of customary water law in Kenya. However, she indicates that human rights to water and sanitation probably have limited application as the issue is recognition of customary autonomy in governing water for irrigation, not water for subsistence. The author argues that making the link between customary governance and human rights is more likely to be effective than

---

[9] Resolution A/RES/64/292. United Nations General Assembly, July 2010 General Comment No. 15. The right to water. UN Committee on Economic, Social and Cultural Rights, November 2002.

[10] Declaration on the Rights of Indigenous Peoples, United Nations General Assembly, New York City, 13 September 2007.

pursuing a customary right to natural resources, because human rights issues are better established in Kenyan jurisprudence, through the Bill of Rights.

Craig's chapter, 'Legal strategies to expand indigenous governance in climate change adaptation', advocates for the incorporation into climate change management of a greater respect for Indigenous peoples' rights. Existing approaches to climate change unthinkingly replicate State-centric governance models that fail to respect Indigenous peoples' rights. New approaches need to move beyond viewing Indigenous peoples merely as stakeholders or participants, and to recognise their distinct rights and interests. Whilst this chapter highlights that indigenous people will be disproportionately represented among populations harmed by climate change, Craig makes a case that focusing only upon vulnerability interests fails to fully recognise the claims and contributions of Indigenous peoples. Indigenous climate change interests arise at three levels – as members of the population of citizens who will suffer economic and welfare impacts; as vulnerable Indigenous people who will suffer additional impacts such as loss of cultural resources and collectivity, who need protection and deserve compensation; and as Indigenous peoples with distinct rights that need to be recognised in governance. This last aspect is virtually absent from dominant concepts of governance and climate change response, and is an argument that is developed further by Aseron, Greymorning and Williams in the following chapter.

The chapter considers that a principled approach requires a move from impacts-based thinking to a rights-based conceptualisation. Part of this is to reconsider sovereignty and the state, and the relationship of Indigenous peoples to the state. The focus would be upon the independent rights of Indigenous peoples to negotiate their relationship with the formal state, participating with a distinct status and rights. Among the basis for rights-based involvement in climate change policy and management are claims to a right to cultural survival, given the impact of climate change. Whilst effective legal recognition of special rights status must come through state sovereignty, she argues that sovereignty relies on other sources of authority. Craig suggests that the failure to recognise existing rights or emerging rights may prejudice currently negotiated arrangements, and become a future source of conflict over justice. She argues that the nature of the state and the relationship of Indigenous people to the state are changing. The meaning of what constitutes law (human rights particularly) is undergoing an evolution. It is becoming more complex particularly with notions of 'soft law' and 'traditional law' being given greater attention through judicial interpretation and new legal venues.

These developments raise the question: if the fundamental structures of the justice system are evolving, then in what ways must environmental law scholarship, policy-making and practice also evolve? The final chapter in this book challenges many assumptions about environmental law scholarship, and suggests that embedded in legal traditions are problems of non-recognition, adverse distribution and inappropriate process. Indigenous peoples offer a wealth of knowledge for dealing with environmental problems, but we do not use culturally appropriate methods to harness this knowledge. Aseron, Greymorning and Williams offer timely suggestions for how to pursue collaboration and avoid marginalisation and commodification of Indigenous knowledge in their chapter, 'Innovative collaboration, inclusive practices, governance and cultural capital'.

This concluding chapter argues that economically and politically dominant cultures systematically oblige Indigenous people to reframe their interactions subservient to that dominance, and that this is more powerful and pervasive than many who are not Indigenous people can ever understand. Institutionalised research approaches largely exclude or at least constrain the perspectives of Indigenous people. This is so even when researchers want to 'empower' their Indigenous colleagues. Two specific illustrations are given: the choice to use modes of communication which do not take into account the significance of ritual for communicating and learning by Indigenous peoples; and the assumed acceptance of the coloniser's language as the only appropriate means of communication.

In part to illustrate the differences the authors use a combination of representative diagrams and Indigenous storytelling to highlight the significance of differences in culture, power relationships, ways of understanding the world and governance mechanisms. The maintenance of dominance and difference through generally used approaches are political choices enforced by scientific cultures. In themselves they limit the capacity of Indigenous people to participate and the capacity of the researchers to come to a true understanding of the knowledge that is available. The authors suggest that even the methods and aspirations of movements like environmental justice and earth jurisprudence may themselves be oppressive of people who have a fundamentally different cultural perspective.

In common with a number of the other chapters, this chapter suggests that at the heart of problems of environmental justice lie power relationships, and the fundamental conflict between dominating and less powerful or oppressed interests. A fundamental consideration is that for one group in society to be given more power requires that another group surrender some power. Decisions about who will be recognised, what processes will be used to allow participation within the legal system, and ultimately how these benefits will be distributed are intrinsically about the exercise of power. This chapter brings that potent fact clearly to our attention.

It suggests that even the desire to act with goodwill may be far from sufficient to address the fundamental problems that stand in the way of true environmental justice.

KEY LESSONS

The chapters in this book provide a rich source of ideas and information about the many dimensions of environmental justice. They do not, nor are they intended to, pretend that there is a settled consensus about the meaning of environmental justice, nor about the ways in which the complex challenges can be solved. The authors approach the topic with different understandings of what environmental justice is, and how it might be achieved. However, it is clear that the foundational commitment to a more just and sustainable world lies at the heart of all of their investigations. In some ways, the heterogeneity represents the richness and depth of commitment rather than presenting an impediment to the pursuit of a more just and sustainable world.

The authors show significant differences in how they see the scope and content of environment and justice. It would be comforting to suggest that these abstract discussions can remain unresolved without adversely affecting the social and environmental interests that all strive to advance. Unfortunately, those chapters which concentrate upon implementation at the 'front line' make it clear that decisions about whether environmental justice is focused upon rights of nature, rights to nature, or some other formulation will impact upon judicial determination of who forms part of the community of justice, what processes for inclusion and determination apply, and ultimately who will be the beneficiaries and whether the benefits will depend upon human use of the environment. As has been well illustrated, moving concepts of environmental justice 'off the page' and into practice requires deep systematic change in governance systems. Whilst the creation of appropriate legal instruments and procedures is an important part of this change, often this will have to be accompanied by more fundamental approaches to empower and support those who are meant to benefit, and to control potential abuses by those from whom power and resources will have to be diverted. True achievement of the outcomes of social justice will require radical reform backed by sustained effort and investment by many people.

The chapters included in this volume reflect the theme of the 11th IUCN Academy of Environmental Law Colloquium. The theme, 'He Tapuwae', a Maori waiata, emphasises that the search for environmental justice is a series of steps towards greater understanding and shared learning.

Realisation of the fundamental nature of the questions raised by the search for environment and justice, and the evidence provided in the chapters of this book, demonstrate that in the pursuit of environmental justice we cannot divorce the political from the practical. Whilst it is important to have leaders who can develop the abstract concepts that will inform environmental justice arrangements, it is at least as important to overcome the many practical challenges. To achieve environment justice requires changes to administrative arrangements, strengthening the capacity of the less powerful, ensuring the integrity of formal governance, changes to land-use and other resourcing titles, creating more effective processes for engagement and substantive desperation, and many other adjustments in society. These practical challenges should be well thought through and aggressively implemented to ensure that the search for environmental justice be expedited so that society can benefit from its implementation.

ACKNOWLEDGEMENTS

The editors wish to thank the Secretariat of the IUCN AEL, Jamie Benidickson, Winnie Carruth and Yves Le Bouthillier; the Chair and members of the Governing Board; and over 200 academic colleagues from around the world who gave presentations at the Colloquium. The editors would also like to thank Justice Antonio Herman Benjamin and Professor Ben Boer of the World Commission on Environmental Law, and Dr Alejandro Iza, the Director of the IUCN Environmental Law Centre, for their support with the Colloquium. We would also like to thank Matthew Ryan, our editorial assistant.

The Colloquium was jointly organised by the University of New England, New South Wales, Australia, and the University of Waikato, New Zealand, and the editors would also like to thank these institutions for their assistance and financial support in organising the Colloquium, and the student volunteers from both universities who helped make the event a success.

Finally, the editors would like to thank the New Zealand Law Foundation for their generous grant funding, and for proudly supporting the Colloquium and the production of this book.

REFERENCES

Crutzen, P. (2002), 'The Geology of Mankind' 415 *Nature* 23.

Crutzen, P. and E. Stoermer (2000), 'The "Anthropocene"' 41 *Global Change Newsletter* 17.

Elias, S. (25 July 2014), 'Righting environmental justice', *RM Theory and Practice* 42
Kuhn, T. (1996), *The Structure of Scientific Revolutions*, (3rd edn, Chicago: University of Chicago Press).
Rawls, J. (2001), *Justice as Fairness: A Restatement* (Cambridge, MA: Belknap Press).
Resource Management Act 1991 (New Zealand).
Shelton, D. (2009), 'Human rights and the environment' *RM Theory and Practice* 91.
Shortle, J. (2012), *Water Quality Trading in Agriculture* (Report to the Organization for Economic Cooperation and Development, Directorate for Trade and Agriculture, OECD Publishing).
Stone, J. (1964), *Legal System and Lawyer's Reasoning* (Redwood, CA: Stanford University Press).
United Nations (2002), *The Right to Water*, Resolution A/RES/64/292.
United Nations (2007), *Declaration on the Rights of Indigenous Peoples* A/61/L.67
Whata, C. (2013), 'Environmental rights in times of crisis: The Canterbury experience' *RM Theory and Practice* 42.

PART I

Framing the search for environmental justice

In this first section we explore perspectives of scholars and judges upon the fundamental nature of environmental justice, and key characteristics of the search for its meaning and its application. The voices heard in this section are of Brian Preston, whose experience as an environmental law judge supports his precise framework for analyzing what is required through the law to deliver environmental justice in practice. Klaus Bosselmann provides a scholar's perspective upon the changing nature of the challenges that must be met if environmental justice is to be achieved through environmental law. Lee Godden and Emily O'Connell consider how innovative environmental policy instruments might in themselves give rise to significant issues of ecological and human justice. These three chapters help to frame the discussions in the chapters that follow.

2. The effectiveness of the law in providing access to environmental justice: an introduction

The Hon Justice Brian J. Preston SC

INTRODUCTION

Environmental justice includes three concepts: distributive justice, procedural justice and justice as recognition.[1] In this chapter, I will consider the ways in which the law supports (or fails to support) these in practice.

Distributive justice concerns the distribution of environmental goods (or benefits) and environmental bads (or burdens). Distributive justice is promoted by giving substantive rights to members of the community of justice to share in environmental benefits (such as clean air, water and land, green space and a healthful ecology) and to prevent, mitigate, remediate or be compensated for environmental burdens (such as pollution and loss of green space, biological diversity or ecological integrity).

Claims about distributive justice involve addressing three questions: who are the members of the community of justice to whom distributive justice is due? What are the environmental benefits and burdens to be distributed? And, what are the principles or criteria of distribution to be applied? Just arrangements should be assessed not only in simple distributive terms, but also in how distributions of benefits and burdens affect the capabilities of members of the community of justice to achieve valuable functionings (both activities and states of existence or being).

Procedural justice is concerned with how decisions, including distributive choices, are made, who is involved and who has influence. Procedural justice is promoted by the law giving rights to access environmental information, participate in decision-making, and access review procedures before a court or tribunal to challenge decision-making or impairment

---

[1] Walker (2012) 10, 42–51.

of substantive or procedural rights. Broad, inclusive and democratic decision-making procedures are a precondition for distributive justice.

Justice as recognition is concerned with who is given respect, and who is (and is not) valued. Access to justice as recognition is promoted by the law giving substantive and procedural rights, but also by affording recognition of social groups and communities, and of the natural environment and components of it.

This chapter highlights how the law is helping or hindering access to environmental justice in these three senses.

DISTRIBUTIVE JUSTICE

Distributive justice is central to environmental justice. It involves substantive justice in that it concerns the environmental benefits and burdens that are received by members of the community of justice. The law establishes the framework for distribution of environmental benefits and burdens. Natural resources laws allocate entitlements to use natural resources, including water, minerals, timber and components of biological diversity. Planning laws spatially designate land and its resources (by zoning), regulate use (by development control), and allocate entitlements to use (land use permits). Pollution laws regulate environmental externalities, including allocating entitlements to cause externalities such as pollution of air, water and land.

The extent to which laws enable distributive justice depends on, first, the community of justice (the recipients of distributive justice) that is recognised by the law, second, the environmental benefits and burdens to be distributed, and third, the criteria governing the distribution. Achieving distributive justice is not only about ensuring just distributions of primary goods, but also about ensuring that distributions enable members of the community of justice to lead fully functioning lives. Achievement of distributive justice is not only a product of the laws' content and terms, but also how laws are applied in practice. Distributive injustice is caused by laws which provide for inequitable distribution, but also by inequitable application or non-application of laws.

The community of justice consists of those entities entitled to be recipients of justice. For distributive justice, they are the claimants for and the recipients of distributions of benefits and burdens. For procedural justice, they are those entitled to access environmental information, participate in environmental policy-making and decision-making, and have access to justice through the courts. For justice as recognition, they are those entitled to social and political recognition.

For distributive justice, laws affect the community of justice in two ways: first, the laws confine membership of the community of justice and, second, the laws affect who (within or without that membership) receives environmental benefits or burdens. I will discuss the latter first.

Laws skew distribution of environmental benefits towards consuming users and environmental burdens towards non-consuming users for at least four reasons. First, environmental laws are inherently biased towards consuming uses instead of non-consuming uses, creating a 'loaded' distributive system. Environmental laws typically prohibit or restrict the use or exploitation of the environment, including natural resources, but that prohibition or restriction can be lifted by a regulatory authority granting approval to use or exploit the environment.[2] Thus, natural resource laws initially prohibit but then enable the consumption of resources such as coal or metalliferous reserves, forests for timber, and ground or surface water, by the granting of a mining, timber or water licence.

Second, environmental laws impose the burden of proof on those seeking to preserve the environment (non-consuming users) rather than on those persons wishing to consume or exploit the environment (consuming users). This again skews distribution of environmental benefits in favour of consuming users.

Laws allowing consuming users to apply for approval do not impose a legal burden of proof on consuming users to establish that the distribution for which they have applied is just and equitable. They do not need to prove an absence of any particular environment harm (such as harm to threatened species, populations or ecological communities), or some acceptable environmental outcome or standard (such as ecologically sustainable development (ESD)), or that the economic or social benefits of the proposed activity will outweigh the environmental costs.

Especially for more significant activities, there seems to be a presumption that approval will be granted unless a good reason is demonstrated to the contrary. This affects a transfer of the burden to those opposing an activity to prove that the approval should not be granted.

In environmental impact assessment and in the determination of an application for approval, undue weight is given to quantifiable over unquantifiable data.[3] This also affects the burden of proof. Consuming uses of the environment yield quantifiable benefits – the products of consumption (such as the minerals extracted) have quantifiable market

---

[2] See Fowler (1984) 18–33 (discussing negative components of environmental law).

[3] Tribe (1974) 1317.

value, as do the costs of production, resulting in net quantifiable benefits. Environmental externalities lack market value or are undervalued and thus the quantified net market benefits of consumption will generally outweigh the non-market environmental burdens. This cost-benefit approach usually results in the consuming use being approved. The burden of establishing that the environmental costs are greater than have been quantified and outweigh the benefits of exploitation falls on those wishing to preserve the environment.

Conventional economic analyses, such as cost benefit analysis, do not consider issues of distributive justice; they are concerned only with the aggregation of costs and benefits, not how or why these are distributed.[4]

The burden of proof problem arises in another way. The loading in favour of consuming users results in allocation of the burden of proof to non-consuming users in any legal action to restrain consumption or exploitation of resources. Consuming users, by exercising their demands for consumption, foreclose non-consuming users from exercising theirs (preservation), but the contrary does not hold true. Even in a system of laws regulating use and exploitation, the leverage inherent in consuming users of the environment means that they can continue until they are restrained by court order. Consuming users will thus be defendants and persons wishing to preserve the environment will be plaintiffs. In our legal system, plaintiffs bear the burden of proving that the defendant's conduct is in breach of the law. In cases of doubt, the plaintiff will not succeed, and use or exploitation of the environment will prevail.[5]

Third, following from the previous two points, environmental laws do not enable holistic determination of competing claims for distribution of environmental benefits and burdens. As noted above, the laws permit an application for approval of consumption or exploitation of the environment, not its preservation. In this sense, there cannot be a resolution of competing applications for approval of consumption versus preservation of the environment.

The laws are structured to deal narrowly with applications for particular consuming uses under the particular law. There is no capacity to consider consuming uses under other laws, or applications that have not yet been made. There is usually no capacity to consider the cumulative impacts of pending applications. This results in a 'tyranny of small decisions' – decisions with small environmental impacts collectively manifest themselves

---

[4] *Bulga Milbrodale Progress Association Inc v Minister for Planning and Infrastructure and Warkworth Mining Ltd* [2013] NSWLEC 48 [485].

[5] Krier (1970); Preston (1986) 221; Preston (2014a) 82.

as significantly adverse to the environment when accumulated at a larger scale, over space and time.[6] This reductionist decision-making approach does not allow for a holistic assessment of issues of distribution. The result is a failure to address the full environmental costs of consuming uses. This skews the cost-benefit analysis in favour of consumption.

Fourth, the laws are inadequate in the distributive decisions that are able to be made. The approval of a consuming or exploitative use usually will not require the full internalisation of the environmental burdens or costs. There usually will be a partial internalisation – conditions of approval may require the avoidance, mitigation or offsetting of certain environmental impacts to a certain degree, but there still will be some externality. The fossil fuel power station will still emit greenhouse gases and the open cut quarry or mine will still emit air or noise pollution. Approval authorises the imposition of these burdens. A legal right only arises where the actual burdens of an activity exceed the burdens that are lawfully approved. The result is to continue distribution of environmental benefits to consuming users and environmental burdens to non-consuming users.

Laws also affect the community of justice by confining the membership of the community. Generally, the entities entitled to be recipients of distributive justice are limited to the present generation of humans. Future generations of humans are excluded, as are present and future generations of non-humans.

Environmental laws usually fail to mandate the implementation of intergenerational equity. Laws do not accommodate the preservation of environmental goods to enable distribution to future generations. Application for approval can only be made for current exploitation, not for non-distribution of environmental resources to conserve the option to consume for future generations. The laws only inadequately permit consideration of intergenerational equity. Some might include intergenerational equity as a statutory object or as a relevant matter within the exercise of discretionary statutory powers. However, laws tend not to oblige that a power be exercised to promote or be consistent with the object of intergenerational equity[7] or that a statutory approval for a consuming use only be granted if to do so will implement the principles of intergenerational equity.[8]

Non-human nature, both current and future, is not included in the community of justice and cannot claim distributive justice. Potential

---

[6] Dwyer and Taylor (2013)186–7.

[7] See generally Fisher (2001) 364–8.

[8] Preston (2014a) 83.

members of non-human nature in the community of justice include sentient animals and non-sentient organisms, as well as species, populations and ecological communities and ecosystems.[9] A case can be made that non-human nature should be included within the community of justice, at least to the extent of being recipients of the distribution of environmental benefits.[10]

The extension of the community of justice to non-human nature would enable all members to make claims against other members. The deliberative task would be to determine the level of environmental resources that various natural organisms, groups and systems need and are entitled to claim against humans and one another.[11]

Non-human nature is usually the recipient of environmental burdens, not environmental benefits, from the law. The point made earlier concerning the inability to apply for the preservation of the environment under laws regulating its exploitation is relevant here. Allocation of environmental resources to non-human nature usually involves preservation of the environmental status quo. Preservation of the environmental status quo involves non-distribution. No application can be made under the laws for statutory approval for non-distribution.

Statutory approval of a consuming use might be conditioned on the protection of some part of the area to be impacted (an on-site offset), or of another area of the environment as an offset for the impacted area (an off-site offset). However, such a condition falls short of achieving distributive justice for non-human nature. First, it does not resolve competing claims by members of the community of justice, but rather only a claim by a member to consume the environment needed by a non-member. Second, it does not involve a distribution of environmental benefits to non-human nature, only a protection (which may not be permanent) from distribution within the protected area. Third, there is always a loss of environmental resources. The loss of the organisms, populations, ecological communities or ecosystems within the area impacted by the activity is not offset by protection of other organisms, populations, ecological communities or ecosystems at the offset sites. This is because the need for environmental resources by the organisms, populations, ecological communities or ecosystems is already satisfied by the resources at those offset sites. There is no transfer of environmental resources from the impact site to the offset sites. There is merely a loss of the environmental resources at the impact

---

9 Schlosberg (2007) 119.

10 Baxter (2005) 75–151.

11 Baxter (2005) chapter 9; Schlosberg (2007) 120, 132.

site and maintenance of the existing resources at the offset sites. Hence, there is no distribution of environmental benefits.

Conversely, environmental laws enable the distribution of environmental burdens to non-human nature. The environmental externalities of approved uses are borne by non-human nature. The upshot is that environmental laws involve distributive injustice to non-human nature.

A question in determining claims about distributive justice is: what is to be distributed? Environmental justice involves both environmental benefits and burdens. Particular environmental features, materials or activities can be viewed as benefits or burdens depending on the claimant and the context. For example, energy consumption can be viewed as a benefit in providing essential energy services and a burden in contributing to carbon emissions and climate change.[12]

Environmental laws tend not to allow multiple contexts or viewpoints. Each law, by its nature, scope and purpose, fixes the claims that can be made and the context for viewing environmental resources, features and activities and hence for characterisation as benefits or burdens. Natural resources laws view the resources the subject of the laws as the benefit; non-human nature dependent on those resources represents a burden as it has the potential to prevent or restrict the consumption or exploitation of the resources. As I have noted, environmental laws do not generally permit a holistic evaluation of the distributive question but confine evaluation according to the law concerned.

Another question to be addressed in determining claims about distributive justice is: what are the principles of distribution? Many different criteria have been suggested for achieving distributive justice. As a general rule, the criteria can be grouped as goal-based, rights-based or duty-based.

Goal-based criteria for distribution are concerned with the welfare of any member of the community of justice insofar as this contributes to some state of affairs stipulated as good apart from the member's choice of that state. Goal based theories include forms of utilitarianism, such as Bentham's hedonistic utilitarianism,[13] bio-happiness utilitarianism,[14] economic utilitarianism[15] and social utilitarianism.[16]

Rights-based criteria are concerned with rights and interests of individuals and not how the welfare of each individual contributes to some

---

12 Walker (2012) 43.

13 See Moore (1912) chs 1 and 2 on utilitarianism.

14 See Swaminathan (2011); Robinson (2013) 7–8, 25–6; Iyer (1996).

15 See Posner (1981) 73–4; Posner (2007) chapter 3.

16 See Elders (2005) 575 (discussion of Jhering's social utilitarianism). See also Pound (1999) 203–5; J Stone (1964) 224–9.

desired state of affairs, including the interests of society. Rights-based theories include those propounded by Rawls[17] and Dworkin.[18]

Duty-based theories concern the moral quality of the acts of individuals that fail to meet certain standards of behaviour. Kant's categorical imperatives are a duty-based theory.[19] Duty-based theories use codes of conduct that set morally accepted standards of behaviour. These codes of conduct may be set by society for the individual or by the individual for himself. The individual at the centre must conform to the code or be liable to be punished or corrupted.[20]

Duty-based criteria might be seen in Leopold's land ethic: 'a thing is right when it tends to preserve the integrity, stability, and beauty of the biotic community. It is wrong when it tends otherwise';[21] or in Baxter's principle: 'we must do right by other life forms, but in a precise kind of way, namely by recognising their claim to a fair share of the environmental resources which all life forms need to survive and flourish'.[22] It is also possible that principles of ESD incorporate duty-based criteria. The principle of intergenerational equity and the polluter pays principle pronounce duties that can be used in distributive choices.[23]

An expansion of the community of justice to include non-human nature could change the criteria for distributing environmental benefits and burdens. Goal-based criteria could be expanded to include desired environmental quality goals. For example, Hillman has suggested (as one of six principles for determining a fair distribution of resources and responsibilities for stream rehabilitation) the principle of utilitarian equality, where the goal is to maximise overall catchment health, balancing costs and benefits in the allocation of resources.[24] Rights-based criteria could be expanded to consider the needs,[25] vulnerability,[26] interests[27] or integrity[28] of non-human nature. Duty-based criteria could be expanded

---

17 See Rawls (1971); Rawls (2001).
18 See Dworkin (1978); Dworkin (1986).
19 Dworkin (n 18) 172.
20 Ibid.
21 Leopold (1949) 262.
22 Baxter (2005) 4.
23 See, eg, Protection of the Environment Administration Act 1991 (NSW), s 6(2).
24 Hillman (2004) 30.
25 Benton (1993) 187–93.
26 Walker (2012) 46.
27 Baxter (2005) 115–25.
28 Schlosberg (2007) 136–8. The concept of ecological integrity has been recognised in environmental soft law instruments, including the World Charter for

to consider land ethics[29] and causal responsibility (such as the polluter pays principle).[30]

Achieving distributive justice is not simply a matter of ensuring distributions of primary environmental goods that are just in themselves, but also of ensuring that such distributions enable individuals and communities to lead fully functioning and flourishing lives. Distributive justice is not solely concerned with the amount of primary goods distributed, but also with what those goods do for individuals and communities.[31] This is the capabilities approach of Sen and Nussbaum.[32] The capabilities approach concerns what is needed to transform primary goods (if they are available) into a fully functioning life and what interrupts that process.[33] The focus of distributive justice under a capabilities approach is on the distribution and access to capabilities of functioning. Distribution may be by the state.[34]

The capabilities approach can be applied to an extended community of justice that includes non-human nature, by considering what capabilities are needed for individual organisms of different species, and of populations of organisms of the same species, as well as of ecological communities and ecosystems, to fully function.[35] Application of the capabilities approach to non-human nature is not without difficulties. One is determining the capability sets for different organisms, populations, ecological communities and ecosystems, or even larger living systems. Another is that there will be different, often competing, capabilities between humans and non-human nature and, within non-human nature, between different organisms, populations, ecological communities and ecosystems. The capabilities approach does not provide criteria for resolving competing claims for distribution. Nevertheless, the capabilities approach does draw attention to the question of what environmental resources and other capabilities are needed for all of non-human nature to lead fully functioning lives.

In general, environmental laws are deficient in setting criteria for the distribution of benefits and burdens. Goal-based criteria are rarely

---

Nature 1982 (cl I(4)), and in the principle of ESD of conservation of biological diversity and ecological integrity.

29 See, eg, Leopold (1949) 237–61.

30 Hillman (2004) 31; Walker (2012) 45–7.

31 Schlosberg (2007) 30.

32 Nussbaum and Sen (eds) (1993); Nussbaum (2006); Sen (2009); Sen (2006) 154; Sen (1999) 10.

33 Schlosberg (2007) 4.

34 Ibid, 31.

35 Ibid, 153–7.

specified or required to be applied in distribution of environmental benefits and burdens. Modern statutes usually contain an objects clause stating the goals of the statute.[36] However, the objects clause is usually unhelpful; it may merely be a form of recital or a historical explanation; even if it is a statement of purpose, its use may be limited to being an interpretive tool supporting the substantive provisions of the statute; it may be drafted at a high level of generality, and be hortatory and aspirational; or it may contain objects that are potentially conflicting, such as encouraging both economic development and environmental protection.[37] Such objects clauses do not set meaningful goals to be applied in distributive decision-making.

Statutes often specify matters to be considered in the exercise of discretionary powers, including to distribute (or effect the distribution of) environmental resources. However, the specification of the matters to be considered may not be helpful in providing criteria for distributive decision-making: the relevant matters may not contain any goals, but only subject matters to be considered; the relevant matters may not involve all relevant goals, in particular goals such as environmental outcomes or standards; the relevant matters may be expressed at a high level of generality; and there may be conflict between relevant matters and goals.[38]

Environmental statutes usually prescribe conditional, not absolute, rules. For example, statutes rarely state that an approval cannot be granted unless some environmental outcome or standard is achieved or protected.[39] Statutes are replete with discretionary powers but rarely burdened with duties or obligations.[40] There is rarely a duty to achieve some environmental outcome or standard, or to ensure that some environmental outcome or standard is not compromised.[41]

In summary, environmental statutes set no meaningful, goal-based criteria for distribution of environmental benefits or burdens. The statutes do not mandate just distributions according to set goals. Instead, distributive decisions are loosely bounded by the statute, leaving considerable discretion. The distributive decision will often turn on the decision-maker's perceptions of justice and how he or she chooses to exercise the statutory discretion.[42] Because environmental statutes do not set meaningful

---

36 See generally Rohde (1995); Barton (2001).
37 Preston (2014a) 76–7; Bates (2010) 211–16.
38 Preston (2014a) 80.
39 Fisher (2001) 364–8.
40 Bullen (2006) 265.
41 Preston (2014a) 83.
42 Dwyer and Taylor (2013) 209.

environmental goals, distributive decisions tend to favour environmental consumption, not conservation.[43]

Rights-based criteria are more commonly specified or required in the distribution of environmental benefits or burdens. Where statutes employ rights-based criteria, they usually prioritise human consuming users. Planning statutes uphold existing (or non-conforming) use rights – the right to continue, and to enlarge, expand or intensify with consent, an existing use of land that has become prohibited, usually because of its environmental incompatibility.[44] Resource guarantee statutes affirm allocation of natural resources, such as timber from native forests, to the relevant industry.[45] These distributions are based on the statutorily accepted rights or entitlements of consuming users.

Occasionally, the interests, needs or vulnerabilities of non-human nature are required to be considered in the exercise of discretionary powers. For example, in Australia, the Water Management Act 2000 (NSW) sets water management principles concerning the interests, needs and integrity of water sources, flood plains and dependent ecosystems (including groundwater and wetlands), and habitats, animals and plants that benefit from water.[46] The legislation requires a state water management outcomes plan to promote the water management principles[47] and management plans to commit water for fundamental ecosystem health or other specified environmental purposes.[48] These provisions provide rights-based criteria for allocation of water to the environment.

Duty-based criteria are rarer in environmental statutes. Insofar as certain principles of ESD could be seen to involve duties, a statute that requires regulatory authorities to apply the principles of ESD might be thought to involve application of duty-based criteria.[49] However, most environmental statutes neither include duty-based criteria nor require

---

43 Bates (2010) 215–16.

44 See, eg, Environmental Planning and Assessment Act 1979 (NSW), pt 4 div 10.

45 See, eg, Forestry and National Parks Estate Act 1998 (NSW) as discussed in Ricketts and Rogers (1999) 161. See also Plantations and Reafforestation Act 1999 (NSW), pt 2.

46 Water Management Act 2000 (NSW), s 5.

47 Water Management Act 2000 (NSW), s 6(2)(b).

48 Water Management Act 2000 (NSW), ss 8(1), 2(A) and (2).

49 See for instance ss 2A(2), (3) of the National Parks and Wildlife Act 1974 (NSW) (but see Basten JA in *Country Energy v Williams* [2005] NSWCA 318; (2005) 141 LGERA 426 [65] that it is possible to read too much into the obligation to give effect to the objects of the Act by applying the principles of ESD) and s 5 of the Environmental Protection Act 1994 (Qld). See also Preston (2014) (n 5) 78.

consideration or application of such criteria in exercising powers that distribute environmental benefits and burdens.

PROCEDURAL JUSTICE

Procedural justice is a widely accepted requirement additional to distributive justice. Procedural justice concerns how decisions are made, who is involved and who has influence. Procedural injustice can be a cause of distributive injustice, but is also an element of justice in itself. Justice involves not only fair distributive outcomes but also just processes by which distributive outcomes are reached.[50] The importance of procedural fairness is evidenced by its centrality in public law for administrative and judicial decision-making.

Procedural justice involves: access to environmental information, entitlement to participate in decision-making, and access to review procedures before a court or tribunal to challenge decision-making or impairment of substantive or procedural rights.

The availability of environmental information is a key condition of effective participation. Principle 10 of the Rio Declaration on Environment and Development provides, in part, that:

> Environmental issues are best handled with participation of all concerned citizens at the relevant level. At the national level, each individual shall have appropriate access to information concerning the environment that is held by public authorities, including information on hazardous materials and activities in their communities, and the opportunity to participate in decision-making processes. States shall facilitate and encourage public awareness and participation by making information widely available.

The United Nations Economic Commission for Europe (UNECE) Convention on Access to Information, Public Participation in Decision-Making and Access to Justice in Environmental Matters (Aarhus Convention) implements Principle 10 of the Rio Declaration. It provides a right of the public to access environmental information held by public authorities.[51]

The UNEP Guidelines for the Development of National Legislation on Access to Information, Public Participation and Access to Justice

---

50 Walker (2012) 47–8.

51 See Convention on Access to Information, Public Participation and Access to Justice in Environmental Matters, 1998, 2161 UNTS 447, arts 1, 4 and 5 (Aarhus Convention).

in Environmental Matters (UNEP Guidelines) recommend norms and principles for facilitating access to information.[52]

Jurisdictions vary in the extent to which their laws facilitate access to environmental information. Environmental laws may provide for access to environmental information about exercises of functions. Environmental laws which provide for public participation, through public notice and exhibition of proposed policies or plans or applications for approval, usually provide for public access to information on those proposals and require publication, such as by a public register, of the adopted policies, plans and approvals.[53]

'Right to know' laws commonly require public authorities to make available public registers of environmental information. The public registers may be of land use permits (such as development consents), environmental permits (such as pollution licences), contaminated land sites, water licences, mining licences, forestry licences and wildlife licences.[54] Laws may require the government or public authorities to produce 'state of the environment' reports.[55] Public authorities may also be required to produce an annual report on their operations.[56]

Environmental laws may require persons who exploit the environment to disclose information about their activities, particularly activities that cause or threaten harm to the environment. Pollution laws commonly impose notification requirements.[57] Conditions of land use or resource permits may also require monitoring and reporting, and notification of incidents. Most jurisdictions have freedom of information laws[58] and laws

---

52 Guidelines 1–7 of the UNEP Guidelines.

53 See, eg, Environmental Planning and Assessment Act 1979 (NSW).

54 See, eg, NSW Environment Protection Authority, 'Public registers' (24 June 2010) <www.epa.nsw.gov.au/publicregister/index.htm> accessed 9 March 2015 and the UK Environment Agency, 'What do the Public Registers Cover? – A Legal Explanation' (7 December 2012) <http://epr.environment-agency.gov.uk/ePRInternet/Info.aspx> accessed 9 March 2015.

55 For example, s 10 of the Protection of the Environment Administration Act 1991 (NSW) requires the Environment Protection Authority to produce a report on the state of the environment every three years and s 516B of the Environment Protection and Biodiversity Conservation Act 1999 (Cth) requires the Minister administering that Act to prepare a report on the Australian jurisdiction every five years.

56 For example, the National Parks and Wildlife Service is required by s 144B of the National Parks and Wildlife Act 1974 (NSW) to produce an annual report under the Annual Reports (Departments) Act 1985 (NSW).

57 See, eg, s 148 of the Protection of the Environment Operations Act 1997 (NSW). See also Lipman and Farrugia (2013).

58 Examples are the Government Information (Public Access) Act 2009 (NSW) and the Freedom of Information Act 1982 (Cth), which facilitate access to

requiring public authorities to provide reasons for decisions affecting a person.[59]

A second element for procedural justice is public participation in decision-making. Principle 10 of the Rio Declaration emphasises the need for public participation in environmental decision-making processes. The Aarhus Convention implements Principle 10.[60] The UNEP Guidelines recommend norms and practices to achieve effective public participation.[61]

Although most jurisdictions meet some of these recommendations, few would fully meet all. Public participation is most commonly found in procedures for environmental impact assessment and project approval.[62] A review of Australian laws dealing with public participation in environmental impact assessment found that they, with some exceptions, satisfy the minimum requirements in Article 6 of the Aarhus Convention.[63]

What is evident, however, is that environmental laws restrict who is entitled to procedural justice to the present generation of humans. Future generations of humans, and non-human nature, have no entitlement to participation. Procedural justice is based in participatory parity – the capability of participating on par with the rest of society.[64] Excluded entities suffer participatory, and hence procedural, injustice. The solution is to afford full status to those who have been excluded to have their viewpoints and interests included in deliberative and discursive decision-making. As I earlier observed, a case can be made for extending the community of justice to include non-human nature.[65]

How might non-human nature be able to participate? Various suggestions have been made. Obviously there needs to be human agency – humans need to act as agents on behalf of non-human nature. Dryzek suggests that we need to enlarge our conception of communication. Nature can communicate non-verbally.[66] The signals emanating from the natural world include disruptions to the physical integrity of nature, such as climate change or species extinction. Schlosberg explains this using the example of climate change. Climate change is demonstrated in not only

---

government information prior to seeking review of government action in courts or tribunals.

59 Administrative Decisions (Judicial Review) Act 1977 (Cth), s 13(1).

60 See Aarhus Convention, arts 1, 6, 7 and 8.

61 Guidelines 8–14 of the UNEP Guidelines.

62 Bates (2010) 302.

63 Lambropoulos (2010).

64 Schlosberg (2007) 157.

65 Ibid, 131–57.

66 Dryzek (2000) 149.

atmospheric studies but also by signals like migratory birds returning earlier, species expanding or contracting their range, insect eggs hatching earlier, glaciers melting, oceans warming, and weather issues such as increased rainfall in some areas and drought in others. These separate warnings together signal climate change.[67]

Baxter suggests that interests of the 'inarticulate' can be articulated through proxies.[68] Proxies can represent those who cannot represent themselves.[69] Non-participants include future generations of humans, and non-human nature. Eckersley uses the concept of 'political trusteeship': persons and groups within the polity speaking on behalf of the interests of those outside the polity.[70] Eckersley suggests a variety of ways that proxy knowledge could enhance environmental decision-making: including environmental monitoring, reporting and impact assessment. Eckersley also suggests that there could be proxy representation through independent Environmental Defender's Offices.[71] Stone argues that natural objects, such as rivers, forests and trees, should have legal rights to make claims to protect against damage or to seek compensation and reparation for damage. Natural objects could vocalise their claims through appointed legal spokespersons.[72]

Needless to say, most jurisdictions' environmental laws have yet to embrace these suggestions. There are few examples where non-human nature has been recognised. One example is in the Constitution of Ecuador[73] and another is the recognition of the Whanganui River in New Zealand.[74]

The third element of procedural justice is review procedures before a court or tribunal to challenge decision-making or impairment of rights. Principle 10 of the Rio Declaration requires provision of access to judicial and administrative proceedings, including redress and remedy. The Aarhus Convention provides the right to challenge public decisions made without respect for rights of access to environmental information or participation in decision-making.[75] The UNEP Guidelines suggest norms and practices for facilitating access to justice.[76]

---

[67] Schlosberg (2007) 192.
[68] Baxter (2000) 54–6.
[69] Schlosberg (2007) 193.
[70] Eckersley (2004) 114.
[71] Ibid, 135.
[72] C Stone (1972); (1985); (1987); (2012).
[73] Article 71 of Ecuador's revised Constitution of 2008. See also Williams (2013) 268.
[74] See Finlayson (2012). See also Williams (2013) 270.
[75] See Aarhus Convention, arts 1 and 9.
[76] Guidelines 18–26 of the UNEP Guidelines.

Jurisdictions vary in the degree to which access to justice principles are satisfied. I have suggested conditions for successful public interest litigation.[77] The conditions are: adequate environmental laws; a justifiable legal action; a willing and able plaintiff; knowledgeable, experienced and willing lawyers; funding; standing to sue; evidence; simple and affordable procedures for commencing litigation; court practice and procedure that are not barriers to justice; little delay in determining the litigation; an independent, impartial and competent court; and adequate remedies.

JUSTICE AS RECOGNITION

Environmental justice also involves recognition. Recognition is distinct from but closely connected to distribution and procedure. Lack of recognition, in the social and political realms, is demonstrated by various insults, degradation and devaluation. It inflicts damage, constrains individuals and communities and leads to ineffective participation in the polity (procedural injustice) and to inequalities in distribution (distributive injustice).[78]

At the core of misrecognition are processes that devalue some individuals, groups or communities compared to others, reflecting unequal patterns of recognition across social groups. Institutions of the state can give unequal recognition to social groups. There is also a wider cultural basis of misrecognition such that 'the conception of justice occupies social and cultural space beyond the bounds of the state'.[79]

Fraser argues that misrecognition is an injury to the institutional or social status of individuals or communities and is not merely psychological damage.[80] Fraser identifies three processes of misrecognition which lead to status injury: first, a general practice of cultural domination and oppression; second, a pattern of non-recognition, equivalent to being rendered invisible; and third, disrespect or being routinely maligned or disparaged in stereotypical public and cultural representations.[81]

Misrecognition is evident with respect to indigenous peoples and cultural minorities. Decisions concerning locating waste, for example, have worked injustice in recognition of indigenous groups and poor communities.[82]

---

77 Preston (2014b) 25.
78 Schlosberg (2007) 14.
79 Ibid 16.
80 Ibid 18.
81 Fraser (1998) 3, 7.
82 Walker (2012) 78–83.

Injustice by misrecognition is also evident of individuals and groups advocating environmental causes. They are routinely described in pejorative terms like busybodies, greenies, NIMBYs,[83] BANANAs,[84] LULUs,[85] or FRUITs.[86] Such labelling is part of a pattern of misrecognition in the form of insults, stigmatisation and devaluation of individuals and groups and their concerns. This cultural domination, non-recognition and disrespect injures their social status, constrains their participation in decision-making, and occasions unequal distribution of environmental burdens.

Schlosberg develops Fraser's status injury approach to examine how non-human nature is disrespected in human culture in these ways.[87] As Schlosberg notes, Fraser's insistence on the status of the misrecognised individual or group makes the application of recognition as an element of ecological justice much easier:

> The status model is not aimed at valorizing individual or group identity or at recognising the psychological plight of individual victims, but instead at overcoming subordination. In this, we can dismiss the criticism that recognition of, for example, the agency or integrity of the natural world necessitates an anthropomorphizing or a psychological need for recognition in the non-human world. We can see nature injured, its interests ignored, autonomy dismissed, or its integrity damaged without resorting to such psychological language or conceptions.[88]

If the community of justice were extended, the status injury approach could be applied to individual organisms and groups of organisms (populations) and also to systems such as ecological communities and ecosystems.[89]

Institutions of the state can address misrecognition by enabling meaningful involvement of non-human nature in policy and decision-making,

---

83 A pejorative term for residents who oppose new development because it is close to them and say it should be: 'Not In My Back Yard' (NIMBY), see Shively (2007).

84 The negative term used to criticise the ongoing opposition of advocacy groups to land development anywhere: "Build Absolutely Nothing Anywhere Near Anyone" (BANANA), see Shively (2007).

85 The negative term used to characterise local opposition to unwanted land uses: "Locally Unwanted Land Uses" (LULU), see Shively (2007).

86 The negative term, used in a development industry article in Vancouver, to refer to allegedly irrational local opponents (fruit cakes or fruit loops) of urban redevelopments: "Fear of Revitalisation, Urban-Infill and Towers" (FRUIT), see Mureşanu and Mureşanu (2013) 235.

87 Schlosberg (2007) 19, 138–42.

88 Ibid, 139.

89 Ibid, 148–9.

and distributions with proper regard to the needs, interests, vulnerabilities and integrity of non-human nature. Non-human nature can be afforded recognition through proxies, trustees, guardians or legal spokespersons.

Misrecognition is only one way in which injustice as recognition can occur. Misrecognition is a failure to give the recognition that is warranted for individuals or groups. Another form of injustice is mal-recognition, involving recognition of a malignant kind. An example is where action is taken against individuals or groups, who have exercised democratic rights (such as public participation or protest), to prevent them from continuing to effectively exercise such rights. This is demonstrated by strategic litigation against public participation, or SLAPP suits.[90] SLAPP suits aim to stifle humans from exercising their rights or to punish them for having done so.[91] People targeted in a SLAPP suit often pay a 'price' for participation in litigation, including lost financial resources and time, and emotional stress.[92] To reduce mal-recognition, environmental laws should afford protection to entities that are vulnerable to mal-recognition.[93] The courts have a role in devising, implementing and following practices aimed at reducing mal-recognition to facilitate environmental justice.[94]

CONCLUSION

Achieving environmental justice requires a holistic and comprehensive approach, tackling the institutional, political, social, economic and legal factors that impede equal justice for all. Restrictions on membership of, and impartial treatment between members of, the community of justice need to be addressed. Misrecognition of individuals and groups, in human society and in non-human nature, needs to be overcome. Participatory parity needs to be extended to all members of the community of justice including future generations and non-human nature. Fair and just distributions of environmental benefits and burdens to members of the community of justice need to be effected. Only by achieving justice as recognition, procedural justice and distributional justice can access to environmental justice be achieved.

---

90 See, eg, Pring and Canan (1996); Pring (1989); Preston (2014b).
91 Pring (1989) 5–6.
92 Ibid.
93 Preston (2014b) 27.
94 See also Pring and Pring (2009) 53.

REFERENCES

Barton, C. (2001), 'Aiming at the Target: Achieving the Objects of Sustainable Development in Agency Decision-Making' 13 Geo Int'l Envtl L Rev 837.

Bates, G. (2010), *Environmental Law in Australia* (7th edn, Chatswood, NSW: LexisNexis).

Baxter, B. (2000), 'Ecological Justice and Justice as Impartiality' 9 *Environmental Politics* 43.

Baxter, B. (2005), *A Theory of Ecological Justice* (Abingdon: Routledge).

Benton, T. (1993), *Natural Relations: Ecology, Animal Rights and Social Justice* (London: Verso).

Bullen, E. (2006), 'Legislative Limits on Environmental Decision-Making: The Application of the Administrative Law Doctrines of Jurisdictional Fact and Ultra Vires' 23 EPLJ 265.

Dryzek, J. (2000), *Deliberative Democracy and Beyond: Liberals, Critics and Contestation* (Oxford: Oxford University Press).

Dworkin, R. (1978), *Taking Rights Seriously* (Cambridge, MA: Harvard University Press).

Dworkin, R. (1986), *Laws Empire* (Cambridge, MA: Belknap Press).

Dwyer, G. and M. Taylor (2013), 'Moving from Consideration to Application: the Update of Principles of Ecologically Sustainable Development in Environmental Decision-Making in New South Wales' 30 EPLJ 185.

Eckersley, R. (2004), *The Green State: Rethinking Democracy and Sovereignty* (Cambridge, MA: MIT Press).

Elders, J. (2005), 'Rudolph Von Jhering, (1818–92) and the Economics of Justice' in Jürgen G Backhaus, *The Elgar Companion to Law and Economics* (2nd edn, Cheltenham, UK and Northampton, MA, USA: Edward Elgar).

Finlayson, C. (2012), 'Whanganui River Agreement Signed' (30 August 2012) accessed 9 March 2015 at www.beehive.govt.nz/release/whanganui-river-agreement-signed.

Fisher, D. (2001), 'Sustainability – the Principle, its Implementation and its Enforcement' 18 EPLJ 361.

Fowler, R., 'Environmental Law and its Administration in Australia' (1984) 1 EPLJ 10.

Fraser, N. (1998), 'Social Justice in the Age of Identity Politics: Redistribution, Recognition, and Participation' in G. Peterson (ed.), *The Tanner Lectures on Human Values* (Vol 19, Salt Lake City, UT: University of Utah Press).

Hillman, M. (2004), 'The Importance of Environmental Justice in Stream Rehabilitation' 7 *Ethics, Place and Environment* 19.

Iyer, K. (1996), 'Nature-Friendly Planning of Humanity's Future: Dialectics and Dynamics of Development Management' 31 *Economic and Political Weekly* 2297.

Krier, J. (1970), 'Environmental Litigation and the Burden of Proof' in M. Baldwin and J. Page (eds), *Law and the Environment* (New York: Walker & Co).

Lambropoulos, V. (2010), 'What Can Australia Learn from the Europeans about Public Participation, Article 6 of the Aarhus Convention and Environmental Impact Statements' 27 EPLJ 272.

Leopold, A. (1949), *A Sand County Almanac* (Oxford: Oxford University Press).

Lipman, Z. and M. Farrugia (2013), 'Obligation to Report and Manage Pollution Incidents' 18 LGLJ 18.

Moore, G. (1912), *Ethics* (London: Thornton Butterworth).
Mureşanu, F. and M. Mureşanu (2013), 'Cannibal Architecture Hates BANANAs: Post-Communist Rebranding of Historical Sites' in S. Sonnenburg and L. Baker (eds), *Branded Spaces: Experience Enactments and Entanglements* (Wiesbaden: Springer), 229.
Nussbaum, M. (2006), *Frontiers of Justice: Disability, Nationality, Species Membership* (Cambridge, MA: Harvard University Press).
Nussbaum, M. and A. Sen (eds) (1993), *The Quality of Life* (Oxford: Clarendon Press).
Posner, R. (1981), *The Economics of Justice* (Cambridge, MA: Harvard University Press).
Posner, R. (2007), *Economic Analysis of Law* (7th edn, New York: Wolters Kluwer).
Pound, R. (1999), *The Spirit of the Common Law* (Piscataway, NJ: Transaction Publishers).
Preston, B. (1986), 'Third Party Appeals in Environmental Law Matters in New South Wales' 60 *Australian Law Journal* 215.
Preston, B. (2014a), 'Internalising Ecocentrism in Environment Law' in M. Maloney and P. Burdon (eds), *Wild Law – In Practice* (Abingdon: Routledge).
Preston, B. (2014b), 'Environmental Public Interest Litigation: Conditions for Success' in K. Uga (ed.), *Towards an Effective Guarantee of the Green Access* (Tokyo: Shinzansha).
Preston, J. (2014), 'Participation from the Deep Freeze: "Chilling" by SLAPP Suits' 31 EPLJ 47.
Pring, G. (1989), '"SLAPPs": Strategic Lawsuits Against Public Participation' 7 Pace Envtl L Rev 1.
Pring, G. and P. Canan (1996), *SLAPPs: Getting Sued for Speaking Out* (Philadelphia, PA: Temple University Press).
Pring, G. and C. Pring (2009), *Greening Justice: Creating and Improving Environmental Courts and Tribunals* (The Access Initiative).
Rawls, J. (1971), *A Theory of Justice* (Cambridge, MA: Harvard University Press).
Rawls, J. (2001), *Justice as Fairness: A Restatement* (Cambridge, MA: Harvard University Press).
Ricketts, A. and N. Rogers (1999), 'Third Party Rights in NSW Environmental Legislation: the Backlash' 16 EPLJ 157.
Robinson, N. (2013), 'Environmental Principles & Norms Amidst the Anthropocene' (11th Annual Colloquium of the IUCN Academy of Environmental Law, Hamilton, 26 June 2013).
Rohde, J. (1995), 'The Objects Clause in Environmental Legislation – The Nature Conservation Act 1992 (Qld) Exemplified' 12 EPLJ 80.
Schlosberg, S. (2007), *Defining Environmental Justice: Theories, Movements and Nature* (Oxford: Oxford University Press).
Sen, A. (1999), *Development as Freedom* (Oxford: Oxford University Press).
Sen, A. (2006), 'Human Rights and Capabilities' 6 *Journal of Human Development* 151.
Sen, A. (2009), *The Idea of Justice* (London: Allen & Lane).
Shively, C. (2007), 'Understanding the NIMBY and LULU Phenomena: Reassessing Our Knowledge Base and Informing Future Research' 21 *Journal of Planning Literature* 255.

Stone, C. (1972), 'Should Trees Have Standing? Towards Legal Rights for Natural Objects' 45 S Cal L Rev 450.

Stone, C. (1985), 'Should Trees Have Standing? Revisited: How Far will Law and Morals Reach? A Pluralist Perspective' 59 S Cal L Rev 1.

Stone, C. (1987), *Earth and Other Ethics – A Case for Moral Pluralism* (New York: Harper & Rowe).

Stone, C. (2012), 'Response to Commentators' 3 *Journal of Human Rights and the Environment* 100.

Stone, J. (1964), *Legal System and Lawyers' Reasonings* (Sydney: Maitland Publications Pty Ltd).

Swaminathan, M. (2011), *In Search of Bio-happiness – Biodiversity & Food, Health and Livelihood Security* (Singapore: World Scientific Publishing Co).

Tribe, L. (1974), 'Ways Not to Think about Plastic Trees: New Foundations For Environmental Law' 83 Yale LJ 1315.

Walker, G. (2012), *Environmental Justice: Concepts, Evidence and Politics* (Abingdon: Routledge).

Williams, C. (2013), 'Wild Law in Australia: Practice and Possibilities' 30 EPLJ 259.

3. The rule of law in the Anthropocene

Klaus Bosselmann

INTRODUCTION

The term *Anthropocene* marks a new geological epoch of significant human impact on the Earth's ecosystems. Human activities have caused climate change, biodiversity loss, ozone depletion, ocean acidification, overuse in land and freshwater, chemical pollution and interference with nitrogen and phosphorus cycles. Scientists believe that each of these ecosystems or processes has a certain 'boundary' (that is, threshold or tipping point) which, if crossed, may trigger non-linear changes in the functioning of the Earth system as a whole. Collectively, therefore, these 'planetary boundaries' define the safe operating space for humanity with respect to the Earth system.[1]

Ensuring a safe operating space for humanity is the central challenge in the Anthropocene. A precondition for meeting the challenge is some coordinated effort based on global responsibility across nations and cultures. It is doubtful, however, that an effort of this nature currently exists. So far, national interests have only allowed for a set of lowest common denominators: general agreements on climate change, biodiversity loss, desertification or poverty and human rights. There is, at this point in time, no real global responsibility and no sense of urgency for lowering humanity's overall impact on the Earth system.

Yet, the Anthropocene requires nothing less. We must revise our ethics and our laws in order to adapt them to conditions that allow for a just, sustainable world within the limits of planetary boundaries. A fundamental rule of self-constraint is needed, a rule that respects the integrity of the Earth's ecosystems.

Such a rule does not yet exist, but is in a *status nascendi*. As will be argued here, international environmental law as well as international law in general follow a certain logic that may well lead to the recognition of such a rule. If

[1] Rockström *et al.* (2009) 472–5. See also its critiques, e.g., Brook and others (2013) 396–401.

it is true that the political legitimacy of nation-states rests on their ability to provide, at least potentially, for the well-being of their citizens,[2] then a globalised and finite world sets new demands, ultimately the demand for transnational cooperation on issues that are pre-conditional to human existence and well-being. Securing peace is one of these issues, securing a safe operating space within planetary boundaries is another. Traditionally, international law had its focus on prevention (of war). With the emergence of international humanitarian and human rights law and international economic and environmental law the focus has shifted from pure prevention to active design. This shift is the signum of a globalised world and will be essential in the Anthropocene where human activities need to be controlled not only in terms of their impact on other people, but on the entire planet. In a finite world, the logic of self-constraint is compelling and it seems only a matter of time until we can meaningfully speak of a rule to live within the limits of the Earth system. The logic is implicit in the traditions of ecological law,[3] sustainability law, sustainable development law and Earth jurisprudence,[4] and the rule derived from this logic manifests itself in the growing literature around a 'rule of law for nature' [5] or a 'rule of ecological law'.[6]

In December 2012, the UN General Assembly heard what may be required here when it discussed the Report 'Harmony for Nature' prepared by the Secretary-General.[7] Here are some excerpts of the Report:

> 45. Numerous scientists, economists, and legal experts have decried the escalating destruction of the Earth's natural systems (. . .) They are insisting that, rather than people and planet serving the infinite growth of the economy, economy must recognize its place as servant to the larger well-being of humans and the Earth itself.
> 46. In this new system, the rule of law, science, and economics will be grounded in the Earth. (. . .)
> 47. A key challenge in developing a global governance system built on the rule of ecological law is reinvigorating a transformed sense of democracy, in which individuals and communities embrace their ecological citizenship in the world and act on their responsibility to respect the complex workings of the Earth's life systems.

---

[2] Barker (1990); Münch (2001); Falk in Balb, Land, Staring, Van Steenbergen, Wilterdink (eds) (2000).

[3] Stone (1972); Bosselmann (1985) 345–361; Bosselmann (1986) 1–22; Bosselmann (1995); Schröter, (1999).

[4] Berry (1999); Cullinan (2003); Burdon (ed.) (2011); Burdon (2013).

[5] Voigt (ed.) (2013).

[6] Garver (2013) 316–37.

[7] UN Report *Sustainable Development Harmony with Nature* of the Secretary-General, A/67/ 17 August 2012.

Such comments hint to new fundamentals of law and governance: the rule of ecological law, a transformed sense of democracy, the concept of ecological citizenship and responsibility for the Earth's life systems. They are the typical categories of law in the Anthropocene.

MORALITY FOR THE ANTHROPOCENE

Some preliminary remarks may be in order on what the Anthropocene entails, what it means morally and what it could mean for the development of law.

The *Anthropocene* (literally 'Age of Man') describes our epoch of *homo sapiens* now roaming the entire globe and pushing planetary boundaries. This epoch began with the Industrial Revolution – triggered by the invention of steam engine, fuelled by coal and oil and driven by the paradigm of progress and growth.[8] But only the last 50 years saw the explosion of population numbers and of economic prosperity, known as the 'Great Acceleration' – the acceleration of socio-economic processes in stark conflict with the carrying-capacity of the planet. Today, humanity uses the equivalent of 1.5 planets to provide the resources we use and absorb our waste.[9]

Humans have now transformed the Earth's life systems in ways that pose a real danger to our own survival and the survival of other life. This is a new phenomenon. It is, however, the result of another transformation of human development that began 12,000 years ago with the emergence of agriculture and the Neolithic Revolution. This provided the base for permanent settlements and niche building that is now manifest in the urban concentrations where the majority of our species live. So as we have transformed the face of the Earth by agricultural and other conversions of landscapes, we have transformed our social organisation – from the equality of hunter-gatherer bands to a hierarchy of privilege based on acquired wealth from the earth and manifested now in territorial behaviour like some other social species have. Hunter-gatherers shared the common

---

[8] There is some debate around the beginning and notion of the *Anthropocene*. The International Commission on Stratigraphy, concerned with issues of geological time, currently explores an exact definition for the Anthropocene (Working Group on the 'Anthropocene' of the Subcommission on Quaternary Stratigraphy http://quaternary.stratigraphy.org/workinggroups/anthropocene accessed 9 March 2015. See also the article by science journalist Voosen (2012).

[9] Global Footprint Network http://www.footprintnetwork.org/en/index.php/GFN/page/world_footprint/ accessed 9 March 2015.

space, but agriculture made us territorial. In legal terms, humanity has shifted from sharing the commons to adopting exclusive property rights.[10]

The significance of this shift can hardly be overestimated,[11] but it took many centuries for the process of the enclosure of the commons to unfold.[12] Exclusive property rights have been created by political liberalism and exercised by individuals, companies and states. They are the legal mechanism that has shaped modern civilization and are the key for its continued existence. It is difficult to imagine how a sustainable future could be achieved without major changes to the system of property rights and land ownership.[13] If we do not find a way of exercising temperance and self-control in the context of property rights, Garrett Hardin's 'Tragedy of the Commons' will finally be complete.

But what might generate such temperance and self-control? We could be pessimistic here considering the power of capitalism with its roots deeply embedded in the European traditions of dualism, anthropocentrism, materialism and expansionism.[14] On the other hand, we could celebrate the European traditions of humanism, human rights and democracy as among humanity's greatest achievements. If we manage to strengthen this part of our common heritage then we can be more optimistic.

The point is that all achievements of modern civilization, good or bad, are manifestations of a morality that has placed humans over nature. Such a morality may have been good enough for the amazing advancements in science, technology and prosperity in the Holocene, but has begun to show its dark side. Its ecological arrogance and ignorance spells our collective downfall, at least, in the long run. The moral challenge in the Anthropocene, therefore, is to move from a human-centric to an Earth-centric (or ecocentric) paradigm.

Not by coincidence the Preamble of the Earth Charter begins with this sentence: 'We stand at a critical moment in Earth's history, a time when humanity must choose its future.' The Earth Charter defines respect and care for the community of life – not just human life – as fundamental to all law and governance. The problem is, of course, that such ethical shift cannot be installed per decree, but only be advocated through the educational and political process.

What we as legal teachers and researchers can do, however, is to show

---

10 Schlatter (1951); Freyfogle (2003).

11 See Polanyi (1944); generally acclaimed as the most influential work of economic history.

12 Gonner (1966); McCloskey (1975) 123–60; Thirsk (1989).

13 Bosselmann in Grinlinton and Taylor (eds.) (2011) 23–42.

14 Bosselmann (2010) 2430.

the failures of the existing legal system and describe the changes needed for a better one.[15] The failures can be seen on a daily basis and are all around us. For example, the huge gap between rich and poor undermines all prospects for sustainability, but governments seem incapable of controlling the rich and transnational corporate power. Here we need to discuss the social dimension of property rights. Or think of climate change. The air is free for everyone and corporates use their power to determine the price that they are prepared to pay. Governments, in turn, fear for the competitiveness of their national economies and do not act. Here we need to discuss the social dimension of property rights. The social and ecological blindness of property rights is at the core of the law's failure to achieve sustainability. Fundamentally, the legal system needs to be organised around sustainability not property.[16]

The good news is that these concerns are beginning to sink in. This makes it more and more absurd to separate the world of economics (around property) from the world of ecology (around sustainability). The paradigm of separation is still dominating legal curricula and scholarship, but environmental law has always been about integration, for 25 years now known as 'sustainable development'. That is why environmental law can function as a vanguard of law in general.

Sustainable development law is the antithesis of current fragmented law as it integrates environmental, economic and social concerns. It cannot succeed, however, as long as it remains a vague idea and rather detached from the ecological reality and disconnected from the basics of the legal system including property rights, state sovereignty and the rule of law.

So here is my suggestion for a two-step strategy.

The first step is to recognise the reality of planetary boundaries. Of the nine boundaries identified thus far,[17] three have already been exceeded (atmospheric greenhouse gas concentrations, rate of biodiversity loss and nitrogen cycle). The recognition of planetary boundaries sets a non-negotiable bottom-line for all human activities. More particularly, and in the context of the concept of sustainable development, it suggests a hierarchical order of its three constituent elements: the natural environment comes first, human society second and economic prosperity third. Such an understanding of sustainable development ('strong sustainability') reflects the reality of planetary boundaries and marks the first step towards a refined rule of law.

---

[15] See, for example, Voigt (2013).

[16] Grinlinton and Taylor (eds) (2011) (n 13).

[17] Rockström and others (2009).

The second step is to take the strong sustainability approach to the design and interpretation of laws governing human behaviour. The rule of law is the most basic tool to ensure control and accountability of governments. It demands that governmental decisions are bound by law and implies that all citizens are subject to the law. But not any law can count for the true meaning of the rule of law. A purely 'formal' or 'thin'[18] recognition of the rule of law, deprived of any values and content, permits any man and his dog claiming compliance. Such formalism is not what I have in mind here and is surely not good enough for nations that describe themselves as civilized and supportive of the virtues of citizenry.

THE RULE OF LAW IN AN ECOLOGICAL CONTEXT

It may not be obvious why the rule of law should have a central importance for the formulation of law in the Anthropocene. It lacks, after all, clear meaning and is not universally defined. On the other hand, any rule of law depends on the existence of a state, a constitution, the law and judicial review. To this end, we can locate the rule of law as a concept to ensure the functioning of these institutions. A state has absolute authority (sovereignty), but is bound by constitutional rights and duties; it governs by way of positive law, but is controlled by independent courts. Such basic arrangements make it possible to speak of the rule of law as a fundamental concept for the way society governs itself. Its practical purpose is to minimise the risk of arbitrariness and inequality.

Historically, the transition from *Rex Lex* ('The King is Law') to *Lex Rex* ('The Law is King') marked the beginning of the modern constitutional state. Despite their different histories, cultures and practices, all European governing regimes share this legal heritage. Today, the entire international system of sovereign constitutional states is based on the rule of law.[19]

Beyond such commonality, there is uncertainty and treatises of the rule of law usually begin with observing that the rule of law is an 'ideal' and a 'highly contested idea'.[20] Yet most agree that the rule of law is a concept of multiple, complexly interwoven strands that reflect certain values and

---

18 Tamanaha (2004).

19 Garner (2009) 1448.

20 Belton (Carnegie Papers 2005); Shklar in Hutchinson and Monahan (eds.) (1987) 1.

ideologies.[21] This calls for a further investigation of which values and ideologies might be relevant here and in the context of the Anthropocene.

A recent report for the European Commission,[22] for example, acknowledges a variety of meanings of the rule of law, but specifically identifies some core elements across legal cultures and expressed in numerous international documents: (1) independence and impartiality of the judiciary, (2) legal certainty, (3) non-discrimination and equality before the law, (4) respect for human rights, (5) separation of powers, (6) the principle that the state is bound by law, and (7) the substantive coherence of the legal framework.[23] The report concludes by stating that it can be deduced there exists a rule in customary international law that demands that the rule of law operates in the states as a precondition for membership in international organisations.[24]

The international recognition is perhaps the most significant feature of the rule of law principle. If the rule of law can be seen as a defining characteristic of the modern state, then any linking with universally accepted principles – in whatever shape or form – would have ramifications for the contents of domestic *and* international law. This is already the case with respect to universally accepted principles such as respect for human rights, the principle of legality or the idea of a constitutional state based on fundamental rights. However, what could be more fundamental as the protection of human life and the physical conditions that human life depends on? Surely, the protection of ecological conditions as prerequisite for human life and well-being can, today, be recognised as a universally accepted principle, at least, morally.

So what would it take to *legally* recognise such a principle in the context of the rule of law?

For several years now, the World Justice Project of the American Bar Association has measured the strength of the rule of law principle around the world and ranks countries according to their governments' accountability, the absence of corruption, clarity and stability of laws, fundamental rights, open government, regulatory enforcement and access to justice. The latest Rule of Law Index 2012–13[25] has the five Scandinavian countries (including Finland and Iceland) topping the list of the world's most respected countries. They are followed by the Netherlands, then

---

[21] E.g. Loughlin (2010) 312; Fallon Jr. (1997); Flores and Himma (eds.) (2013) 1 *et pass.*

[22] Ehm (2010).

[23] Ibid. at 7.

[24] Ibid. at 16.

[25] Agrast, Botero, Martinez, Ponce and Pratt (2013).

Germany, Austria and New Zealand (with the USA way down the list). The interesting thing here is that, with the exception of New Zealand, the top ten countries do not even refer to the 'rule of law' in their respective jurisdictions.

Instead, they speak of *Rätt staat* (Danish/Swedish/Norwegian) and *Rechtsstaat* (German/Dutch) or *Rechtsstaatsprinzip* and *Rechtsstaatlichkeit* (German). The literal translation of 'rule of law' (for example, *Herrschaft des Rechts*) would be far too limiting to capture the system of principles and values associated with the *concept* of the rule of law. One obvious difference is that virtually all continental European countries relate the idea of law (*Recht, Rätt, Droit, Derecho, Diritto*) to the idea of the state (*Staat, Etat, Estado, Stato*). Both ideas are intertwined and describe the expectation that a government gains legitimacy and legality only through adherence to predefined standards and principles.

It is typical for the Romano-Germanic legal tradition to derive the content of the rule of law from an entire system of mutually reinforcing and limiting principles. Depending on what principles are invoked and how they are defined, it is possible to give the *Rechtsstaat* certain content. In Germany we speak of *sozialer Rechtsstaat* ('social constitutional state'), *Umweltstaat*[26] ('environment state') or *ökologischer Rechtsstaat*[27] ('eco-constitutional state'). Such contextualised understanding allows for a fruitful discourse on the importance of ecological responsibilities and the rule of law. In Germany, this discourse started in the mid-1980s and prompted a very promising investigation of the Joint Constitutional Commission of Bundestag and Bundesrat. The 1989 final report of the Joint Commission concluded that the question of an ecological rule of law is of such importance that only a wider public debate among the relevant sectors of society could advance this matter. German unification and full-blown neoclassic economics has silenced this debate, but it never really stopped. Michael Kloepfer, a pioneer of German environmental law, recently observed the ongoing 'ecologicalization of the legal system' and an increasing 'ecologicalization of society'.[28] As the ecological crisis continues to evolve, it is likely that we will see more of this fundamental debate in the years to come.

Like in Germany, the past two decades saw moves towards an ecological rule of law in many other civil law jurisdictions such as Switzerland, Austria, France, Spain, Portugal, South Africa, and Latin American countries including Brazil, Venezuela and particularly Bolivia and

---

26 Kloepfer (ed) (1994); Callies (2001).

27 Bosselmann (1992) and Bosselmann (1995) (n 3); Steinberg (1998).

28 Kloepfer in Kube *et al.* (eds.) (2013) 869.

Ecuador. What we could learn here is that, conceptually, the rule of law can be expanded to include ecological responsibilities.

Arguably, the same is true for the rule of law outside civil law jurisdictions including international law and the Anglo-Saxon common law system. To illustrate this I want to particularly acknowledge Scandinavian legal scholarship and briefly discuss two important achievements.

One is Environmental Law Methodology (ELM) as developed by one of the pioneers of environmental law, the late Staffan Westerlund. Taking a system-theoretical approach, ELM looks at law and the environment from an external point of view. Rather than conventional legal theory with its focus on internal structure and content, ELM is interested in the reality of natural systems and their representation in legal systems. This opens the view for the mismatch between ecological realities and legal construct. From an ELM perspective it is obvious that environmental law has largely failed. In the words of Staffan Westerlund: 'Environmental Law as an academic discipline has not really achieved anything of significance for ecological sustainability'.[29] He adds: 'Not even in New Zealand with its 1991 Resource Management Act'. We here in New Zealand certainly know what Westerlund was talking about. After a promising start with the so-called environmental bottom-line approach to interpret the purpose of the RMA, the supposed overall judgment approach took over and reduced ecological sustainability to just one concern among others. The latest chapter in the NZ experience is that the current government wants to rip the heart out of the RMA altogether by favouring economic development over environmental concerns. So NZ is perfectly in line with the rest of the world and sustainable development remains a distant illusion.

If Westerlund is right, and I think he is, then environmental law needs to focus on ecological sustainability as its central point of reference.

Other achievements of Scandinavian scholarship include insights into the effectiveness (or lack of it) of international environmental law. Apart from Westerlund, the work by Jonas Ebbesson,[30] Inga Carlman,[31] Martti Koskenniemi,[32] Tina Korvela,[33] Hans-Christian Bugge,[34]

---

[29] Westerlund in Bugge and Voigt (eds.) (2008) 48–65.

[30] E.g. *Compatibility of International and National Environmental Law* (1999).

[31] E.g. 'The rule of sustainability and planning adaptivity' (2005) 34(2) *Ambio*, 163–8.

[32] E.g. 'Hegemonic Regimes', in Young (ed) (2012); Koskenniemi (2009).

[33] *Taking Aims Seriously: How legal ecology affects judicial decision-making* (unpubl. Helsinki 2012).

[34] E.g. '"Our common future" revisited' in Bugge and Voigt (eds) (n 29) 3 – 83.

Christina Voigt[35] and many others has shown that international environmental law lacks coherence, direction and fundament.[36] There is no clear guidance, essentially no specific law. In her book 'The Significance of the Default',[37] Adalheidur Johannsdottir from the University of Iceland has asked what happens when there is no specific law: What is the law if there is no law? If a treaty contains no specific duties around ecological sustainability, then the default position is state sovereignty with its traditional right to exploit and use natural resources. And that is the problem. There is little incentive for states to be serious about global responsibilities if they can rely on their default position. So any lack of global commitment goes in their favour of national sovereignty which is the equivalent to exclusive private property. To reverse this bizarre logic, the default position needs to be ecological sustainability. That is the result of Johanndottir's remarkable research.

International law as well as domestic law need to include the principle of sustainability as a fundamental norm, a *grundnorm*.[38]

A *grundnorm* can be defined as a basic norm to bind governmental power in the same sense as the rule of law is generally perceived as a basic norm to bind governmental power. This understanding differs from Kelsen's definition[39] and is closer to Immanuel Kant's argument that any positive law must be grounded in a 'natural' or 'basic' norm of general acceptance and reasonableness. The existence of an environmental *grundnorm*, therefore, rests on the assumption that respecting the planet's ecological boundaries is a dictate of reason (*Gebot der Vernunft*) and general acceptance (*allgemeine Gültigkeit*).[40] According to Kelsen's Pure Theory of Law any basic norm can be a *grundnorm* so long as its bindingness can somehow be established. By contrast, Kant puts any candidate to the test of reasonableness. It certainly seems reasonable to assume the physical reality of a finite planet as generally acceptable and require all social and legal norms to be informed by it. In this vein we can postulate that keeping within planetary boundaries and protecting the integrity of ecological systems are a fundamental requirement for all human actions.

---

35 E.g. Voigt (2012) 164–6; Voigt (2009).

36 See also Kim and Bosselmann (2013) 285–309.

37 Johannsdottir (2009).

38 *Ibid.* at 292 and Bosselmann in Voigt (ed.) (2013) 75–93.

39 According to Kelsen's pure legal theory, the validity of positive law is conditional to the acceptance of a (not predefined) *Grundnorm*.

40 Kant (1907). Similarly, Robert Alexy asserts that Kant's basic norm 'may include moral elements' (2002, 147) and argues for a *grundnorm* to include 'content' (*ibid.* at 120).

Surely, ecological sustainability has *grundnorm* qualities that any legal norm, including the rule of law, ought to respect.[41]

THE MEANING AND FUNDAMENTALITY OF SUSTAINABILITY

The case for sustainability is not only scientifically and ethically strong, it can also be traced back to history. Virtually all cultures have historically followed the wisdom of sustainability, some more successfully than others, but all mindful of the basic human need to maintain and nurture the conditions on which life depends.

Western civilization is no exception. The concept of sustainability has been part of European cultural history. It can be found in medieval monasteries (first appearing in the Canticle of the Sun by Saint Francis of Assisi), in the writings of the philosophers of the enlightenment (Spinoza, Leibniz, Humboldt, Goethe), and in energy sciences and macro-economics.[42]

Three hundred years ago, in 1713, the economist Hans von Carlowitz published his book *Sylvicultura Oeconomica* (The Economy of Forestry)[43] that defines *Nachhaltigkeit* as the foundational principle of successful economic strategies. Through translations of this book first into French and then English the German word *Nachhaltigkeit* became known as sustainability. Essentially, the sustainability principle had importance in European economics and law until the beginning of the Industrial Revolution when it rapidly became forgotten and replaced by the idea of economic growth driven by fossil fuel, investment capital and associated debt.

So, the very origins of the Anthropocene can be described as the disappearance of long-term sustainability in favour of short-term gain. This gives us a clue about where our thinking about the Anthropocene must focus. As we are facing a collapse of ecological, social and economic systems we realise sustainability as the antonym, the opposite of collapse. In this sense, the authors of the 1972 Report to the Club of Rome[44] aimed for a world model that was 'sustainable, that is, without sudden and uncontrollable collapse'.[45]

We should acknowledge, therefore, that our modern sustainable development discourse following the 1987 Brundtland Report, did not start

---

41 Godden (2009) 808.
42 See Grober (2012).
43 von Carlowitz (2000 [1713]).
44 Meadows and Meadows and others (1972).
45 Grober (2012) 117.

from scratch. Rather it was informed by the idea that infinite growth in a finite world is not possible. Again, this was not a new idea itself as it was first raised by theorists such as Thomas Malthus and Friedrich Engels. However, the Club of Rome Report made the connection between economic growth and prospects for sustainability predicting eventual global collapse if the growth paradigm remains unchanged.

Today we can see just how destructive the obsession with growth is. Everything is sacrificed at its altar. Until quite recently, perhaps governments could have been excused for giving priority to growth over sustainability. The thinking was that only a growing economy allows for policies that make environmental protection possible in the first place. Sustainability-thinking aims for the opposite: only functioning ecological systems allow for policies that make economic prosperity possible in the first place. This is clear to see for everyone who observes what is going on. Governments are tragically trapped as they force their own citizens into austerity for the sake of upholding the growth paradigm. They rather accept social and environmental decline including climate collapse than reorganising financial and economic markets. What we see is crisis management around market failures, not governance for the commons.

Our only hope is governments do not forget sustainable development altogether, but start thinking about what it *really* means. As Staffan Westerlund pointed out: 'The core problem lies in achieving and maintaining ecological sustainability as the necessary foundation for sustainable development.'[46] The integrity of ecological systems should indeed be the starting-point for any considerations around sustainability and sustainable development.

The notion of ecological integrity[47] is by no means new and has been used in numerous legal documents including domestic law and international treaties. The concept first appeared in the international arena in 1978 with the Great Lakes Water Quality Agreement signed bilaterally between Canada and the United States,[48] whose purpose was 'to restore and maintain the chemical, physical, and biological integrity of the waters of the Great Lakes Basin Ecosystem'.[49] The first multilateral environmental treaty to include the notion of integrity was the

---

46 Westerlund in Bugge and Voigt (eds.) (2008).

47 E.g. the extensive work of over 20 years by the Global Ecological Integrity Group http://www.globalecointegrity.net (accessed 9 March 2015).

48 Agreement between the United States of America and Canada on Great Lakes Water Quality, Ottawa (Canada), 22 Nov. 1978, into force 22 November 1978, available at: http://www.ijc.org (accessed 9 March 2015).

49 Art. II GLWQA, ibid.

Convention on the Conservation of Antarctic Marine Living Resources adopted in 1980.[50] The parties to the Convention recognised 'the importance of safeguarding the environment and protecting the integrity of the ecosystem of the seas surrounding Antarctica'.[51] Since then, more than a dozen international environmental treaties have been adopted with some reference to ecological integrity in their preambular or operative parts.[52] Among soft law agreements designed around ecological integrity as a core concept are the 1982 World Charter for Nature,[53] the 1992 Rio Declaration on Environment and Development,[54] Agenda 21,[55] the Draft International Covenant on Environment and Development,[56] the Earth Charter,[57] the Plan of Implementation of the World Summit on Sustainable Development,[58] and The Future We Want.[59]

Today, it seems almost forgotten that the 1992 Rio Declaration commits, in its preamble, the UN member states to 'international agreements which respect the interests of all and protect the integrity of the global environmental and developmental system'.[60] Furthermore, Principle 7 obligates states to 'cooperate in a spirit of global partnership to conserve, protect and restore the health and integrity of the Earth's ecosystem'.[61] This was in the spirit of the World Charter for Nature of 1982, which firmly established the integrity of ecosystems or species as a non-negotiable bottom line when achieving 'optimum sustainable productivity' of natural resources.[62]

The Earth Charter, which was adopted in 2000 as global civil society's

---

[50] Convention on the Conservation of Antarctic Marine Living Resources, Canberra (Australia), 20 May 1980, in force 7 April 1982.

[51] Ibid., preamble.

[52] See Kim and Bosselmann (2013) 305.

[53] UNGA Resolution A/RES/37/7, 28 October 1982.

[54] Adopted by the UN Conference on Development and Environment, Rio de Janeiro (Brazil), 3–14 June 1992, UN Doc. A/CONF.151/26/Rev.1 (Vol. I), 14 June 1992.

[55] Agenda 21: Programme of Action for Sustainable Development, UN Doc. A/CONF.151/26, 14 June 1992.

[56] IUCN Environmental Law Programme (2010).

[57] The Earth Charter Initiative (2000).

[58] Report of the World Summit on Sustainable Development, Plan of Implementation of the World Summit on Sustainable Development, UN Doc. A/ CONF.199/20, 4 September 2002.

[59] UNGA Resolution A/RES/66/288, of 11 September 2012, Annex, The Future We Want.

[60] Rio Declaration (n 54).

[61] Principle 7 Rio Declaration.

[62] Principle 4 World Charter for Nature (n 53).

response to the Rio Declaration, is in its entirety designed around the concept of ecological integrity. Here, 'all individuals, organizations, businesses, governments, and transnational institutions' are urged to '[p]rotect and restore the integrity of Earth's ecological systems, with special concern for biological diversity and the natural processes that sustain life'.[63] Similarly, the 2010 IUCN Draft International Covenant on Environment and Development states as a first fundamental principle: 'Nature as a whole and all life forms warrant respect and are to be safeguarded. The integrity of the Earth's ecological systems shall be maintained and where necessary restored.'[64] Although still a draft, the inclusion here is significant because the Covenant is a codification of existing environmental law, and was intended as a blueprint for an international framework convention.

Such repeated references in legal and semi-legal documents *per se* would not suffice to suggest that the notion of protecting Earth's ecological integrity has become the ultimate goal of international environmental law. However, the concept of ecological integrity is emerging as one of the common denominators among the plethora of international environmental legal instruments. In this sense, the concept has the potential to be recognised and accepted as an environmental *grundnorm* of international law.[65]

CONCLUSION

Sometimes, the rule of law appears as a monstrance carried in front of a solemn procession. There was something eerily disturbing when President Bush said: 'America will always stand firm for the non-negotiable demands of human dignity, i.e. the rule of law' or when President Putin declared 'the principles of the rule of law amongst the country's highest priorities'. or when President Robert Mugabe explained: 'Only a government that subjects itself to the rule of law has any moral right to demand from its citizens obedience to the rule of law.' With such rhetoric the rule of law becomes elusive and a weapon in the hands of the powerful.

It may be true that appeals to the rule of law have too often escaped serious analysis.[66] It perhaps shares this fate with other foundational

63 Principle 5 World Charter for Nature.
64 Art. 2 Draft International Covenant (n 56).
65 See Kim and Bosselmann (2015).
66 Fallon (n 21) 55.

concepts such as fairness, justice or sustainability. Yet, none of these are in any way dispensable or negotiable if humanity is to flourish. This is even more true in the Anthropocene with its new global dimensions of responsibility.

Understood as a value-based, complex and dynamic concept, the rule of law needs ongoing and never-ending attention. It may be time now to remind ourselves that the law has no intrinsic value, but is a mere human construct intended to govern ourselves in a civilized manner. However, what could be more civilized than caring for the conditions that make human life possible in the first place. It is here where the concern for the integrity of life as a whole has its place. And it is here where a renewed sense of the rule of law must have its beginning.

REFERENCES

Agrast, M., J. Botero, J. Martinez, A. Ponce and C. Pratt (2013), *Rule of Law Index 2012–13* (The World Justice Project).

Agreement between the United States of America and Canada on Great Lakes Water Quality, Ottawa (Canada), 22 November 1978, into force 22 November 1978, available at: www.ijc.org.

Alexy, Robert (2002), *The Argument from Injustice* (Oxford: Clarendon Press).

Barker, R. (2001), *Political Legitimacy and the State* (Oxford: Clarendon Press).

Belton R. (2005), *Competing Definitions of the Rule of Law* (Carnegie Papers).

Berry, T. (1999), *The Great Work: Our Way into the Future* (New York: Bell Tower/Random House).

Bosselmann, K. (1985), 'Wendezeit im Umweltrecht. Von der Verrechtlichung der Ökologie zur Ökologisierung des Rechts' Kritische Justiz 345–61.

Bosselmann, K. (1986), 'Eigene Rechte der Natur? Ansätze einer ökologischen Rechtsauffassung', *Kritische Justiz* 1–22.

Bosselmann, K. (1992), *Im Namen der Natur: Der Weg zum ökologischen Rechtsstaat* (Minich: Scherz).

Bosselmann, K. (1995), *When Two Worlds Collide: Society and Ecology* (Auckland: RSVP).

Bosselmann, K. (2010), 'Losing the Forest for the Trees: Environmental reductionism in the law', *Sustainability* 2424–48.

Bosselmann, K. (2011), 'Property Rights and Sustainability: Can they be reconciled?' in D. Grinlinton and P. Taylor (eds), *Property Rights and Sustainability: The Evolution of Property Rights to Meet Ecological Challenges* (Leiden: Martinus Nijhoff).

Bosselmann, K. (2013), 'Grounding the Rule of Law' in C. Voigt (ed.), *Rule of Law for Nature: New Dimensions and Ideas in Environmental Law* (Cambridge: Cambridge University Press).

Brook, B. *et al.* (2013), 'Does the Terrestrial Biosphere Have Planetary Tipping Points?' 28(7) *Trends in Ecology & Evolution* 396–401.

Bugge, H. (2008), '"Our Common Future" revisited', in H. Bugge and C. Voigt

(eds), *Sustainable Development in International and National Law* (Groningen: Europa Law).
Burdon, P. (ed.) (2011), *Exploring Wild Law: The Philosophy of Earth Jurisprudence* (Adelaide: Wakefield Press).
Burdon, P. (2013), *Earth Jurisprudence: Private Property and the Environment* (Abingdon: Routledge).
Callies, C. (2001), *Rechtsstaat und Umweltstaat* (Tuebingen: Mohr Siebeck).
Carlman, I. (2005), 'The Rule of Sustainability and Planning Adaptivity' 34(2) *Ambio* 163.
Convention on the Conservation of Antarctic Marine Living Resources, Canberra (Australia), 20 May 1980, in force 7 Apr. 1982, available at http://www.ccamlr.org (accessed 9 March 2015).
Cullinan, C. (2003), *Wild Law: A Manifesto for Earth Justice* (Cambridge: Green Books).
Ebbesson, J. (1999), *Compatibility of International and National Environmental Law* (Berlin: Springer).
Ehm, F. (2010), *The Rule of Law: Concept, Guiding Principle and Framework* (CDL-UDT).
Falk, R. (2000), 'The Quest for Humane Governance in an Era of Globalization' in D. Balb, M. Land, R. Staring, B. Steenbergen, and N. Wilterdink (eds) *The Ends of Globalization: Bringing Society Back In* (Lanham, MD: Rowmart Littlefield).
Fallon Jr., R. (1997), 'The Rule of Law as a Concept in Constitutional Discourse' (1997), *Columbia Law Review* 1.
Flores, I. and K. Himma (eds) (2013), *Law, Liberty, and the Rule of Law* (Berlin: Springer)
Freyfogle, E. (2003), *The Land We Share: Private Property And The Common Good* (Washington DC: Island Press).
Garner, B. (2009), *Black's Law Dictionary* (9th edn, London: Thomson Reuters) 1448.
Garver, G. (2013), 'The Rule of Ecological Law: The Legal Complement to Degrowth Economics' (2013), 5 *Sustainability* 316–37.
Godden, L. (2009), 'Book Review: The Principle of Sustainability' 47 *Osgoode Hall Law Journal* 807.
Gonner, E. (1966), *Common Land and Inclosure* (London: Cass).
Grober, U. (2012), *Sustainability: A Cultural History* (Cambridge: Green Books).
Johannsdottir, A. (2009), *The Significance of the Default: A Study in Environmental Law Methodology with Emphasis on Ecological Sustainability in International Biodiversity Law* (Uppsala universitet, Edita Västerås).
Kant, I. (1907), *Die Metaphysik der Sitten*, Bd. VI (Akademieausgabe).
Kim, R. and K. Bosselmann (2013), 'International Environmental Law in the Anthropocene: Towards a Purposive System of Multilateral Environmental Agreements', 2(2) *Transnational Environmental Law* 285.
Kim, R. and K. Bosselmann (2015), 'Operationalizing Sustainable Development: Ecological Integrity as a *Grundnorm* of International Law', 24:2 *Review of European, Comparative & International Environmental Law* forthcoming.
Kloepfer, M. (ed.) (1994), *Umweltstaat als Zukunft* (Bonn: Economica).
Kloepfer, M. (2013), 'Umweltschutz', in H. Kube *et al.* (eds.) *Leitgedanken des Rechts. Festschrift für Paul Kirchof* (Heidelberg: CF Müller).

Korvela, T. (2012), *Taking Aims Seriously: How Legal Ecology Affects Judicial Decision-Making* (unpubl. Helsinki).
Koskenniemi, M. (2009), 'The Politics of International Law – 20 Years Later' 20(1) *The European Journal of International Law* 7.
Koskenniemi, M. (2012), 'Hegemonic Regimes', in M. Young (ed.), *Regime Interaction in International Law. Facing Fragmentation* (Cambridge: Cambridge University Press).
Loughlin, M. (2010), *Foundations of Public Law* (Oxford: Oxford University Press).
McCloskey, D. (1975), 'The Economics of Enclosure' in W. Parker and E. Jones (eds), *European Peasants and Their Markets: Essays in Agrarian Economic History* (Princeton, NJ: Princeton University Press).
Meadows, D. and D. Meadows *et al.* (1972), *The Limits to Growth. A Report to the Club of Rome's Project on the Predicament of Mankind* (Berkeley, CA: Earth Island).
Münch, R. (2001), *Nation and Citizenship in the Global Age* (Basingstoke: Palgrave-Macmillan).
Polanyi, K. (1944), *The Great Transformation* (Boston, MA: Beacon Press).
Rockström, J. *et al.* (2009a),'A Safe Operating Space for Humanity' 461 *Nature* 472.
Rockström, J. *et al.* (2009b), 'Planetary Boundaries: Exploring the Safe Operating Space for Humanity' 14(2) *Ecology and Society* 32.
Schröter, M. (1999), *Mensch, Erde, Recht: Grundlagen ökologischer Rechtstheorie* (Baden-Baden: Nomos).
Schlatter, R. (1951), *Private Property: The History of An Idea* (New Brunswick, NJ: Rutgers University Press).
Shklar, J. (1987), 'Political Theory and the Rule of Law' in Allan Hutchinson and Patrick Monahan (eds), *The Rule of Law: Ideal or Ideology?* (Toronto: Carswell Legal Publications).
Steinberg, R. (1998), *Der Ökologische Verfassungsstaat* (Frankfurt: Suhrkamp).
Stone, C. (1972), 'Should Trees Have Standing?' 45 *Southern California Law Review* 450.
Tamanaha, B. (2004), *On the Rule of Law: History, Politics, Theory* (Cambridge: Cambridge University Press).
The Earth Charter Initiative (2000), *The Earth Charter* (The Earth Charter Initiative), accessed 9 March 2015 at http://www.earthcharterinaction.org.
Thirsk, J. (1989), *Tudor Enclosures* (2nd edn. Vol. 41 of the Historical Association (UK)).
United Nations (1992), Agenda 21: Programme of Action for Sustainable Development, UN Doc. A/CONF.151/26, 14 Jun. 1992, accessed 9 March 2015 at www.unep.org.
United Nations General Assembly (UNGA) Resolution A/RES/37/7, 28 October 1982, accessed 9 March 2015 at http://www.un.org/documents/ga/res/37/a37r007.htm.
United Nations Report (2012), *Sustainable Development Harmony with Nature* of the Secretary-General, A/67/ 17 August 2012.
Voigt, C (2009), *Sustainable Development as a Principle of International Law: Resolving Conflicts between Climate Measures and WTO Law* (Leiden: Martinus Nijhoff).

Voigt, C. (2012), 'Rule of Law for Nature – Ideas and Developments' 42 *Environmental Policy and Law* 3.
Voigt, C. (ed.) (2013), *Rule of Law for Nature: New Dimensions and Ideas in Environmental Law* (Cambridge: Cambridge University Press)
von Carlowitz, H. (2000 [1713]), *Sylvicultura Oeconomica, Anweisung zur Wilden Baum Zucht* [*Forest Economy or Guide to Tree Cultivation Conforming with Nature*] (TU Bergakademie Freiburg und Akademische Buchhandlung).
Voosen, P. (2012), 'Geologists Drive Golden Spike Toward Anthropocene', Greenwire, 17 September 2012, accessed 9 March 2015 at http://www.eenews.net/stories/1059970036.
Westerlund, S. (2008), 'Theory for Sustainable Development Towards or Against?' in H. Bugge and C. Voigt (eds), *Sustainable Development in International and National Law* (Groningen: Europa Law).
World Summit on Sustainable Development (2002), *Report of the World Summit on Sustainable Development, Plan of Implementation of the World Summit on Sustainable Development*, UN Doc. A/CONF.199/20, 4 Sep. 2002, available at http://www.johannesburgsummit.org (accessed 9 March 2015).

4. Biodiversity justice in a climate change world: offsetting the future

Lee Godden and Emily O'Connell

INTRODUCTION

The concept and practice of 'offsetting' has become endemic in many aspects of environmental law and governance. However, there is limited analysis of whether the concept of offsets can contribute effectively to preserving biodiversity under climate change conditions. Many regions are still experiencing biodiversity decline, which will be exacerbated by climate change impacts.[1] The latest IPCC Assessment confirms the likelihood of continued climatic changes that will increase the likelihood of severe impacts such as droughts and floods.[2] Offsets therefore need to ensure the integrity of biodiversity conservation outcomes over broad spatial and temporal parameters, given the uncertainty and variability of impacts under climate change.

Accordingly, this chapter examines offsetting in biodiversity conservation and explores how climate change may bring added pressure to bear where biodiversity losses are offset, due to the additional difficulties of predicting how adaptation will need to occur into the future.[3] It discusses whether offsets provide an effective instrument for biodiversity 'justice' in a climate change future given a need to ensure equity between current offsets and future climatic risks to biodiversity. Biodiversity offsets are one potential method, among other forms of adaptation, to counter the predicted accelerating decline of biodiversity. However, it is argued that the focus should remain on achieving a net-gain for biodiversity, spatially and temporally, not simply no-net loss (or even substantial losses) in order to achieve long-term viability for many at-risk species and populations. By contrast, many approaches seem to adopt a perspective of 'offsetting of the future' as opposed to 'offsetting for the future'.[4] This

1 Locke and Mackey (2009).
2 Christensen and Kanikicharla (2013) ch14, 1224.
3 Barnett and O'Neill (2010) 213.
4 Bekessey and others (2010) 152.

creates intergenerational inequities as it fails to maintain strict equivalence between the current loss and the corresponding offset given accelerating risks over time. Case studies of offsetting models illustrate some entrenched difficulties.

In order to 'offset for the future', a return to the basic premise of a priority for preservation is needed as the first step for biodiversity protection.[5] Policy frameworks and legal instruments should reflect such goals when adopting offset measures. A stronger insistence on prioritising the integrity of biodiversity values can assist in dealing with enhanced risks to biodiversity from extreme events, such as flood and fire.[6]

OFFSETS: THE CONCEPT

The concept of an offset has many interpretations, with varying legal and policy formulations. Globally, the idea underpins the flexibility mechanisms of the Kyoto Protocol under the United Nations Framework Convention on Climate Change ('UNFCCC').[7] Greenhouse gas emissions produced in one country can be offset elsewhere through actions to sequester carbon or reduce deforestation, using the mechanism of emissions' credits.[8] Offsetting is not confined to the climate change context. The European Commission defines a biodiversity offset as:

> Measures taken to compensate for any residual significant, adverse impacts that cannot be avoided, minimised and/or rehabilitated or restored, in order to achieve 'no-net-loss' or a 'net-gain' of biodiversity. Offsets can take the form of positive management interventions such as restoration of degraded habitat, arrested degradation or averted risk, protecting areas where there is imminent or projected loss of biodiversity.[9]

The biodiversity offset has become a standard 'condition' on development control and project authorisation under many environmental impact assessment and approval regimes in a growing number of countries. For

---

5 Grigg (2014).

6 For a discussion of enhanced risks under climate change, see generally IPCC Fourth Assessment Report *Climate Change 2007: Impacts Adaptation and Vulnerability* (2007).

7 United Nations Framework Convention on Climate Change (UNFCCC 1994); Kyoto Protocol to the United Nations Framework Convention on Climate Change (1998).

8 Zahar, Peel and Godden (2012) 339–72.

9 For example see European Commission (2013), *Guidance on Integrating Climate Change and Biodiversity into Strategic Environmental Assessment*, 6.

example, where vegetation clearance occurs in a proposed development, an offset of (ideally) equivalent habitat may be implemented, other than on the development site. The core of the biodiversity offset or banking concept is that the loss of biodiversity resulting from development will be offset by biodiversity protection elsewhere. Losses sustained in one area are mitigated by biodiversity benefits in other spatial locations and temporalities.

Issues raised around distributive justice relate to the potential for differential impacts for biodiversity where offset measures are adopted – for example, losses in high value biodiversity areas may be 'offset' in areas of lower quality biodiversity values and current losses 'offset' against speculative equivalence in the future. There has been limited examination of longer term outcomes for biodiversity under offset mechanisms, leaving aside the wetland mitigation program in the USA. Nor has there been substantial assessment of the cumulative effects upon biodiversity retention over time. Cumulative impacts may have considerable distributive implications as long-term biodiversity loss under climate change over larger, regional scales has not been fully explored.[10] Yet, even given the relatively sparse 'evidence-based assessment' of offsets, these measures have been adopted in a growing number of jurisdictions.

In tandem, biodiversity loss continues apace in many areas, despite concerted efforts to redress the decline. Climate change will introduce another major stress to factors that are precipitating biodiversity decline.[11] Potentially, biodiversity can adapt to changing habitats and species ranges under climate change. Yet to be effective this process will require an adaptive and flexible, spatial and temporal approach to managing biodiversity. Potentially offsetting mechanisms can assist, but only if the equivalence between loss and the corresponding offset is rigorously maintained.

BIODIVERSITY DECLINE AND CLIMATE CHANGE

Biodiversity has become a signifier for a larger complex of objectives that drive law and policy across a diverse range of environmental protection, resource management and planning laws in many countries.[12] The *Convention on Biological Diversity* (1992) identifies biodiversity as 'the variability among living organisms from all sources including, inter alia,

---

10 Locke and Mackey (2009) 12–13.

11 Keenan (2012).

12 Sands and Peel with Fabra and Mackenzie (2012) 449.

terrestrial, marine and other aquatic ecosystems and the ecological complexes of which they are part; this includes diversity within species, between species and of ecosystems'.[13] The Convention Preamble expresses the concern that 'biological diversity is being significantly reduced by certain human activities'.[14] Some 20 years on, the picture emerging from Rio+ 20 offers little reassurance.[15] Despite extensive efforts and expenditure, internationally and nationally, the rate of decline in biodiversity has not been stemmed in most countries. Many reasons are put forward for failure to redress the decline, but the development of effective legal and regulatory measures for biodiversity protection remain elusive.

While some commentators suggest that biodiversity itself may be an 'unclear concept',[16] the term is predicated upon constructs of ecological systems and populations; with processes operating within, and between, the constituent elements. Given such interdependencies, biodiversity loss under climate change is likely to be highly disparate in its extent and occurrence,[17] with significant distributive justice implications. Moreover, there is a problematic relationship between what biodiversity is protected under current conservation parameters, and what species will remain viable in a climate change future. Thus, offsetting policies and practices, depending upon the extent to which various species and populations are 'substituted' or 'offset', may closely affect the probability of various species and populations remaining viable under climate change conditions.

The *Convention on Biological Diversity* was adopted in the same United Nations forum that gave rise to the Framework Convention on Climate Change. To date, there has been variable success in addressing climate change through the UNFCCC process. The Convention itself contains no firm commitments for countries to reduce GHG emissions, and current pledges by nations to reduce greenhouse gas emissions are non-binding.[18] The future international response is uncertain; highlighting the challenges of integrating governance and legal frameworks across political boundaries. Given the stalling of many climate change mitigation measures, attention increasingly has turned toward adaptation.[19]

---

13 Convention on Biological Diversity (1993) art 2.

14 Ibid, Preamble.

15 The United Nations Conference on Sustainable Development (UNCSD 2012) also known as Rio 2012 or Rio+20.

16 Hamilton (2005) 91.

17 Intergovernmental Panel on Climate Change (2013).

18 United Nations Environment Programme (UNEP 2010).

19 Gerrard and Fischer Kuh (eds 2012) 4.

BIODIVERSITY AND ADAPTATION TO CLIMATE CHANGE

Adaptation to climate change impacts and the fostering of resilient ecological communities has assumed increasing policy and legal importance. Accordingly, climate change regulation should be understood as extending beyond measures for mitigating global warming to encompass aspects of the existing environmental law and associeted legal framework as part of broad adaptation strategies.[20] In particular, spatial planning and protected areas models will be a key means to assist adaptation to climate change impacts for biodiversity.[21] It is vital that the environmental legal and governance frameworks are modified accordingly to assist biodiversity protection. To date, in many countries such transformation remains partial at best. Few national biodiversity protection laws and environmental impact assessment measures have been comprehensively revised to deal with climate change or to instigate long-term adaptive strategies.

By contrast, the projected impacts of climate change on biodiversity are relatively well understood for many regions. There are efforts to integrate measures to reduce biodiversity decline and to redress climate change impacts.[22] Climate change is recognised as a key driver of biodiversity loss worldwide, along with habitat loss; fragmentation and degradation; invasive species; unsustainable levels of natural resource harvesting and extraction; and pollution. Direct impacts of climate change on biodiversity may include changes and reductions in the climatic and geographic range of species; changes to population dynamics and the timing of species' lifecycles; together with an alteration in the structure and composition of ecosystems and communities. More indirectly, climate change will compound ongoing threats to biodiversity. For example, temperature rise and changes to precipitation patterns will exacerbate the impact of unsustainable levels of water allocation on aquatic ecosystems.

Even leaving aside the intrinsic value of the various creatures that will perish, there will be substantial interference with essential ecological functions.[23] From an anthropocentric viewpoint, biodiversity decline will have major distributional effects where the loss will impact food supplies, opportunities for recreation and tourism, and sources of fuel, medicines and energy. In turn, this creates challenges for the legal system in terms

---

[20] Ruhl (2010) 371–5, 381–2.
[21] Foerster, Macintosh and McDonald (2013).
[22] European Commission (2013) 28.
[23] Secretariat of the Convention on Biological Diversity (2000).

of how it regulates the risks created by climate change, especially for biodiversity protection where cascading risks due to climate change pose a particular problem for fragile ecosystems.

Climate change demands a fundamental rethink of legal and policy objectives, and practices of biodiversity conservation. The magnitude of changes to natural systems, and the increased variability and uncertainty posed by climate change, also means that goals of *preserving* existing conditions or *restoring* conditions to some historical reference point are becoming increasingly unrealistic. If we are entering a period of 'non-stationarity' of data where future situations cannot be predicted on the basis of past trends,[24] it has particular implications when seeking to implement environmental protection and biodiversity offsets. Against what 'data' is an offset to be measured or valued? Is it possible to accurately predict what will be 'equivalent' when the future conditions include enhanced probabilities of severe natural hazards?

Those charged with responsibility for making decisions about biodiversity protection have to enter into difficult trade-offs about the future. Decisions must be made on the likely success of preserving a species or ecosystem in light of uncertain threats, in the context of competing conservation objectives and limited resources. Already there are moves towards a triage approach, where it is recognised that not all species can be saved or where default measures, such as gene banks of endangered species, are becoming commonplace; together with ideas of restoring fundamentally altered or degraded ecosystems.[25]

The 'Age of the Anthropocene' has profound implications for biodiversity conservation, which historically has been tied to legally protecting specific natural areas and associated biodiversity. Climate change is likely to precipitate a shift in overarching objectives from positive conservation scenarios based on static spatial arrangements towards ecological restoration measures that may range from: minimising, where possible, extensive biodiversity loss; preventing total ecosystem collapse; and ensuring the bare functioning of ecosystem services, for possible regeneration into the future.[26] This context raises central questions around the role of offsets for biodiversity conservation under climate change, when such profound changes are taking place in the 'background conditions'.

---

24 Craig (2010).

25 See Harris and others (2006).

26 See McCormack and McDonald (2014) 117.

BUILDING BIODIVERSITY RESILIENCE?

Given the profound shifts that are predicted to occur under climate change, there is a need for varied and flexible forms of adaptation that utilise a range of legal and policy measures. Biodiversity offsets represent one of a spectrum of policy and legal instruments that might be adopted. Experimentation with a range of measures would seem prudent given the current biodiversity decline and increasing uncertainties about the timing, frequency and severity of extreme weather events, such as bushfires; together with the spatial and temporal diversity of their impacts. On the other hand, the role of biodiversity as part of building resilience is not widely canvassed.[27]

Biodiversity retention is a key factor for climate change mitigation. Climate change policy at the international and national levels now places emphasis on the contribution of bio-sequestration activities and more sustainable land use practices to emissions' mitigation.[28] Accordingly, biodiversity justice must be a layered concept that operates across multiple temporal and spatial scales, connecting current decision-making around offsets with future biodiversity risk scenarios, as well as policy and legal measures for climate change adaptation. To achieve effective interconnection though, decision-makers must have a firm understanding of both the potential advantages and limitations of utilising offset mechanisms in the context of climate change.

OFFSETTING: POLICY AND LEGAL EXPERIMENTATION

The long engagement with sustainable development has seen various attempts to manage biodiversity decline, while still allowing economic growth, including the adoption of market approaches based upon ecosystem services and offsets.[29] Ecosystem services emerged as part of an evolution towards complex legal structures, frequently with a reduced role for direct state intervention.[30] The concept of environmental trading has figured prominently:

---

27 See generally Ruhl and Saltzmann (2010).
28 Long (2013).
29 Costanza and others (1997).
30 Gunningham (2009) 185.

> In establishing a market, the government first creates a new form of property—legal entitlements to emit pollutants, catch fish, develop habitat—and then imposes a set of rules governing their exchange.[31]

The trends involve greater reliance on private sector forms of biodiversity conservation.[32] Offsetting has become pervasive, but it is a relatively recent policy and legal instrument added to the 'toolkit'. Offsets now cover a range of environmental situations, but began with vegetation clearance. Thus, as Gibbons and Lindenmayer note:

> [o]ffsetting (also known as setasides, compensatory habitat, mitigation banks) is a policy instrument used to permit some continued clearing within an overall no-net loss or net-gain objective. Offsetting is based on the assumption that impacts from clearing can be offset if sufficient habitat can be protected, enhanced and/or established elsewhere. Offsetting is used widely by government organizations and the private sector globally.[33]

Biodiversity offsets under this model are often associated with wetland mitigation banking or bio-banking. This policy experiment in biodiversity management has attracted both advocates and censure. A fundamental assumption is that the offset 'exchange' involves a fungible commodity. As Salzman and Ruhl argue, a basic aspect of offsetting has been overlooked, '[p]erhaps because it *is* so obvious there has been scant consideration of the simple question—*what is actually being traded*'.[34] Intangibles, such as the level of threat to a species, may become particular pressure points under climate change impacts, where risk assessments of biodiversity exchange and substitution need to deal with high levels of uncertainty.

HOW DO OFFSETS WORK?

Under the biodiversity offset or bio-banking model, proponents of a project development that involves vegetation clearance, biodiversity degradation or other habitat loss, are required to identify (or, can now often choose from designated private sector providers) an offset of equivalent or enhanced biodiversity value. The equivalence of the offset is assessed using a metric that is designed to 'score' the biodiversity value of various areas.[35]

---

31 Salzman and Ruhl (2000) 617.
32 Dempsey and Robertson (2012).
33 Gibbons and Lindenmayer (2007) 27–8.
34 Salzman and Ruhl (2000) 611 (Emphasis in original).
35 Ibid, 659.

A trading or banking approach relies on the commensurability (equivalence) between the area being cleared and the offset. In turn, this relies on a sufficiently coherent metric or assessment method that can manifest the complimentary values. The most well-known model is wetland mitigation banking in the USA.

Wetland Mitigation in the USA

Wetland Mitigation Banking was initiated in the US under the federal Clean Water Act of 1977.[36] Regulators, in partnership with private-sector interests, initiated 'a market in privately owned "wetland ecosystem services", such as duck habitat, flood protection and biodiversity'.[37] In general terms, to develop a market in these services, the relevant regulatory prohibition is wetland pollution (or filling) under the Clean Water Act of 1972.[38] Permits to fill in wetlands could be obtained from the federal Corps of Engineers on the condition that the wetland loss is mitigated. Prior to the advent of wetland mitigation trading, the Corps and Environment Protection Agency preferred onsite mitigation. With the support of developers, environmentalists and the government, the Corps allowed offsite mitigation as wetland trading was seen as a solution for both environmental protection and development.[39] Strict equivalence of value between the biodiversity that is lost and what is substituted is the ideal regulatory basis on which the trade is predicated. Yet some commentators argue that many trades do not meet these goals as most trades are organised on an 'area for area' basis.[40] The problem of ensuring commensurability (instead of simply matching the sheer areas substituted) has been identified in wetland banking schemes in the USA.[41]

If a bare 'area for area' metric is used, then the offsetting leaves unaccounted for many types of intrinsic biodiversity characteristics. In a climate change context, this may mean – for example – that vulnerable species with restricted ranges dislocated due to changing habitat may not be accounted for. Not all wetland acres are created equal—they are nonfungible' across time, space and type 'when their ecosystem service values are considered'.[42] This variable distribution will need to be care-

36 Clean Water Act of 1977 (1977); National Research Council (USA) (2001).
37 Robertson (2004) 361.
38 Clean Water Act of 1972 (1972).
39 Salzman and Ruhl (2005) 3–4.
40 Salzman and Ruhl (2000) 611–12.
41 Salzman and Ruhl (2005) 8.
42 Salzman and Ruhl (2000) 657.

fully assessed if offsets are to play a role in building resilient ecosystems under climate change conditions. Moreover, the need to ensure commensurability for the biodiversity that is exchanged, points to challenges for ensuring systemic biodiversity protection – often already at risk with climate change. The difficulties in achieving adequate metrics, and therefore commensurability, at the point of exchange can be exacerbated where regulators are constrained in setting overall systemic goals; for example, no net loss rather than net gain. This highlights the critical role played by the governance of the system where long-term adaptation is required.

Governance of Offset Schemes

The importance of effective systemic governance is highlighted by the decision of the United States Supreme Court in the case of *Solid Waste Agency of Northern Cook County v US Corps of Engineers* (SWANCC).[43] In the SWANCC decision, the Supreme Court disallowed a practice under the Clean Water Act that had been used to protect 'isolated wetlands' – which are those wetlands that do not have observable connectivity to a navigable stream. The result created chaos in the wetland banking industry. Many developers openly disregarded regulations and filling wetlands.[44] Local and regional initiatives to restore the platform for offset trading created a very disparate banking system that ultimately proved unviable in some localities. The result was a haphazard, spatial patchwork of regulatory regimes controlling wetland banking.[45] Such a spatial patchwork may exacerbate a perennial problem of biodiversity protection – the 'death by a thousand cuts'. Increasingly isolated pockets of biodiversity often become surrounded by development, and ecosystem vulnerability is increased by climate change. Federal regulations for wetland mitigation became more systematised with the adoption of a new compensatory mitigation regulation in 2008 that, 'represents a significant turning point in the program's integration of ecosystem services into mitigation decision making'.[46]

43 531 US 159 (2001).
44 Robertson (n 37) 370.
45 Ibid.
46 Ruhl, Salzman and Goodman (2008–2009) 263.

mandatory levels of 'controlled burning' and clearance around residential areas that may exacerbate biodiversity and habitat loss.[55]

Native Vegetation Framework

Native vegetation removal is primarily managed through the Planning and Environment Act 1987 (Vic). The removal of native vegetation requires permission from the responsible authority, usually the local government authority. Certain applications will require approval from a state government department, as a referral authority. In deciding whether to permit clearance of native vegetation – often critical habitat – the decision-maker must take into account the *Permitted clearing of native vegetation: Biodiversity Assessment Guidelines* ('Permitted Clearing Guidelines'). The Permitted Clearing Guidelines came into force in September 2013 and represented a significant change in the policy framework. The new goal for native vegetation management in Victoria is to achieve: 'No net loss in the contribution made by native vegetation to Victoria's biodiversity'.[56] Previously, the primary goal under *Victoria's Native Vegetation Management: A Framework for Action* ('Framework for Action') had been to increase the extent and quality of native vegetation across Victoria under a 'Net Gain' objective.[57]

The policy change affects the Framework for Action. Originally, the Framework required a sequencing of actions called a 'three step approach' for native vegetation removal:

(1) the removal of native vegetation must first be avoided;
(2) if the removal cannot be avoided then it must be minimised; and
(3) after attempting to avoid and minimise the removal, it may be mitigated by 'offsetting' the removal.

Offsetting native vegetation removal is a last resort under this hierarchy. When a permit for native vegetation removal is granted, the offset is required to be similar to the native vegetation being removed. The requirement for 'like for like' offsets is an effort to address the commensurability issue. The value of habitat to be lost is assessed and measured, and then

---

[55] 'The Commission proposes that the State make a commitment to fund a long-term program of prescribed burning, with an annual rolling target of a minimum of 5 per cent of public land each year. . .': 2009 Victorian Bushfires Royal Commission (2010) 15.

[56] State Government Victoria (2013) 5.

[57] State Government Victoria (2002).

transferred into a scoring metric called 'habitat hectares'. The 'equivalence measure' is the number of habitat hectares that are required to be offset. Despite the Framework being in place for over a decade, an overall net gain in native vegetation has not been achieved.[58] The Environmental Defender's Office argues in particular that:

- the first two steps in the three-step approach (avoid and minimise) are regularly bypassed in favour of moving directly to offsetting; and
- the process for measuring Net Gain is poorly documented and so inadequate for regulating or measuring Net Gain.[59]

The change in policy priority to no-net loss may escalate biodiversity loss. Offsetting, where it undercuts the first two stages of the Action Framework, may contribute to that decline. In a region already experiencing high degrees of climatic variability and extreme events, such a policy may exacerbate losses to biodiversity. It remains to assess whether sufficient safeguards can be incorporated into the offsets' concept, to provide greater biodiversity protection and adaptation under climate change.

CAN OFFSETS BE EFFECTIVE IN PROMOTING ADAPTATION?

The commentators remain divided. Walker *et al.* argue that there are fundamental flaws in the approach:

> Viable trading requires simple, measurable, and interchangeable commodities, but the currencies, restrictions, and oversight needed to protect complex, difficult-to-measure, and noninterchangeable [sic] resources like biodiversity are costly and intractable. These safeguards compromise trading viability.[60]

Biodiversity trading (i.e. offsets), is promoted to enable both conservation and development; while achieving 'no net loss' or even 'net gain'. Instead it has facilitated development, while perpetuating biodiversity loss.[61] Some commentators are more optimistic, yet caution about the

---

58 Environment Defender's Office (Vic) (2013) 19.
59 Ibid, 27.
60 Walker and others (2009) 149.
61 Ibid, 150.

need for rigorous design for the exchange process to ensure the integrity of biodiversity benefits.[62]

Beckessey *et al.* offer a realistic appraisal of the utility of offsets, but stress that the 'biodiversity bank cannot be a lending bank'.[63] They identify positive incentives from bio-banking. Requiring project proponents to pay the substantial costs of habitat loss, for example, promotes careful planning approaches. They see a complex of mechanisms, such as offsetting, biobanking and biodiverse carbon sequestration playing an important role in conserving biodiversity under increasing development pressures.[64] Significantly, they do not expressly address the function of offsets in terms of climate change adaptation.

The commensurability between the biodiversity losses and that which is substituted is questioned:

> [p]olicies that allow habitat destruction to be offset by the protection of existing habitat are guaranteed to result in further loss of biodiversity. Similarly, schemes that allow trading the immediate loss of existing habitat for restoration projects that promise future habitat will, at best, result in time lags in the availability of habitat that increases extinction risks, or at worst, fail to achieve the offset at all.[65]

In particular, they raise concerns about schemes that allow present day losses of biodiversity to be offset by future restoration projects; for example, when old growth forest matures. The 'gap' between current loss and the promised future habitat protection may never eventuate – particularly given enhanced risks of extreme events, such as flood and fires as a consequence of climate change. 'Loading' offsets into a future time frame should be prevented by ensuring that a bio-bank should be 'a savings bank not a lending bank'.[66]

> [T]he only workable and equitable system is one in which [biodiversity] assets are banked for the future and trading is only possible once it can be demonstrated that assets have matured (reached ecological equivalence with whatever losses they are being traded against).[67]

The value of biodiversity assets must be demonstrated before allowing-them to offset future losses. Thus, despite refinements to the design of

62 Salzman and Ruhl (2000) 614.
63 Bekessey and others (2010) 151, 151.
64 Ibid.
65 Ibid.
66 Ibid.
67 Ibid.

offset schemes, problems remain in terms of developing rigorous and equitable measures of biodiversity equivalence. There is an implicit discounting of future biodiversity values built into the framing of commensurability in many offset and bio-banking schemes.[68] The skew toward present-day values of biodiversity 'assets' echoes the discount valuation argument in environmental impact assessment – this methodology significantly discounts future costs against present-day benefits. The appropriate discount rate to be adopted has been a vexed issue in accounting for climate change costs into the future. Similar difficulties apply when accounting for future biodiversity values under climate change conditions, when adopting metrics for commensurability in offset schemes. Unless the metric is robust (that is, with effective values for future commensurability) and able to take into account increased climate change risks, then current losses of biodiversity will be devalued. Without future complementarity in the exchange, it may impede ecosystem resilience and the capacity for adaptation. Offsetting schemes need to operate within more expansive temporal dimensions to adequately factor in enhanced risks due to climate change.

Few legal instruments for offsets appear to have the flexibly to match the current losses with future values and adaptation options for biodiversity. Such matching will be necessary to produce schemes geared toward systemic gains to promote ecosystem resilience. The need to take account of the wider effects of trading biodiversity raises a familiar cumulative impact problem. Under climate change conditions, there will be a stronger need to incorporate multi-temporal and multi-scalar cumulative impact considerations into offsetting regimes.

CONCLUSION: OFFSETTING BIODIVERSITY FOR THE FUTURE?

Offsetting, is now an accepted part of the environmental policy and legal spectrum, which began as a specific regulatory and private sector response to off-site mitigation of development impacts. The concept appears in a wide range of regulatory frameworks and practices. Many offset schemes for vegetation clearance and biodiversity conservation depend on policy settings, executive action or private law models, such as negotiation and contract. These forms may introduce some flexibility in approach, but

---

[68] A concise summary of the difficulties of ensuring interchangeability over type, space and time is provided by Walker and others (2009) 151–2.

their long-term capacity to produce equitable outcomes for biodiversity under climate change conditions remains to be thoroughly tested.

The construct of biodiversity justice is proposed as part of any evaluative platform. It can be used to explore key assumptions, such as the commensurability of biodiversity values that are integral to the offset model. The principles are directed to assess whether offset mechanisms are well-suited to enhancing biodiversity adaptation to climate change. The chapter has canvassed two case studies of biodiversity offsetting. The first examined whether offsets can provide systemic biodiversity gains in wetland mitigation banking when governance is fragmented. Integrated and systemic protections for biodiversity are a key factor in biodiversity adaptation under climate change conditions. The second case study examined difficulties in developing measures of commensurability across time and diverse locations. It is also important to ensure offsets are not the 'first option' when assessing proposals for vegetation clearance.

As a first principle, banking for the future and building a stronger margin of loss to account for the increased risks and uncertainties of climate change impacts will be important in building biodiversity resilience under climate change. Offsets will likely continue to form part of the legal and regulatory measures for biodiversity management. Given the complexity of biodiversity protection and the uncertainty of how adaptation to climate change will occur, it indicates that offset schemes should be limited in scope, unless appropriate safeguards are in place. If offsets are to be used in a period of increasing climate variability and risk, a core principle for such schemes is to adhere to a hierarchy of avoid, minimise, and *then* offset biodiversity loss. Adoption of the precautionary principle is needed where serious or irreversible harm may occur.[69] The first principle is to preserve biodiversity, where and when possible; a principle endorsed in the *Convention on Biological Diversity*. Secondly, the measures of commensurability should incorporate a principle of 'for the future', and not 'into the future'. This will assist to avoid the problems of time lags and the enhanced risks of climate change impacts that may render any offset nugatory into the future. Thirdly, the principle of biodiversity protection should be a fundamental part of climate change adaptation law and policy. Offsets schemes should be integrated into systemic management for building ecosystem resilience to climate change. The steps should lead us toward biodiversity justice by offsetting for a climate changed future.

[69] Peta Norris, 'The Promise and Reality of Biodiversity Offsetting' (2014) 31 *Environmental and Planning Law Journal* 137, 140.

REFERENCES

2009 Victorian Bushfires Royal Commission (2010), *Final Report Summary* (Parliament of Victoria, July) accessed 10 March 2015 at http://www.royalcommission.vic.gov.au/finaldocuments/summary/PF/VBRC_Summary_PF.pdf.

Australian Government, Department of Sustainability, Environment, Water, Population and Communities (2012), *Environment Protection and Biodiversity Conservation Act 1999* Environmental Offsets Policy accessed 10 March 2015 at http://www.environment.gov.au/.

Barnett, J. and S. O'Neill. (2010), 'Maladaptation' 20 *Global Environmental Change* 211.

Bekessy, S., B. White, D. Lindenmayer, M. McCarthy, M. Colyvan, M. Burgman and H. Possingham (2010), 'Policy Perspective: The Biodiversity Bank Cannot be a Lending Bank' 3 *Conservation Letters* 151.

Christensen, J. and K. Kanikicharla (Lead Authors) (2013), 'Climate Phenomena and their Relevance for Future Regional Climate Change' in IPCC, *Climate Change 2013: The Physical Science Basis*, ch 14, 1224.

Clean Water Act of 1972, Pub L No 92–500, 86 Stat 816 (1972).

Clean Water Act of 1977, Pub L No 95–217, 91 Stat 1566 (1977).

Costanza, R. *et al.* (1997), 'The Value of the World's Ecosystem Services and Natural Capital' 387 *Nature* 253.

Craig, R. (2010), '"Stationarity is Dead" – Long Live Transformation: Five Principles for Climate Change Adaptation Law' 34 *Harvard Environmental Law Review* 9.

Dempsey, J. and M. Robertson (2012), 'Ecosystem Services: Tensions, Impurities, and Points of Engagement within Neoliberalism' 36 *Progress in Human Geography* 758.

Environment Defender's Office (Vic 2012), 'A Framework for Action? Implementation and Enforcement of Victoria's Native Vegetation Clearing Controls' (Monitoring Victoria's Environmental Laws Report No. 4, EDO Report Series, July 2012) accessed 10 March 2015 at http://www.edovic.org.au/

Environment Defender's Office (Vic 2013), 'Reforming Native Vegetation Offset Rules in Victoria' (May 2013) accessed 10 March 2015 at http://www.edovic.org.au/.

European Commission (2013), *Guidance on Integrating Climate Change and Biodiversity into Strategic Environmental Assessment* (European Commission 2013) accessed 10 March 2015 at http://ec.europa.eu/environment/eia/.

Foerster, A., A. Macintosh and J. McDonald (2013), 'Transferable Lessons for Climate Change? Managing Bushfire and Coastal Climate Hazards in Australia' 30 *Environmental and Planning Law Journal* 469.

Garnaut, R. (2011), *The Garnaut Review 2011: Australia in the Global Response to Climate Change* (Cambridge: Cambridge University Press).

Gerrard, M. and K. Fischer Kuh (eds) (2012), *The Law of Adaptation to Climate Change: U.S. and International Aspects* (Chicago: American Bar Association, Section of Environment, Energy, and Resources).

Gibbons, P. and D. Lindenmayer (2007), 'Offsets for Land Clearing: No Net Loss or the Tail Wagging the Dog?' 8 *Ecological Management & Restoration* 26.

Grigg, B. (2014), 'Biodiversity Offsets: The Dangerous Trade in Wildlife' in M. Maloney and P. Burdon (eds), *Wild Law – In Practice* (Abingdon: Routledge) 213.

Gunningham, N. (2009), 'Environmental Law, Regulation and Governance, Shifting Architectures' 21 *Journal of Environmental Law* 179.

Hamilton, A. (2005), 'Species Diversity or Biodiversity?' 75 *Journal of Environmental Management* 89.

Harris, J. *et al.* (2006), 'Ecological Restoration and Global Climate Change' 14 *Restoration Ecology* 170.

Intergovernmental Panel on Climate Change Working Group 1 (2013), *Climate Change 2013: The Physical Science Basis: Working Group I Contribution to the Fifth Assessment Report Intergovernmental Panel on Climate Change*, T. Stocker and others (eds) (Cambridge: Cambridge University Press).

Keenan, R. (2012), 'Adaptation of Forests and Forest Management to Climate Change: An Editorial' 3 *Forests* 75.

Locke, H. and B. Mackey (2009), 'The Nature of Climate Change: Reunite International Climate Change Mitigation Efforts with Biodiversity Conservation and Wilderness Protection' 15 *International Journal of Wilderness* 7.

Long, A. (2013), 'REDD+, Adaptation and Sustainable Forest Management: Toward Effective Polycentric Global Forest Governance' 6 *Tropical Conservation Science* 384.

McCormack, P. and J. McDonald (2014), 'Adaptation Strategies for Biodiversity Conservation: Has Australia got what it takes?' 31 *Environmental and Planning Law Journal* 114.

Norris, P. (2014), 'The Promise and Reality of Biodiversity Offsetting' 31 *Environmental and Planning Law Journal* 137, 140.

Robertson, M. (2004), 'The Neoliberalization of Ecosystem Services: Wetland Mitigation Banking and Problems in Environmental Governance' 35 *Geoforum* 361.

Ruhl, J. (2010), 'Climate Change Adaptation and the Structural Transformation of Environmental Law' 40 *Environmental Law* 363.

Ruhl, J. and J. Saltzmann (2010), 'Climate Change, Dead Zones and Massive Problems in the Administrative State: A Guide for Whittling Away' 98 *California Law Review* 59.

Ruhl, J., J. Salzman and I. Goodman (2008–2009), 'Implementing the New Ecosystem Services Mandate of the Section 404 Compensatory Mitigation Program – A Catalyst for Advancing Science and Policy' 38 *Stetson Law Review* 251.

Salzman, J. and J. Ruhl (2000), 'Currencies and the Commodification of Environmental Law' 53 *Stanford Law Review* 607.

Salzman, J. and J. Ruhl, (2005), '"No Net-Loss" – Instrument Choice in Wetlands Protection' *Faculty Scholarship* 1 accessed 10 March 2015 at http://scholarship.law.duke.edu/faculty_scholarship/1238.

Sands, P. and J. Peel with A. Fabra and R. Mackenzie (2012), *Principles of International Environmental Law* (3rd edn, Cambridge: Cambridge University Press).

Secretariat of the Convention on Biological Diversity (2000), *Sustaining Life on Earth: How the Convention on Biological Diversity Promotes Nature and Human Well-being* (Secretariat of the Convention on Biological Diversity) accessed 10 March 2015 at https://www.cbd.int/doc/publications/cbd-sustain-en.pdf.

State Government Victoria, Department of Natural Resources and Environment (2002), 'Victoria's Native Vegetation Management: A Framework for Action' accessed 10 March 2015 at http://www.pyrenees.vic.gov.au/.
Swainson, B. and R. de Loe (2011), 'The Importance of Context in Relation to Policy Transfer: A Case Study of Environmental Water Allocation in Australia' 21 *Environmental Policy and Governance* 58.
United Nations (1993), Convention on Biological Diversity (opened for signature 5 June 1992, entered into force 29 December 1993) 1760 UNTS 79.
United Nations (1994), United Nations Framework Convention on Climate Change (adopted 9 May 1992, entered into force 21 March 1994) 1771 UNTS 107 (UNFCCC).
United Nations (2012), The United Nations Conference on Sustainable Development (UNCSD), 20–22 June 2012, also known as Rio 2012 or Rio+20.
United Nations Environment Programme (2010), *The Emissions Gap Report: Are the Copenhagen Accord Pledges Sufficient to Limit Global Warming to 2°C or 1.5°C?: A Preliminary Assessment. Full Report* (Joseph Alcamo and others, UNEP) accessed 10 March 2015 at www.unep.org/publications/ebooks/emissionsgapreport/.
Walker, S., A. Brower, R. Theo Stephens and W. Lee (2009), 'Why Bartering Biodiversity Fails' 2 *Conservation Letters* 149.
Zahar, A., J. Peel, and L. Godden, (2012), *Australian Climate Law in Global Context* (Cambridge: Cambridge University Press).

PART II

Rights-based conceptualisations

Environmental justice exists at the intersection between environmental law and the pursuit of social justice. Central to the pursuit of social justice has been a focus upon the development and implementation of legal rights, particularly legal rights of the vulnerable to be protected and to be able to share more equitably in the opportunities of society. Many of these rights have emerged through international agreements, and have been generally focused upon the protection of the interest of vulnerable human beings.

However, some versions of environmental justice extend the idea of protection of the vulnerable from the protection of human interests derived from the environment towards the protection of the interests of the environment *per se.* This Part takes a pragmatic perspective on the ways in which human interests are being pursued, and the implications of this for justice.

5. Human rights and the environment

Justice Susan Glazebrook[1]

INTRODUCTION

Ko au te whenua, Ko te whenua ko au
I am the land and the land is me[2]

The protection of the environment should be a priority on both the individual and state level. The Māori proverb set out above describes a link between people and the environment that is both intrinsic and interdependent. Humans have the power to protect or destroy the environment. Yet it is also the environment that ultimately sustains the earth's population. The importance of the environment to human well-being, health and ultimately survival is self-evident. We rely on the environment for food, air, water and mineral resources, not to mention for its natural beauty.

The first part of this chapter will consider whether there is already a human right to an environment of quality and, if not, whether existing human rights adequately address environmental issues. Following this, it will examine the arguments for and against an environmental human right. In the second part of the chapter I will discuss the special relationship between indigenous peoples and the environment. I will then briefly address the issues relating to environmentally displaced or disadvantaged persons. The chapter concludes by examining the contents of any human right to a quality environment, should it be considered desirable.

---

[1] I am grateful to my clerk, Claire Brighton, for her invaluable assistance with this chapter. This chapter builds on aspects of my earlier papers, 'Human Rights and the Environment' (2009) 1 *VUWLR* 293; and 'Keeping it Clean and Green: The Case for Constitutional Environmental Protection Rights' in Morris, Boston and Butler (2011) 425. The views expressed in these papers are my own and do not represent those of the Supreme Court.

[2] This is a Māori proverb or whakatauki. The Māori are the indigenous people of New Zealand and have a strong connection to the land. Whakatauki play a large role within Māori culture. This particular whakatauki is associated with the Whanganui River.

A RIGHT TO ENVIRONMENTAL QUALITY?[3]

Most commentators consider that there is insufficient support for the existence of a substantive right to a quality environment.[4] One of the main difficulties, in my view, is that any right to the environment has become intermingled with the right to development and, in particular, with the principle of sustainable development.[5] This has rendered the existence of a stand-alone environmental right even more uncertain. It is true, however, that environmental rights are contained in a number of constitutions around the globe.[6]

Procedural environmental rights enjoy greater support than any substantive right, in part because of their comparability with civil and political rights.[7] As environmental participation rights become more widespread, it may be more promising to postulate a right to participation as constituting customary international law, rather than to argue for an existing substantive right.

A number of existing substantive human rights have been interpreted as covering environmental issues.[8] The right to life, for example, has been accepted as including the right to pollution-free water and air and to include positive obligations on the state to act to remedy environmental risks that threaten life.[9]

The ability of existing rights to provide adequate protection for the environment is, however, limited in a number of ways. The focus of existing rights is not specifically on the environment. They will only apply where environmental concerns happen to coincide with their immediate focus. Another limitation arises from the tendency to frame existing rights in the negative, as an obligation not to breach the right, rather than a duty to take action. This significantly limits the ability of many existing rights to address environmental issues.

---

[3] For a more comprehensive discussion of these issues see Glazebrook (2009) 294–312.

[4] Hill, Wolfson and Targ (2004) 400; Weston and Bollier (2013) 34.

[5] See Boyle (1996) 46.

[6] In 2005 some 60% of national constitutions had provisions protecting the environment. Asia Pacific Forum of National Human Rights Institutions (2007) 187.

[7] Rodriguez-Rivera (2001) 16.

[8] These include the right to privacy and family life; right to freedom of expression; the right to health; and the right to judicial review. The rights to culture, self determination and property may also be relevant: Taylor (1998) 343–5.

[9] See for example the Indian cases: *Charan Lal Sahu v Union of India* AIR 1990 SCF 1480 and *Kumar v State of Bihar* (1991) 1 SCC 598; and *Farooque v Bangladesh* (1997) 49 Khaka Law Reports (AD) 1.

Existing economic, social and cultural rights are probably the easiest to interpret as encompassing environmental protections (such as threats to health due to environmental damage). The issues that arise in relation to the justiciability of these rights, however, may limit the practical protection they can afford.[10] Their usefulness in the environmental field is further limited by the fact that such rights are subject to progressive implementation, meaning that rather than requiring immediate performance, states are permitted to fulfil them over time as resources become available.[11]

ARGUMENTS AGAINST THE RIGHT TO A QUALITY ENVIRONMENT

I turn now to the question of whether there should be a specific right to an environment of quality. The arguments against such a right can be grouped into four broad propositions:

(a) Recognition will not improve environmental protection.
(b) An environmental right would be incompatible with the existing human rights framework.
(c) It is difficult to fit environmental concerns into a rights framework.
(d) There is no need for a substantive right because participation rights suffice.

I will discuss each of these arguments in turn.

Recognition Will Not Improve Environmental Protection

Whether a right would fulfil the goal of aiding environmental protection is an important consideration in deciding whether or not the right ought to be recognised. The discussion of this issue can be subdivided into five propositions.

There is a lack of concentration on the environment for its own sake

This argument reflects the concern that, if framed as a human right, environmental protection would give way to the right for humans to

---

[10] For a discussion of justiciability in the environmental context see Du Bois (1996) 153–75.

[11] International Covenant on Economic, Social and Cultural Rights, art 2; Boyd (2012) 23.

use and abuse the environment to the detriment of other species and the ecosystem.[12] In my opinion, this criticism takes too narrow a view of human rights. Rights do not have to be related only to the physical needs of humans. They can and should also relate to spiritual, cultural and aesthetic needs and desires. The Association of Southeast Asian Nations Charter, for example, refers to the need to protect the cultural heritage of the environment.[13]

It might devalue and confuse existing international environmental law

Any right to the environment should be framed so as to support international environmental law and not be incompatible or inconsistent with it.[14] The content of the right would be moulded by international environmental law and vice versa.

A right to the environment would not add to existing environmental protection measures

My response rests partly on terminology and is partly systemic. In terms of terminology, individuals are more likely to comply with the duties placed on them if they consider themselves to be doing so as part of the enjoyment of a right. Turning to systemic issues, even if an environmental right adds little to existing environmental protections (but every little bit surely helps), such a right can be seen as necessary to give a proper balance to human rights discourse itself. An environment of quality is essential to the exercise of many existing human rights. Framing environmental protection as a right draws it into the more general rights framework, where it would need to be weighed against other rights, thus preventing the environment from being overlooked.[15]

The creation of a right to environment would result in duplication of remedies

A right to environment may herald a welcome and necessary strengthening in human rights remedies generally.[16] The development of new remedies relating to human rights and the environment will provide an opportunity

---

[12] Redgwell in Boyle and Anderson (n 5) 71–87.

[13] Charter of the Association of Southeast Asian Nations 2007 (ASEAN 2007) art 9.

[14] de Sadeleer (2002) 275.

[15] APF Background paper (2007) 86.

[16] There is a concern that human rights remedies are not being applied consistently: see Shelton (2005) 1. See also *Basic Principles and Guidelines on the Right to a Remedy and Reparation for Victims of Gross Violations of International*

to ensure that remedies are complementary rather than inconsistent with or duplicative of existing environmental remedies.

It draws attention away from the root causes of environmental degradation
Humans are the cause of environmental degradation. A human rights approach, properly coupled with an emphasis on individual, collective, business and state responsibility, should provide impetus for addressing the root (human) causes of degradation.

An Environmental Right Would Be Incompatible with the Existing Human Rights Framework

The introduction of an entirely incompatible right would clearly be undesirable. I address below the arguments that such a right would not fit easily into the current framework.

There should not be a proliferation of new rights
I agree that a proliferation of new rights could, in some circumstances, devalue existing rights. However, an unwillingness to expand rights to meet changing circumstances would have the same effect. New rights should not be added if they are trivial, but a right to an environment of quality can effectively be seen as one of the foundation stones on which all other rights depend. Vice-President Weeramantry, in his separate opinion in the *Case Concerning the Gabčíkovo-Nagymaros Project (Hungary/Slovakia)*, certainly saw it in this way. He said that it was:[17]

> . . . a vital part of contemporary human rights doctrine, for it is a *sine qua non* for numerous human rights such as the right to health and the right to life itself. It is scarcely necessary to elaborate on this, as damage to the environment can impair and undermine all the human rights spoken of in the Universal Declaration and other human rights instruments.

There are difficulties in linking any such new right with other rights
Those who are in decision-making roles are always engaging in an exercise of weighing rights. If a right is not articulated, however, it may not be considered at all. Equally, if an issue is seen as being outside a human rights framework, it may become too important and overshadow human rights

---

Human Rights Law and Serious Violations of International Humanitarian Law GA Res 60/147, A/RES/60/147 (2006).

[17] *Case concerning the Gabčíkovo-Nagymaros Project (Hungary v Slovakia)* [1997] ICJ Rep 7, separate opinion of Vice-President Weeramantry at 91–2.

altogether. Accordingly, one of the reasons for including environmental protection as a right is that it would allow it to be balanced against other rights, rather than being isolated in its own legal framework.

Human rights bodies are not appropriate organs to supervise environmental protection

Current human rights bodies may well lack environmental expertise. This, however, is a concern in itself given the importance of the environment to human survival. It might equally be argued that existing environmental bodies lack human rights expertise. This may suggest the need for a combined approach.[18]

It is Difficult to Fit Environmental Concerns into a Rights Framework

A number of reasons have been put forward to suggest that an environmental right cannot be properly placed in a human rights framework. For the reasons that follow, I think in fact that it would be a relatively easy task to do so.

There is general difficulty in characterising the right

The difficulties in terminology have, in my view, been exaggerated. A wide range of words has been used in various domestic and international instruments to describe the level of environmental quality protected, including 'healthy', 'safe', 'adequate', 'clean' and 'ecologically balanced'.[19] The basic concepts, however, are well understood. The application to particular situations will be a matter of interpretation for supervisory institutions and courts, in the same way as for other human rights.[20]

It may lead to ambiguity regarding the identity of the rights holder

There is no doubt that the right to a quality environment could not be framed solely as an individual right. It must also be a right enjoyed by communities and peoples. This, however, strengthens rather than devalues it as a right. The dual collective and individual nature of environmental rights is recognised in a number of constitutions[21] and in the African Charter on Human and Peoples' Rights.[22]

---

[18] Pillay (2012).

[19] Boyd 2012) 33.

[20] See comments of Boyle (1996) 50–51.

[21] For example the Constitution of Colombia 1991, art 79.

[22] Article 24 refers to the right of 'all peoples' to a general satisfactory environment. This term is undefined, but is capable of encompassing both collective

The focus on individual rather than collective rights and responsibilities is inappropriate

The fact that there is an individual right does not mean that there is not a community right.[23] Indeed environmental rights and the right to sustainable development may be best understood as community or collective rights as they are more naturally enjoyed within and by communities. Collective rights and duties are not new. They are referred to in the preambles of both the International Covenant on Civil and Political Rights (ICCPR) and the International Covenant on Economic, Social and Cultural Rights (ICESCR) and in art 29(1) of the Universal Declaration of Human Rights (UDHR), which explicitly acknowledges that everyone has 'duties to the community in which alone the free and full development of his [or her] personality is possible'.

The focus on rights rather than responsibilities is inappropriate

States are responsible for both their own unlawful acts and those of state entities and persons carrying out state functions.[24] The obligation 'to protect' contained in many human rights instruments imposes an obligation on states to take measures that prevent third parties from interfering with human rights.[25] Further, rights are not one-sided. The modern view is that obligations are to be applied horizontally as between individuals,[26] groups and corporations as well as the traditional vertical application between individuals and the state.[27]

In 2008, the UN Human Rights Council endorsed a human rights framework developed by UN special representative John Ruggie, containing a set of guiding principles for addressing human rights in the business context. The principles, commonly referred to as the 'Protect, Respect and Remedy' framework, recognise the relationship between states and business obligations in the area of human rights and the role that business entities should fulfil in the protection of human rights.[28] This framework could be adapted to apply to individuals and communities.

---

and individual rights: see Kiwanuka (1988) 82.

[23] Reeves (1998) 15.

[24] United Nations Draft Articles of State Responsibility: *Responsibility of States for Internationally Wrongful Acts* U.N. Doc. A/56/10 (2001) arts 4–8.

[25] APF (2007).

[26] Regarding individual duties under international law see Praust (1992).

[27] See Knox (2012).

[28] United Nations Human Rights Council (UNHRC 2011).

There is No Need for a Substantive Right because Participation Rights Suffice

Participation rights are important. They encourage transparency and accountability in policy decisions and strengthen environmental justice.[29] Further, serious damage to the environment is often linked to repression of affected groups and denial of access to information.[30] In my view, however, procedural and participation rights alone are not sufficient. Without being attached to an explicit right to environment, participation rights may exist in somewhat of a vacuum. The reverse is also true. For example, despite the existence of substantive environmental rights, the lack of enforceable participation and procedural rights in a number of South Asian communities has inhibited their ability to enjoy those substantive rights.[31] Both procedural and substantive rights are required for the full protection of individual (and communal) environmental interests.

ARGUMENTS IN FAVOUR OF THE RIGHT TO A QUALITY ENVIRONMENT

Many of the arguments in favour of an explicit right to a quality environment have been traversed in the course of countering the arguments against such a right. One of the strongest arguments for recognition is the intrinsic link between environmental preservation and the enjoyment of other internationally guaranteed rights.[32] I now turn to some more specific arguments in support of recognising the substantive right to a quality environment.

A Specific Right Would Give Greater Prominence to the Environment

Recognising a right to the environment would give environmental protection issues a more 'human face'.[33] Without drawing connections between environmental protection and people, 'the environment' can, contrary to the words of the International Court of Justice,[34] seem something

---

29 See for example Du (2009) 139.

30 See discussion in Anderson, in Boyle and Anderson (1996) 5.

31 Razzaque (2002) 133.

32 Shelton (2002) 6.

33 Australian Human Rights and Equal Opportunity Commission (AHREOC) (2008) 12.

34 See the comments in *Legality of the Threat or Use of Nuclear Weapons* [1996] ICJ Rep 226, 241.

of an abstraction. The importance of winning the hearts and minds of people and the role of rhetoric in protecting the environment cannot be overemphasised.

A Specific Right Would Address the Needs of the Vulnerable More Clearly[35]

There is a growing body of evidence suggesting that the burden of environmental damage is borne more heavily by poor and developing nations.[36] Recognition of a right to a quality environment would concentrate attention on their plight, although it would at the same time be necessary to ensure that any environmental protection measures that were taken were not unduly onerous on those who could afford it least, both between and within states.[37]

The Environment Would Be Balanced as a Separate Right

Humans depend on the environment. Yet, human interests may conflict with the interests of environmental protection. Recognising a right to the environment would ensure a more balanced analysis of the competing interests within the rights framework.[38] One area where such conflicts are likely to arise is in relation to property rights. The right to property includes the right to own, use and not be arbitrarily deprived of property.[39] Where property rights are recognised, but environmental rights are not, the risk is that property rights may be more likely to override non-rights based environmental interests. An additional benefit of affording rights-status to environmental protection is that it may alter public perception of the issues underlying use restriction and compulsory acquisition. Rather than being viewed as state interference with private property use, greater recognition may be afforded to how the use of private property affects the rights and interests of other citizens.[40]

---

[35] Ksentini, F. (1994) Annex 1: 'Draft Principles on Human Rights and the Environment' [Draft Principles] principle 25 required special attention to be given to vulnerable persons and groups.

[36] Dupont and Pearman (2006) 27.

[37] AHREOC (2008) 14–15.

[38] Boyd (2012) 30.

[39] UDHR, art 17. Property rights are also recognised in other international instruments.

[40] Waldron (2012). See especially ch 3, 'In Defence of Legislation'.

Health

For those who still need convincing of the need for a right to environment, I refer to the following data:[41]

(a) Worldwide, 13 million deaths (23 per cent of all deaths) could be prevented each year by making our environment healthier.
(b) For children under 14, over one-third (36 per cent) of all disease is caused by environmental factors such as unsafe water or air pollution. There are more than four million environmentally-caused deaths of children each year.
(c) Better environmental management could prevent 42 per cent of deaths from malaria, 41 per cent of deaths from lower respiratory infections in developing countries[42] and 94 per cent of deaths from diarrhoeal disease. These are three of the world's biggest childhood killers.

INDIGENOUS PEOPLES, COLLECTIVE RIGHTS AND THE ENVIRONMENT

The unique relationship between indigenous peoples and the environment has been recognised at the international level.[43] Although not binding, the most significant international recognition of indigenous rights and interests is the Declaration on the Rights of Indigenous Peoples 2007, which recognises that indigenous peoples have the right to the conservation and protection of the environment and the productive capacity of their lands or territories and resources.[44] The connection between indigenous peoples and the land is both cultural and spiritual.[45] Most indigenous peoples also

---

41 Prüss-Üstün and Corvalán (2006).

42 The figure is 20% in developed countries.

43 Gillespie (2003) 69; United Nations (2002) [5], and *World Summit on Sustainable Development Johannesburg Declaration on Sustainable Development* A/CONF.199/20 (2002) (Johannesburg Declaration) [25].

44 Article 29. Focus has been placed on participation rights for indigenous peoples: see arts 5 and 18 of the Declaration. See also the Indigenous and Tribal Peoples Convention 1989, arts 5 and 15. Twenty-two states have ratified the Tribal Peoples Convention.

45 See for example New Zealand Law Commission *Converging Currents: Custom and Human Rights in the Pacific* (NZLC SP17, 2006) at [5.27]. In New Zealand, the special relationship between the New Zealand Māori and the land has been recognised in a number of Treaty of Waitangi settlements. The

view environmental preservation as a duty owed to generations to come. The Declaration recognises this and provides that:[46]

> Indigenous peoples have the right to maintain and strengthen their distinctive spiritual relationship with their traditionally owned or otherwise occupied and used lands, territories, waters and coastal seas and other resources and to uphold their responsibility to future generations in this regard.

Closely associated with the interests of indigenous people is the issue of collective rights. In Pacific cultures, for example, environmental responsibility is collective and supported by collective decision-making[47] while territorial and resource 'ownership' is based on collective customary interests.[48] A healthy environment is intrinsically linked to the collective well-being of the people[49] and traditional customs and customary laws are created in harmony with environmental sustainability. Some commentators have criticised the focus on environmental issues, arguing that this obscures more important issues, such as property rights and self-determination.[50] These concerns are valid but, in my view, do not point away from recognising an environmental right. Indeed, given the close connection between indigenous cultures and the environment, it can be seen as quintessentially an indigenous right. It is, however, important to ensure that any such right is framed in a way that honours, recognises and accommodates indigenous culture, practices and aspirations, including self-determination.

ENVIRONMENTALLY DISPLACED PERSONS

The negative effects of climate change will not be experienced in the same way in all areas of the globe. The impact will differ depending both on the level of exposure and the capacity of an area to adapt to the resulting changes. In many cases, it will be poorer, developing areas that bear the greatest burden.[51]

Waikato-Tainui settlement, for example, acknowledges that respect for *te mana o te awa* (the spiritual authority, protective power and prestige of the Waikato River) is at the heart of the relationship between the tribe and their ancestral river: The Waikato-Tainui Raupatu Settlement: Waikato-Tainui Raupatu Claims (Waikato River) Settlement Act 2010.

46 Article 25.

47 Vegter (2005) 570.

48 Manus (2005) 566.

49 Reeves (1998) 11–16.

50 Jeffery (2005) 11.

51 UN Human Rights Council (2011) 1.

Indigenous peoples are particularly vulnerable to environmental harm because of the reliance they place on their lands and resources and the cultural and religious links they maintain with their traditional territories.[52] As the UN Permanent Forum on Indigenous Issues has stated, climate change exacerbates difficulties already faced by indigenous peoples, including political and economic marginalisation, loss of land and resources, human rights violations, discrimination and unemployment.[53] Most of the 200 million indigenous people in the world live in highly vulnerable ecosystems – from semi-arid rangelands to rainforests and low-lying islands.[54] Preserving these ecosystems is not just about preserving livelihoods. It is about preserving a way and understanding of life and the unique relationship that indigenous people have with the environment. Land loss due to rising sea levels and the increased incidences of serious natural disasters are of special concern.[55] In addition to the obvious potential violations of the rights to life, adequate food, water, health and adequate housing, displaced persons are also at risk of being denied their rights to self-determination, culture, language and religion.[56]

It is unlikely that the vast majority of those who may end up as environmentally displaced persons would fall under the protection of the Refugee Convention.[57] While there have been suggestions that the definition of 'refugee' under the Convention ought to be changed to include environmentally displaced persons,[58] this is probably not likely to occur in the short term.[59] The plight of environmentally displaced persons must be pre-emptively and urgently addressed by the international community. The first priority should be to avoid displacement but, if unsuccessful, there must be plans for relocation in a way that does the least damage to the way of life of displaced persons. The relevance of a right to the environment in such circumstances is that it would provide a degree of standing for environmental refugees. Their displaced status would be linked to a violation of the right to an environment capable of sustaining them.

---

52 For an overview of the effects of climate change on indigenous populations see Secretariat of the UN Permanent Forum on Indigenous Issues (2007) from 5.

53 Ibid 3–4.

54 Anton and Shelton (2011) 545.

55 Displacement as a result of climate change induced conflict is also an increasing concern: Hsiang, Burke, Miguel (2013).

56 See McAdam and Saul (2008) 10. See also McAdam (2012).

57 Convention Relating to the Status of Refugees 1951; Black (2001) 11.

58 See Warnock (2007) 269–74; Cartagena Declaration on Refugees (1984) [III(3)].

59 Solomon and Warner in Gerrard and Wannier (eds) (2013) 258.

SUGGESTED CONTENT OF THE RIGHT

I now discuss the elements I think should be encompassed in any right:[60]

(a) biodiversity and the environment for its own sake;
(b) rights and duties;
(c) collective as well as individual rights and duties;
(d) indigenous peoples and minorities;
(e) future generations;
(f) participation and process;
(g) a separate sustainable development right; and
(h) remedies.

Biodiversity and the Environment for its Own Sake

A right to the environment should not be defined solely in terms of human needs. This is not to suggest that it is inappropriate to relate the right to human needs. Indeed, as already discussed, one of the reasons for recognising a right is the connection between realising existing human rights and preserving the environment. Human needs must, however, be balanced with express recognition of the right to biological diversity and a balanced eco-system.[61]

Rights and Duties

To be effective, a substantive right to the environment must include both rights and duties. Of course, the existing human rights framework already includes duties, and environmental duties do already exist.[62] The

---

60 Most of these elements are contained in the recommendation of the Advisory Council of Jurists (ACJ) of the Asia Pacific Forum of National Human Rights Institutions (APF). APF Final Report (2007) 38. The APF was established in 1996 and its prime purpose is to support the establishment and strengthening of national human rights institutions. The ACJ is a body of jurists from the region and advises the APF on the interpretation and application of international human rights law: www.asiapacificforum.net (accessed 11 March 2015). At the time of the environmental report, I was a member of the ACJ.

61 The importance of ecosystems is being increasingly recognised pursuant to the ecosystem approach at international law: United Nations *Report of the United Nations Conference on Sustainable Development* A/CONF.216/16 (2012) [Rio 20+ Report] including at [4], [30], [39], [40], [56], [61].

62 States are subject to duties not to injure the environment of other states: *Legality of the Threat or Use of Nuclear Weapons* (1996) [29]. A breach of this

argument is that existing duties would be strengthened and supported by the recognition of a right and by explicit articulation of the duties of the state and of individuals, communities and businesses to take action to protect, promote and improve[63] the environment.[64] While there needs to be some care with the concept of improving the environment, it should certainly include remedying environmental degradation, and, for example, improvements in terms of better sanitation. Any duty to 'improve' would also have to recognise the need to preserve biodiversity and a balanced ecosystem.

Collective as well as Individual Rights and Duties

Substantive environmental rights and duties ought to apply not only to individuals but to communities and peoples and perhaps even to families, given the importance of kinship in many indigenous societies.

Indigenous Peoples and Minorities

The explicit (and culturally appropriate) recognition of the relationship between indigenous peoples and the environment would also be essential, as would the recognition and protection of the rights of minorities as they too may be particularly vulnerable to environmental risks, including in situations of environmental displacement.

Future Generations

The notion of guardianship and the need to preserve the environment for future generations should be explicit. While a number of non-binding international human rights instruments recognise future generational rights and interests,[65] the concentration on the living is a weakness of the current human rights framework. The concept of intergenerational

---

obligation could give rise to states responsibility under art 1 the Draft articles on state responsibility (2001), art 1.

[63] The concept of a duty to 'improve' the environment is included under the Association of Southeast Asian Nations' Charter, discussed above, and the Additional Protocol to The American Convention on Human Rights in the Area of Economic, Social and Cultural Rights 1999.

[64] This could mirror the duties placed on corporations to protect, respect and remedy human rights under the United Nations 'Protect, Respect and Remedy' Framework (n 28).

[65] Article 25 of the Declaration of the Rights of Indigenous Peoples, for example, recognises that resources are held on trust for future generations.

equality is grounded on the notion that members of the present generation are both trustees, responsible for the robustness and integrity of the planet, and beneficiaries, with the right to use and benefit from it for themselves.[66] Climate change issues have a significant intergenerational dimension.[67]

Participation and Process

It would also be necessary to deal with participation and procedural rights in the context of any environmental right.[68] Participation rights must include the right to all information necessary to enable effective public participation in environmental decision-making.[69] It must also include the right to participate in planning and decision-making activities and the right to a prior assessment of the environmental, developmental and human rights consequences of proposed actions.[70] The participation rights of indigenous peoples and minorities ought to be dealt with specifically in a manner that is appropriate for the particular peoples.[71]

A Separate Sustainable Development Right

I would include a right to sustainable development separate from the right to an environment.[72] Coupling the environment and development makes it impossible to balance the environment for its own sake against the right

---

[66] Weiss (1992) 19 at 20. There is recognition of the environmental rights of future generations in a number of national constitutions. See for example the Constitution of Brazil 1988, s 225. The Constitution of Chile 1833, art 19(8) and Constitution of the Republic of the Philippines 1987, art II s 16 have been held to extend to future generations: see respectively *Communidad de Chanaral v Codeco Division el Saldor (1998) S/Recurso de Protection* and *Oposa v Factoran* (1995) 33 I.L.M. 173.

[67] Redgwell in Churchill and Freestone (eds) (1991) 47.

[68] Ksentini (1994) at [70]. United Nations (2012) principles 10, 20, 22. See also APF Final Report (n 25) 56–7.

[69] 1994 Draft Principles (n 35) art 15. By comparison, art 19(2) of the ICCPR gives the right to 'receive and impart' information.

[70] 1994 Draft Principles (n 35) art 18. Article 25(a) of the ICCPR provides a right to participate freely in the government of their country, either directly or through freely chosen representatives.

[71] See the Convention on Access to Information, Public Participation in Decision-making and Access to Justice in Environmental Matters 1998 (Aarhus Convention), and APF Final Report (2007) 15.

[72] It has been argued that, like the environmental right, the right to energy has also been inappropriately subsumed into the right to development. Currently,

to development. The focus on sustainable development that still exists within environmental rights discourse[73] suggests that environmental interests are important only to the extent that the environment is valuable for human use. Keeping the right to the environment and that of sustainable development separate would mean that the two rights would be balanced and weighed against one another, should they come into conflict. This should lead to an overall result which meets the broader concept of sustainability, which requires environmental, social and economic demands to be balanced to ensure that human activity does not surpass the planet's limited resources.[74]

Remedies

A separate right to the environment would also require consideration of specific remedies, both judicial and administrative, for environmental harm or threat of such harm.[75] The remedies should not only address the human cost of any breach but should also provide for restoration and preservation of the environment.

CONCLUSION

Protecting the environment is of paramount importance. Our well-being and very survival is intrinsically linked to the environment in which we live. In this chapter, I have presented the case for a substantive right to the environment and addressed the opposing views. My conclusion is that many of the arguments raised against such a right can be addressed by a proper framing of the content of any right to a quality environment. It is fitting to end as I began, with a whakatauki:[76]

> Whatungarongaro he tangata, toitū he whenua hoki
> *As man disappears from sight, the land remains*

---

however, a human right to energy is accepted as a moral right, but is not accepted in international law: see Clemson (2012).

[73] Sustainable development was, for example, still a central concept in the outcomes of the Rio 20+ conference in 2012; see n 61.

[74] Bosselmann (2008) 9.

[75] 1994 Draft Principles (n 35). Art 20 addresses remedies.

[76] A Māori proverb.

REFERENCES

Anderson, M. (1996), 'Human Rights Approaches to Environmental Protection: An Overview' in A. Boyle and M. Anderson (eds), *Human Rights Approaches to Environmental Protection* (Oxford: Oxford University Press).

Anton, D. and D. Shelton (2011), *Environmental Protection and Human Rights* (New York: Cambridge University Press).

Asia Pacific Forum of National Human Rights Institutions (APF 2007), *Human Rights and the Environment: Background Paper* accessed 11 March 2015 at www.asiapacificforum.net (APF Background paper).

Asia Pacific Forum of National Human Rights Institutions (2007), *APF Human Rights and the Environment: Final Report and Recommendations* accessed 11 March 2015 at http://www.ohchr.org.

Association of South East Asian Nations (ASEAN 2007), *Charter of the Association of Southeast Asian Nations* (adopted at the 13th ASEAN Summit, November 2007) accessed 11 March 2015 at www.aseansec.org.

Australian Human Rights and Equal Opportunity Commission (2008), *Human Rights and Climate Change: Background Paper* accessed 11 March 2015 at https://www.humanrights.gov.au.

Basic Principles and Guidelines on the Right to a Remedy and Reparation for Victims of Gross Violations of International Human Rights Law and Serious violations of International Humanitarian Law GA Res 60/147, A/RES/60/147 (2006).

Black, R. (2001), *Environmental Refugees: Myth or Reality?* (New Issues in Refugee Research, Working Paper No 34 provided for UNHCR).

Bosselmann, K. (2008), *The Principle of Sustainability: Transforming Law and Governance* (Cornwall: Ashgate Publishing Ltd).

Boyd, D. (2012), *The Environmental Rights Revolution: A Global Study of Constitutions, Human Rights, and the Environment* (Vancouver: University of British Columbia Press).

Boyle, A. (1996), 'The Role of International Human Rights Law in the Protection of the Environment' in A. Boyle and M. Anderson (eds) *Human Rights Approaches to Environmental Protection* (Oxford: Oxford University Press).

Cartagena Declaration on Refugees (Adopted by the Colloquium on the International Protection of Refugees in Central America, Mexico and Panama, 22 November 1984).

Case concerning the Gabčíkovo-Nagymaros Project (Hungary v Slovakia) [1997] ICJ Rep 7, separate opinion of Vice-President Weeramantry.

Charan Lal Sahu v Union of India AIR 1990 SCF 1480.

Clemson, M. (2012), 'Human Rights and the Environment: Access to Energy' 16 NZJEL 39.

Communidad de Chanaral v Codeco Division el Saldor (1998) S/Recurso de Protection.

Constitution of Brazil (1988).

Constitution of Chile (1833).

Constitution of the Republic of the Philippines (1987).

Convention on Access to Information, Public Participation in Decision-making and Access to Justice in Environmental Matters 1998 (Aarhus Convention).

Convention Relating to the Status of Refugees (1951).

de Sadeleer, N. (2002), *Environmental Principles: From Political Slogans to Legal Rules* (Oxford: Oxford University Press).
Du, Q. (2009), 'Public Participation and the Challenges of Environmental Justice in China' in J. Ebbesson and P. Okowa (eds), *Environmental Law and Justice in Context* (Cambridge: Cambridge University Press).
Du Bois, F. (1996), 'Social Justice and the Judicial Enforcement of Environmental Rights and Duties' in A. Boyle and M. Anderson (eds), *Human Rights Approaches to Environmental Protection* (Oxford: Oxford University Press).
Dupont, A. and Pearman, G. (2006), *Heating Up the Plant: Climate Change and Security* (Lowy Institute Paper 12, New South Wales: Lowy Institute for International Policy).
Farooque v Bangladesh (1997), 49 Khaka Law Reports (AD) 1.
Hill, B., S. Wolfson and N. Targ (2004), 'Human Rights and the Environment: A Synopsis and Some Predictions' 16 Geo Int'l Envtl L Rev 359.
Hsiang, S., M. Burke, and E. Miguel (2013), 'Quantifying the Influence of Climate on Human Conflict' (accessed 11 March 2015 at www.sciencemag.org, 1 August 2013).
Gillespie, A. (2003), 'Small Island States in the Face of Climatic Change: the End of the Line in International Environmental Responsibility' 22 UCLA J Envtl L & Pol'y 107.
Glazebrook, S. (2009), 'Human Rights and the Environment' (2009) 1 VUWLR 293.
Glazebrook, S. (2011), 'Keeping it Clean and Green: The Case for Constitutional Environmental Protection Rights' in C. Morris, J. Boston and P. Butler (eds), *Reconstituting the Constitution* (Berlin, Heidelberg: Springer).
Jeffery, M. (2005), 'Environmental Governance: A Comparative Analysis of Public Participation and Access to Justice' 9 JSPL 1.
Kiwanuka, R. (1988), 'The Meaning of "People" in The African Charter on Human And Peoples' Rights' 82 Am J Int'l L 80.
Knox, J. (2012), 'Horizontal Human Rights Law' 102 AJ Int L 1.
Ksentini, F. (1994), *Review of Further Developments in Fields with which the Sub-Commission has been Concerned Human Rights and the Environment: Final Report of Sub-Commission on Prevention of Discrimination and Protection of Minorities* UN Doc E/CN.4/Sub.2/1994.
Kumar v State of Bihar (1991), 1 SCC 598.
Legality of the Threat or Use of Nuclear Weapons [1996] ICJ Rep 226.
McAdam, J. (2012), *Climate Change, Forced Migration, and International Law* (Oxford: Oxford University Press).
McAdam, J. and B. Saul (2008), *An Insecure Climate for Human Security? Climate-Induced Displacement and International Law* (Sydney Centre for International Law, Working Paper 4).
Manus, P. (2005), 'Sovereignty, Self-Determination, and Environment-Based Cultures: The Emerging Voice of Indigenous Peoples in International Law' 23 Wis Int'l L J 553.
New Zealand Law Commission *Converging Currents: Custom and Human Rights in the Pacific* (NZLC SP17, 2006).
Oposa v Factoran (1995), 33 I.L.M. 173.
Pillay N. (2012), *Strengthening the United Nations Human Rights Treaty Body System: A Report by the United Nations High Commissioner for Human Rights* A/66/860 (June).

Praust, J. (1992), 'The Other Side of Right: Private Duties under Human Rights Law' 5 Harv. Hum. Rts. J. 51.

Prüss-Üstün, A. and C. Corvalán (2006), *Preventing disease through healthy environments: Towards an estimate of the environmental burden of disease* (Geneva: World Health Organisation).

Razzaque, J. (2002), *Background Paper No 4 Human Rights and the Environment: The National Experience in South Asia and Africa* (Joint UNEP-OHCHR Expert Seminar on Human Rights and the Environment, Geneva, January 2002).

Redgwell, C. (1991), 'Intergenerational Equity and Global Warming' in R. Churchill and D. Freestone (eds), *International Law and Global Climate Change* (London: Graham and Trotman).

Redgwell, C. (1996), 'Life, the Universe and Everything: A Critique of Anthropocentric Rights' in A. Boyle and M. Anderson (eds), *Human Rights Approaches to Environmental Protection* (Oxford: Oxford University Press).

Reeves, P. (1998), 'Collective Human Rights of Pacific Peoples' in N. Tomas and Haruru (eds), *Collective Human Rights of Pacific Peoples* (International Research Unit for Māori and Indigenous Education, University of Auckland).

Rodriguez-Rivera, L. (2001), 'Is the Human Right to Environment Recognized Under International Law? It Depends on the Source' 12 Colo J Int'l Envtl L & Pol'y 1.

Secretariat of the UN Permanent Forum on Indigenous Issues (November 2007), *Climate Change: An Overview* (New York: United Nations).

Shelton, D. (2002), *Human Rights, Health and Environmental Protection: Linkages in Law and Practice* (Health and Human Rights Working Paper Series No 1: A Background Paper for the World Health Organization 2002).

Shelton, D. (2005), *Remedies in International Human Rights Law* (Oxford: Oxford University Press).

Solomon, M. and K. Warner (2013), 'Protection of Persons Displaced as a Result of Climate Change' in M. Gerrard and G. Wannier (eds), *Threatened Island Nations: Legal Implications and a Changing Climate* (New York: Cambridge University Press).

Taylor, P. (1998), 'From Environment to Ecological Human Rights: A New Dynamic in International Law?' 10 Geo Int'l Envtl L Rev 309.

United Nations (1966), *International Covenant on Economic, Social and Cultural Rights*, (Office of the High Commissioner of Human Rights: Geneva), accessed 11 March 2015 at http://www.ohchr.org.

United Nations (2002), *Report of the World Summit on Sustainable Development* A/CONF.199/20.

United Nations (2002), *World Summit on Sustainable Development Johannesburg Declaration on Sustainable Development* A/CONF.199/20.

United Nations (2012), *Report of the United Nations Conference on Sustainable Development* A/CONF.216/16.

United Nations Draft Articles of State Responsibility: *Responsibility of States for Internationally Wrongful Acts* U.N. Doc. A/56/10 (2001).

United Nations Human Rights Council (2011), *Human Rights and the Environment* HRC Res 16/11, A/HCR/RES/16/11.

United Nations Human Rights Council (2011), *Human Rights and Transnational Corporations and Other Business Enterprises* HRC Res 17/4, A/HRC/17/4.

Vegter, A. (2005), 'Forsaking the Forests for the Trees: Forestry Law in Papua

New Guinea Inhibits Indigenous Customary Ownership' 14 Pac Rim L & Pol'y J 545.
Waikato-Tainui Raupatu Settlement: Waikato-Tainui Raupatu Claims (Waikato River) Settlement Act 2010.
Waldron, J. (2012), *The Rule of Law and the Measure of Property* (The Hamlyn Lectures, New York: Cambridge University Press).
Warnock, A. (2007), 'Small Island Developing States of the Pacific and Climate Change: Adaptation and Alternatives' 4 NZYIL 245.
Weiss, E. (1992), 'In Fairness to Future Generations and Sustainable Development' 8 Am U.J. Int'l & Policy 19.
Weston, B. and D. Bollier (2013), *Green Governance: Ecological Survival, Human Rights, and the Law of the Commons* (Cambridge: Cambridge University Press).

6. No private property rights in the atmosphere

Ben France-Hudson

INTRODUCTION

The New Zealand Emissions Trading Scheme ('NZ ETS') does not create private property rights in either the atmosphere or greenhouse gases. Neither does it confer a private property right to emit greenhouse gases. Rather, it employs a very restricted private property right that can only be used for an extremely limited range of purposes. In particular, the primary purpose of the private property right at the heart of the regime is simply to enable its holder to discharge a liability that arises as a consequence of undertaking activities that result in greenhouse gas emissions.

This observation is important because it addresses the criticism that environmental management regimes which employ private property to solve the tragedy of the commons[1] actually create 'rights to pollute'.[2] The structure of the NZ ETS neatly avoids creating such a right and this suggests that the risks associated with using private property as a tool of environmental management can be ameliorated. More generally, the way the NZ ETS utilises private property indicates that private property itself may be far more flexible than is often acknowledged. This may provide a further source of support for a number of modern property law theories that stress private property's essentially social function.

This chapter begins by focusing on the concerns surrounding rights to pollute, and particularly the criticism that an 'unattenuated' private property right sends the wrong ethical and moral message about greenhouse gas emissions by transmuting an environmental problem into an economic

---

[1] Hardin (1968). The basic premise of Hardin's now ubiquitous metaphor is that the tragedy will unfold whenever it would be in everybody's best interest to look after a common resource, but because nobody owns it, each person has a direct incentive to take what they can now and 'let the devil take the hindmost'. See Rose (1999) 45, 46.

[2] Wiener (1999) 724.

one. It then undertakes a careful analysis of the emissions unit relied on by the NZ ETS and concludes that it does not create a right to pollute. By focusing on the question of exclusivity, it is clear that the private property right employed by the NZ ETS is best described as a right to avoid a penalty, which is separate from the resource being managed. It does not confer a right to pollute.

Finally, this chapter explores the positive implications this conclusion has on our search for environmental justice. If it is possible to use private property to manage greenhouse gases without transferring an ownership right to the atmosphere, the same will also be true for other resources. This chapter demonstrates that private property is a far more flexible and social institution than it is often given credit for. Its use within the NZ ETS indicates that we can use it in a positive and just way, in order to mediate our relationships with each other and the complex ecologies in which we live.

CONCERNS ASSOCIATED WITH USING PRIVATE PROPERTY TO RESOLVE THE TRAGEDY OF THE COMMONS

One of the great ironies of the tragedy of the commons is the fact that some of the greatest risks associated with using private property to solve the tragedy arise as a result of the very attributes that underpin private property's attractiveness as a solution. On one hand, private property is attractive as a tool of environmental management because it has the happy effect of encouraging individuals to look after, invest in and trade the resources they own without the concern that someone else can simply take 'their' things at will.[3] This idea underpins the theory behind regimes such as the NZ ETS; that by simply defining and enforcing private property rights in a resource, and letting the resulting market function freely, all environmental problems will eventually be solved.[4] On the other hand, however, there is a general concern that using private property as a tool of environmental management may lead to increased environmental degradation and to entrenched private property rights that may stranglehold flexibility and change. This is a risk because the rights ostensibly required by these sorts of regimes stem from a tradition that sees private property as providing rights, but demanding no duties.

This concern was brilliantly captured by Leopold in his classic *A Sand*

---

[3] Rose (1990) 262.
[4] Sinden (2007) 537.

County Almanac[5] where he noted that our 'Abrahamic' concept of land (and by extension private property) was one that entailed privilege but no obligation.[6] His broad point was that the culturally dominant idea of private property, which stems from the classical liberal tradition, is often the key source of environmental destruction. This is an idea that has been repeated time and again by a diverse range of academics.[7] Consequently, in criticising the private property approach to environmental management, scholars have suggested that it is perilous to trust the solution to environmental problems to the very institution that is the root cause of the problems in the first instance.[8]

A RIGHT TO POLLUTE

A primary way in which this general concern is manifested with regard to emissions trading schemes is the risk that an entitlement to emit greenhouse gases can also be framed as a 'right to pollute'.[9] This view of the right arises because, at least on some levels, emissions trading schemes treat greenhouse gas 'pollution' as a simple cost of doing business.[10] The whole purpose of these regimes is to establish a system whereby individuals and corporate entities can choose not to pollute, or alternatively, to pay and continue to pollute, whichever is cheaper.[11] Essentially, by establishing a market in private rights to undertake emitting activities, critics say that environmental protection is translated into the dominant language of private property and the classical liberal emphasis on individual autonomy, commodity and trade.[12]

Moreover, critics argue that by creating a 'right to pollute' emissions trading schemes actually encourage substitute performance, in the sense that polluters can pay someone else to achieve reductions on their behalf, rather than behaving in an environmentally sustainable way. While levels of pollution may actually be reduced, these schemes sometimes operate to obscure the difficult questions about which polluters are actually reducing their environmental impact and exactly where and how pollution

5 Leopold (1949).
6 Ibid, vii and 167–8.
7 For a review see: Taylor and Grinlinton (2011).
8 Babie (2010b).
9 Guerin (2003) 18.
10 Merrill (2000) 277.
11 Rose (2006) 1919.
12 Wiener (1999) 724.

is occurring. Many find this deplorable, and are concerned that there is a real risk that a genuine ecological problem will be translated into a simple exercise of economics.[13] The risk is that those who are involved may lose sight of the very real environmental problems at issue and become caught up in the 'logic of prices, sale, purchase, registration, transfer and return'.[14] Thus, the creation of private property rights in natural resources can mean that people no longer place any intrinsic value on the things that have been commodified.[15] In essence, the purchase of a right to pollute sends the wrong ethical or moral message about the activity of pollution.[16] It may be seen as permitting the holder of an emissions unit to do something that is wrong simply because he or she has acquired a private property right. There is a risk that the adoption of property-based measures to regulate environmental resources may work against 'moral suasion' creating a 'climate in which one is not expected to do the right thing unless it is in one's direct interest to do so'.[17]

However, while there are undoubtedly risks associated with rights to pollute, this risk is not realised in relation to the NZ ETS. The emissions units created by the regime do not grant any sort of entitlement that could be characterised as a right to pollute. Demonstrating this point requires a careful consideration of the structure and operation of the NZ ETS, beginning by briefly outlining the contours of the scheme.

THE NZ ETS

The NZ ETS is established under the Climate Change Response Act 2002 ('the Act') which was implemented in order to facilitate New Zealand in discharging its obligations under two international treaties: the United Nations Framework Convention on Climate Change and the Kyoto Protocol ('the Protocol'). The scheme requires participants to monitor and report their emission of various greenhouse gases. Participants must also surrender to the Crown one emissions unit for each tonne of emissions made over the relevant compliance period.[18] Surrendering a unit means that it cannot be used again or transferred to another participant. The emissions unit is the private property right created (or adopted from the

---

13 Guerin (2003) 18.
14 Winter (2010) 15.
15 Rose (2006) 1919.
16 Ibid.
17 Rose (1991) 34.
18 Cameron (2011) 252.

Protocol) by the NZ ETS to achieve its purpose. Failure to surrender sufficient emissions units is met with both criminal and financial sanctions.[19] In particular, a participant who fails to surrender units sufficient to discharge their obligations must either: surrender sufficient units; or pay to the Crown an excess emissions penalty of NZ$30 for each unit they should have surrendered.[20]

The requirement to surrender a unit has the effect of altering the price associated with undertaking a particular emitting activity.[21] Activities that require emission units to be surrendered should become more expensive. Over time, the changes in price should affect incentives and behaviour. If structured appropriately, this should lead to a reduction in greenhouse gas emissions, at least in comparison with what the situation would have been in the absence of the NZ ETS.

Of course, in assessing whether or not the NZ ETS creates a right to pollute, it is necessary to consider the nature of the private property right that lies at the heart of the regime. In particular, it is instructive to consider the strength of the private property right represented by an emissions unit, because the theory suggests we should see a private property right that is strong and unattenuated. The contention is that the more complete the private property right is, the more the private and social benefits of the resource use are meshed, eliminating externalities and the losses to the common pool.[22] In other words, in order for natural resources to be put to their 'best' and 'most efficient' use, the private property rights recognised or created must be full and complete. It follows that the predominant literature in this area is overlaid by the expectation that the property rights should not be vulnerable to direct political interference.[23] It is claimed that only an unattenuated right will provide the necessary incentives for innovation and resource conservation that will enable the tragedy of the commons to be avoided.[24]

This idea reaches its apogee in the work of the 'free market environmentalists' who argue for regimes of natural resource management based on the free market, strong private property rights and limited government.[25] The argument is that private property rights must be well defined in order to facilitate exchange. If they are not well defined there will be conflict

---

19 Climate Change Response Act 2002, ss 132 and 134.
20 Ibid, s 134(2)(b).
21 Wilson (2011) 158.
22 Libecap (2009).
23 Martin and Verbeek (2002) 2.
24 Ibid, 3.
25 Rose (1999) 51.

between parties who may all consider they have a legitimate interest in a particular resource. As well as being clearly specified, rights need to be transferable so that an owner can take full advantage of the potential for gains made through trade. The use of strong private property rights should harness the power of human self-interest and in so doing solve environmental problems along the way.[26] However, as canvassed above, it is the creation of such a right that gives rise to the risks associated with rights to pollute.

Assessing the strength of a private property right can be a difficult exercise. While there are different ways to approach the question,[27] this chapter focuses on the characteristic of exclusivity, which is often described as private property's *sine qua non*. Querying the degree to which emissions units reflect an exclusive private property right suggests that the private property right in emissions units is far from absolute. It also indicates that the NZ ETS does not create anything that could be characterised as a 'right to pollute'.

In property law theory exclusivity denotes the extent to which the owner of the resource can enjoy its use while remaining free from interference.[28] The more a right is subject to interference, the less exclusive it is. The right to exclude is considered essential to private property because it protects secure possession. It does this by forbidding the use or acquisition of the resource by others. As a result, where one has a 'private property right' in a resource, one can use that resource to the exclusion of all others,[29] and can use it in any way one sees fit.[30] It is this characteristic that provides the small domain of complete mastery and self-direction that is so important to classical liberal thought.

However, when we consider the nature of emission units it becomes evident that, while they are exclusive in some respects, this exclusivity is extremely limited. The Act does not confer either an exclusive right to a part of the atmospheric sink or the right to emit greenhouse gases. Instead, what is created is a narrow right that can only be used in a few specified circumstances.

26 For an excellent survey see Medema (2011).
27 See Radin (1993) 120 and Scott (2008) 6.
28 Hamilton and Bankes (2010) 25.
29 Babie (2010a) 532.
30 Ibid.

THE NATURE OF AN EMISSIONS UNIT

Although the language of the Act avoids the term 'ownership',[31] it is clear that, to a certain extent, emission units confer an exclusive right. The Act confers an exclusive right to deal with the units held in the holder's account. This is made explicit by s 7(2), which indicates that, with a few narrow exceptions, no other person is entitled to transfer or otherwise deal with emissions units.[32] The interesting point, however, is that the ability to deal exclusively with the right is extraordinarily narrow. Dealings with emissions units are limited to surrender, cancellation, retirement, transfer and (to a certain extent) use as security. Moreover, once surrendered, cancelled or retired units cease to be of any practical benefit to market participants in the NZ ETS (although they maintain a degree of utility to the Crown in meeting its international obligations). In reality, therefore, there is little that this exclusivity is protecting the right holder from. Because of the way that the regime is structured, the holder of an emissions unit does not have any 'neighbours' who might adversely interfere with the use of his or her right.

Essentially, the NZ ETS establishes a new market. The commodity traded in the market is the emissions unit. Although the different types of units are identified in the interpretation section of the Act (s 4), the Act does not further define the nature of these units.[33] What the Act does do,

---

[31] With one exception the Act does not address the question of 'ownership' or title to units. Instead, the Act generally refers to the 'holding' of units. For example: the language used in s 10, which outlines the purpose of the registry, states that the register's purpose is to ensure the accurate, transparent and efficient accounting of the 'holding' of units; a 'holding account' is defined as an account in the register for the purpose of 'holding units' (s 4). The only section which suggests that holders of emissions units can be said to 'own' those rights, and therefore have the exclusive right to deal with the units held in their accounts, is s 29 which states that:

> **29 Printed search result receivable as evidence**
> A printed search result, or a copy of a printed search result, that purports to be issued by the Registrar is receivable as evidence and is, in the absence of evidence to the contrary, proof of any matter recorded in the unit register, including . . .—
> (a) the *ownership* of units; . . .
> (emphasis added)

Consequently, although the Act eschews the language of ownership we can accept that a degree of 'ownership' is envisaged by the Act. This is supported by the fact that the Act does provide for a degree of exclusive use as discussed in the main body of the text. See also: Cameron (2011) 269.

[32] Cameron (2011) 269.

[33] Indeed, the nature of Kyoto units is governed by the international agreements underpinning the Kyoto Protocol itself. The Act essentially incorporates

however, is to specify that participants have a liability to surrender one unit for each whole tonne of emissions emitted over a specified period (currently this is on an annual basis).[34] This is at the heart of the NZ ETS and it is this that gives emissions units both purpose and value. Without this they would be meaningless.

However, scholars almost always paraphrase this structure by saying that the holder of an emissions unit has the 'right to emit' one tonne of carbon dioxide (or equivalent) for each unit he or she holds. For example, Wilson notes that: 'In the case of a trading regime covering greenhouse gases, the "property right" is permission to emit a certain amount of gas into the atmosphere at a certain time; for example, one tonne of CO2 in a given year.'[35] This is often the source of claims that emissions units create a 'right to pollute'. The reality of what the Act does, however, is more complicated than this.

The structure of the Act suggests that it is not granting 'the right' to emit a tonne of emissions. Neither is it granting 'permission' to emit. Rather, if a participant does emit a tonne of carbon dioxide they are liable to surrender one emissions unit. Failure to do so leads to specified consequences. Participants can face criminal sanctions, but also face a charge of NZ$30 for each unit they ought to have surrendered.[36] The exclusive right created by the Act is not a right to emit greenhouse gases, but actually the ability or right to avoid being stung with the penalties under the Act. Consequently, it is impossible to even roughly equate the ownership of an emission unit with ownership of the atmosphere or other greenhouse gases. The two are conceptually distinct. An emissions unit can only be used to discharge obligations under the Act or fulfil various Kyoto processes.[37] It does not grant any interest in the atmosphere or the relevant gases.

The precise form of an emissions unit is surprising given the theory underpinning the use of such tools. On a purely theoretical basis the best way to deal with the problem of greenhouse gas emissions would be to somehow establish private property rights in the atmosphere itself. However, due to the practical difficulty of achieving this, scholars have suggested the second best approach is to explicitly assign private property rights to the greenhouse gas emissions themselves and set up a market in

these by reference. New Zealand Units ('NZU') (the domestic emissions unit) are simply defined as a unit issued by the Registrar and designated as a NZU (Climate Change Response Act 2002, s 4).

[34] Climate Change Response Act 2002, ss 63 and 65.

[35] Wilson (2011) 148.

[36] Climate Change Response Act 2002, s 134(2)(b).

[37] Such as cancellation, retirement, or carry over. See Cameron (2011) 272.

them.[38] Other scholars have suggested achieving this result by privatising access to the resource (that is, greenhouse gases). As Tietenberg notes: [39]

> Although the popular literature frequently refers to the tradable-permit approach as 'privatising the resource' . . . in most cases it does not actually do that. Rather, it privatizes the right to access the resource to a pre-specified degree. Economists have consistently argued that tradable permits should be treated as secure property rights to protect the incentive to invest in the resource. Confiscation of rights or simply insecure rights could undermine the entire process.

However, the Climate Change Response Act 2002 does not create a property right in the atmosphere, nor does it provide a property right in the relevant greenhouse gases. Moreover, it is arguable that an emissions unit does not actually 'privatise the right to access the resource to a pre-specified degree'. Rather, an emissions unit simply enables its holder to avoid the consequences of non-compliance under the Act. It gives neither an interest in the relevant resources, nor the right to access the resources. The fact that the primary use of an emission unit is to escape a liability severs any relationship between the property right and the resource.

This is a particularly interesting observation from the point of view of exclusivity and the attraction of using a system of private property to manage greenhouse gases. The environmental benefits of an exclusive right are said to flow from the fact that exclusivity functions to forbid others from taking or using the resource.[40] This means that one can then use the resource in any way one sees fit, protected from interference by others.[41] This should, in turn, create an incentive to use resources in a way that rationally secures long-term sustainability.[42] Overall, one of the key things that exclusivity usually provides is a say in how the resource is managed.[43] However, an emissions unit does not confer any power of management over the resources in question. In fact an emissions right does not reflect an interest in a specific resource at all. While the market created may provide incentives to reduce one's own emissions profile, in order to profit by selling any excess units, it does not actually give a right in the greenhouse gases, or atmosphere itself.

It is very difficult to argue that emissions units reflect the exclusive

---

38 Goldemberg *et al.* (1995) 29.
39 Tientenberg (2003) 408.
40 Hamilton and Bankes (2010) 25.
41 Babie (2010a) 532.
42 Winter (2010) 16.
43 Scott (1999) 112.

right demanded by the classical liberal conception of absolute property (let alone a lesser right that is easier to achieve in practice). The NZ ETS has not granted participants a share of the atmosphere over which they have absolute property rights.[44] Neither has it granted an interest in, or the right to access, the relevant greenhouse gases. The property right in an emissions unit is much more narrow than this. It was created to serve what is essentially a single purpose; allowing participants to engage in a market comprised of a commodity that allows them to discharge particular obligations. Nevertheless, an emissions unit is a form of private property, albeit one that is aimed at a very specific purpose, and which has few practical uses.

Overall, an emission unit does not provide exclusivity in a strict sense or in the sense anticipated by those who advocate private property as a solution to the tragedy of the commons. Emissions units do not reflect the 'strong' or 'unattenuated' private property rights predicted by the theory. An emissions unit only entitles the holder to discharge an obligation. This is crucial to the creation of a functioning market in emissions units but it is clear the Act is not providing access, or a right to, a resource either shared or exclusive. It is simply an exclusive property right that can be used for the purposes of discharging obligations imposed by the Act.

It is, therefore, erroneous to characterise emissions units under the NZ ETS as creating a 'right to pollute'. Rather, the Act has created an extremely limited private property right that is quite separate from the resources being managed. While the right has sufficient exclusivity to protect its holder from any interference that would prevent him or her from using the property right in the limited range of ways available under the Act, it is difficult to reconcile this structure with the far greater degree of control envisaged by the theory.

GENERAL OBSERVATIONS

The observation that the NZ ETS does not create private property rights in the atmosphere or greenhouse gases has important ramifications, not only for the way we view the NZ ETS, but also for our conception of private property as an institution and the way it is employed to solve environmental problems.

Plainly, the Act neatly sidesteps concerns surrounding 'rights to pollute' by creating a restricted private property right that is quite separate from

---

44 Page (2009) 20.

the resource being managed. This observation leads to the conclusion that the architects of the NZ ETS have done a good job of balancing the tension between the utility of private property and its potential to cause environmental damage. In particular, it insulates the Crown from criticism if it changes the regulations surrounding emitting activities. Unit holders cannot argue that rule changes will illegitimately interfere with their private property rights, as their rights are limited and do not represent an interest in the resource that can be 'taken away' by regulation.

This is not to say that the NZ ETS will achieve its environmental goals. Indeed, it is fair to say that the NZ ETS is currently faced with manifold difficulties, including the flow on effects of New Zealand's decision to cease participation in the Kyoto scheme itself.[45] Rather, the point is that by adopting a restricted form of private property right, the designers of the NZ ETS have happened upon a structure that restricts the likelihood of some of the particular risks associated with private property being borne out. By adopting a property right that is limited both in relation to its strength and its use, the NZ ETS demonstrates that it is possible to create a private property regime to manage resources that has the potential to achieve positive environmental outcomes while ameliorating some of the associated risks.

This also has more general implications for our understanding of private property, particularly as a tool of environmental management. The theory underpinning the use of private property as a solution to the tragedy of the commons is ostensibly grounded in classical liberal thought and its approach to private property. We use private property in the environmental sphere precisely because we wish to harness the power of the market to tap individual energy and industry. The hope is that, almost as a by-product, we will be able to solve environmental problems along the way, simply by restricting access to the commons. Consequently, one can be forgiven for assuming that regimes such as the NZ ETS are overtly embracing the classical liberal idea of property, which employs the market as a way of regulating the commodities that we regard as desirable. As we create more of these goods, there is more to go around, which grows the economy and leads to society, as a whole, becoming better off.

With the NZ ETS, however, the theory is exactly the *opposite*.[46] We

---

[45] On 9 November 2012 the New Zealand government announced that it would not be signing up for a second commitment under the Kyoto Protocol. See Minister for Climate Change Issues, 'New Zealand Commits to UN Framework Convention' (press release, 9 November 2012) accessed 11 March 2015 at www.beehive.govt.nz.

[46] Alexander (2004) 78.

want to mitigate the effects of anthropogenic climate change by emitting fewer tonnes of greenhouse gases. We are not using private property in this regime in order to generate more greenhouse gases, but instead to limit our use of them so that we do not overwhelm the delicate balance underpinning the Earth's climate. It follows that the true aim of employing private property in a scheme such as the NZ ETS is not the classical liberal aim of satisfying individual preference in order to achieve aggregate wealth maximisation; but rather, the goal is resource conservation for the benefit of the entire community.

This suggests that as an institution, private property has a much broader role in our society than that suggested by classical liberal theory. In particular, these observations lend credence to some of the modern theories of private property grounded in conceptions of human flourishing and social obligation, which make affirmative demands of property owners.[47]

These theories suggest that the core purpose of private property is to secure sufficient property to individuals in order to allow them to flourish. This theory recognises that humans are social creatures whose individual autonomy is enabled by their social nature and the communities in which they live.[48] As a result, private property rights are inherently relational and sometimes an owner will have obligations to others. This fact tempers the scope of the individual's ability to use his or her property solely as he or she wishes and recognises that sometimes individuals owe obligations to the community in relation to the resources they control. In some circumstances, the collective community interest may take priority over the private interests of the individual. Consequently, property holders may have obligations regarding how they use their property that reflect the broader interests of the community.[49]

The fact that the NZ ETS does not create a private property right in the atmosphere is one piece of evidence that this alternative idea of private property may indeed be at work in our legal institutions. Conceptions of private property grounded in ideas of human flourishing and social obligation help to explain the structure and limitations placed on the rights created by the NZ ETS. It also assists in explaining why, notwithstanding the absence of strong property rights, these sorts of regimes can be quite successful in mediating the balance between the community interests in the form of environmental protection, and individual rights and interests.

These observations suggest that regimes such as the NZ ETS need not

---

47 See, for example, Alexander (2009); Alexander and Peñalver (2009).

48 Alexander and Peñalver (2009).

49 Ibid.

necessarily be mistrusted. The NZ ETS demonstrates that it is possible to balance the negative and positive aspects of private property and deploy the institution to help address environmental problems. Rather than worry about these regimes for the reasons captured by Leopold, they can, perhaps, be viewed as counter-intuitively positive. In combination with other tools of 'smart regulation'[50] the way these regimes are being experimented with may well augur approaches that can actually assist us to address the ecological challenges with which we are faced. While private property may be the root cause of many ecological ills, at least in relation to the NZ ETS we see its use in a positive way. The NZ ETS employs a vision of private property that seeks an explicitly social goal; that is to limit the emission of greenhouse gases in an attempt to mitigate the effects of climate change.

Finally, we can speculate that as we all become more familiar with schemes similar to the NZ ETS we may also learn to mediate the belief that we have an unrestricted ability to deal with our own property in any way we chose. We may be able to accept that while many uses of property have negative environmental consequences, private property can also be a powerful tool for addressing ecological concerns. There is a real possibility that regimes such as the NZ ETS may not only achieve the desired environmental outcome, but may also assist us to change our cultural perception of private property from one that sanctions behaviour likely to lead to negative environmental results to one that promotes environmentally sustainable conduct.

CONCLUSION

In the search for environmental justice the place of private property as a tool of resource management is a troubling one. There is no doubt that the dominant idea of private property as entailing rights but imposing no duties runs the risk of entrenching environmental problems rather than solving them. However, despite the concerns surrounding rights to pollute, the NZ ETS appears to have found a way to sidestep the anxieties while still harnessing the utility of private property as a resource management tool.

The NZ ETS demonstrates that private property rights can be coupled with inherent limitations. The explicitly social goal of the scheme illustrates that private property is, at heart, a social institution. Recognising

---

50 See Gunningham (2009).

this means that private property need not be seen as incompatible with environmental protection and environmental justice. It follows that private property based resource management should not necessarily be mistrusted; instead, it should be viewed as potentially *positive*. Regimes such as the NZ ETS provide possible pathways toward a refreshed approach to private property and practical mechanisms for resilient ecosystems and flourishing communities.

REFERENCES

Alexander, G. (2004), 'Propreity Through Commodity? Why have Legal Environmentalists Embraced Market-based Solutions?' in H. Jacobs (ed.), *Private Property in the 21st Century: The Future of an American Ideal* (Cheltenham, UK and Northampton, MA, USA: Edward Elgar).

Alexander, G. (2009), 'The Social-Obligation Norm in American Property Law' 94 Cornell L Rev 745.

Alexander, G. and E. Peñalver, (2009), 'Properties of Community' 10 Theo Inq L 127.

Babie, P. (2010a), 'Idea, Sovereignty, Eco-colonialism and the Future: Four Reflections on Private Property and Climate Change' 19 GLR 527.

Babie, P. (2010b), 'Private Property: The Solution or the Source of the Problem' 2 *Amsterdam Law Forum* 17.

Cameron, A. (2011), 'New Zealand Emissions Trading Scheme' in A. Cameron (ed.), *Climate Change Law and Policy in New Zealand* (Lexis NZ).

Goldemberg, J. *et al.* (1995), 'Introduction: Scope of the Assessment' in J. Bruce, L. Hoesung and E. Haites (eds), *Climate Change 1995: Economic and Social Dimensions of Climate Change. Contribution of Working Group III to the Second Assessment Report of the Intergovernmental Panel on Climate Change* (Cambridge: Cambridge University Press).

Guerin, K. (2003), *Property Rights and Environmental Policy: A New Zealand Perspective* (New Zealand Treasury: New Zealand Treasury Working Paper 03/02).

Gunningham, N. (2009), 'Environmental Law, Regulation and Governance: Shifting Architectures' 21 JEL 179.

Hamilton, J. and N. Bankes (2010), 'Different Views of the Cathedral: The Literature on Property Law Theory' in Aileen McHarg *et al.* (eds), *Property and the Law in Energy and Natural Resources* (Oxford: Oxford University Press).

Hardin, G. (1968), 'The Tragedy of the Commons' 162 *Science* 1243.

Leopold, A. (1949), *A Sand County Almanac: and Sketches Here and There* (Oxford: Oxford University Press).

Libecap, G., (2009), 'The Tragedy of the Commons: Property Rights and Markets as Solutions to Resource and Envrionmental Problems' 53 AJARE 129.

Martin, P. and M. Verbeek (2002), 'Property Rights and Property Responsibility' in *Property: Rights and Responsibilities Current Australian Thinking* (Land & Water Australia).

Medema, S. (2011), 'Of Coase and Carbon: The Coase Theorem in Environmental

Economics, 1960 – 1979' accessed 11 March 2015 at http://ssrn.com/abstract=1929086.

Merrill, T. (2000), 'Explaining Market Mechanisms' 2000 U Ill L Rev 275.

Minister for Climate Change Issues, (2012), 'New Zealand Commits to UN Framework Convention' (press release, 9 November 2012) accessed 11 March 2015 at www.beehive.govt.nz.

Page, E. (2009), 'Licenses to Kill? Cosmopolitanism, Climate Change and Global Emissions Trading' (5th ECPR General Conference, Potsdam University, Potsdam).

Radin, M. (1993), *Reinterpreting Property* (Chicago: University of Chicago Press).

Rose, C. (1990), 'Energy and Efficiency in the Realignment of Common-Law Water Rights' 19 JLS 261.

Rose, C. (1991), 'Rethinking Environmental Controls: Management Strategies for Common Resources' Duke LJ 1.

Rose, C. (1999), 'Expanding the Choices for the Global Commons: Comparing Newfangled Tradable Allowance Schemes to Old-Fashioned Common Property Regimes' 10 DELPF 45.

Rose, C. (2006), 'The Moral Subject of Property' 48 Wm & Mary L Rev 1897.

Scott, A. (1999), 'Moving Through the Narrows: From Open Access to ITQS and Self-Government' (FishRights99 Conference, Fremantle, Western Australia).

Scott, A. (2008), *The Evolution of Resource Property Rights* (Oxford: Oxford University Press).

Sinden, A. (2007), 'The Tragedy of the Commons and the Myth of a Private Property Solution' 78 U Colo L Rev 533.

Taylor, P. and D. Grinlinton (2011), 'Property Rights and Sustainability: Toward a New Vision of Property' in D. Grinlinton and P. Taylor (eds), *Property Rights and Sustainability: The Evolution of Property Rights to Meet Ecological Challenges* (Leiden: Martinus Nijhoff).

Tientenberg, T. (2003), 'The Tradable-Permits Approach to Protecting the Commons: Lessons for Climate Change' 19 Oxf Rev Econ Pol 400.

Wiener, J. (1999), 'Global Environmental Regulation: Instrument Choice in Legal Context' 108 Yale LJ 677.

Wilson, P. (2011), 'The Economics of Emissions Trading' in Alastair Cameron (ed.), *Climate Change Law and Policy in New Zealand* (Lexis NZ).

Winter, G. (2010), 'The Climate is No Commodity: Taking Stock of the Emissions Trading System' 22 JEL 1

7. On the theory and practice of the rights of nature

Joel I. Colón-Ríos

INTRODUCTION

The human right to a healthy environment is now present in more than 100 national constitutions, and some of these constitutions contain strong mechanisms to assure its enforcement.[1] For example, the Constitution of Bolivia 2009, states in Article 33 that human beings 'have a right to a healthy, protected, and balanced environment', and in Article 34, it recognises standing to 'any person, acting in their own name or representing a collectivity', to 'exercise the legal actions in defence' of this right.[2] There is no question that the constitutional recognition of the right to a healthy environment is an important development that contrasts with the approach that prevailed for most of the 20th century, according to which nature was, above all, a collection of resources to be used, and the constitutional protection of the environment was only possible indirectly, that is, through the protection of another right (such as the right to property).

As is well known, in 2008 Ecuador moved beyond the idea of using the human rights framework as the main constitutional tool for the protection of the environment, becoming the first country to formally attribute rights to nature itself.[3] The specific legal form the rights of nature take in the Constitution of Ecuador, and the mechanisms available for their protection, have not yet been fully canvassed. This chapter aims to examine this legal framework in some detail and then look at the way it was put into practice in a 2011 judgment in favour of the rights of the Vilcabamba River. Part I of the chapter briefly considers the philosophical debate about the coherence of the very idea of the rights of nature, as well as

---

[1] See Boyd (2012).

[2] Constitución Política del Estado (Bolivia 2009).

[3] In 2011 Bolivia adopted the *Law of Mother Earth*, which also attributes rights to nature.

the relevance of that debate in the context of Ecuador's constitution. Part II explores in some detail the legal framework established by the Constitution of Ecuador for the protection of the rights of nature. Part III examines the application of that legal framework through an analysis of the Vilcabamba case. Finally, Part IV offers a critical reflection on the case as well as some thoughts on the promises and limits of the constitutional recognition of the rights of nature.

THE PROBLEMS OF THE RIGHTS OF NATURE

The reasons why, perhaps with the exception of corporations, only human beings have been traditionally conceived as rights-holders have been extensively discussed.[4] Carl Wellman, for instance, maintains that rights 'allocate autonomy within some defined sphere to one party vis-à-vis second parties in the event of any conflict of wills or confrontation between these parties'.[5] Under that view, only beings capable of rational action can have rights (that is, only adults, not young children, can possess rights).[6] For example, according to Wellman, it does not make sense to say that a young child has the right to freedom of movement if she is incapable of rational movement.[7] Other authors, even though rejecting Wellman's thesis and presenting not only children but also non-human animals as potential rights-holders, defend theories that at first sight seem to be inconsistent with recognising the rights of other natural entities.

For example, Joel Feinberg maintains that only those beings with 'interests' can have rights.[8] The reason is that a rights-holder must be able to make rights-claims either by herself or through a representative, but it is only possible to *represent* those that possess interests that can be known by the representative (otherwise, how can one know what is 'good' or 'bad' for the represented?).[9] Under that view, at least some non-human animals could be rights-holders since, as a minimum, they have interests in satisfying their basic needs and in living according to their natural instincts; in short, there are things that are 'good' and 'bad' for animals. If one pushes Feinberg's conception to a place he expressly says it should not be taken

4 See Acosta and Martinez (eds) (2011).
5 Wellman (1997) 127.
6 Ibid.
7 Wellman (1997) 128.
8 Feinberg (1980) 159–84. See also Wellman (2005) 213.
9 McCloskey (1965).

(as he does not believe that trees may be rights-holders),[10] one could argue that plants may have rights as well; as there are things that plants may need, such as sunlight and water, and those basic needs may be understood as equivalents to the 'interests' that, for instance, would guide someone called to make a rights-claim on behalf of a group of trees.

But this would not apply to other types of natural entities, such as rocks, minerals, and rivers. Those 'non-living' things cannot have interests since they lack desires, instincts, or objectives that could be identified (and therefore protected) by a representative (after all, what could be 'good' or 'bad' for a rock?). As put by Feinberg, a '"mere thing" -a beautiful natural wilderness, or a complex ornamental artefact, like the Taj Mahal . . . however valuable to others, has no good of [its] own'.[11] That is, it has 'no conscious wishes, desires, and hopes; or urges and impulses, or unconscious drives, aims, and goals; or latent tendencies, direction of growth, and natural fulfilments'.[12] Put differently, if I say that a garden *needs* rain or that my computer *needs* an upgrade, I don't really mean that *they* need rain or an upgrade (as these entities are simply incapable of forming those desires), much less that I or someone else has a duty to provide it to them.

This is neither the place for examining these views in any detail, nor to consider whether the idea of attributing rights to nature can be defended at a theoretical level. However, I would like to briefly explore one of the *socially* necessary conditions for the recognition of rights: for someone or something to be attributed with rights, such an entity must be seen by society as having a non-instrumental value, a value that exists independently of the benefits that it is able to offer to other beings.[13] Using Feinberg's terminology, there must be a social belief that something has interests of its own (however problematic that idea might be from a Western point of view). This belief, present in the view of many indigenous groups, was one of the forces behind the recognition of the rights of nature in the new Constitution of Ecuador. 'According to the indigenous world

---

[10] Feinberg thinks that even though plants may have necessities, these do not amount to interests:

> Having no conscious wants or goals of their own, trees cannot know satisfaction or frustration, pleasure or pain . . . Plants may need things in order to discharge their functions, but their functions are assigned by human interests, not their own.

Feinberg (1980) 168–70. For a critique, see Attfield (1981).

[11] Feinberg (1980) 165.

[12] Ibid.

[13] Stone (2010) 3. See also Tribe (1974). For a critique, see Herguedas (2006).

view', writes Nina Pacari (a Quechua woman and former judge of the Constitutional Court of Ecuador), 'all beings of nature are invested with an energy that we call *samai* and, as a consequence, they are living beings: a rock, a river (water), a mountain, the sun, the plants, that is, all beings are alive and also enjoy being part of a family, [and feel] happiness and sadness as human beings do'.[14]

Under this view, rivers and mountains are conceived as living beings with interests of their own: interests in maintaining their own existence through time, interests in the existence of the systems of life that they help to sustain, and interests in the protection of the conditions that allow for the reproduction of those systems. The idea, as put by Esperanza Martinez, is that according to the Andean indigenous perspective, 'there is nothing without a heart or life principle; everything lives, and in a society in which everything lives, there are only relations among subjects, not among subjects and objects'.[15] This conception, of course, belongs to what we may call a different paradigm, one that does not fit within the traditional philosophical debates on whether non-human entities can be attributed with rights. And discarding it as 'unscientific' or as theoretically unsound will not do, at least not in places like Ecuador, because it has already being accepted at the level of constitutional practice.

The same point may be put as follows. If from a philosophical perspective one were to agree with Wellman that young children cannot be coherently attributed with rights, the fact is that constitutions and international treaties routinely attribute rights to children, and that this attribution has clear legal consequences at least in some cases. In a similar way, Feinberg might be correct that attributing rights to 'rocks', 'whole species' or 'trees' is absurd[16] from a traditional philosophical perspective since those things lack interests of their own. However, once the opposite conception is what has socially prevailed, the philosophical and theoretical arguments inevitably lose some, if not all, of their practical force. In Ecuador, that opposite conception has not only prevailed, but it has been translated into a number of constitutional provisions. In the next section, I will provide an overview of those provisions and I will then look at how they were applied in a judgment that sought to enforce the rights of the Vilcabamba River.

---

14 See Pacari in Acosta and Martínez (eds) (2009) 33.

15 Martínez (2011) 2.

16 Feinberg (1980) 160.

THE LEGAL FRAMEWORK FOR THE PROTECTION OF THE RIGHTS OF NATURE IN ECUADOR

The Constitution of Ecuador was formally drafted by an elected Constituent Assembly that sat in Montecristi, and it was ratified in a referendum in 2008. The recognition of the rights of nature in that constitution was controversial, and a number of delegates, including some of the supporters of the government of President Rafael Correa, strongly opposed it (not because they were opposed to environmental protection, but because – just as the authors mentioned above – they thought nature could not be properly designated as a rights-holder).[17] After intense debates and public discussions (as well as contributions by indigenous movements, non-governmental organisations and academics), the majority of the delegates supported the inclusion of the rights of nature into the new constitution.[18] From its Preamble, the new constitution makes clear that it will be a different sort of fundamental law, stating (among other things) that it was adopted by the people 'celebrating nature, the Pacha Mama, of which we are a part and which is vital to our existence'.

There are a number of provisions in the Constitution of 2008 that are directly or indirectly related with the rights of nature; here I will make special emphasis of the ones that are more relevant in the context of the case that will be discussed in the next section. In order to properly understand the place of the rights of nature within the framework of the constitution, it will also be necessary to briefly consider a number of articles of a more general nature. The main operative provisions are contained in the articles listed in Chapter Seven of Part II, titled 'Rights of Nature'. Article 71 defines nature (or Pacha Mama), as the place 'where life is reproduced and occurs', and states that it has the 'right to integral respect for its existence and for the maintenance and regeneration of its life cycles, structure, functions and evolutionary processes'. It also expresses that 'all persons, communities, peoples and nations can call upon public authorities to enforce the rights of nature', and that in the enforcement and interpretation of these rights 'the principles set forth in the Constitution shall be observed, as appropriate'.

These last provisions are of the utmost importance since, even though it could be argued that nature can exercise these rights without the help of

[17] See Acosta in Acosta and Martinez (2011) 341.

[18] According to Alberto Acosta, who presided the Constituent Assembly (before his resignation in June 2008), an essay written by Eduardo Galeano, which was read in a plenary meeting of the assembly, was fundamental in gaining the support of a number of delegates. Ibid, 344. See also Murcia Riaño (2012) 18.

any human being (for example, regenerating itself without the need of any human intervention), only an individual or group can ask the authorities for their judicial enforcement. Article 72 recognises nature's 'right to be restored', specifying that this 'restoration shall be independent from the obligation of the State and natural persons or legal entities to compensate individuals and communities that depend on affected natural systems'. This is a way of stressing that it is nature's rights that are being recognised, not the rights of the particular human beings that utilise nature for their benefit or subsistence. Article 72 creates a governmental duty on the state in those cases of 'severe or permanent environmental impact, including those caused by the exploitation of non-renewable natural resources', to 'establish the most effective mechanisms to achieve the restoration' and to adopt 'adequate measures to eliminate or mitigate harmful environmental consequences'.

Article 73 creates the additional public duty of applying 'preventive and restrictive measures on activities that might lead to the extinction of species, the destruction of ecosystems and the permanent alteration of natural cycles', and forbids 'the introduction of organisms and organic and inorganic material that may definitively alter the nation's genetic assets'. Article 74 of that same chapter recognises the relationship between the protection of the rights of nature and individual and collective well-being, by stating that 'persons, communities, peoples, and nations shall have the right to benefit from the environment and the natural wealth enabling them to enjoy the good way of living [*el buen vivir* or *sumak kawsay*]'.[19] Article 396 states that 'In case of doubt about the environmental impact stemming from a deed or omission, even if there is no scientific evidence of the damage, the State shall adopt effective and timely measures of protection'. Moreover, that same provision establishes strict liability for cases of environmental damage.

Article 397(1) gives even more force to that provision, establishing that with respect to environmental harm 'the burden of proof regarding the absence of potential or real danger shall lie with the operator of the activity or the defendant'.[20] Consistent with its recognition of the rights

---

[19] For a discussion of the meaning of the concept of *sumak kawsay* and a comparison to the Western conception of development, see Gudynas (2011). See also Article 277(1), which states that 'The general duties of the State in order to achieve the good way of living shall be: (1) To guarantee the rights of people, communities and nature . . .'.

[20] The reverse burden of proof in environmental law is also present in other jurisdictions and has also been the object of many discussions in the context of international environmental law. See Ambrus (2012).

of nature, the constitution establishes a correlative duty on all Ecuadorian citizens to 'respect the rights of nature, preserve a healthy environment and use natural resources rationally, sustainably, and durably'. In order to understand the place of these rights within the Ecuadorian constitution, it is necessary to examine a number of general constitutional provisions. After establishing that 'persons, communities, peoples, and nations are bearers of rights', Article 10 states that 'nature shall be the subject of those rights that the Constitution recognizes for it'. Article 11(1) states that 'rights can be exercised, promoted and enforced individually or collectively before competent authorities' and that these authorities shall guarantee their enforcement. Article 11(3) establishes that the rights and guarantees set forth in the constitution 'shall be directly and immediately enforced by and before any civil, administrative or judicial servant, either by virtue of their office or at the request of the party'.

That is to say, recognised rights, including the rights of nature are 'fully actionable' and the 'absence of a legal regulatory framework cannot be used to justify their infringement . . . or to deny their recognition'. Article 11(5) contains a mandate to all public officials to 'abide by the interpretation more favourable to the enforcement' of rights and constitutional guarantees. Section One of Chapter Two (Part II), titled 'Nature and the Environment', strengthens that provision by enshrining what is sometimes identified as the principle of *in dubio pro natura*, according to which 'in the event of doubt about the scope of legal provisions related to environmental issues, the interpretation most favourable to nature shall prevail'. Importantly, Article 11(6) establishes that 'all principles and rights are unalienable, obligatory, indivisible, interdependent and of equal importance'. This means that, since there are no rights of a higher hierarchy, when there is a collision between the rights of nature and human rights, a balancing exercise will be needed to determine which right should be given protection and which right will be restricted.

As can be seen, the Constitution of Montecristi does not merely affirm the rights of nature in an abstract way, but contains a systematic legal framework for the enforcement of those rights. This framework goes beyond issues of legal standing and includes mandates to public officials about how to interpret and apply them. It is, of course, too early to tell whether this legal framework will be effective in the long term or, as it happens with many human rights regimes in different parts of the world, it will become a dead letter when confronted with powerful economic actors and governments committed to a version of development that does not sit comfortably with the protection of nature. The case of the Vilcabamba River, discussed below, provides an example of a judicial application of the rights of nature by a local court, showing some of the promise of this new paradigm, as well as providing an opportunity to reflect on its limits.

THE JUDICIAL APPLICATION OF THE RIGHTS OF NATURE: THE CASE OF THE VILCABAMBA RIVER

In 2008, the Provincial Government of Loja, as part of the works involved in the widening of the Vilcabamba-Quinara road, deposited large amounts of rocks and excavation materials in the Vilcabamba River. These works were done without an environmental impact study and without the required permits. In 2009 (after the seasonal rains of March and April), the river flow increased to unprecedented levels, causing large floods that affected the riverside populations. By 2010, large areas of land belonging to Eleanor Geer Huddle and Richard Frederick Wheeler, U.S. citizens residing in the area, were flooded. The river itself was affected in important ways, as a result of the deposit of rocks, sand, gravel and trees. Even though they had suffered considerable economic harm, Huddle and Wheeler decided to file a 'protective action' (*acción de protección*) before the courts of Loja 'in favour of nature, particularly in favour of the Vilcabamba River'. Huddle and Wheeler had legal standing to present this action to protect the rights of the river by virtue of the previously mentioned Article 71.

The *acción de protección* is one of the most important mechanisms provided by the Constitution of Ecuador for the protection of rights.[21] Article 88 defines it as an action 'aimed at ensuring the direct and efficient safeguard of the rights enshrined in the Constitution'. The action is of a remedial character: its purpose is to remedy a violation of rights that has already occurred.[22] Such an action 'can be filed whenever there is a breach of constitutional rights as a result of deeds or omissions by any non-judicial public authority'.[23] In a judgment of 15 December 2010, a trial judge refused to grant the protective action on procedural grounds (as one of the representatives of the Provincial Government had not been formally notified of the proceedings). That judgment was appealed to the

21 See Echeverría and Suárez (2013) 104.

22 See Montaña Pinto (2011).

23 It can be also filed '. . . when the violation proceeds from a particular person, if the violation of the right causes severe harms, if [the perpetrator] provides public services in an improper manner, if he acts by delegation or concession, or if the affected person is in a status of subordination, defencelessness or discrimination' (Article 88).

Provincial Court, and a final judgment was rendered on 30 March 2011.[24] The Provincial Court disagreed with the finding of the trial judge. The Court noted that the protective action is the appropriate means to remedy particular harm to the environment and that, unless it can be objectively demonstrated to a court that the environmental harm (or the risk of it) did not exist, 'it is the duty of constitutional judges to order the immediate and effective protection of the rights of nature'.

In this context, the Court noted, the certainty of the harm is not necessary; all that is required is its 'probability'. This is, of course, an indirect reference to the precautionary principle contained in Article 396, cited above. In light of these considerations, and taking into account the summary character of the protective action, the Court stated that the trial judge should have ordered the notification of the action to all the relevant public officials and continued with the proceedings. Moreover, for the Court, the Provincial Government could not defend itself simply by showing that a particular functionary was not notified, when it was otherwise fully aware of the proceedings. The Court then moved to consider the case on its merits. It began by recognising the connections between the rights of nature and the interests of future generations. Favourably quoting Alberto Acosta (who initially presided over the Constituent Assembly that drafted the Constitution of Montecristi), the Court stated:

> [T]here are some premises that are fundamental to advance what can be identified as the 'democracy of the earth'; [these include a recognition that]: a) individual and collective human rights must be in a relation of harmony with the rights of other natural communities in the Earth; b) ecosystems have a right to exist and to continue their vital processes; c) the diversity of life, as expressed in nature, has a value of its own; d) ecosystems have a value independent of their utility to human beings; and e) a legal framework in which ecosystems and natural communities have an inalienable right to exist and flourish, would situate Nature at the highest level of value and importance.

Such an approach, the Court continued, would have 'as a direct effect the prevention of environmental harm, and the reconsideration of many human activities for which the environmental cost is too high'. The Court stated that in this case, no one had questioned the basic facts that a road was being widened, and that as part of these works certain materials were being deposited in the Vilcabamba River. Applying the reverse burden of proof contained in Article 397(1), quoted above, the Court maintained that for an *acción de protección* in favour of the rights of nature to be successful, it was not necessary for the plaintiffs to prove that the relevant

---

[24] Juicio No: 11121-2011-0010.

environmental harm resulted from the actions of the defendant: on the contrary, it was the defendant, in this case the Provincial Government of Loja, who had the burden of proving that the activity of widening a road did not (and would not) harm the environment.

The Court stated that, upon an inspection, a number of examples of environmental damage were identified in the river and surrounding areas, and the government had not demonstrated that they were not the result of its actions. Accordingly, the Court granted the protective action against the Provincial Government (as there had been a violation of Article 71, quoted above). During the proceedings, the Provincial Government had argued that the works on the Vilcabamba-Quinara road were necessary, and that not allowing the local government to widen the road was contrary to the interests of the population. The Court noted that whenever there is a collision among two constitutionally protected interests (presumably the interest of the population of having better roads and the interests of nature), the solution reached must take into account the facts of the concrete case as well as the values and principles contained in the constitution.

If looked at from the perspective of the population of Loja, the Court suggested, the interest in an improved road was not as important as 'the interest in a healthy environment which concerns a much greater number of people' (including the population of Loja). However, the Court maintained that in this case such an analysis was unnecessary, since there was no collision of rights: no one was requesting the Court to issue a permanent injunction prohibiting the widening of the Vilcabamba-Quinara road, only that 'the widening was done paying due respect to the constitutional rights of nature'.[25] The Court concluded that, by affecting the river flow and depositing excavation materials in it, the Provincial Government 'was violating Nature's right to integral respect for its existence and for the maintenance and regeneration of its life cycles, structure, functions and evolutionary processes' (Article 71, quoted above).

The orders issued against the Provincial Government included the submission of a Remediation and Rehabilitation Plan of the affected areas of the river and surrounding properties (this plan would presumably involve the clean-up of the river itself), and to immediately put in place a number of corrective actions directed at stopping the contamination of the river (such as establishing special sites for the disposal of excavation materials, and cleaning the soil that had been contaminated with combustibles).

---

[25] In any case, expressed the court, the need of new or better roads does not give the Provincial Government an authorisation to build or widen them without first obtaining the required environmental permits.

Moreover, the Court ordered the Provincial Government to periodically notify it of the implementation of these orders. Finally, but no less important, it was ordered that the defendant 'must publicly apologise for initiating the construction of a road without the required permits'. Such an apology was to be published in a local newspaper.

THE RIGHTS OF NATURE ON BALANCE: A BRIEF REFLECTION

Even though the judgment in the Vilcabamba case was initially celebrated by many, the Provincial Government of Loja has failed to fully implement the Court's orders (thus failing to repair the harm suffered by the river as a result of the violation of its rights). For example, although the government initially presented a Remediation and Rehabilitation Plan, this document was determined to be insufficient by the Ministry of the Environment.[26] The Provincial Government nevertheless placed some signs prohibiting the deposit of excavation materials into the river and it has partially cleaned up the riverside (although at the time of writing it had not removed the excavation materials that were deposited in the river).[27]

This partial and limited implementation of the judgment, however, does not necessarily mean that there is something fundamentally wrong with the constitutional recognition of the rights of nature. Partial non-implementation of judgments is a common theme in debates about social and economic rights, but that is not generally seen by social movements as a reason against the recognition of second generation rights in national constitutions. Moreover, even if not fully complied with, the judgment in the Vilcabamba case forced the Provincial Government of Loja to perform a number of reparative actions that it may have otherwise not performed. More importantly, however, it opened an avenue that did not exist before: that is, it showed that the rights of nature are susceptible of judicial application in ordinary and local contexts. Since the Vilcabamba case, several actions based on the rights of nature have been filed, including an action against British Petroleum for the oil spill in the Gulf of Mexico.

These cases, regardless of their results and success in terms of the

---

26 See Programa Andino de Derechos Humanos *Informe sobre Derechos Humanos,* (Compilador) (Ecuador 2011) 20.

27 As reported by the Pachamama Foundation http://derechosdelanaturaleza.org/rights-of-nature-laws/vilcabamba-river-1-year-after/ (accessed 11 March 2015), and stated in presentation given by Eleanor Wheeler http://www.youtube.com/watch?v=f2aUscCJMPs (accessed 11 March 2015).

implementation of judgments, contribute to the creation of a new popular discourse around the rights of nature, and provide new opportunities for social movements and non-governmental organisations to transform their demands into a language officially recognised by the state. Whether this is a good thing might be controversial,[28] but it is difficult to see something particularly problematic about the rights of nature that is not present also in the context of human rights generally. Nevertheless, this does not mean that the constitutional recognition of the rights of nature is a development undistinguishable from the recognition of other rights (for example, the recognition of the right to political participation of non-propertied males or the extension of the right to vote to women). Extending rights to nature involves a challenge to one of the core principles of liberal constitutionalism: the idea that the true goal of a constitution is to protect the rights of individuals.

However, there is an aspect of the reasoning of the Court in the Vilcabamba case that should be looked at more closely, since it points towards some of the main issues that judges will confront when applying the rights of nature to particular situations. As will be recalled, the Court maintained that, had there been a collision of rights in this case, the interest of the entire population to a healthy environment (here the Court seemed to consider the rights of nature and the right to a healthy environment together) would have prevailed over the interest of the population of Loja in the widening of the Vilcabamba-Quinara road. However, in the view of the Court there was no collision because the eventual widening of the road was not at issue, all that was asked by the plaintiffs was that the widening took place in a way that did not involve a violation of nature's rights.

That analysis might be correct in relation to the rights of the Vilcabamba River, but not in relation to the other natural entities destroyed in the process of widening the road. For example, the judgment mentions that trees and other excavation materials were being deposited in the river. The rights of those trees that died in the process (and that were probably home to a number of ecosystems), were obviously affected by the widening of the road. Of course, the action before the court was filed on behalf of the river, not on behalf of the trees (although the claimants presented their action '*in favour of nature*, particularly in favour of the Vilcabamba River'),[29] so in

---

[28] There is an old debate in U.S. legal theory about whether the language of rights is in fact capable of advancing the interests of progressive social movements. See for example, Hunt (1990); Roithmayr (2001).

[29] Emphasis added.

that sense the Court was arguably on solid legal ground when it said that there was no collision between the rights of the parties (that is, the river, on the one hand, and the Provincial Government acting on behalf of the population of Loja, on the other). But the point is that if one is to take the rights of nature seriously (to use Ronald Dworkin's famous phrase),[30] recognition must be made of the fact that all sorts of human endeavours negatively affect nature's rights.

As a result, balancing the rights of nature and the rights of humans will be necessary in most cases as these rights will frequently (if not almost always) collide. And this means that sometimes the rights of humans (for example, rights to housing, rights of property, and so on)[31] will (and should) prevail. For example, if the Court in Loja had been presented with a situation in which no excavation materials were being deposited in the river and in which the only environmental harm was the cutting of a limited number of trees, perhaps the court would have been correct to conclude that nature's rights needed to be limited in order to give way to the widening of the road.[32] In fact, in the Vilcabamba case, the Court implicitly (and perhaps unconsciously) engaged in that balancing exercise when suggesting that the widening of the road could take place as long as a number of 'remedial and reparative' measures were taken.

The result of that (implicit) balancing exercise was that the negative impact on the rights of nature that would result from the cutting of trees (which would likely involve the partial destruction of the habitats of a number of birds and lizards) did not reach the level of importance that would justify limiting the right of the Provincial Government to widen the Vilcabamba-Quinara road (or the right to development of the inhabitants of the province). Such a conclusion might be sensible enough, but it is

---

[30] Dworkin (1977).

[31] An application of the rights of nature in which there was a clear collision with property rights took place in Ecuador in 2011, where a court ordered (at the request of the Minister of the Interior) the destruction of the tools and machinery used by a number of illegal miners that were causing significant harm to a number of rivers. Oficio No. 0626-2011 J22GPP, 20 May 2011. See also Programa Andino de Derechos Humanos, *Informe sobre Derechos Humanos* (Compilador) (Ecuador 2011) 90–1.

[32] Nevertheless, even in that case, a deeper analysis was needed. For example, was the widening of the road really necessary? Was there a way of widening the road without cutting the trees or perhaps by only cutting a lesser number of trees? In other words, it was necessary to justify the restriction of the rights of the trees, and this justification required a balancing exercise in which the impact of the action in question (that is, cutting some trees to widen a road) is balanced against the degree in which the rights of the trees are affected or restricted.

based on a balancing exercise that should have been made explicit. This is one of the reasons why academic discussions about the scope and meaning of the rights of nature, as well as their relationship to human rights, are necessary. Only those discussions, together with a developing body of case law, can result in a coherent jurisprudence in this area. Otherwise, judges would be setting the basic standard of what may be considered as a legally relevant violation (or restriction) of the rights of nature in an unprincipled way and, if the standard is set too high, then only the most brutal violations of these rights will be sufficient to trigger a judicial remedy.

REFERENCES

Acosta, A. (2011), 'Los Derechos de la Naturaleza: Una Lectura sobre el Derecho a la Existencia' in A. Acosta and E. Martínez (eds), *La Naturaleza con Derechos: De la Filosofía a la Política* (Quito: Abya-Yala).

Acosta, A. and E. Martínez (eds) (2011), *La Naturaleza con Derechos: De la Filosofía a la Política* (Quito: Abya-Yala).

Ambrus, M. (2012), 'The Precautionary Principle and a Fair Allocation of the Burden of Proof in International Environmental Law' 21(3) *Review of European Community & International Environmental Law* 259.

Attfield, R. (1981), 'The Good of Trees' 15 *Journal of Value Inquiry* 35.

Boyd, D. (2012), *The Environmental Rights Revolution* (Vancouver: University of British Columbia Press).

Constitución Política del Estado (Bolivia 2009).

Constitución de la República de Ecuador (2008).

Dworkin, R. (1977), *Taking Rights Seriously* (London: Duckworth).

Echeverría, H. y Suárez, S. (2013), *Tutela Judicial Efectiva en Materia Ambiental: El Caso Ecuatoriano* (Quito: CEDA).

Feinberg, J. (1980), *Rights, Justice, and the Bounds of Liberty* (Princeton: Princeton University Press).

Gudynas, E. (2011), 'Buen Vivir: Today's Tomorrow' 54(4) *Development* 441.

Herguedas, A. (2006), 'Del Valor Intrínseco de la Naturaleza' 34 *Isegoría* 261.

Hunt, A. (1990), 'Rights and Social Movements: Counter-Hegemonic Strategies' 17(3) *Journal of Law and Society* 309.

Juicio No: 11121-2011-0010 (Acción de Protección).

Martínez, E. (2011), 'Pachamama y Sumak Kawsay' (Quito).

McCloskey, H.J. (1965), 'Rights' 15 *Philosophical Quarterly* 115.

Montaña Pinto, J. (2011), 'Aproximación a los Elementos Básicos de la Acción de Protección' in *Apuntes de Derecho Procesal Constitucional: Parte Especial 1: Garantías Constitucionales en Ecuador*, Tomo II (Quito: Centro de Estudios Constitucionales).

Murcia Riaño, D. (2012), *La Naturaleza con Derechos: Un Recorrido por el Derecho Internacional de los Derechos Humanos, del Ambiente y del Desarrollo* (Quito: Universidad del Bosque).

Oficio No. 0626-2011 J22GPP, 20 May 2011 (Medida Cautelar).

Pacari, Nina. (2009), 'Naturaleza y Territorio Desde la Mirada de los Pueblos

Indígenas' in Alberto Acosta and Esperanza Martínez (eds) *Derechos de la Naturaleza: El Futuro es Ahora* (Quito: Abya-Yala).

Programa Andino de Derechos Humanos *Informe sobre Derechos Humanos* (Compilador) (Ecuador 2011).

Roithmayr, D. (2001), 'Left (Over) Rights' 5 *Law Text Culture* 407.

Stone, C. (2010), *Should Trees Have Standing?* (3rd edn, Oxford: Oxford University Press).

Tribe, L. (1974), 'Ways Not To Think About Plastic Trees: New Foundations for Environmental Law' 83(7) Yale LJ 1315.

Wellman, C. (1997), 'The Growth of Children's Rights' in *An Approach to Rights: Studies in the Philosophy of Law and Morals* (The Netherlands: Kluwer Academic Publishers).

Wellman, C. (2005), 'Feinberg's Two Concepts of Rights' 11 *Legal Theory* 213.

PART III

Implementation challenges of environmental justice

The third Part considers the ways in which approaches to environment governance are (or are not) embracing the concept of environmental justice. Chapters in this section consider policy innovation in response to emerging environmental issues that are often very contentious. The section considers the institutional structures that are necessary to give effect to legal principles and to implement philosophical values. Reflecting back upon the first section, the chapters highlight significant implementation difficulties (but also opportunities) in attempting to pursue any concept of environmental justice. They highlight the inevitability of political dynamics as part of the pursuit of environmental justice.

8. REDD+ implementation in Thailand – legal and institutional challenges

Wanida Phromlah and Paul Martin[1]

INTRODUCTION

Environmental justice emphasises equitable distribution of opportunities, benefits and risks over natural resources, and public participation in decision making and management. The distribution of costs and benefits of natural resources should be allocated without discrimination on the basis of caste, gender, religion or economic status, and all citizens should be able to exercise rights to natural resources upon which their livelihoods depend. These aims require effective legal and institutional arrangements.[2]

REDD+ is a carbon trading mechanism for reducing emissions from deforestation and forest degradation, and for conservation and sustainable management of forests, using a market instrument to help achieve environmental and social justice values in developing countries. A key aspect is the intention that carbon units accredited to a developing country will be 'traded' to offset emissions from developed country sources. [3,4]

In this regard REDD+ aims to support social justice, economic opportunity and inclusion for (particularly) forestry communities and indigenous people in developing countries.[5] At the heart of the achievement of such an ambitious set of goals is the necessity of having effective forest law and institutional systems.

---

1 The advice of Alastair I. Fraser is gratefully acknowledged.

2 Moore and Pastakia (2007) xiii–xviii.

3 Bluffstone, Robinson, and Guthiga (2012). See also Larson (2011).

4 For a detailed discussion of REDD+ in the Asian context see the 2013 International Journal of Rural Law & Policy Special Edition, 'REDD+ and legal regimes of mangroves, peatlands and other wetlands: ASEAN and the world'. accessed 12 March 2015 at http://epress.lib.uts.edu.au/journals/index.php/ijrlp/issue/view/271.

5 Bluffstone, Robinson, and Guthiga (2012). See also Larson (2011) 540.

This chapter diagnoses legal and institutional challenges for Thailand in pursuing the environmental justice aspects of REDD+ implementation. The chapter begins with a discussion of the main challenges. It then suggests directions for securing environmental justice in implementation of REDD+ for Thailand, with particular attention to forest property rights, including absolute and partial ownership by communities. The chapter is informed by an examination of relevant Thai laws and REDD+ commentaries, and by an in-depth investigation of forest management within Thailand between 2011 and 2013. The research took the form of a series of interviews and discussion groups conducted with forest community members, front-line government forestry personnel, experts and policy makers.

GOVERNANCE, INSTITUTIONAL AND LEGAL CHALLENGES

Thailand has substantial forest-related institutions and legislation that ought to support the achievement of emissions offsets obligations under the REDD+ scheme.[6] These include six acts aimed at conserving forests, and Sections 66 and 67 of the Constitution which support participation of the public in natural resource management.[7] At first sight it therefore seems that Thailand has the constitutional provisions, legal rules and institutional structures that might form the backbone of an effective REDD+ implementation system.[8] What is less clear, given the number of rules, actors and administrative structures, is whether such a system can be made efficient and effective in practice, or whether internal co-ordination challenges will frustrate the achievement of effective and equitable governance of the type required by REDD+.

---

[6] The discussion in this paragraph is based on Korhonen-Kurki *et al.* (2012) 94–5. See also Forsyth (2009) 113 and 115–16 and Wertz-Kanounnikoff and Angelsen (2009) 13, 24.

[7] The six forest-related acts are: the Forest Act B.E. 2484, the National Reserved Forest Act BE 2507, the Wildlife Conservation and Protection Act BE 2535, the National Park Act BE 2504, the Forest Plantation Act BE 2535, and the Chainsaw Act BE 2545; see Lasimbang and Luithui (2006) 15–31. See also FAO-Regional Office for Asia and the Pacific (2009) 75–88.

[8] Asia Indigenous Peoples CCMIN (2011). See also Praurasiddhi *et al.* (2013) 8–12.

INSUFFICIENT INCENTIVES FOR FOREST PRESERVATION

Successful implementation of REDD+ requires sufficient incentives for stakeholders, particularly forestry dependants, to invest in REDD+ activities.[9] Managing a forest for biodiversity and social outcomes, as well as to secure carbon values, will require additional management instruments beyond those required where the amount of carbon sequestered (or trees harvested) is the only economic value. It will require distinct management regimes for biodiversity and other ecological services, and for social outcomes. Managing these values concurrently will complicate management and measurement, and may involve additional economic investments. Arguably, achieving social outcomes is likely to require granting secure rights to communities, providing them with opportunities to generate income from forest management or adapting forests to provide commercial benefits in order to offer communities necessary incentives to invest in long-term REDD+ activities.[10] In brief, managing forests for REDD+ social and ecological values that go beyond carbon or timber values will involve additional costs and complexities compared to management for the narrower set of values. As many of these surrounding values will not have a tradeable economic value, the economic incentive and economic resources to deliver these non-market values may prove difficult to provide.

National aspirations for community participation in managing and using forests as a means to economic and social welfare are apparent from the Thai Constitution. Sections 66 and 67 of the Constitution recognise the rights of the community to participate in (and benefit from) forest management, but there has been no revision of forestry laws to implement these Constitutional provisions.[11] The government conducts forest management through restrictive laws that largely overlook community interests, and decision-making power for forest management remains with state agencies.[12] This restricts the security of community interests in forest management, as community decisions can be readily overruled by state officers (should the community get to make these decisions at all). Insecurity of interests and control can cause forest users to exploit as much forest as possible as quickly as possible, to maximise their short-term

---

[9] Wertz-Kanounnikoff and Angelsen (2009), 24. See also Tacconi (2007) 338.

[10] Larson (2011) 542. See also Bluffstone, Robinson, and Guthiga (2012) 48.

[11] FAO (2011) 39. See also Constitution 2007 ss 66–7 (Thailand).

[12] Fischman (2012) 8–9. See also Community Forest Management Bureau (2011) and Wataru (2003) 213–14.

communities. This diversity of interests raises questions, such as: Who will have rights to carbon stocks (the government or community members)? Can the private sector and NGOs share in the benefits of these carbon stocks? Who is going to pay for REDD+ implementation, particularly for the non-market social and ecological values? Will the protection of carbon and biodiversity values involve limiting other community uses?

To achieve effective REDD+ implementation, it is important that consensus among stakeholders is ensured. The example of drafting and ratification of the Community Forest Bill in Thailand illustrates why this is necessary, and some of the difficulties that this may meet. This Bill was passed by the Parliament on 21 November 2007,[19] but has not come into effect as it has been opposed by some stakeholders on constitutional grounds.[20] The conflict highlights that many forest stakeholders in Thailand have competing views on fundamental forest governance issues. Such differences include diverse views of what legal rights to forest are (or should be), what is common property within forests, how a forest community should be defined, concerns about whether the community ought to have the right to live within protected forest lands, and different views about whether people can live in harmony with forests being managed for different values.[21]

The history of the Community Forest Bill in Thailand suggests that for REDD+ implementation, negotiating consensus among stakeholders who have different perspectives and interests is essential. Without underlying agreement, REDD+ implementation may prove too difficult. However, the lack of a tradition of negotiated compromise among community interests, and reliance on authoritarian models of resource governance, suggests that there will be a lot of social learning required in making these changes.

A LACK OF EFFECTIVE COORDINATION

REDD+ is complex. It involves many technically or socially difficult issues which include the maintenance of biodiversity; conservation of forests; the measurement, verification and trading of carbon stocks; advancing social justice; social inclusion for forest people; and land use

---

[19] Rights and Resources Initiative (RRI) (2008).

[20] FAO (2011) 39.

[21] Fisher (2011) 69, 75–8.

management.[22] Thai forest governance involves a number of organisations and authorities at different levels.[23] Lack of effective coordination and competing roles is apparent. Confusion between agencies over who has responsibility for different aspects of this mix already exists. This could create difficulties, such as transaction costs and inaccuracies in relevant databases which can frustrate reliable forestry policy analysis.[24] Poor institutional design probably cannot be compensated for by political appeals to cooperate.

Compounding the inconsistent roles of key land-management departments, the Royal Forest Department (RFD) and the Department of National Parks, Wildlife, and Plant Conservation (DNWPC),[25] is a lack of coordination between central and local government. The RFD, at central government level, pursues the establishment of eucalyptus plantations that involves government in processes to regain land from villagers, to increase commercial forest lands. This is inconsistent with other policies to increase community forestry. Local authorities, including forestry staff working with the communities, argue that this forestry centralisation is counterproductive and villagers resist the plantations policy.[26] Such institutional problems have the adverse effect of creating volatile and inconsistent policy settings:

> The current authorities very often pursue their own agendas without consideration of previous policies or consultation with the agencies who previously implemented forest governance. As a result the outcomes of previous practices are ignored. This is a key source of confusion and inconsistency between previous and current forest related law and policy.[27]

The competing interests of different parts of government exacerbate an underlying lack of coordination among agencies. This is likely to lead to the tension in REDD+ implementation.

---

22 Korhonen-Kurki *et al.* (2012) 94–5. See also Forsyth (2009) 115–16.

23 Lasimbang and Luithui (2006) 15–31. See also FAO-Regional Office for Asia and the Pacific, (2009) 75–88.

24 Peskett and Brockhaus (2009) 25, 32–5. See also Korhonen-Kurki *et al.* (2012) 99.

25 Gine (2005) 5.

26 Lakanavichian (2007) 325, 343.

27 Wataru (2003) 219.

DEFICIENCIES IN LEGAL AND INSTITUTIONAL STRUCTURES

Effectively implementing REDD+ requires an integrated approach involving multilevel governance spanning the international to the local governance levels.[28]

As has been discussed, Thai forest law is complex and internally inconsistent. The interests of many people are unclear and insecure. These are not conditions conducive to successful implementation of REDD+. The authority charged with managing climate sustainability, the Thailand Greenhouse Gas Management Organization (TGO), is not formally linked to forest authorities such as RFD and DNWPC. The TGO has a role in greenhouse gas (GHG) emission reduction in Thailand through promoting low carbon activities, providing GHG reduction information, approval of carbon sequestration projects, and as the Designated National Authority for the Clean Development Mechanism (DNA-CDM) office in Thailand.[29] However, effectively implementing REDD+ involves far more than GHG emissions reduction. It requires effective land use management, maintaining forest areas, advancing economic opportunity for less powerful stakeholders, and ensuring social equity for indigenous and local people. At the very least a powerful central agency with a mandate to deliver significant administrative reform of forest governance seems to be required to overcome the structural impediments we have highlighted.

DIRECTIONS FOR EFFECTIVE IMPLEMENTATION OF REDD+

The above discussion has identified major challenges of forest governance for REDD+ implementation in Thailand. This section suggests potential reform directions for more effective implementation of REDD+. The approach we have taken to proposed reforms is based upon institutional systems logic. Rather than focus upon a narrow aspect of institutional performance (for example, law reform, or economic incentives) we have attempted to prescribe a set of mutually reinforcing interventions. The issues span property right reform, investment, incentives, safeguards

---

28 Korhonen-Kurki *et al.* (2009) 92 and 94–5. See also Forsyth (2009) 115–16 and Westholm *et al.* (2011) 8 and 16.

29 Office of Natural Resources and Environmental Policy and Planning: Thailand (ONEP) and United Nations Development Program (UNDP 2010) 10–11.

against perverse effects of reform, conflict and consultation mechanisms, and the building of social capital. Because effective implementation will be only as good as the weakest link in the institutional system, systemic reform is essential to fully satisfy what REDD+ implementation will require.

The proposals pay particular attention to forest property rights (including absolute and partial ownership by communities). Tenure reform is a pivotal component (or a prerequisite) for successful REDD+ implementation.[30] This is not intended to discount the other institutional reforms that are also needed, including reconciliation of the competing aims of the agencies that will be involved, streamlining many laws and administrative systems, tackling corruption, and creating legal arrangements that do more than lip-service to the Constitution. However, while all of these reforms are necessary, they will not be sufficient unless the fundamental power imbalances in forest governance are addressed. Given the elements of environmental justice mentioned above, property rights[31] have the potential to better enable environmental justice in REDD+ implementation, particularly equitable sharing of benefits and opportunities involving natural resources in society.

PROPERTY RIGHTS TO FOREST RESOURCES

A meta-analysis of 69 cases conducted worldwide in 2006 revealed that the two most significant attributes for successful community forestry are tenure security and clear ownership of forest resources.[32] Property rights help organise how forest resources can be used and can provide incentives for more effective forest management. The property right holder can be assured of the future benefits of their investment in forest management (assuming a functioning institutional structure that adequately defends property rights).

If forest users have insecure rights to their interests in forests, lacking assurance that their beneficial interest will be long lasting, they may be reluctant to invest in forest management.[33] Insecure rights can also

---

[30] Larson (2011) 542. See also Westholm *et al.* (2011) 8 and Dahal, Larson and Pacheco (2010) 183, 207.

[31] Meinzen-Dick and Knox (2001) 41, 49. See also Ellsworth and White (2004) 6.

[32] Pagdee, Kim and Daugherty (2006).

[33] Robinson, Holland and Naughton-Treves (2011) 30. See also Bruce, Wendland and Naughton-Treves (2010) 7.

encourage users to exploit the forest for short-term profit – a situation that can lead to accelerated degradation. This has occurred in the Brazilian Amazon, where insecure land rights have resulted in significant deforestation.[34] A study of patterns of loss and regeneration of tropical dry forest in Madagascar found that deforestation occurred mainly in areas where property rights were insecure, whereas areas with well-defined property rights showed either regenerating or stable forest cover.[35] This is consistent with the study of the Centre for International Forestry Research (CIFOR) conducted in 2009 which revealed that full-scale implementation of REDD+ in many countries faces challenges including unclear forestry rights. In most deforestation hotspots, land rights are unclear, overlapping and contested.[36]

A more positive example of the benefits of creating security for forest communities is the community forest user groups (CFUGs) in Nepal, who have been granted secure rights by their government. These groups have effectively restored forest lands in response to the incentive that has been created. In 2009, the deforestation rates in forest lands managed by the CFUGs were independently assessed as being better than the rates in forest lands administered by the government. The deforestation rate in forest land managed by CFUGs was 0.88 per cent, compared to the rate in forests administered by the government of approximately 1.5 per cent.[37]

The evidence suggests that granting rights to disadvantaged groups, such as indigenous people, particularly women and the poor, should help to ensure social justice[38] from REDD+ implementation. Allocation of property rights can help determine who benefits from forests and property rules can embed responsibilities as well as beneficial interests. For this reason it seems that property rights are likely to help to ensure that stakeholders, particularly the poor, benefit from REDD+ implementation.[39]

They can also be a mechanism for adjusting political power structures. Rights over natural resources are an important source of power. Granting secure rights to forest resources for a particular group, such as a community or women within a community, empowers them by granting control over resources, reducing the ability of government or others

---

34 Araujo *et al.* (2009) 2461, 2464.
35 Elmqvist *et al.* (2007) 1 and 9.
36 Angelsen (2009) 125 and 135.
37 Hatcher (2009) 2.
38 FAO (2011) 56.
39 Bruce, Wendland and Naughton-Treves (2010) 1–2.

with entrenched sources of power to control how forest resources are exploited.[40]

A clear delineation of rights to forests is needed to ensure mutual understanding and to reduce competing claims.[41] Right holders can be individuals (private property) or a group of people (common property).[42] Granting rights to individuals (private property) is likely to be more secure than common property. However, experience in Thailand suggests that private property approaches can also entrench corruption and unfairness by limiting checks and balances. Effective common property regimes reinforced by strong social self-sanctions[43] have proven to be an effective means for sustainable forest management in some situations.[44]

Property rights to forests may be usefully separated from property rights to land.[45] Property rights to forests provide restricted rights to forest resources,[46] concerned with who is entitled to use, manage, and make decisions about forest resources, and in what way, for how long, and under what conditions.[47] In order to provide reasonable security it may not be necessary for people to have rights to underlying forest lands. The design of forest interests (rather than land interests) can be done in a manner to discourage the practice of clearing forest areas in order to claim property rights.

Right reforms can have systematic effects on social equity, through social processes that can accompany legal changes. For example, within the community forest projects conducted in the Banke District of Nepal in 2007, governance literacy, gender equality and women's rights classes, were conducted with special attention given to educating women. The women became more confident and able to express their opinions in public. They discovered that there were legal provisions for forest user groups to set aside funds for income-generating activities for poor and marginalised households, and they requested that funds be provided to ten households. Some of the women subsequently ran for executive office in the community forest user group.[48] The results of this initiative highlight that under supportive conditions empowerment through forest property rights can be transformative for marginalised groups.

---

40 Harrison (2003) 78.
41 RRI (2008) 12.
42 Bromley (1991) 24–5.
43 Martin and Verbeek (2006) 136.
44 Ostrom (1999) 3–7.
45 Bruce (1998) 1.
46 Bruce (1998) 1.
47 Larson, Barry and Dahal (2010) 3, 12.
48 FAO (2011) 57.

Property rights help to ensure people are able to secure and negotiate benefits associated with forest products.[49] Rights to forests can also provide collateral for funding for communities and indigenous people who might otherwise have limited opportunities for securing a loan from a bank. In China, forest tenure reform has enabled farmers to broaden their funding options, and this has relieved the shortage of funding in forestry. The farmers and forestry enterprises use the documents identifying their rights (the Certificate of Forest and Woodland Tenure Right issued by the local government) as collateral documents to secure a loan. To obtain this certificate, communities and forestry companies list their forest interest claims on an application document. The claim is independently assessed by the local government and, if approved, the local government will then issue the Certificate.[50]

OTHER RIGHT CONSIDERATIONS

REDD+ incentives should not be less than the compensation, income, or the rewards from alternative uses of the same asset, particularly the use of the resource for commercial forests. This is important for the sustainability of REDD+ security, but also to ensure that the communities who are meant to benefit from management of their forests are not locked into a 'second-best' economic model compared to other uses of their assets. Reduced economic opportunity from a public good investment would increase, not reduce, social inequity. There is an economic and management issue (beyond the scope of this investigation) in the expectation that unpriced non-market values (social justice, biodiversity) will be delivered through REDD+, where the carbon price may not provide any (or an insufficient) premium over other carbon units in the marketplace to fund these activities. One result is that REDD+ management is likely to have an incentive to stint on investment in these non-market values, to remain competitive in the carbon market. This is a systemic risk of REDD+ that does not seem as yet to have been given a great deal of consideration.

Forest-related traditional knowledge reflects the long-term interdependence between communities and forests. Local communities which have long settled in forest areas have practical forest-management skills that allow them to exploit forests for subsistence.[51] Legally recognising

---

49 Cunningham *et al.* (2008) 10–11.
50 Zhu, Zhang and Peng (2011) 154–5.
51 Forest People Programme (2011) 21.

traditional forest-related knowledge for forest management holds the promise of advancing social justice and social inclusion for disadvantaged (particularly forestry community) people under REDD+, whilst better protecting carbon, social and biodiversity values.

Legal arrangements may be needed to ensure recognition of the non-timber forest products (NTFPs) including subsistence, local trade, non-timber commercial trade, culture and recreation. This too is not a simple matter of legal protection. The recognition of NTFPs must be sensitive to the nature and scale of diverse activities, where local economic and cultural conditions can significantly alter the effects of pursuing these values. For example, it can be argued that in the interests of social justice subsistence use should not be tightly regulated unless there are clear risks of overharvesting, but greater governance attention should be paid to traded industrial-scale NTFPs.[52] This reflects the expectation that risks of harm from international-scale industrial exploitation are naturally far greater than from local-scale, community uses, and the social justice dividend is greater for the latter than the former. However, the continuum between 'communal' and 'industrial' trade is contingent on local conditions and the robustness and resilience of the values being exploited.

THE NEED FOR SAFEGUARDS

Whilst the case for stronger property interests in forests is compelling, perverse effects of badly designed land tenure strategies could contribute to deforestation, by creating counterproductive financial incentives.[53] In the Amazon, forest conversion under customary and statutory law is strengthened by evidence of having occupied and cleared the land. Deforestation therefore becomes a way to establish property rights.[54] Perverse incentives – such as the direct payment of subsidies and concessions that serve selective economic interests and stimulate deforestation and forest degradation – are always a governance concern. To again illustrate this risk, subsidies for developing plantations in Indonesia encouraged overharvesting of logging concessions and clearing of 'degraded' natural forests.[55] Both these examples suggest that a simplistic approach to creating secure forest titles also carry a significant risk.

52 Laird, Wynberg and McLain (2010) 367.
53 Tacconi (2007) 338.
54 Angelsen (2009) 125, 134.
55 Sunderlin and Atmadja (2009) 45, 48.

There is particularly a risk where there are deeply entrenched power imbalances, and where safeguards against corruption are weak. An example of this risk can be found in Nepal where the Community Forest User Group (CFUG) program provides communities secure rights to forests, particularly in the Terai (Jungle area). We have previously pointed to some positive effects of this program, but few programs are perfect. An initial survey of implementing this program identified the Dhankheti CFUG as one of the worst performing CFUGs in the country. This was because its Executive Committee members were involved in a well-organised illegal timber trade network.[56] Corruption risk may increase if absolute secure rights mean that some people are prevented from benefitting from forest resources. These people may then attempt to benefit from forest resources in whatever way – illegal or corrupt – they can. The exclusionary nature of property rights implies that strengthening security of interest of one group can mean eroding the interests of subordinated groups.

Such concerns are likely to be significant in Thailand where formal governance systems are often underdeveloped and where corruption is too frequently encountered. For this reason forest rights may need to be conditional, and subject to regular external monitoring and assessment. When there is a breach of conditions, legal authority is needed to extinguish formal rights subject to requirements of due process for cancellation, or compensation where justified on public policy grounds, or to apply other sanctions.[57] A number of possible models of conditional but secure forestry rights can be envisaged. For example, Nepal has designed two types of forestry rights – primary and secondary. The members of a village have primary use rights to forests, while non-village members have specific secondary rights. Non-village members are allowed to extract grass and some fruits that should be common to everyone, but they are never permitted to collect firewood.[58] However, any such design would have to be tailored to the specific Thai situation.

At least in the early years until forest communities do become more powerful and sophisticated in protecting and using these rights, Thai forest tenure arrangements may need to be conditional and subject to independent oversight to ensure that environmental, social and economic policy objectives are being met. The governance oversight requirement of REDD+ provides the opportunity to establish independent scrutiny

---

56 Paudyal (2010–2011) 1.

57 RRI (2012) 22 and 31.

58 FAO (2011) 24–5.

backed by some degrees of sanction power should abuses be identified. Where the line between property right certainty and attenuation for the purposes of governance should be drawn for REDD+ purposes is a complex matter needing further research.

To minimise conflict, sustainable forest management should reflect an understanding of the needs and interests of all affected parties. Public participation and consultation with stakeholders are essential. These processes can build trust between the forest agencies and stakeholders, promote transparency, and ensure inclusive solutions that incorporate stakeholders' views and needs.[59]

To ensure genuine public participation, decisions and proposed actions should be widely communicated. Feedback from consultation should also be published to show how ideas discussed have been considered. These are not merely matters of general principle. Ensuring transparency and participation requires strong institutional structures rather than vague policies or generalised administrative instructions. This is particularly the case in Thailand where a top-down and non-inclusive approach is deeply embedded. Changes to information flow will be essential to better, more participative decisions about forest management.

COORDINATION AND MUTAL UNDERSTANDING

We have outlined some of the structural complexities of the existing forest governance system. A starting point for reform would be to review overlaps and inconsistent responsibilities of authorities to simplify the processes of administration and approval. This would require identification of the sectoral linkages between agencies, and the enhancement and promotion of cooperation to limit competitive actions, and maximise synergies and collaboration.[60] All relevant agencies should be involved in the process of reviewing and reforming their responsibilities.

Authorities responsible for, or participating in, forest management in Thailand would need to jointly develop a mutual understanding about future forest management objectives and principles, and develop a collective management program. Conventional management requirements such as performance measures and evaluation methods would be incorporated in this design. Coordination of reforms might be documented in the form of memoranda or agreements. Relevant agencies could also make joint

---

[59] Kishor and Rosenbaum (2012) 48.

[60] FAO and ITTO (2005) 44.

budgetary commitments or share common databases of information (for example, forestry inventories and maps). There is a great deal which could be done to reduce wasted complexity, even short of regulatory reform.

Regular meetings between the relevant forestry authorities should be established to evaluate and to improve their performance. The meetings might be informal (such as meeting of leaders, staff or related authorities), or formal arrangements (such as a committees, boards, councils, or commissions). The argument for greater formality is the advantage of oversight, but the risk is of 'bureaucratic proceduralism'. Whilst Thailand could achieve much improvement by these administrative steps, statutory reform is likely to be ultimately needed.

REFORM OF FUNDAMENTAL STRUCTURES

Seeking to improve inefficient of ineffective laws and institutions by establishing new ones can lead to further contradictions, overlaps, and complexity. Systematic analysis[61] should be employed to reform fundamental legal and institutional structures.

All key transactions and actors relevant to REDD+ implementation, (particularly relating to interests or rights that people can gain from REDD+) should be identified. Existing laws and institutions should be analysed to identify the supports and constraints Thailand has for the transactions required for REDD+ implementation. Supports should be retained and developed, while constraints should be eliminated or reduced. Two things should particularly be considered: the feasibility of implementation and the consistency with social and economic contexts. The feasibility of implementation depends upon the availability of resources, and the context consistency refers particularly to alignment with the belief and values of people.[62] An important consideration is the alignment of the desirable changes with Thai social structures and culture. Modifications to rights and reforms drawn from other jurisdictions may be needed to ensure that REDD+ implementation does suit the national context and needs.

---

[61] Martin and Verbeek (2006) 28–35.
[62] Martin *et al.* (2007) 23–4.

CONCLUSION

Environmental justice puts an emphasis on fair distribution of opportunities, benefits and risks over natural resources in society, and genuine public participation in decision making and management. Both elements require effective legal and institutional arrangements.

REDD+ is intended to enhance environmental justice – enhancing social justice, economic opportunity, and inclusion, particularly for forestry communities and indigenous people in developing countries, whilst delivering the environmental benefits of reducing carbon in the atmosphere.

At the heart of the achievement of such an ambitious set of REDD+ goals is the necessity of having an effective forest governance system. There are five key challenges that Thailand must meet if it is to secure environmental justice in REDD+ implementation. These are: (1) strengthening the insufficient incentives for investing in forest preservation; (2) mistrust and potential tensions; (3) weak and competing forestry rights; (4) a lack of effective coordination among relevant authorities; and (5) deficiencies in fundamental legal and institutional structures.

This paper points to some necessary legal and institutional reforms. These would help to ensure greater environmental justice in implementation of REDD+ for Thailand, particularly addressing property rights, by granting secure right over forest resources, in order to improve incentives for investing in REDD+ compatible forest management. However, we argue that rights granted should not be absolute, as Thailand's history suggests this could lead to corruption. We propose that, forest tenure arrangements need to be conditional and subject to independent oversight to ensure that environmental, social and economic policy objectives are truly being met. Additional arrangements needed for REDD+ implementation in Thailand include: effective management of tensions and trust, reform to deal with weak and competing forest rights (viz. a clear delineation of rights to forests to ensure mutual understanding and to reduce competing claims), coordination and mutual understanding between agents holding key roles, and reform of fundamental legal and institutional structures.

REDD+ can act as a catalyst for essential reforms to Thailand's forest governance system. If this were to occur, Thailand would not only secure the economic benefits of the carbon market. It would also make substantial strides in strengthening environmental governance and social justice outcomes from its vital forest resources.

REFERENCES

Angelsen, A. (2009), 'Policy Options to Reduce Deforestation', in A. Angelsen *et al.* (eds) (2009) *Realising REDD+: National Strategy and Policy Options* (Center for International Forestry Research (CIFOR)).

Araujo, C. *et al.* (2009), 'Property Rights and Deforestation in the Brazilian Amazon', 68(8–9) *Ecological Economics* 2461.

Asia Indigenous Peoples CCMIN (2011), 'REDD+ Implementation in Asia and the Concerns of Indigenous Peoples' Asia Indigenous Peoples CCMIN, accessed 12 March 2015 at http://www.iwgia.org/iwgia_files_publications_files/0654_REDD_Plus_Implementation_in_Asia_and_the_Concerns_of_Indigenous_Peoples.pdf.

Bluffstone, R., E. Robinson and P. Guthiga (2012), 'REDD+ and Community-Controlled Forests in Low-Income Countries: Any Hope for a Linkage?', 87 *Ecological Economics* 43.

Bromley, D. (1991), *Environment and Economy: Property Rights and Public Policy* (Oxford: Blackwell).

Bruce, J. (1998), 'Review of Tenure Terminology' July(1) Tenure Brief: University of Wisconsin-Madison 1.

Bruce, J., K. Wendland and L. Naughton-Treves (2010), 'Whom to Pay? Key Concepts and Terms Regarding Tenure and Property Rights In Payment-Based Forest Ecosystem Conservation' December (15) Tenure Brief: University of Wisconsin-Madison.

Community Forest Management Bureau (2011), *The Manual of Implementation of Community Forest Project* (The Royal Forest Department).

Cunningham, A. *et al.* (2008), 'Sustainable Trade and Management of Forest Products and Services in the COMESA Region: An Issue Paper' (Bogor: CIFOR).

Dahal, G., A. Larson and P. Pacheco (2010), 'Outcomes of Reform for Livelihoods, Forest Condition and Equity', in A. Larson, D. Barry and G. Dahal (eds) (2010), *Forests for People: Community Rights and Forest Tenure Reform* (London: Earthscan).

Ellsworth L. and A. White (2004), *Deeper Roots: Strengthening Community Tenure Security and Community Livelihoods* (New York: Ford Foundation).

Elmqvist T. *et al.* (2007), 'Patterns of Loss and Regeneration of Tropical Dry Forest in Madagascar: The Social Institutional Context' (5:e402) *PLoS ONE* 1.

Engel, A. and B. Korf (2005), 'Negotiation and Mediation Techniques for Natural Resource Management', Prepared in the framework of the Livelihood Support Programme (LSP): An interdepartmental programme for improving support for enhancing livelihoods of the rural poor, FAO.

FAO-Regional Office for Asia and the Pacific (2009), 'Thailand Forestry Outlook Study', Asia-Pacific Forestry Sector Outlook Study II-Working Paper Series No APFSOS II/WP/2009/22, FAO.

FAO (2011), 'Reforming Forest Tenure: Issues, Principles and Process', FAO Forestry Paper 165, FAO.

FAO and ITTO (2005), 'Best Practices for Improving Law Compliance in the Forest Sector', FAO Forestry Paper No 145.

Fischman, E. (2012), *The Relevance of Tenure and Forest Governance for Incentive Based Mechanisms: Implementing Payments for Ecosystem Services in Doi Mae*

Salong (International Union for Conservation of Nature (Gland, Switzerland: IUCN)).

Fisher, R. (2011), 'Thailand's Forest Regulatory Framework in Relation to the Rights and Livelihoods of Forest Development People', in H. Scheyvens (ed.) (2011), *Critical Review of Selected Forest-related Regulatory Initiatives: Applying a Rights Perspective* (Kanagawa, Japan: Institute for Global Environmental Strategies (IGES)).

Forest Peoples Programme (2011), 'Customary Sustainable Use of Biodiversity by Indigenous Peoples and Local Communities: Examples, Challenges, Community Initiatives and Recommendations Relating to CBD Article 10(c)', A Synthesis Paper based on case studies from Bangladesh, Cameroon, Guyana, Suriname, and Thailand, Forest People Programme.

Forsyth, T. (2009), 'Multilevel, Multiactor Governance in REDD+: Participation, Integration and Coordination', in A. Angelsen *et al.* (eds) (2009), *Realising REDD+: National Strategy and Policy Options* (Barat, Indonesia: CIFOR).

Gine, X. (2005), *Land Security in Rural Thailand: Evidence from a Property Rights Reform* (World Bank, Development Research Group, Finance Team).

Harrison, S. (2003), 'Property Rights Issues in Small-Scale Forestry in the Philippines' 25(2) *Annals of Tropical Research* 77.

Hatcher, J. (2009), 'Securing Tenure Rights and Reducing Emissions from Deforestation and Degradation (REDD): Costs and Lessons Learned', Social Development Working Papers No 120/December 2009, Social Development Department: The World Bank.

Hoare, A. (2010), *Community-Based Forest Management in the Democratic Republic of Congo: A Fairytale or a Viable REDD Strategy?* (Cambridge: Forests Monitor: Rights, Research, Policies, People).

Kishor, N. and K. Rosenbaum (2012), *Assessing and Monitoring Forest Governance: A User's Guide to a Diagnostic Tool* (Washington, DC: Program on Forests (PROFOR)).

Korhonen-Kurki, K. *et al.* (2012), 'Multiple levels and multiple challenges for REDD+' in A. Angelsen *et al.* (eds) (2012), *Analysing REDD+: Challenges and Choices* (Barat, Indonesia: CIFOR).

Laird, S., R. Wynberg and R. McLain (2010), 'Recommendations' in S.A. Laird, R.J. McLain and R.P. Wynberg (eds) (2010), *Wild Product Governance: Finding Policies that Work for Non-Timber Forest Products* (London: Earthscan).

Lakanavichian, S. (2007), 'Trends in Forest Ownership, Forest Resources Tenure and Institutional Arrangements: Are They Contributing to Better Forest Management and Poverty Reduction? Case study from Thailand', Forestry Policy and Institutions Working Paper 14: Understanding Forest Tenure in South and Southeast Asia, Food and Agriculture Organization, FAO.

Larson, A. (2011), 'Forest Tenure Reform in the Age of Climate Change: Lessons for REDD+', 21(2) *Global Environmental Change* 540.

Larson, A., D. Barry and G. Dahal (2010), 'Tenure Change in the Global South' in A. Larson, D. Barry and G. Dahal (eds) (2010), *Forests for People: Community Rights and Forest Tenure Reform* (London: Earthscan).

Lasimbang, J. and C. Luithui (2006), *Natural Resource Management Country Studies: Thailand* (United Nations Development Programme: Regional Indigenous Peoples' Programme, United Nations).

Martin, P. *et al.* (2007), *Developing a Good Regulatory Practice Model for*

Environmental Regulations Impacting on Farmers (Research Report, Australian Farm Institute and Land & Water Australia).

Martin, P. and M. Verbeek (2006), *Sustainability Strategy* (Annandale, NSW: The Federation Press).

Meinzen-Dick, R. and A. Knox (2001), 'Collective Action, Property Rights, and Devolution of Natural Resource Management: A Conceptual Framework' in R. Meinzen-Dick, A. Knox and M. Di Gregorio (eds) (2006), *Collective Action, Property Rights and Devolution of Natural Resource Management: Exchange of Knowledge and Implications for Policy* (DSE/ZEL).

Moore, P. and F. Pastakia (eds) (2007), *Environmental Justice and Rural Communities: Study from India and Nepal* (Gland, Switzerland: IUCN).

Office of Natural Resources and Environmental Policy and Planning: Thailand (ONEP 2010), *Thailand's National Capacity Self-Assessment: United Nations Framework Convention on Climate Change* (Office of Natural Resources and Environmental Policy and Planning: Thailand (ONEP) and United Nations Development Program (UNDP)).

Ostrom, E. (1999), 'Self-governance and Forest Resources', Occasional Paper No 20, (Center For International Forestry Research (Barat, Indonesia: CIFOR)).

Pagdee, A., Y. Kim and P. Daugherty (2006), 'What Makes Community Forest Management Successful: A Meta-Study from Community Forests Throughout the World', 19(1) *Society and Natural Resources* 33.

Paudyal, B. (2010–2011), 'Curbing Corruption in Forestry Management through User Groups in Nepal', (16) Partnership for Transparency Fund (PFT) Case Study Series 1.

Peskett, L. and M. Brockhaus (2009), 'When REDD+ Goes National: A Review of Realities, Opportunities and Challenges' in A. Angelsen, *et al.* (eds) (2009) *Realising REDD+: National Strategy and Policy Options* (Barat, Indonesia: CIFOR).

Praurasiddhi, T. *et al.* (2013), *Readiness Preparation Proposal (R-PP) for Country: Thailand* (World Bank, Forest Carbon Partnership Facility (FCPF)).

RRI (2008), 'The Thailand Community Forest Bill', Rights and Resources Initiative, 3 January 2008, accessed 12 March 2015 at http://www.rightsandresources.org/news/the-thailand-community-forest-bill/.

RRI (2012) *What Rights?: A Comparative Analysis of Developing Countries' National Legislation on Community and Indigenous Peoples' Forest Tenure Rights*, accessed 12 March 2015 at http://www.rightsandresources.org/documents/files/doc_4924.pdf.

Robinson, B., M. Holland and L. Naughton-Treves (2011), 'Does Secure Land Tenure Save Forest?: A Review of the Relationship between Land Tenure and Tropical Deforestation', CGIAR Research Program on Climate Change, Agriculture and Food Security (CCAFS) Working Paper No 7, (Consortium of International Agricultural Research Centers (CGIAR) Research Program on Climate Change, Agriculture and Food Security (CCAFS)).

Sunderlin, W. and S. Atmadja (2009), 'Is REDD+ An Idea Whose Time has Come, or Gone?' in A. Angelsen *et al.* (eds) (2009), *Realising REDD+: National Strategy and Policy Options* (Barat, Indonesia: CIFOR).

Tacconi, L. (2007), 'Decentralization, Forests and Livelihoods: Theory and Narrative' 17(3–4) Global Environmental Change 338.

Wataru, F. (2003), 'Dealing with Contradictions: Examining National Forest Reserves in Thailand', 41(2) *Southeast Asian Studies* 206.

Wertz-Kanounnikoff, S. and A. Angelsen (2009), 'Global and National REDD+ Architecture Linking Institutions and Actions' in A. Angelsen *et al.* (eds) (2009), *Realising REDD+: National Strategy and Policy Options* (Barat, Indonesia: CIFOR).

Westholm, L. *et al.* (2011), 'REDD+ and Tenure: A Review of the Latest Developments in Research, Implementation and Debate', Focali Report 2011:02, Forest, Climate and Livelihood research network (Focali) in collaboration with Sida's Environmental Economics Helpdesk, at Department of Economics, University of Gothenburg.

Zhu, B., Y. Zhang and F. Peng (2011), 'Research on Forestry Credit Innovation Mode Based on Collateral Mechanism of Extension and Substitution' Eastern Academic Forum 152.

9. Indonesia REDD+: beyond carbon, more than just forest

Mas Achmad Santosa,[1] Josi Khatarina,[2] and Aldilla Stephanie Suwana[3]

BACKGROUND

Indonesia's Reducing Emissions from Deforestation and Forest Degradation plus (REDD+) is not merely a mitigation tool to tackle deforestation and forest degradation. Indonesia's REDD+ strategy is designed to be *Beyond Carbon and More Than Forest*. In its National REDD+ Strategy, the vision of REDD+ is 'to sustainably manage forest and peatland as national assets for the ultimate welfare of the people'. Thus, the peoples' welfare is one ultimate goal of REDD+. Consequently, the principles of REDD+ also include fairness (which is elaborated upon as equality to everyone) and human rights protection, including for groups that are vulnerable to social and economic change. To realise the vision, the initial priority of REDD+ in Indonesia is to improve governance, strengthen spatial plans and improve the investment climate. The intent is to achieve two goals at the same time, first to reduce emissions and second to maintain sustainable growth with equity. This is because the root causes of deforestation and forest/peatland degradation in Indonesia relate to failings of governance which in some cases have resulted in violation of justice principles. Therefore, REDD+ in Indonesia is not only a way to reduce Green House Gas (GHG) emissions through such endeavours as carbon trading, but is also a catalyst for governance reform in natural resources management including more effective law enforcement. This is seen as a means to enhance equality of access to natural resources, thereby to enhance the rights of disadvantaged people

---

[1] Founder of Indonesian Center for Environmental Law (ICEL) and Deputy Head of President's Delivery Unit for Development Monitoring and Oversight.

[2] Senior legal counsel of Indonesia REDD+ Agency.

[3] Legal counsel of Indonesia REDD+ Agency.

including *Masyarakat Hukum Adat* (MHA).[4] REDD+ in Indonesia is therefore seen as an entry point to promote sustainable growth with equity.[5]

This chapter will elaborate problems of forest and peatland governance that give rise to social injustice and how the REDD+ preparation program was designed to confront this situation. The focus will be on the progress of Indonesia's governance of REDD+ including the establishment of the REDD+ Agency.[6] It will first describe the REDD+ framework, the REDD+ institutional arrangements, and each of the programs of REDD+ that are intended to build up the basic elements reflected in its motto, *Beyond Carbon More Than Forest*. The chapter will describe and discuss progress and conclude with outlining the way forward to environmental and social justice.

REDD+ FRAMEWORK DESIGN: THE ENHANCEMENT OF FOREST AND PEATLAND GOVERNANCE IN PURSUIT OF ENVIRONMENTAL AND SOCIAL JUSTICE

There are several drivers of deforestation and forest/peatland degradation that need to be addressed in order to meet the target of reducing emissions from deforestation and forest/peatland degradation.[7] First is the absence of clarity over land tenure that is manifested in the number of agrarian conflicts.[8] Second is the situation where there are many conflicting laws and regulations at the national level. This is a result of a traditional sectoral approach in natural resources management.[9] Third is the nation's approach to decentralisation that still struggles in many areas to fulfil its promise of better governance in all areas of policy including management of natural resources. This is obvious from the reports that highlight many overlapping licenses, which in themselves increase the amount

---

[4] The Government of Indonesia does not use the term 'indigenous people.' The term which is used is *Masyarakat Hukum Adat*, roughly translated as 'custom-based society', meaning groups living according to traditional customs and rules in geographically isolated and rural areas.

[5] REDD+ Task Force (2012).

[6] For a comprehensive overview of the progress of governing REDD+ before the establishment of REDD+ Agency, see Santosa, Khatarina and Suwana (2013).

[7] See Indrarto *et al.* (2012).

[8] Indrarto *et al.* (2012).

[9] Indrarto *et al.* (2012). See UKP4 and MOLHR (2013).

and severity of tenurial conflict[10] and further weaken the investment climate.[11] Fourth (and most important) is the absence of a systematic or coherent design to protect the rights of forest dependent communities and other vulnerable groups. This is very important from a public policy perspective as many vulnerable groups are forest dependent communities. The most recent information conveyed in the Gini Index[12] indicates a growing wealth gap between the rich and the poor.[13] Indonesia's Gini Index has deteriorated from 0.37 to 0.413 over four years and has hit its highest rate since 1996 (0.355).[14] While this figure still compares very well with other countries in Southeast Asia and certainly to nations in Latin America and Africa, the inequity of income figure is the worst in modern Indonesian history.

As will be elaborated below, the improvement of forest and peatland governance under the banner of adoption of REDD+ is designed as a response to those issues. Without substantial governance reforms in forest and peatland management, any strategy to reduce emissions from deforestation and forest degradation will not be effective in addressing Indonesia's basic challenges. The designs have developed a strategy and institutional reforms comprising a complete set of steps and implementing actors. A fundamental assumption is that once Indonesia raises standards of governance in management of forest and peatland, environmental and social justice will also be enhanced.

To provide support for the necessary reforms one of the first formal actions ordered by the President in the beginning of the REDD+ era was Presidential Instruction No 10/2011 on the Suspension of New Licenses and Improving Governance of Primary Forest and Peatland (Presidential Instruction on Moratorium). As obvious in its title and specified in the decree, the Presidential Instruction on Moratorium suspends the issue of further licenses on primary forest and peatland in conservation forests, protected forests, production forests and other specified land areas, subject to certain conditions. It instructs all relevant ministries/institutions

---

10 Indrarto *et al.* (2012). See UKP4 and MOLHR (2013). See also Yasmi *et al.* (2012) and Working Group on Forest Land Tenure (2012).

11 See *Churchill Mining and Planet Mining Pty Ltd v Republic of Indonesia* (ICSID Case No. AEB/12/40 and 12/14). Churchill filed a claim to ICSID because the licenses to operate on the concession site were revoked. The revocation was based on evidence of non-procedural licenses and the issuance of overlapping licenses.

12 Gini index of 0 represents perfect equality, while an index of 1 implies perfect inequality.

13 Sambijantoro (2014).

14 Badan Pusat Statistik (2014).

and heads of local government at the district and provincial levels to improve forest and peatland management while reducing emissions from deforestation and forest/peatland degradation. This policy is important as it provides space for policy makers to design strategies to improve forest and peatland governance while making sure forest and peatland areas that are still in good condition remain protected, as well as protecting the operations of businesses that have legitimate licenses.

This Presidential Instruction on Moratorium as with other Presidential Instructions were elaborated into measurable and specific action plans by the President's Delivery Unit on Development Oversight and Monitoring (*Unit Kerja Presiden Bidang Pengawasan dan Pengendalian Pembangunan* or UKP4). These action plans include programs such as those expediting forest gazettal, mapping the areas occupied by *Masyarakat Hukum Adat*, harmonising laws and regulations, reviewing land based licenses, and improving the effectiveness and integrity of law enforcement. Based on the agreed indicators for these programs, there has been tangible progress in the improvement of forest and peatland governance.[15] However, further time is needed to make sufficient progress, and so after evaluation, this instruction was extended by a Presidential Instruction No 6/2013 on Suspension of New Licenses and Improving Governance of Primary Forest and Peatland for a further two years.

Pursuant to the Presidential Instruction on Moratorium (a policy instrument), a regulation was passed. On 20 September 2010, Presidential Regulation No 61/2011 on a National Action Plan to Reduce GHGs Emissions (Presidential Regulation on GHGs Emissions Reduction) was issued. The Presidential Regulation on GHGs Emissions Reduction establishes mandatory actions to reduce GHGs emissions from various sources, including improving forest and peatland governance. The action plans are not exhaustive and inclusive lists; the action plans will be further elaborated in more detailed plans. For instance, the REDD+ Provincial Strategy and Action Plans are derived from the REDD+ National Strategy.

Further, the enactment of the Presidential Decree No 19/2010 on the Task Force for the Preparation of the REDD+ Agency established an implementation institution.[16] The role of the Task Force was not only to establish the REDD+ Agency and implement other instruments of REDD+, but also to supervise the implementation of the Presidential

15 Working Group of Moratorium Monitoring (2013).

16 The Task Force is extended by two other Presidential Decrees, Presidential Decree No 25/2011 and Presidential Decree No 05/2013.

Instruction on Moratorium. Hence, the Task Force was also a tool to accelerate the enhancement of forest and peatland governance more generally.

The most recent regulation was Presidential Regulation No 62/2013 on the Agency for the Reducing Emission from Deforestation and Degradation of Forest and Peatland (Presidential Regulation on REDD+ Agency). The Presidential Regulation on REDD+ Agency provides a legal basis for the establishment of the REDD+ Agency. The REDD+ Agency has to carry forward the work undertaken by the Task Force and further improve the forest and peatland governance through its functions. One of the tasks of the REDD+ Agency is to the increase of environmental services, biodiversity, and the welfare of local people or *Masyarakat Hukum Adat*. The scope of the REDD+ Agency's tasks has proven that the Indonesia REDD+ scheme goes far beyond reducing GHGs emissions and carbon sequestration and encompasses supporting biodiversity, engagement with and empowerment of local and customary communities and promotion of governance reform in areas such as land and natural resource management.

As indicated above, the enhancement of forest and peatland governance to support the achievement of environmental and social justice outcomes are considered to be prerequisites for REDD+. The link between the desired outcomes, policies and regulations are described as forming the five pillars of the REDD+ National Strategy (see Figure 9.1). These five pillars highlight the importance of governance reform in order to achieve the ultimate goals of REDD+, namely to advance environmental and social justice.

REDD+ INSTITUTIONAL ARRANGEMENTS: REDD+ AGENCY, FUNDING INSTRUMENTS, MEASUREMENT, REPORTING AND VERIFICATION

To support the implementation of the above-mentioned laws, regulations and policies, REDD+ suitable institutional arrangements are crucial. These have to be able to carry out the function of coordination while independently monitoring and evaluating performance and providing payments based on that performance. The need for independence and transparency is the reason for the division of Measurement, Reporting and Verification (MRV) and Funding Instruments from the main REDD+ Agency.

Thus, the Presidential Regulation on REDD+ Agency has become one of the most pivotal milestones in the progress of REDD+ in Indonesia. It

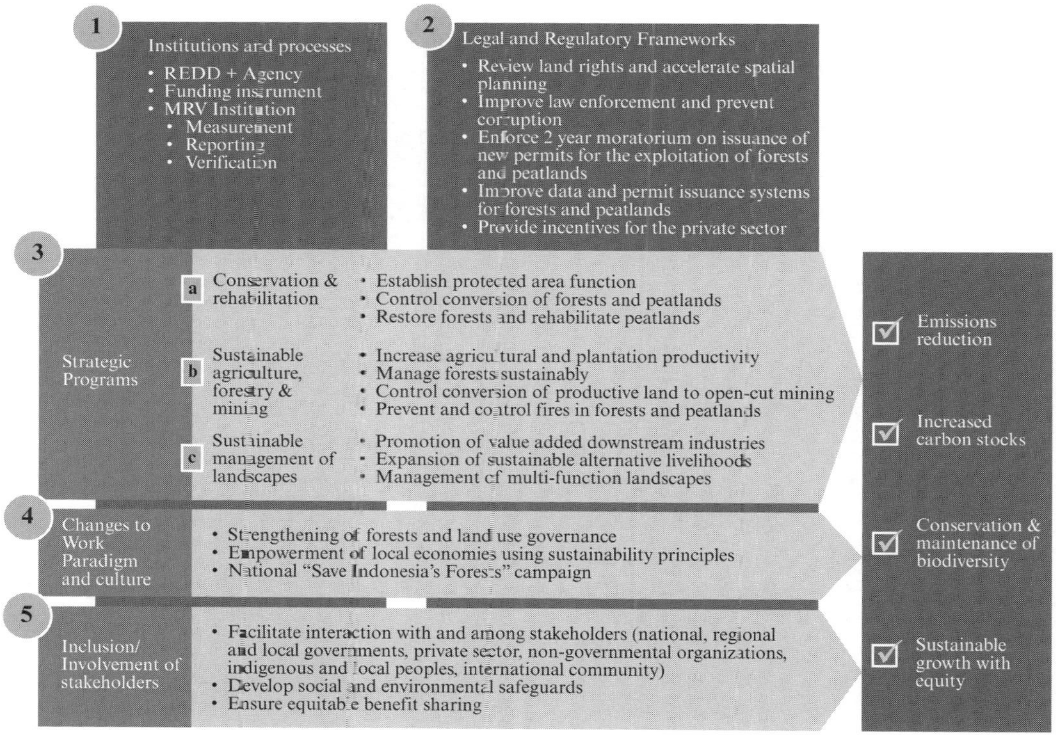

Source: Adapted from the Framework of National Strategy.

Figure 9.1 The five main pillars

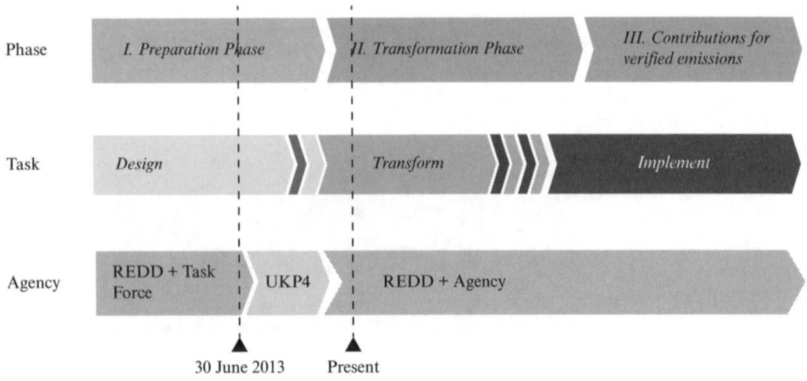

Figure 9.2 The phases of REDD+ in Indonesia[17]

provides a legal basis for the establishment of the Government REDD+ Agency and for the MRV and Funding Instruments and a proper framework of arm's length relationships between the implementation and the evaluation aspects of REDD+.

The establishment of the REDD+ Agency marked the completion of Phase I (preparation and design) in a three stage process leading up to realising economic contributions for emission reductions through REDD+. In Phase III, when MRV and Funding Instruments are fully functioning, REDD+ will be fully operational in Indonesia. (See Figure 9.2.)

Moving into Phase II (transformation and implementation), the REDD+ Agency will act as the designated national authority for REDD+. It is responsible for achieving the objectives of REDD+. The Presidential Regulation on REDD+ Agency states clearly that the purpose of REDD+ is to have an impact beyond forests, and beyond carbon sequestration, in achieving social goals. Article 2 of the Presidential Regulation on REDD+ Agency states that REDD+ aims to:

(a) reduce emissions from deforestation;
(b) reduce emissions from forest degradation and/or peatland degradation;
(c) sequester and increase carbon stocks through forest conservation, sustainable forest management, and/or rehabilitation and restoration of damaged forest areas; and

---

[17] Mangkusubroto (2013).

(d) provide benefit to the increase of environmental services, biodiversity, and the welfare of local or *Masyarakat Hukum Adat*.

To achieve the purpose, the REDD+ Agency is empowered to coordinate, synchronise, plan, facilitate, manage, monitor, oversee and control REDD+ activities in Indonesia.[18] This includes 13 key tasks mainly categorised in four types of functions. These are new functions (functions that do not exist in other ministries/institutions), strengthening functions (functions that exist in other ministries/institutions), coordinating functions and open functions (tasks assigned by the President). To support the REDD+ Agency's coordination function, the REDD+ Agency is not given direct power to grant or issue licenses. Other ministries such as Ministry of Forestry will grant licenses that have correlation with REDD+ projects. It is expected that, liberated from the responsibility to grant licenses, the REDD+ Agency will be able to effectively supervise the full implementation of REDD+ programs, projects and/or activities.

Details of the REDD+ Agency functions are as follows:[19]

(a) Four New Functions
    (1) developing the National REDD+ Strategy to implement REDD+ in Indonesia;
    (2) developing a REDD+ safeguards framework for social, environmental and funding matters;
    (3) preparing and coordinating instruments and mechanisms for REDD+ funding and the distribution of benefits to parties implementing REDD+ programs, projects and/or activities in accordance with regulations; and
    (4) developing standards and methodology to measure GHGs emissions and sequestration from REDD+ programs, projects or activities, and consolidation and reporting of data on GHGs emissions and sequestration from REDD+ programs, projects or activities.
(b) Four Strengthening Functions
    (1) managing aid in the form of funds or other legally acceptable forms related to REDD+ in accordance with regulations;
    (2) increasing the capability and capacity of ministries/agencies, partners and communities and the quality of instruments for implementing REDD+;

---

18 Art 4 Presidential Regulation on REDD+ Agency.

19 Art. 5 Presidential Regulation on REDD+ Agency.

- (3) preparing recommendations related to Indonesia's position in international fora; and
- (4) monitoring and evaluating the implementation of REDD+ programs, projects and/or activities.

(c) Three Coordinating Functions

- (1) coordinating the formation and development of REDD+ policies and the mainstreaming of REDD+ in national development;
- (2) coordinating law enforcement as relates to the implementation of REDD+ programs, projects and/or activities; and
- (3) coordinating and facilitating the resolution of disputes and conflicts related to REDD+ programs, projects and/or activities in accordance with regulations.

(d) One Open Function

- (1) Carrying out tasks assigned by the President.

Further, the last task is to carry out the administration of the REDD+ Agency. Until the REDD+ Agency is fully independent and operational, the UKP4 will provide ongoing support to the REDD+ Agency.[20] In order to be fully operational, REDD+ Agency will need to establish its own funding instruments and facilitate the establishment of an independent MRV system. Moreover, a stakeholder committee will be institutionalised to ensure the REDD+ Agency's accountability and to enable public participation. These organisational structures are detailed below.

We believe that the REDD+ institutional arrangements reflect good governance principles, for three reasons. First, the creation of a Stakeholder Committee as a permanent organ inside the REDD+ Agency. This arrangement is designed to institutionalise public interest participation in REDD+ programs, projects and/or activities and to strengthen public accountability of the REDD+ Agency. Second, the division of functions of the REDD+ Agency, MRV and Funding Instruments distinguishes development of policy from the powers to conduct monitoring and to fund activities. This division of power is expected to provide a balance to ensure the REDD+ Agency and its officials encounter minimal possibilities for abuse of power. Third, Presidential Regulation on REDD+ Agency specifically requires that the funding instruments should be supported by a framework of safeguards. In the latest governance design of funding instruments, concepts for a Board of Trustees, Safeguard Committee and

---

[20] Art. 27(2) Presidential Regulation on REDD+ Agency.

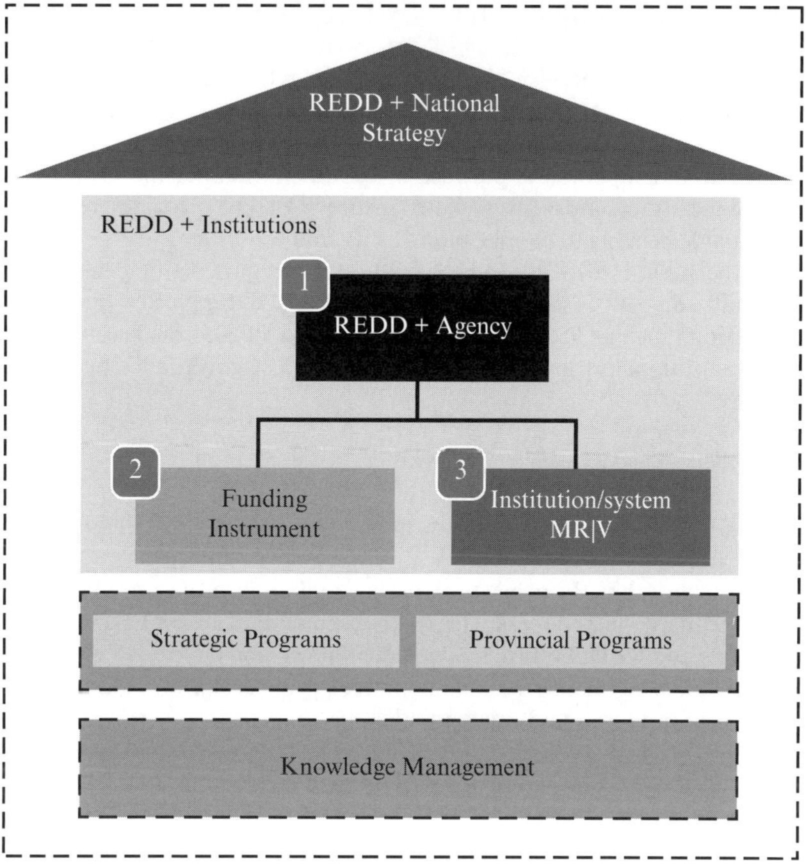

Figure 9.3 REDD+ institutional arrangements[21]

a Disbursement and Investment Committee under the FREDDI ('Fund for REDD+ in Indonesia') structure will be discussed. This design should guarantee that the REDD+ programs, projects and/or activities operate in accordance with good governance principles to provide transparency and accountable benefits to the people, biodiversity and ecosystems. Figure 9.3 depicts these institutional arrangements to govern Indonesia's REDD+ program.

[21] UKP4 (2013).

THE FUND FOR REDD+ IN INDONESIA

The fund for REDD+ in Indonesia (FREDDI) provides the funding instruments for REDD+. In the context of pursuing social justice through REDD+, two principles are relevant. First, the funding instruments should support the purpose of REDD+. Second, the instrument will reflect safeguards designed to ensure REDD+ provides real and sustainable benefits to people, biodiversity and ecosystem.

In the period 2013–2014, FREDDI is in the process of being institutionalised. The institutionalisation of FREDDI requires amending regulations such as Presidential Regulation No 80/2011 on Trust Funds. The institutionalisation of FREDDI is to reflect governance principles such as:

1. effectiveness, efficiency, fairness;
2. transparency and accountability;
3. leadership in design, management and governance of FREDDI by the Government of Indonesia;
4. ensuring that Principles, Criteria, and Indicators for REDD+ Safeguards in Indonesia (PRISAI) become part of FREDDI operations and REDD+ Project implementation; and
5. flexibility to finance national initiatives, provincial priorities, demand-driven proposals and small grants.[22]

As noted above the structure of FREDDI will involve a Board of Trustees, a Safeguard Committee and a Disbursement and Investment Committee (see Figure 9.4).

In assessing and reviewing proposals, the Safeguard Committee will use safeguard guidelines known as *Prinsip, Kriteria, dan Indikator Safeguard REDD+ di Indonesia* (Principles, Criteria, and Indicators for REDD+ in Indonesia or PRISAI). PRISAI is intended to ensure that REDD+ provides real and sustainable benefits to people, biodiversity and ecosystems, and supports improved governance, whilst ensuring that REDD+ programs are effective and reduce the risk of non-permanence.[23]

---

[22] Working Group Funding Instrument (2013) *FREDDI*.

[23] Working Group Funding Instrument (2013), *Safeguards REDD+ Indonesia*.

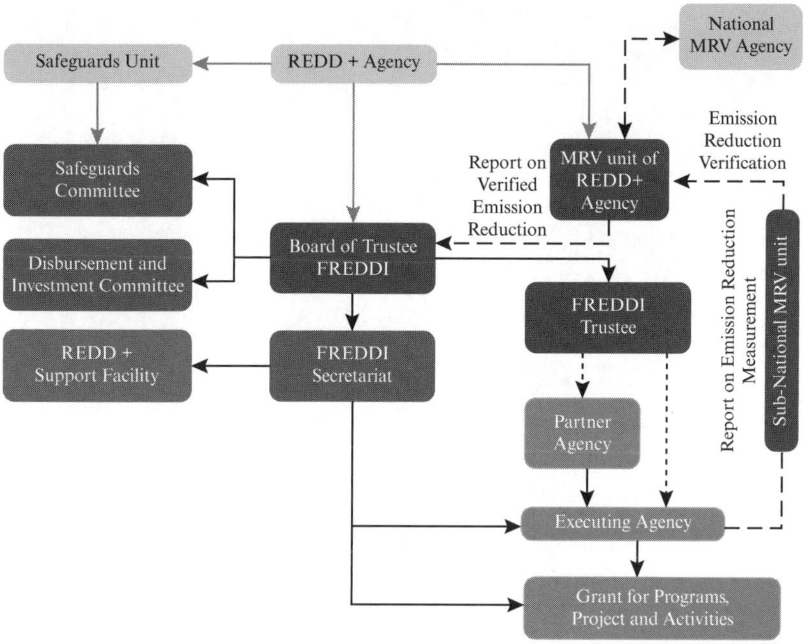

Figure 9.4 Illustration of FREDDI's structure[24]

MEASUREMENT, REPORTING AND VERIFICATION

MRV is an important activity to ensure that REDD+ achieves its promise and goals. The REDD+ Agency has continued the work through the REDD+ Task Force to develop the strategy and implementation plan for REDD+ MRV. The framework for Indonesia's MRV approach is shown in Figure 9.5.

The Verification will be conducted by the Ministry of Environment based on the Minister of Environment Regulation No 15/2013 on Measurement, Reporting and Verification of Climate Change Mitigation Action.

24 UKP4 (2013).

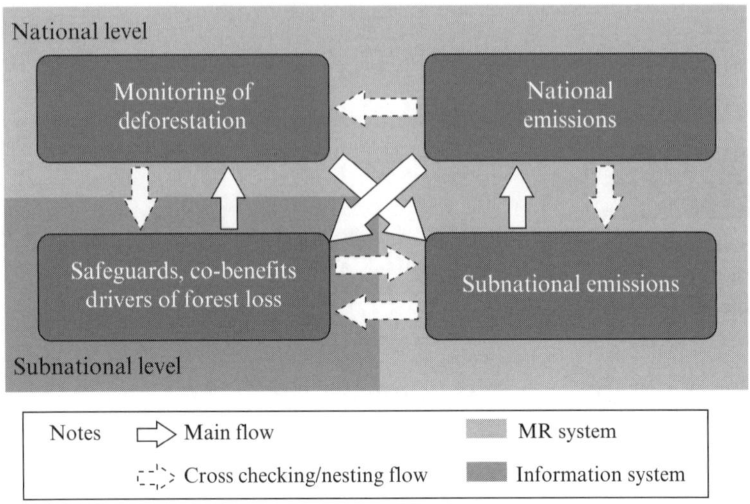

Figure 9.5 *Preliminary MRV architecture as laid out by the National MRV Strategy*

STAKEHOLDER COMMITTEE (*KOMITE PEMANGKU KEPENTINGAN*)

In order to ensure good governance, specifically to enhance public participation, a stakeholder committee will be one of the organs of the REDD+ Agency. The stakeholder committee will be established under and directly responsible to the Head of the REDD+ Agency and will provide advice regarding implementation of REDD+ programs, projects and/or activities.[25]

The members of this Committee will not be staff of the REDD+ Agency. The Committee will consist of figures with standing, repute and expertise in fields as diverse as the environment, community and *Masyarakat Hukum Adat* empowerment, women's empowerment, the role of business in development, good governance, and science and technology.[26]

With its make up of independent members from various fields, the Stakeholder Committee is an important tool to guarantee that REDD+ programs, projects and/or activities uphold the principles of accountability and public participation.

---

[25] Art 20 and 21 Presidential Regulation on REDD+ Agency.

[26] Art 22 Presidential Regulation on REDD+ Agency.

REDD+ AGENCY: FIVE PREREQUISITES AND TEN IMPERATIVE ACTIONS

Following the earlier discussion of the institutional set-up of the REDD+ Agency, this section discusses action for the agency's initial year in accordance with the mandate for Phase II (transformation and implementation). The action plan covers strengthening the governance pillars for REDD+. By 2014 the REDD+ Agency has initiated ten imperatives for action and five prerequisites for action at the national and sub-national levels. The imperative actions represent continuing programs of the UKP4 and the REDD+ Task Force.[27] The ten imperative actions focus on forest and peatland governance in general, while the five prerequisites are basic requirements for implementation of the imperative actions. The ten imperative actions and five prerequisites are as follows:

(a) Ten imperative actions:
   (1) monitoring the moratorium;
   (2) promoting legal reform, including license review and forest gazettals;
   (3) support for law enforcement;
   (4) mapping, capacity building and the implementation of the customary forest program;
   (5) forest fire management;
   (6) green village program;
   (7) green school program;
   (8) support for the completion of spatial planning;
   (9) support for conflict resolution; and
   (10) strategic program for saving national parks and protected forests.

(b) Five prerequisites are the existence of:
   (1) provincial strategy and action plans;
   (2) baseline data and cadastral maps;
   (3) institutionalisation at the sub-national level;
   (4) Memorandums of Understanding (MoU) with the provincial and district governments; and
   (5) MRV and Reference Emissions Level (REL).

The REDD+ programs are going to be implemented in eleven provinces that hold the majority of Indonesia's land with forest cover and

---

27 Art 27(2) Presidential Regulation on REDD+ Agency.

peatland. The provinces are Central Kalimantan, East Kalimantan, Jambi, West Sumatra, Central Sulawesi, West Kalimantan, Aceh, Riau, South Sumatra, West Papua and Papua. The first five provinces have entered into an MoU with UKP4 and the REDD+ Agency on REDD+ implementation in the province. By focusing on the eleven provinces, it is expected that Indonesia will be able to significantly reduce its GHG emissions from forest and peatland.

Imperative actions on REDD+ must be implemented at the local level because Indonesia's governmental system have been decentralised since 1999. In addition, this also allows a test of the jurisdictional approach in the context of REDD+.

As imperative actions represent a continuation of programs from the REDD+ Taskforce, some progress in those areas has already been achieved.[28] The performance to date of several REDD+ programs related to the improvement of social justice in the context of general development will be discussed later in this chapter.

LAW AND REGULATORY REFORM

Conflicting laws and regulations have created flaws and weaknesses in forest and peatland governance.[29] In response, the REDD+ Agency together with Ministry of Law and Human Rights has been developing a Road Map for Legal Reform to ensure harmonisation and synchronisation of laws and regulations horizontally and vertically.[30] It is understood that in some cases there is an urgent need to amend, revoke or enact particular pieces of legislation. Thus, in parallel, there are efforts to improve implementing regulations, such as by revoking the Minister of Agriculture Regulation No 26/2007 on Guidelines of Plantation License, enactment of Law No 18/2013 on Prevention and Eradication of Forest Destruction, and the issuance of several presidential instructions. Outside the government sphere, there are efforts from civil society organisations (CSOs) to ensure the harmonisation of laws with the Constitution through the Constitutional Court. Constitutional Court Case No 35/2012 regarding customary forests (*Hutan Adat*) is one such example. This decision will be discussed below in relation to protecting the rights of *Masyarakat Hukum Adat* (MHA), as it is an important new interpretation of the Forestry Law under the Constitution.

---

28 See Santosa, Khatarina and Suwana (2013).

29 See Arnold (2008). See also UNDP and UN-REDD+ Programme (2013).

30 See UKP4 and MOLHR (2013).

The Minister of Agriculture Regulation No 26/2007 on Guidelines of Plantation Licensing was revoked by the Minister of Agriculture Regulation No 98/2013 (Minister Regulation on Plantation License). This enactment has a strategic role in enhancing governance standards for plantation licensing. Some issues that had created problems at the implementation level were clarified or new rules introduced in this regulation. Some examples of improvements are limitations on land ownership by groups of companies,[31] obligations for free, prior and informed consent (FPIC) in the areas where MHA exist,[32] clarification of obligations towards the development of community plantations[33] and allotment of shares in the crude palm oil manufacturing industry to local plantation cooperatives,[34] promoting transparency in licensing processes and strengthening regulations on second line enforcement.[35] These new policies are expected to improve and guarantee the access of smallholders or farmers in general in modern plantation businesses such as palm oil. The limitation of occupation of land by groups of companies aims to ensure harmonisation with the Agrarian Law No 5/1960 which controls the scale of land ownership.[36] This is important, as there are indications that plantation enterprises such as palm oil are being dominated by large groups of companies.

The enactment of Law No 18/2013 on Prevention and Eradication of Forest Destruction (Prevention and Eradication of Forest Destruction Law) is expected to improve law enforcement in six main aspects. First, the Prevention and Eradication of Forest Destruction Law mandates the establishment of an institution, the Prevention and Eradication of Forest Destruction Institution (*Lembaga Pencegahan dan Pemberantasan Perusakan Hutan*) which is responsible directly to the President. It consists of representatives from the Ministry of Forestry, Police Department of the Republic of Indonesia, Attorney General and other related ministries/institutions.[37] The institution will improve coordination and augment the effectiveness of law enforcement as it has discretion to carry out investigations and to manage coordination between all law enforcement agencies. Prior to the law, each ministry/institution had segregated (and poorly linked) powers to investigate crimes in forest areas.

Second, the Prevention and Eradication of Forest Destruction Law

---

31 Art. 17 Minister Regulation on Plantation License.
32 Art. 24 Minister Regulation on Plantation License.
33 Art. 15 Minister Regulation on Plantation License.
34 Art. 14 Minister Regulation on Plantation License.
35 Art. 47 Minister Regulation on Plantation License.
36 Art 7 and 17 Agrarian Law.
37 Chapter V. Prevention and Eradication of Forest Destruction Law.

focuses on organised forest crime rather than petty crime.[38] Logging related activities conducted by people living in or near forest areas who previously legitimately exploit forest for traditional cultivation or for private usage (not for commercial use) with proper licenses as long as it is conducted outside conservation forests (*hutan konservasi*) or protected forest (*hutan lindung*) will not be sanctioned.[39] Third, the scope of the Law is wider than the Law No 41/1999 on forestry (Forestry Law) as it controls not only destruction and encroachment of forest but also illegal activities such as plantations and mining located in the forest areas.[40]

Fourth, the Prevention and Eradication of Forest Destruction Law allows the use of evidence outside the scope of evidence authorised in the Criminal Procedures Code, such as wire-tapping[41] and removal of bank secrecy.[42] Fifth, sanctions are established for authorities who grant licenses that are not in accordance with laws and regulations.[43] Finally, the laws allow utilisation of corporate criminal liabilities within law enforcement.[44] Corporate criminal liability provides the legal basis to incarcerate not only field actors (physical perpetrators) but also corporate directors (functional perpetrators).

Along with the new laws and regulations, some additional policies are also being adopted by the government. Apart from the Presidential Instruction on Moratorium, the President has issued Presidential Instruction No 2/2013 on Handling National Security Disturbances and Presidential Instruction No 8/2013 on Completion of Spatial Plans of Provinces, Regencies and Municipalities. The Presidential Instruction on Handling National Security Disturbances promotes and supports the settlement of tenurial conflict,[45] while the Presidential Instruction on the Completion of Spatial Plans will expedite the finalisation of spatial plans for each province, regency and municipality. Resolution of tenurial conflicts will hopefully improve clarity of tenure through a peaceful process.

---

38 Art 11(1) and (2) Prevention and Eradication of Forest Destruction Law and general elucidation.

39 Art 11(3), (4), and (5) Prevention and Eradication of Forest Destruction Law. It remains to be seen whether the licenses issuances for the above-mentioned activities will be made complicated or not.

40 Art 1(5), and 17 Prevention and Eradication of Forest Destruction Law.

41 Art 34 Prevention and Eradication of Forest Destruction Law. The wire-tapping will be conducted by Ministry of Telecommunication and Information.

42 Art 35 Prevention and Eradication of Forest Destruction Law.

43 Art 28, 105 Prevention and Eradication of Forest Destruction Law.

44 Art 18 and Chapter X Prevention and Eradication of Forest Destruction Law.

45 See Santosa, Khatarina and Suwana (2013).

At the same time, finalising of spatial plans will provide clear reference to all parties on which areas can be used for production and which are protected for reasons including for conservation. This means that those who clearly have ownership of a particular piece of land should also have their right to use the land in accordance with its function clarified as well as protecting the land from illegal use. In combination with the Presidential Instruction on Moratorium, the two Presidential Instructions are important policy instruments to improve the governance of forests and peatland.

ENHANCING *MASYARAKAT HUKUM ADAT'S* RIGHTS

An historic milestone for the protection of *Masyarakat Hukum Adat*/MHA (custom based society) was Constitutional Court Decision No 35/2012. This decision recognises that MHA have rights over their land that has forest cover, known as customary forest. This decision has a very important role in strengthening legal protection of MHA's interests. Previously, Article 1(6) of the Act 41/1999 stated that: 'Customary forest means a state forest located in the area of MHA'. The Constitutional Court granted the plaintiffs' request, declaring the phrase 'state' to be unconstitutional and unenforceable. Article 1(6) now reads: 'Customary forest means a state forest located in the area of MHA.'

Furthermore, in its judgment the Court decided that '. . . the forest based on its status is differentiated into two status, state forest and private forest. Moreover, private forest is differentiated into customary forest and personal/legal entity forest. The status of the three forests is at the same level and all forests are managed by the State.' Therefore, customary forest is no longer part of State Forest as stated in the Forestry Law but is a form of private forest. Consequently, MHA, similar to other right owners have rights and obligations toward utilisation of their land under existing laws and regulations, including laws on spatial planning. For example, in a protected area (*Kawasan Lindung*), as it is with other private rights ownership, activities that can be carried out by rights owner, including MHA, should reflect the legal function of this area. Neither open pit mining nor large scale industrial plantations can be developed in that area. On the other hand, in forest production areas, MHA as rightful owners, are to be consulted and can confer (or withhold) their consent on the use of their areas in accordance with the law. Other than the change of status of customary forest, there are several other legal developments that can be extracted from the Constitutional Court Decision. These relate to the legality of existing regulations, conditions on which MHA are to be recognised and recognition in the context of the Unitary State of the Republic of Indonesia (*Negara Kesatuan Republik Indonesia*/NKRI).

On the first aspect, the Court rejected the plaintiff's proposal to dismiss the Article 67(2) and (3) provisions.[46] The plaintiff argued that because those articles require that acknowledgement and revocation of MHA's right should be conducted through the issuance of Local Regulations and Government Regulations, then these provisions should be dismissed as they contradict Article 18B(2) of the Constitution. Article 18B(2) of the constitution stated 'The States recognises and respects MHA and their traditional rights as long as it is in accordance with society's development and the principles of NKRI under prevailing laws.' The Constitutional Court rejected this argument because the effect of granting the proposal would create loopholes in the legal framework on MHA as there would be no legal instrument for acknowledging MHA. Thus, before a specific law on MHA interests, the existing legal framework should prevail.

On the aspect recognition of MHA standing, the Court emphasised the real existence of MHA and their rights are to be respected so long as this is not against national interest. To be recognised, MHA should not only 'exist' but in fact be 'still alive'.[47] The Constitutional Court stressed that 'if in the progress of development, some MHA does not exist anymore, the customary forest management rights shall be returned to the State, hence the customary forest status will be changed to forest state'.[48] The Court clearly stated that recognition of customary forest is subject to the national interest.[49]

On the third aspect, the Court stated that the existence of MHA is within the framework of the Negara Kesatuan Republik Indonesia (NKRI), the unitary state.[50] Therefore in the context of forest management there will be no 'state within a state'.[51] The Constitutional Court rejected the plaintiff's argument that MHA have rights to freely decide their own fate, political status and to pursue their own economic, social and cultural development.[52] In this context, the Constitutional Court stated that 'the argument

[46] Art 67 (2) stipulates that 'acknowledgement and revocation of MHA as referred to in paragraph (1) is declared by Regional Regulation'.

Art 67 (3) stipulates that 'further provisions as referred to in paragraph (1) and (3), shall be regulated by Government Regulation'.

[47] Consideration part of the Constitutional Court Decision [3.13.2].

[48] Consideration part of the Constitutional Court Decision [3.13.7].

[49] Consideration part of the Constitutional Court Decision [3.13.2].

[50] Decision part of the Constitutional Court Decision [1.3] and [1.4].

[51] Consideration part of the Constitutional Court Decision [3.13.2].

[52] Consideration part of the Constitutional Court Decision [3.13.2].

proposed by the plaintiffs might cause the implication of separatist acts by the MHA', hence contradicting the State's interest and the concept of the NKRI.[53] The amendment of the above mentioned two articles (Article 1(6) and 4(3)) impacted on other articles in the Forestry Law such as Article 5(1) and its explanation, Article 5(2), (3), and (4) and further Article 67(1), (2), and (3).

There exists a regulation of the Head of the National Land Agency No 5/1999 on Settlement Guidelines for MHA's Customary Rights. This provides mechanisms to recognise MHA through Local Regulation. Despite some critiques of this regulation, the Constitutional Court's decision has affirmed that the current laws and regulations should be applied before a specific law is passed. Thus, local government can utilise this particular regulation to recognise the existence of MHA and their areas.

It should also be noted that the access to forest and forest land use should not only rely on the recognition of the idea of customary forest. Other mechanisms for social forestry (*pengelolaan hutan berbasis masyarakat* or PHBM) such as community plantation forests (*hutan tanaman rakyat* or HTR), village forest (*hutan desa* or HD), and community forest (*hutan kemasyrakatan* or HKm) can also be used to provide opportunities for forest dependent communities.[54] Currently, the Ministry of Forestry plans to expand the area of forest granted under these types of licenses to 2.5 million hectares.[55] In a considerably short period of time, the percentage of village forests has reached 3 per cent[56] compared to the percentage in 2009 which was less than 1 per cent.[57]

LICENSING INFORMATION SYSTEM

UKP4 has been developing a prototype for a Licensing Information System (*Sistem Informasi Perizinan* or SIP). It is an online-based platform for licensing, with a database, online application, monitoring and communication features specifically for land-based licenses. This program is intended to strengthen coordination mechanisms between different agencies that have authority over land-based licensing, as well as between local and central level government.

The Licensing Information System initiative reflects the license audits

---

53 Consideration part of the Constitutional Court Decision [3.13.2].
54 See Rahmina (2011).
55 Minister of Forestry (2010).
56 Sadewo (2014).
57 Minister of Forestry (2011).

for forestry, plantation and mining activities. The license audits assess five main aspects of licenses such as management, regulatory and administrative compliance, tenurial, environment, and state revenues. The license reviews have been conducted in eight districts in the provinces of Central Kalimantan, East Kalimantan and Jambi.

The combination of the SIP and license audit is designed to pursue four goals those being: (1) resolving and reducing tenurial conflicts, (2) reducing bureaucratic red-tape, (3) reducing GHGs, and (4) ultimately increasing state revenues, as called '3R+I formula'.

LAW ENFORCEMENT

Forestry and natural resources crimes are multi-sectoral crimes often involving other crimes such as money laundering, gratification, bribery and tax evasion. The prevailing laws and regulations tend to promote a sectoral approach, for example only applying Forestry Law in forest areas rather than also using other laws that might be applicable. This approach has limitations in handling forestry and other natural resources crimes. Encouraging more effective law enforcement, UKP4 coordinated with the Ministry of Forestry, the Ministry of Environment, the Ministry of Finance, the Attorney General, Police Department of Republic of Indonesia and the Indonesian Financial Transaction Reports and Analysis Center (anti money laundering agency) to jointly prepare the Guidance to Handle Criminal Acts Related to Environment/Natural Resources in Forest and Peatland by using a Multi-door Approach (Multi-door Guidelines).

The Multi-door Guidelines have been implemented with success in recent cases of illegal slash and burn activities in the Province of Aceh. PT Kalista Alam was convicted through both civil and criminal charges. With regard to the civil charges, the District Court of Meulaboh declared that PT Kalista Alam was guilty of burning and clearing forest and peatland in violation of Law 32/2009 on Environmental Protection and Management. The court granted the prosecutor's (Ministry of Environment) claims for the company to pay compensation of IDR 114 billion ($10 million) to the state and an environmental restoration fee of IDR 251 billion ($23 million).[58] The related criminal law suit has reached the trial process stage.

Learning from the last two years of experience in preparing REDD+, UKP4 and REDD+ the Presidential Task Force have developed and

---

[58] Satriastanti (2014).

supported better coordination among enforcement agencies, strengthened the integrity of the enforcement officers and enhanced the skill and knowledge in investigation and prosecution natural resources related crimes.

CONCLUDING REMARKS: ARE WE IN THE RIGHT TRACK TO REACH REDD+ BEYOND CARBON, MORE THAN FOREST?

Indonesia REDD+ aims to be *Beyond Carbon, More Than Just Forests*. REDD+ is not merely a tool to reduce emissions from deforestation and degradation, but also an entry point to enhance environmental justice, protect forest, promote profound governance reforms in natural resources management and empower forest dependent communities.

Key factors to promoting good environmental governance and reducing corruption risks include promoting transparency; access to information; genuine public participation together with a clean and responsive bureaucracy; coherent and even-handed legal framework; together with strong law and regulatory enforcement mechanisms. Those key factors are built up through the REDD+ frameworks, REDD+ institutional arrangements and each of the REDD+ programs.

In pursuing its goals of *Beyond Carbon, More Than Just Forests*, the Government of Indonesia, especially the REDD+ Agency has been constantly faced with formidable challenges. The critical challenges are the ongoing prevalence of 'stove pipe' or 'silo' and sectoral defined regulatory and administrative systems that inhibit effective cross-sectoral coordination; poorly structured systems of local governance that discourage sustainable natural resource management; the incapability and incapacity of civil society organisations (CSOs) to effectively advocate to reduce the rapid expansion of natural resource exploitation; and the poor capacity of local political society to strike a better balance between sustainable and unsustainable natural resource exploitation. The 'stove pipe' sectoral approaches severely inhibit if not cripple efforts to create programmatic coherence and integrity at the national level. They contribute to conflicting and disjointed and even corrupted natural resource management. Poorly defined incentive systems that ought to favour sustainable natural resource management locally have led governors, regents, and mayors to enjoy powers and authorities to conduct unsustainable and short term focused natural resources exploitation. A lack of public/citizens control coupled with ineffective law enforcement have contributed to worsening the negative impacts of decentralisation and led to patterns of corruption at local levels. Last, CSOs have not been able to develop optimally a role in criticising and influencing prevailing laws and regulations at the national and sub-national levels. If REDD+ is going to be the entry point to pursue environmental and social justice, those challenges will need to be addressed as matters of highest priority.

REFERENCES

Arnold, L. (2008), 'Deforestation in Decentralised Indonesia: What's Law Got to Do with It?' 4/2 LEAD, accessed 12 March 2015 at http://www.lead-journal.org/content/08075.pdf.

Badan Pusat Statistik, 'Gini Ratio based on Province Year 1996, 1999, 2002, 2005, 2007–2013', accessed 12 March 2015 at http://www.bps.go.id/tab_sub/view.php?kat=1&tabel=1&daftar=1&id_subyek=23&notab=6.

Graef, A. (2014), 'Palm Oil Company Ordered to Pay $30 Million for Illegal Rainforest Destruction' *EcoWatch* (16 January 2014), accessed 12 March 2015 at http://ecowatch.com/2014/01/16/palm-oil-company-to-pay-for-illegal-rainforest-destruction/.

Indrarto, G. *et al.* (2012), 'The Context of REDD+ in Indonesia: Drivers, Agents and Institutions' CIFOR Working Paper 92, accessed 12 March 2015 at http://www.cifor.org/publications/pdf_files/WPapers/WP92Resosudarmo.pdf.

Mangkusubroto, K. (2013), 'Transition Toward REDD+ Agency Operationalization', REDD+ Implementation Conference, Jakarta, October 2013.

Minister of Forestry of the Republic of Indonesia (2010), Minister of Forestry Regulation No. P.51/Menhut-II/2010 on Strategic Plan 2010–2014, accessed 12 March 2015 at http://www.dephut.go.id/uploads/files/P51_2010.pdf.

Minister of Forestry of the Republic of Indonesia (2011), Minister of Forestry Regulation No P.49/Menhut-II/2011 on Forestry Plan at the National Level Year of 2011–2030, accessed 12 March 2015 at http://www.dephut.go.id/uploads/files/DitRenHut_RKTN_2011.pdf.

Rahmina *et al.* (2011), 'Ordinances and Procedures of Community Based Forest Management Program in Framework of Law No 41/1999', accessed 12 March 2015 at http://www.redd-indonesia.org/pdf/Buku_Saku_PHBM_web.pdf.

REDD+ Task Force (2012), Decree of Head of REDD+ Task Force No REDD 02/SATGAS REDD PLUS/09/2012 on REDD+ National Strategy, accessed 25 March 2015 at http://www.reddplus.go.id/program/strategi-nasional-redd.

Sadewo, J. (2014), 'Community Access to Forest is Expanded' Republika, 28 February 2014, accessed 12 March 2015 at http://www.republika.co.id/berita/nasional/umum/14/02/28/n1p8ww-akses-rakyat-atas-hutan-makin-diperluas.

Sambijantoro, S. (2014), 'Rich Benefit Most from RI's Growth, Says Deputy Minister' The Jakarta Post (Jakarta, 7 February 2014), accessed 12 March 2015 at http://www.thejakartapost.com/news/2014/02/07/rich-benefit-most-ri-s-growth-says-deputy-minister.html.

Santosa, M., J. Khatarina and A. Suwana (2013), 'The Progress on Governing REDD+ in Indonesia', International Journal of Rural Law and Policy, accessed 12 March 2015 at http://epress.lib.uts.edu.au/journals/index.php/ijrlp/article/view/3356.

Satriastanti, F. (2014), 'Aceh Peatland Ruling Only First Step in Restoring

Corporate Damage' Thomson Reuters Foundation, 23 January 2014, accessed 12 March 2015 at http://www.trust.org/item/20140123103924-5edrg/.

UKP4 (2013), 'REDD+ in Indonesia: The Road to Implementation' (UKP4); the document was distributed in the Nineteenth Session of the Conference of the Parties (COP 19), 11–22 November 2013, Warsaw, Poland.

UKP4 and MOLHR (2013), '*Peta Jalan Pembaruan Peraturan Perundang-undangan untuk Mendorong Penyempurnaan Tata Kelola Hutan dan Lahan Gambut dalam Kerangka*'/ '*REDD+*/Policy paper on Legislation Road Map to Improve Forest and Peatland Governance and REDD+ Legal Framework', REDD+ Task Force/REDD+ Special Team UKP4 and Ministry of Law and Human Rights of the Republic of Indonesia/MOLHR.

UNDP and UN-REDD+ Programme (2013), *Participatory Governance Assessment: The 2012 Indonesia Forest, Land and REDD+ Governance Index*, UNDP Indonesia, accessed 12 March 2015 at http://www.id.undp.org/content/dam/indonesia/docs/envi/PGA%20Report%20English%20Final.pdf.

Working Group Funding Instrument (2013), 'FREDDI (Fund for REDD+ Indonesia) *Nota Konsep Instrumen Pendanaan REDD+ di Indonesia*' (REDD+ Task Force); the paper was distributed in the 'REDD+ in Indonesia: Preparation to Implementation', 19 December 2013, Four Seasons.

Working Group Funding Instrument (2013), '*Nota Konsep Prinsip Kriteria dan Indikator Safeguards REDD + Indonesia – PRISAI*' (REDD+ Task Force); the paper was distributed in the 'REDD+ In Indonesia: Preparation to Implementation', 19 December 2013, Four Seasons.

Working Group of Moratorium Monitoring (2013), '*Laporan Pemantauan Instruksi Presiden No 10/2011: Hasil Capaian dan Tindak Lanjut*/Report on the Monitoring of President Instruction No 10/2011: Outcomes and Follow-up' (UKP4 and REDD+ Task Force).

Working Group on Forest Land Tenure (2012), 'Konflik, Land Tenure, dan REDD (Conflict, Land Tenure and REDD)' Warta Tenure 10, accessed 12 March 2015 at http://wg-tenure.org/category/warta-tenure/.

Yasmi, Y. *et al.* (2012), 'The struggle over Asia's forests; An overview of forest conflict and potential implications for REDD+', 14(1) *International Forestry Review* 99, accessed 12 March 2015 at http://www.cifor.org/library/3770/the-struggle-over-asias-forests-an-overview-of-forest-conflict-and-potential-implications-for-redd/.

10. Consensus federalism and freshwater regulation

Amelia Keene*

INTRODUCTION

At what level of governance should environmental regulation most effectively be carried out? This chapter reframes and responds to that federalism question by focusing not only on the level of government, but also on how stakeholders are incorporated into the process. It poses as a case study the current freshwater reforms in New Zealand, which are centralising water quality regulations through consensus-based decision-making at both a national and regional level. It labels this process consensus federalism. These reforms can usefully be compared to the environmental federalism[1] of the 1970s in the United States.

Although federalism has been extensively debated,[2] the debate has been preoccupied with constitutional concerns, with little attention paid to the role of consensus-based decision-making. Overall, consensus federalism is a positive development for New Zealand and, based on the United States experience with environmental federalism, can be predicted to lead to improved environmental outcomes. However, some specific criticisms are made of the reforms.

---

* This chapter is an abridged version of an LLM thesis completed in 2013 at Columbia University. My thanks to Professor Michael Gerrard for his supervision and comments, to the lively participants at the 2013 IUCN Colloquium, and to the Andrew Sabin Family Foundation for supporting my attendance.

1 Sovacool (2008); Federalism encapsulates the challenge of 'assigning government authority to the correct level of government in our constitutional structure': Kendall (2004) 2.

2 See eg, Adler (2005); Bulman-Pozen and Gerken (2009); Butler and Macey (1996); Engel (2006); Kincaid (1990); Schapiro (2005); Revesz (1992).

THE FRESHWATER PROBLEM

New Zealand does not suffer the water scarcity issues that make management of freshwater resources so challenging in many countries. Yet it is struggling to sustainably manage its freshwater resources. Climate change will put greater pressure on the quantity of water available, exacerbating existing water quality issues.[3] Studies of freshwater quality in New Zealand belie its clean and green image. In 2012, 69 per cent of freshwater beaches were graded as fair, poor or very poor for the purposes of summer recreation, with 45 per cent deemed unsuitable for swimming.[4] The biggest source of water quality pollution in New Zealand is diffuse pollution, particularly sediment, and nitrates, ammonia and phosphorous pollution from sewage and animal effluent.[5] Overall water quality is declining. Thus in evaluating any reform of clean water regulation, special consideration should be given to control of diffuse pollution.

REGULATION IN NEW ZEALAND

This section analyses New Zealand's existing environmental law framework from the perspective of environmental federalism, to illustrate the extent to which significant matters of freshwater regulation have previously and are currently left to regions to determine with limited national guidance. This is true historically.[6] Before the Resource Management Act 1991 (RMA), and leaving aside the complex question of Maori customary law,[7] water quality was principally the responsibility of local-level government. While the enactment of the RMA in 1991 heralded a statutory change towards greater centralisation on its face, local and regional councils retained control in practice.[8]

---

3 Hennessy *et al.* (2007) 508.

4 Ministry for the Environment, Indicator Update: INFO 653, (October 2012).

5 Parliamentary Commissioner for the Environment, 'Water Quality in New Zealand: Understanding the Science' (March 2012, Wellington) 6; Parliamentary Commissioner for the Environment, 'Water Quality in New Zealand: Land use and nutrient pollution' (November 2013, Wellington) 65.

6 Wheen (1997).

7 Patterson (1994); Wheen (1997); Dawson (2008).

8 Randerson (1999).

The Resource Management Act 1991

Since 1991, the principal environmental statute in New Zealand, the RMA, has provided a number of legal mechanisms to regulate freshwater quality. Subsection 5(1) provides the principal goal: to promote the 'sustainable management of natural and physical resources'. This recognises the importance of the 'life-supporting capacity of water', and of managing water in a way that provides social, economic and cultural well-being for communities today and in the future.[9] While 'sustainable management' has been interpreted broadly,[10] its inter-relationship with the other principles set out in sections 5 to 8 remains contested.[11] The purposive section does not provide useful guidance about the level of pollutants permissible in specific waterways. Neither does the RMA provide any concrete indication of what polluting activities might be permitted or prohibited, or what life supporting means.

Instead, decisions are delegated to the council with little guidance. Section 15 of the RMA prohibits any discharge of a contaminant into water, unless permitted by a rule in a regional plan, a resource consent, or regulations made under the RMA. Under s 30, regional councils must control land uses to maintain and enhance water quality, and to control the taking, damming, diversion and discharge of contaminants into water. Such discharges are managed through the resource consent process, and through the regional plan and regulations.

It could be argued that s 15 prohibits diffuse pollution without resource consent. Unlike the United States Clean Water Act, which provides expressly that NPDES permits are required only for point source discharges,[12] s 15 uses broader language, prohibiting any 'discharge' of contaminants, defined to include 'emit, deposit, and allow to escape'.[13] In practice, however, consents for diffuse discharges are not required,[14] and few councils have imposed rules on diffuse discharges.[15] At least one case has suggested that councils should adopt more stringent measures to

---

9 Resource Management Act 1991 (NZ), s 5(2) (RMA).

10 *North Shore City Council v Auckland Regional Council* [1997] NZRMA 59, 94 (EC); *Watercare Services Ltd v Minhinnick* [1998] 1 NZLR 294, 305 (CA).

11 Dawson (2013).

12 Clean Water Act 1972 (US), §502(12)(A) [CWA]: 'discharge of a pollutant' means 'any addition of any pollutant to navigable waters from any point source'; §301

13 RMA, s 2; *McKnight v NZ Biogas Industries Ltd* [1994] 2 NZLR 664 (CA).

14 *Carter Holt Harvey Ltd v Waikato Regional Council EC Auckland* A123/08, 6 November 2008.

15 Drummond (2006). Canterbury is an exception.

address diffuse discharges, but the court declined to rule on whether they could constitute a discharge under s 15.[16]

The national government can step in if councils are failing to implement an effective freshwater management framework, but this provision has rarely been used.[17]

The RMA attempts to provide some policy direction through the water quality system established by s 69 and the Third Schedule. It sets out different water classes that a council may adopt to manage a water body. However it is a purely voluntary system that provides little meaningful guidance.[18] Many of the standards are circular and do not quantify a base-load level of contaminants for each class.[19] It is not easy to translate the classes into practical reference points to control actual discharge levels. While councils cannot put blanket rules in their plans permitting the most conspicuous forms of pollution,[20] the RMA does not prevent resource consents being granted for the same activity. Nothing tells councils to what standard they must manage water supplies, or sets baselines for the amount of contaminants a waterway can reasonably bear. Water quality management under the RMA occurs at a regional level through the use of the consenting process, which are granted in accordance with regional rules and plans.

While the RMA provides procedures for national policies to be set, through national environmental standards,[21] or national policy statements,[22] no national guidance on freshwater quality was issued until the NPSFM in 2011. As cabinet documents recognise:[23]

---

16 *Day v Manawatu-Wanganui Regional Council* [2012] NZEnv 182, para 5.77; not affected by subsequent decisions: [2012] NZEnvC 285; [2013] NZEnvC 44.

17 RMA, ss 25(1), 25A and 25B. But see: Brower (2010).

18 Even if implemented in the plan, the standards may be breached by the council, as long as it considers the breach as part of the overall assessment of a resource consent application: *Director-General of Conservation (Nelson-Marlborough Conservancy) v Marlborough DC* [2010] NZEnvC 403.

19 For instance, the standard for water being managed in its natural state is water in its natural state: RMA, Schedule 2(9), Class NS Water.

20 RMA, s 70.

21 RMA, s 43; New Zealand Law Society Submission on Proposed Amendments to the National Policy Statement for Freshwater Management 2011, 4 February 2014, arguing that an NES is the correct mechanism for water quality attributes to be set.

22 RMA, s 45.

23 New Zealand Cabinet Paper, Office of the Minister of Agriculture, 'New Start for Fresh Water' (CAB Min (09) 20/12), at [28], available at www.mfe.govt.nz (accessed 20 March 2015).

> New Zealand's highly devolved resource management frameworks mean that regional councils make almost all the most technically and politically difficult decisions on water management, including the setting of community outcomes, often with limited guidance or support from central government.

Thus the original intent of the RMA, to set a national 'biophysical bottom line that must not be compromised',[24] is only now being realised through the reforms.

Reforms: 2010 to 2014

New Zealand adopted a novel approach to reforming the regulatory system. Policy-makers decided on a consensus-based approach (modeled on Danish participatory decision-making)[25] both for the reform process and for decision-making under the new regulatory framework. Formed in 2008, the Land and Water Forum comprises of a range of industry groups, environmental and recreational non-governmental organisations, indigenous Maori representatives, scientists and others. In 2010, the Ministry for the Environment commissioned and funded it to recommend potential reform of New Zealand's freshwater management.[26] The Forum has released three reports. One of its key points was that water was not being managed according to limits, in part due to a failure by central government to use national instruments to provide direction.[27] This has particular implications for diffuse discharges, and means cumulative effects on water bodies are not properly being taken into account.

In response to the first report, the government gazetted the NPSFM. It recognises freshwater management as a nationally significant issue requiring central government direction, and is intended to establish clear limits for water management. However it gives little more than aspirational guidance for regional councils. For instance, the first objective is to: 'safeguard the life-supporting capacity, ecosystem processes and indigenous species including their associated ecosystems of fresh water, in sustainably managing the use and development of land, and of discharges

24 (July 1991) 51b Hansard, Resource Management Bill, 3rd reading; RMA, s 5(2).

25 Andersen and Jaeger (1999).

26 See Letter from Office of Hon. Dr Nick Smith, Minister for the Environment, to Alastair Bisley, Chairman of the Land and Water Forum, setting out the mandate for the project, (14 September 2009), available at www.landandwater.org.nz (accessed 20 March 2015).

27 Land and Water Forum, 'Report of the Land and Water Forum: A Fresh Start for Fresh Water' (September 2010, Wellington) viii.

of contaminants.' Councils must establish their own freshwater objectives and water quality limits in regional plans, and establishing methods to avoid over-allocation of water bodies, either through rule-making or conditions placed on discharge resource consents. The NPSFM must be implemented: 'as promptly as is reasonable in the circumstances, and so it is fully completed no later than 31 December 2030', more than 20 years after the NPSFM was first proposed in 2009.[28]

One legal issue arising out of the NPSFM concerns transitional application. Section 55 of the RMA stipulates that national policy statements must be implemented 'as soon as practicable', or 'within the time specified in the national policy statement'. The standard provided by the NPSFM is 'as promptly as is reasonable in the circumstances', arguably allowing more time than the standard otherwise set by s 55, since it allows for all circumstances to be considered. Prima facie, s 55 provides two alternatives, so that the policy statement might stipulate a longer implementation period thereby displacing the 'practicable' s 55 standard. But the NPSFM does not explain its application to plans already proposed, but not implemented, before the NPSFM came into force. It is not clear whether those plans must take the NPSFM into account at all, and if so, whether under the s 55 practicable standard, or the reasonable standard in the NPSFM. If the latter, this raises retrospectivity issues. In practice, proposed plans should probably be brought into compliance where possible.[29]

While the NPSFM can be seen as an example of cooperative federalism,[30] it continues to prioritise regional expertise over national centralisation. This philosophy is reflected in the implementation guidance: 'it is up to local authorities and their communities to determine appropriate local objectives and methods'. [31] Moreover, it provides abstract objectives that are not quantified so as to allow council implementation. At worst, it could be read as mandating a netting approach since it is focused on protecting the 'overall' water quality and 'ecosystem' of a region, expressly

---

[28] Ibid, policy 1(b).

[29] *Day v Manawatu-Wanganui Regional Council* [2012] NZENV 182 paras 5–186–5.190.

[30] Sovacool (2008) 418: 'broad, overlapping authority between levels of government is essential to promoting regulatory activity and ensuring environmental protection'.

[31] Ministry for the Environment, 'National Policy Statement on Freshwater Management 2011: Implementation Guide' (Wellington, 2011) para 1.3; Cabinet paper, 'Fresh Start for Fresh Water – High level Government Response to the Land and Water Forum Report' (8 August 2011) 13.

recognising that: 'a bottom line of at least maintaining all aspects of water quality everywhere is not possible'.[32]

By failing to provide meaningful water quality standards, the NPSFM makes little progress on the status quo. Moreover, the long implementation period means that changes to the water quality may not be seen for another 20 years. This creates a risk that during the transition period polluters will have an incentive to pollute more to preserve their position once the regime is tightened.[33]

The NPSFM can also be criticised for not setting out how the policies will be enforced, except through self-monitoring. Where objectives are not met, councils are directed to 'specify targets and implement methods' to assist the improvement of water quality in water bodies 'within a defined time frame', and can use any method appropriate (voluntary or rule-based).[34] The council defines the time frame and the methods to be adopted.

The NPSFW was not an independent product of the Land and Water Forum. The government had already drafted it when it commissioned the first report. The Forum had a broader mandate for its second and third reports, to consider how the government should set objectives for the state of water bodies and limits on takes and discharges, how to manage within those limits, and how to improve the decision-making processes.[35] It used this broader mandate to emphasise the need for central regulation capable of being implemented by regional councils.

In its second report the Forum pushed for a set of national 'bottom lines' for water quality, and argued that it was appropriate for the numeric freshwater state objectives to be set at a regional level, noting the difficulty in setting these on a national scale.[36] Water quality standards should be generated at a central level, with different quantified levels of pollutants. It would then be up to local government to decide the level to which water sources should be managed. This proposal would entail the creation of national bottom lines, whereby the lowest water standard that regional councils could choose would constitute a national minimum standard for all waterways.[37]

---

32 Ibid., Objective A2, 12.

33 Land and Water Forum, 'Second Report of the Land and Water Forum: Setting Limits for Water Quality and Quantity, Freshwater Policy and Plan-Making Through Collaboration' (April 2012), xi.

34 National Policy Statement on Freshwater, Policy A2, 6.

35 Land and Water Forum, 'Second Report', iii.

36 Ibid, viii, 12.

37 Ibid, viii.

In its Third Report, the Forum considered how the freshwater objectives and limits would be implemented through the regional planning process.[38] It recommended that a set of management techniques and tools be developed at a national level, while recognising that different tools might be appropriate for different physical, economic and community features of a catchment. It recommended that thresholds be developed, at which greater management of discharges will become necessary; and that regional councils should be able to implement a system of tradeable discharge allowances. Finally, it suggested interim measures be put in place during the transition period to the new regime.

The Land and Water Forum also made some comments about the process of regulatory decision-making. It proposed a consensus decision-making system similar to the process it had adopted in writing the reports, which could also apply at the regional level. It argued that a collaborative approach to freshwater governance should be adopted whereby stakeholders come together to directly negotiate and explore the values and interests of all participants early on in the planning process. This would lead to more durable and resilient outcomes. Somewhat ironically, one of the few areas on which the Forum did not reach a consensus was on this recommendation.[39]

In response to these reports, the government issued a discussion paper endorsing most of the proposals in the Land and Water Forum reports but restricting initial progressing to what it defined as the Forum's core proposals: collaborative planning and the national objectives framework.[40] This ignored the fact that the Forum had several times stressed that its suggested reform proposals be adopted as a package, since it had been negotiated as such.

The proposed National Objectives Framework would replace s 69 and Schedule 3 of the RMA. It would set numerical attribute bands to which waterways can be measured for different values. The bottom band would set the bottom-line, representing the minimum acceptable state at which the water must be managed. For example, the value 'natural form and character' would have attribute bands assigned for temperature, slime, sediment, flows and connectivity. The regional council would make the decision about which values to manage to. However, the national government would prescribe certain values and attributes for all water bodies, thus setting a national bottom line.

---

38 Land and Water Forum, 'Third Report of the Land and Water Forum: Managing Water Quality and Allocating Water' (October 2012).

39 Ibid, iii.

40 Ministry for the Environment, 'Freshwater reform 2013 and beyond' (2013, Wellington).

The efficacy of these proposals will turn on the stringency of the limits and how they are implemented and enforced. The Ministry for the Environment has proposed calling a panel of scientific experts to set the bands. One issue not clearly articulated in the reform proposals is what the 'bottom-lines' will represent. They cannot simply reflect the current bottom line since some waterways are already over-allocated. But neither should they reflect the 'tipping-point' at which water bodies cannot recover. It is important that this issue is clarified before being referred to the panel. Some guidance is provided by the language in the NPSFM, which provides that the 'life-supporting capacity, ecosystem processes and indigenous species including their associated ecosystems' of freshwater must be protected. This suggests a relatively high environmental standard but may be challenging for scientists to quantify in practice. Unfortunately, early indications from leaked copies of the proposed bottom lines suggest that this process is not independent of political pressure, the draft limits have been criticised as being 'extremely weak' on key measures, including on nitrates in rivers and streams.[41]

Implementation by regional councils will be done largely through regional plans and in the issuance of resource consents subject to those plans. But the government will also provide non-binding guidance in the form of 'sector-based user-friendly good management practice toolkits' that will suggest practical measures to reduce contaminant discharges into water, such as upgrading effluent treatment facilities, changing wintering practices or fencing off streams or waterways. This matches the Forum recommendations that deciding which tools to use would be a local decision. But certain recommendations of the Forum were not taken up, such as the idea of tradeable discharge allowances.

REGULATION IN THE UNITED STATES

The Clean Water Act 1972

This section offers a brief overview of the history of water regulation in the United States as a comparison point to the New Zealand reforms. The Clean Water Act (CWA), first adopted in 1972 as the Amendments to the Water Pollution Control Act, heralded a shift towards centralisation of environmental regulation. Its aim was 'to restore and maintain the

---

41 Adam Bennett, 'Draft water plan a "licence to pollute"', The New Zealand Herald, 11 September 2013.

chemical, physical, and biological integrity of the Nation's waters'.[42] As the Senate subcommittee noted in voting unanimously to support the proposed bill, states had been 'lagging' in the setting of water quality standards, resulting in many of the nation's navigable waters being 'severely polluted'.[43]

The cornerstone of the CWA is a ban on the discharge of any pollutants to navigable waters from any point sources except with a permit under the Act.[44] The Act establishes the National Pollutant Discharge Elimination System (NPDES) system, to be administered by the Environmental Protection Agency (EPA), or by the states under delegated authority.[45] The permits must be issued in accordance with the technology-based effluent limitations set under the CWA,[46] which vary according to the pollutant and where it is being discharged.[47] EPA also set new source performance standards for new pollution sources[48] and pre-treatment standards necessary for the public treatment facilities funded by the Act to operate correctly.[49] States remain responsible for adopting and reviewing water quality criteria and standards, and for establishing total maximum daily loads (TMDL).[50] The TMDLs define the maximum amount of a pollutant that can be discharged into the water segment without violating the water quality standard. Whilst subject to EPA approval, this is rarely withheld. States bear responsibility for regulating diffuse discharges.

The CWA represented a significant shift of power to the federal level. It reflects a cooperative federalism model, since responsibility for implementation was delegated to the states. It also heralded a shift from state-level water quality standards to national-level base limitations unrelated to water quality and given effect through the NPDES permits. The division of responsibilities between federal and state level is not necessarily logical or coherent.[51] Water permitting is overseen at a federal level, but delegated to states.[52] States retain primary authority over water quality requirements, although the federal government acts as a backstop. States

---

42 CWA, § 101(a).

43 S.Rep.No.92–414, 92d Cong. 92 (1971), in 2A 'Legislative History of the Water Pollution Control Act Amendments of 1972', at 1422–5 (1973).

44 CWA, § 301, "point sources" is defined in §502(14).

45 CWA, § 402.

46 CWA, § 301(b).

47 CWA, § 302.

48 CWA, § 306.

49 CWA, § 304.

50 CWA, § 303.

51 Craig (2010), 203.

52 CWA, §§ 306(b), 404(g), 101(g).

also have exclusive authority over nonpoint source regulation[53] and waters that are not 'navigable waters'.[54] The CWA sets a federal 'floor' for water quality degradation, through the effluent limitations, but states are free to impose more stringent water quality protections within their respective borders through the TMDL provisions.

Environmental Federalism and the Clean Water Act

Environmental federalism in the United States has been effective in improving environmental protection overall. The CWA significantly reduced point source effluent and raised the quality of waterways.[55] Point source discharges from industry dropped 98 per cent.[56] Many polluted waterways made remarkable recoveries.

The challenge that still remains is that of diffuse pollution, which was left to state and local governments by the CWA. Approximately 82 per cent of the rivers and streams that fail to meet water quality standards, and 77 per cent of lakes, are impaired due to agricultural run-off and hydrological modifications. Diffuse discharges could be addressed in part by water quality standards such as TMDLs being fully implemented.[57] But this method has had limited success in dealing with run-off from agricultural facilities,[58] meaning that new innovation is probably necessary.

It would an error to attribute environmental improvements in the United States wholly to environmental federalism, or to state failings.[59] The introduction of the CWA coincided with growing awareness of environmental issues in the United States.[60] The environmental movement may be responsible for some of the improved environmental outcomes, as it created new social and economic incentives for industrial polluters to stop obvious forms of pollution.

Moreover, the CWA was the culmination of a long period of 'creeping federalisation'.[61] Congress had been incrementally increasing federal

---

53 CWA, § 208.

54 CWA, § 402(a).

55 Andreen (2003).

56 Ibid, 591.

57 Houck (1999) 10471; *Pronsolino v Nastri* (2002) 291 F.3d 1123 (9th Cir); *Friends of Pinto Creek v EPA* (2007) 504 F3d 1007 (9th Cir).

58 *Assateague Coastkeeper v Maryland Dept. of the Environment* (2011) 200 Md App 655.

59 Caputo (1997); Adler (2004).

60 Sovacool (2008) 410–11 also points to the growing nationalisation of American politics, frustration with the states, and a rise in rent-seeking.

61 Percival (1995) 1155.

involvement in water regulation since 1948, and simultaneously, the states had been gradually improving their environmental regulation. State and local legislatures had taken steps through the 1950s and 1960s to recognise the importance of water quality, and by 1966 every state had some water pollution legislation.[62]

Nevertheless, serious environmental concerns remained. The federalisation of water regulation came after a long history of state inadequacy.[63] The enactment of the CWA represented an effective power shift away from the states.[64]

COMPARATIVE ANALYSIS

Some important lessons can be taken from the American experience. The United States centralised much of its freshwater quality regulation in the CWA in 1972, and its federal system works both through quality standards (TDMLs) and permits, whereas the RMA in New Zealand remains solely a consent-based system. The American system also emphasises dialogue and cooperation between the federal government and the states, but does not focus on community involvement.

Substantively, New Zealand is moving closer to the American model, by implementing a dual system of quality limits and permits. Both countries are now focusing on effluent limits to deal with diffuse pollution. Yet it is significant that the United States has not so far succeeded in dealing with diffuse discharges under the CWA, particularly agricultural discharges. This suggests the New Zealand reforms may not be sufficient to deal with diffuse discharges.

Instead, two changes to the New Zealand reforms are advisable. First, a renewed focus on technology standards. For instance, some of the tools in the 'toolbox' of good management techniques could be made mandatory, such as a nationally mandated rule that all stock are fenced off from water supplies where possible,[65] or requiring all farms to have nutrient management plans. This would make enforcement easier to manage since there would be clear minimum steps that all polluters were required to

---

62 Revesz (2009) 578–9.

63 Percival (1995) 1144.

64 Craig (2010) 203.

65 The Dairying and Clean Streams Accord signed by the country's major dairy companies and central and regional government agencies, sets a voluntary target of excluding dairy cattle from 90% of streams, rivers, and lakes by 2012. A binding measure would be preferable.

take regardless of overall limits. This is particularly important since the science and modelling of effluent discharges is not exact, meaning it may be difficult to enforce quality standards.

Another option would be to use the reforms to clarify that diffuse pollution constitute a 'discharge' and thus require a resource consent under s 15. Arguably, the wording of s 15 already covers diffuse pollution, but it is not being interpreted in this way. The easiest way to effect this change would be through a statutory amendment to s 15. Alternatively, or in conjunction, a specific National Environmental Standard could be developed that deals with diffuse pollution and prescribes land use so as to control diffuse pollutants.[66]

A few other brief comments on the reforms are appropriate. First, one potential problem is that enforcement mechanisms are not well-articulated:[67]

> Where a freshwater body is below the minimum acceptable state it would need to be improved over time. There is no proposal to set a deadline at the national level for when minimum states must be met. It is more important for the focus to be on choosing regionally appropriate improvement pathways and timeframes to minimise costs to resource users and communities.

One important lesson from the American experience is the importance of having a stipulated timeframe for compliance with environmental law, with clear consequences and enforcement mechanisms if this is not done.[68] Secondly, the proposal to reduce appeal rights where the consensus approach is used should be abandoned.[69] Preserving robust alternative decision-making processes, including appeals, support the consensus process by providing a fall back where it fails.

CONSENSUS FEDERALISM

There is limited comparative literature on freshwater quality regulation in New Zealand,[70] and even less comparing the United States and New Zealand.[71] However, such comparative study is rewarding. In the United

---

66 Green Party of Aotearoa New Zealand, 'Freshwater reform 2013 and beyond: Submission guide' (April 2013).

67 Ministry for the Environment, 'Freshwater reform 2013 and beyond', 34.

68 Wiseman (2012).

69 Ministry for the Environment, 'Freshwater reform 2013 and beyond', 26.

70 Anker (2003); Peart (2001).

71 Summits and Morrison (2001).

States, environmental federalism is a dominant legal framework used to study environmental regulation. It has provoked a rich academic literature.[72] This compares with New Zealand, where limited consideration has been given to the question of the level of government at which environmental policy is set and implemented. New Zealand federalist concerns rarely went beyond a lament for the lack of national policy statements despite the promise of the RMA.[73]

The reform process in New Zealand has been based on the concept of consensus. The Land and Water Forum represents a landmark shift in the way that environmental regulation is being set. Rather than having environmental policy dominated by the politics of the government in power, the political trade-offs are being made between the key stakeholders, industry, government, indigenous people and environmentalists. This consensus-based process thus helps insulate the process from overt politicisation. While the minister ultimately makes the final decisions in conjunction with cabinet, the government has so far substantially adopted the recommendations of the Land and Water Forum.[74] One can predict that similar results will emerge at a regional level also, with the possibility for local communities, by consensus, to surpass the limits prescribed by national government. It is likely that this consensus-based process will not be used only in setting the water quality objectives, but may be implemented more broadly in environmental planning in New Zealand in future. The process will also enable inclusion of indigenous Maori more directly than has occurred in the past.

One risk of a consensus model is that it does not lead to the best environmental results.[75] Consensus decisions may be skewed in favour of those with the most at stake or the strongest voices, or simply result in adoption of the lowest common denominator. Yet, as a case study, the Land and Water Forum process suggests such fears are not justified. Its recommendations are for far-reaching reforms that will significantly progress environmental protection.[76] Its success reflects the recognition by all stakeholders of a common interest for environmental protection and preservation of freshwater resources, and adequate institutional support. The Forum was given a unique political space in which to operate, and

---

72 See eg Engel (2006); Adler (2005) 153.

73 Drummond (2006).

74 See Cabinet paper, 'Fresh Start for Fresh Water – High Level Government Response to the Land and Water Forum Report' (8 August 2011).

75 Lavigne (2003) 38; McCloskey (2000).

76 Although this is difficult to quantify empirically, particularly at this stage of the reform process. See further: Wondolleck and Yaffee (2000), xiii.

its participants engaged in the process in good faith and a willingness to make hard compromises, none more than its core recommendation for national water quality values. The same common interest in protecting water quality also exists at a local level, meaning that similar results may be possible.

While past work on consensus-decision-making in environmental law has focused on ensuring legitimacy,[77] it is also important that a fall back process is available. The consensus process should complement, not replace, democratic governance.[78] An available alternative reduces pressure on participants to reach an unsatisfactory decision for the sake of a decision. Even if a consensus decision is not possible, however, the process may still serve to narrow the sphere of disagreement to be resolved by the final adjudicator or decision-maker.

New Zealand's freshwater reform process does not fit previous models of federalism.[79] The cooperative or collaborative federalism models do not take into account the process by which stakeholders are incorporated into the decision-making process.[80] Instead, they simply assume that local regulation will be more inclusive.[81] By contrast, consensus federalism ensures that environmental decision-making is being made by all stakeholders at both a national and local level.

As with cooperative federalism, the national framework sets bottom lines without pre-empting more stringent local controls. However the consensus-based approach changes the role of officials from primary decision-maker to mediator and final decision-maker. The concept of consensus federalism encompasses the process and people involved in decision-making, as well as the level of government that makes the ultimate decision. It ensures that communities are concretely incorporated into the process of setting environmental regulation, whilst allowing core baselines to be set at a national level.

The unique aspect of consensus federalism is that, in the event that a consensus can be reached, the outcome is more durable, less-politicised, and less likely to be litigated than if made by traditional decision-makers. As New Zealand's Deputy Secretary at the Ministry for the Environment put it, since 'the stakeholders have all lobbied each other' there has been

---

[77] Mascarenhas and Scarce (2004).

[78] Compare McCloskey (2000) 426.

[79] See eg, Adler (2005); Bulman-Pozen and Gerken (2009); Butler and Macey (1996); Engel (2006); Kincaid (1990); Schapiro (2005); Revesz (1992).

[80] Burleson (2012).

[81] Sovacool (2008).

limited political pressure on the national government.[82] It can be predicted that the same result will occur at a regional level.

CONCLUSION

The Freshwater reform process in New Zealand provides a model for how the balance between top-down environmental policies and community participation might be struck. Labelled 'consensus federalism' by this paper, its methodology is to set national bottom-lines through a science-driven and consensus-based approach that incorporates all the relevant stakeholders, and to allow communities an ongoing role in a consensus-based forum to set specific environmental objectives within national parameters. While much has been written on consensus decision-making,[83] the contribution of this chapter is to consider its role in constitutional terms by looking at the New Zealand freshwater reforms as a case study. Whilst highlighting some substantive concerns, particularly the response to diffuse pollution, the paper concludes that overall the reforms will be a positive development for New Zealand. The New Zealand government should be commended for finally returning to the vision in the RMA for nationally driven environmental policies and should follow through by fully implementing the recommendations of the Land and Water Forum. Consensus federalism promises a more centralised, dynamic regulatory system that will address water quality issues in a multi-faceted and effective way whilst allowing for the input of community knowledge and concerns. The concept of consensus federalism may transcend domestic legal systems and have application in international law contexts also.

REFERENCES

Adler, J. (2004), 'The Fable of Federal Environmental Regulation: Reconsidering the Federal Role in Environmental Protection' 55 Case W Res L Rev 93.

Adler, J. (2005), 'Jurisdictional Mismatch in Environmental Federalism' 14 NYU Envtl LJ 130.

Andersen, I. and B. Jaeger (1999), 'Scenario Workshops and Consensus Conferences: Towards More Democratic Decision-Making' 26(5) *Science and Public Policy* 331.

---

[82] Author interview with Guy Beatson, Deputy Secretary, Policy, Ministry for the Environment, 4 March 2013.

[83] See further: Coglianese (1997).

Andreen, W. (2003), 'The Evolution of Water Pollution Control in the United States – State, Local and Federal Efforts 1782–1972: Part II' 22 Stan Envtl L J 215.

Anker, H. (2003), 'The Resource Management Act and Protection of Water Quality – A Comparison with European Initiatives' 7 NZ J Envtl L 1.

Bennett, A. 'Draft Water Plan a "Licence to Pollute"' The New Zealand Herald, 11 September 2013.

Brower, A. (2010) 'Legislation Note: Environment Canterbury (Temporary Commissioners and Improved Water Management) Act 2010' 14 NZ J Envtl L 309.

Bulman-Pozen, J. and H. Gerken (2009), 'Uncooperative Federalism' 118 Yale LJ 1256.

Burleson, E. (2012), 'Cooperative Federalism and Hydraulic Fracturing: A Human Right to a Clean Environment' 22 Cornell JL & Pub Poly 289.

Butler, H. and J. Macey (1996), 'Externalities and the Matching Principle: The Case for Reallocating Environmental Regulatory Authority' 14 YLLPR 23.

Caputo, D. (1997), 'A Job Half Finished: The Clean Water Act After 25 Years' 27 Envtl L Rep 10574.

Coglianese, C. (1997) 'Assessing Consensus: The Promise and Performance of Negotiated Rulemaking' 46 Duke LJ 1255.

Craig, R. (2010), 'Adapting Water Federalism to Climate Change Impacts: Energy Policy, Food Security, and the Allocation of Water Resources' 5 Envt'l & Energy L & Pol'y 183.

Dawson, A. (2013) 'How to Defend (and Attack) the Resource Management Act: The Principled Consequences of Reducing Public Participation in Environmental Decision-making' Otago Yearbook of Legal Research accessed 20 March 2015 at http://www.otago.ac.nz/law/research/journals/.

Dawson, J. (2008) 'The Resistance of the New Zealand Legal System to Recognition of Maori Customary Law' 12(1) J Sth Pac L 56.

Drummond, L. (2006) 'Managing the Environmental Effects of Agriculture under the Resource Management Act: Non-point Source Discharges' 10 NZ J Envtl L 255.

Engel, K. (2006), 'Harnessing the Benefits of Dynamic Federalism in Environmental Law' 56 Emory LJ 159.

Hennessy, K. *et al.* (2007), '2007: Australia and New Zealand. Climate Change 2007: Impacts, Adaptation and Vulnerability'. Contribution of Working Group II to M.L. Parry and others (eds), *The Fourth Assessment Report of the Intergovernmental Panel on Climate Change* (CUP).

Houck, O. (1999), 'TMDLs IV: The Final Frontier' 29 Envtl L Rep 10469.

Kendall, D. (2004) 'Redefining Federalism' in D. Kendall (ed.) Redefining Federalism: Listening to the States in Shaping 'Our Federalism' (Washington, DC: ELI).

Kincaid, J. (1990) 'From Cooperative to Coercive Federalism' 509 Annals Am Pol and Soc Sci 139.

Lavigne, P. (2003), 'The Movement for American Ecosystem Restoration and Interactive Environmental Decisionmaking: Quagmire, Diversion, or Our Last, Best Hope' 17 TLNEJL 1.

Mascarenhas, M. and R. Scarce (2004), '"The Intention Was Good": Legitimacy, Consensus-Based Decision Making, and the Case of Forest Planning in British Columbia, Canada' 17 *Society and Natural Resources* 17.

McCloskey, M. (2000), 'Problems with Using Collaboration to Shape Environmental Policy' 34 Val U L Rev 423.

Patterson, J. (1994), 'Maori Environmental Virtues' 16 *Environmental Ethics* 397.

Peart, R. (2001), 'Innovative Approaches to Water Resource Management: A Comparison of the New Zealand and South African Approaches' 5 NZ J Env L 127.

Percival, R. (1995), 'Environmental Federalism: Historical Roots and Contemporary Models' 54 Md L Rev 1141.

Randerson, A. (1999), 'Environmental Law and Justice – A Perspective on Three Decades of Practices and Some Possibilities for the Future' 3 NZ J Envtl L 1.

Revesz, R. (1992), 'Rehabilitating Interstate Competition: Rethinking the "Race-to-the-Bottom" Rationale for Federal Environmental Regulation' 67 NYU L Rev 1210.

Revesz, R. (2009), 'Federalism and Environmental Regulation: A Public Choice Analysis' 115 Harv L Rev 533.

Schapiro, R. (2005), 'Towards a Theory of Interactive Federalism' (2005) 91 Iowa L Rev 243.

Sovacool, B. (2008), 'The Best of Both Worlds: Environmental Federalism and the Need for Federal Action on Renewable Energy and Climate Change' 27 Stanford Envtl LJ 397.

Summits, A. and J. Morrison (2001), 'Creating a Framework for Sustainability in California: Lessons Learned from the New Zealand Experience, A Report of the Pacific Institute for Studies in Development, Environment, and Security' (December).

Wheen, N. (1997), 'A Natural Flow – A History of Water Law in New Zealand' 9 Otago L Rev 71.

Wiseman, H. (2012), 'Fracturing Regulation Applied' (2012) 22 Duke Envtl L and Poly F 361.

Wondolleck, J. and S. Yaffee (2000), *Making Collaboration Work: Lessons from Innovation in Natural Resource Management* (Washington, DC: Island Press).

11. International environmental governance in the Pacific island region

Justin Gregory Rose

INTRODUCTION

Upon achieving independence in the second half of the twentieth century the national governments of the Pacific island region commenced participating actively in the processes and institutions of international environmental law. Pacific island countries (PICs) can be seen to have 'taken to heart the keynote concepts of the magnificent declarations in the preamble of the UN Charter, including the reaffirmation of the equal rights of nations large and small, and respect for international law'.[1] Cooperation among the states of the region for the purpose of engaging with international environmental legal processes is also common, in large part because '[f]or the small, there is always safety and strength in numbers'.[2]

The outcomes of Pacific engagement in international environmental governance are mixed. On one hand there is clearly a need to join the international community in developing and implementing multilateral environment agreements (MEAs) of relevance to the region. Pacific environments and societies have undoubtedly benefited from various protections and entitlements enshrined in international legal regimes. Perhaps ironically, during the past two decades the institutional and financing activities surrounding global conventions can be seen to have rendered irrelevant existing Pacific regional environmental treaty law and smothered its further development. Key stakeholders have recently begun voicing concerns identifying a substantial disconnect between international environmental governance and national and sub-national planning and priority-setting in PICs. This disconnect, combined with the costs and burdens required of small PIC governments of maintaining national MEA participation and

[1] Slade (2003) 531–2.
[2] Ibid.

compliance, is recognised as preventing optimal environmental, social and administrative outcomes from being achieved.

In assessing questions of environmental justice as embodied within international legal systems, it is appropriate to investigate how effectively and equitably those systems are serving the smallest, and in some respects most vulnerable, members of the international community.

This chapter describes and critically re-evaluates the role and impact of international and regional environmental law in the Pacific island region. It commences by summarising the historical and geographic context of Pacific island involvement in the development and implementation of regional and international environmental law, the status of that involvement is then reviewed, and the final section analyses the consequent outcomes and discusses possible reforms.

THE PACIFIC ISLAND REGION

The 22 Pacific Island Countries and Territories (PICTs) control a vast expanse of more than 38 million square kilometres.[3] Only 2 per cent of this area is land, which is divided between approximately 30,000 islands. The Exclusive Economic Zone (EEZ) of the Federated States of Micronesia (FSM), for example, is 4,000 times the size of its landmass, larger than the land area of Argentina. Within this region of island nations there is a diverse array of societies and cultures, as well as a variety of legal systems. Fourteen of the 22 PICTs are either independent countries or are governed in free association with New Zealand or the United States.[4] The remaining eight are dependent territories governed by the United States, France, New Zealand or the United Kingdom. Samoa was the first PIC to gain independence in 1962; the most recent was the Republic of Palau in 1994.

The social and environmental character of PICTs is highly diverse.

---

[3] For the purposes of this chapter the 14 independent Pacific island countries are: Cook Islands, Federated States of Micronesia, Fiji, Kiribati, Republic of the Marshall Islands, Nauru, Niue, Palau, Papua New Guinea, Samoa, Solomon Islands, Tonga, Tuvalu, and Vanuatu. The eight dependent Pacific island territories are: American Samoa, French Polynesia, Guam, New Caledonia, Commonwealth of the Northern Mariana Islands, Pitcairn Islands, Tokelau, and Wallis and Futuna Islands.

[4] Free association refers to a treaty-based arrangement wherein an otherwise independent country cedes specified sovereign powers to another country in return for benefits such as preferential migration status or increased levels of development assistance.

Language is a good indicator of socio-cultural diversity and there are more than 2,000 languages spoken in PICTs which means that the Pacific island region is easily the most linguistically diverse area of the world. Linguistic diversity is most pronounced in Melanesia, one of the Pacific's three sub-regions, the other two being Micronesia and Polynesia. Geographically, Melanesia (Papua New Guinea, Solomon Islands, Vanuatu, Fiji and New Caledonia) is characterised by larger islands with substantial forest and mineral resources. Micronesia, a name meaning 'small islands', comprises countries and territories (Kiribati, Republic of the Marshall Islands, FSM, Palau, Guam, Commonwealth of the Northern Mariana Islands and Nauru) with comparatively tiny areas of land and vast marine resources. Some Polynesian countries (Cook Islands, French Polynesia, Niue, Tokelau, and Tuvalu) have similarly small land resources to those in Micronesia whereas others, such as Samoa and Tonga, possess substantial terrestrial and marine resources although the land areas are not on the scale of the Melanesian nations.

PICTs identify as a regional grouping for many purposes, including those relating to environmental protection and natural resource management. Regional cooperation in the Pacific is facilitated by the ten organisational members of the Council of Regional Organisations of the Pacific (CROP). The peak body of CROP is the Pacific Islands Forum (PIF), established in 1971 as the South Pacific Forum. The PIF meets annually with most members being represented by their heads of state. The key CROP organisation for environmental matters is the Secretariat of the Pacific Regional Environment Programme (SPREP). SPREP's programs include regional coordination and capacity building in the areas of multilateral treaty negotiations, waste, pollution, and biodiversity conservation.[5] There are several other CROP agencies with roles relating to environmental management, including the Pacific Islands Forum Fisheries Agency and the Secretariat for the Pacific Community (SPC). Since 2011 the work of SPC has also included that of a former CROP agency of importance for the sustainable management of the region's resources, the Pacific Islands Applied Geoscience Commission (SOPAC).

---

[5] SPREP (2013).

REGIONAL ENVIRONMENTAL LAW IN THE PACIFIC

Modern intergovernmental cooperation in the Pacific island region was initiated in 1947, 15 years prior to the first island country, Samoa, gaining independence. The Canberra Agreement, a treaty between the six 'participating governments' with territorial claims in the region (Australia, New Zealand, United States, United Kingdom, France and the Netherlands) established what was then known as the South Pacific Commission (SPC, later re-named the Secretariat of the Pacific Community).[6] The agreement created the Commission as 'a consultative and advisory body to the participating governments in matters affecting the economic and social development' of the non-self-governing Pacific territories.[7] SPC was invested with various powers and functions, including formulating and recommending measures for the development of the economic and social rights and welfare of Pacific peoples, 'particularly in respect of agriculture (including animal husbandry), communications, transport, fisheries, forestry, industry, labour, marketing, production, trade and finance, public works, education, health, housing and social welfare'.[8] As the island nations of the Pacific gained independence or autonomy in the 20 years following 1962, SPC evolved from a colonialist's club into an organisation representing the interests of the region's governments. At the 23rd South Pacific Conference in Saipan in 1983 all 22 Pacific island member countries and territories were recognised as full voting members of SPC.

SPC was pivotal in initiating regional environmental law in the Pacific. In 1974, in the aftermath of the 1972 Stockholm Conference and following catalysing activities by the International Union for the Conservation of Nature (IUCN), SPC initiated a project aimed towards promoting and developing protected areas in PICTs. Included in this project was the development of a regional treaty. The Convention on the Conservation of Nature in the South Pacific (Apia Convention) was drafted with technical assistance from IUCN and was first discussed at a conference on Pacific national parks and reserves held in New Zealand in 1975.[9] The following year SPC and IUCN jointly hosted a meeting in Samoa for delegates of SPC member countries to consider the draft text. 'The 1976 meeting was

---

[6] *Agreement Establishing the South Pacific Commission* (adopted 6 February 1947, entered into force 29 July 1948) 97 UNTS 227.

[7] Ibid, art 6.

[8] Ibid.

[9] *Convention on the Conservation of Nature in the South Pacific* (adopted 12 June 1976, entered into force 26 June 1990) [1990] ATS 41.

seen as the first major attempt in the Pacific Region to bring about a regional approach to the management of natural resources.'[10] While the text of the Apia Convention was finalised in 1976, the first instrument of accession was not deposited until 1987 and the Convention only entered into force after the fourth instrument was deposited by Australia in March 1990. The Apia Convention's five parties (Australia, Cook Islands, Fiji, France and Samoa) decided to suspend the operation of the Convention in 2006 on the grounds that it had not attracted broad membership from countries of the region and it had been superseded by the 1992 Convention on Biological Diversity (CBD).[11] The SPREP Director commented in 2008 in relation to the suspension of the Pacific's first environmental treaty:

> The work of the Apia Convention had become increasingly sidelined by global conservation conventions, primarily the Convention on Biodiversity. The comprehensive work programmes under the CBD and other conservation conventions and the [associated] availability of funds rendered redundant the necessity for a separate work programme under the Apia Convention. The suspension of the Apia Convention in 2006 came only after exhaustive efforts were made to revitalise it.[12]

The Apia Convention was typical of many of the region's early post-independence environmental governance initiatives in that its development was driven by conservation-minded stakeholders external to the Pacific island region, and consequently the strategies for nature conservation embodied within it mirrored those in place in developed countries. The core obligation of the Apia Convention was for member states to 'encourage the creation of protected areas which . . . will safeguard representative samples of the natural ecosystems occurring therein as well as superlative scenery, striking geological formations, and regions and objects of aesthetic interest or historic, cultural or scientific value'.[13] While Article IV of the Convention, which recognised customary use of protected areas and species in accordance with traditional cultural practices within protected areas, was acknowledged as a provision that was progressive for its time, the general thrust of the treaty was for PICTs to develop national parks systems broadly equivalent to those in Australia, New Zealand and the United States.[14] For this reason the Apia Convention failed to gain

---

10 Pulea (2002) 3.

11 SPREP (2008).

12 Ibid, 11.

13 *Convention on the Conservation of Nature in the South Pacific* (adopted 12 June 1976, entered into force 26 June 1990) [1990] ATS 41, art II.

14 Comment on the progressive nature of art VI: Pulea (2002) 5–6.

widespread support among PICs as their preferred strategy to achieve this aim is establishing networks of community-based or co-managed protected areas.[15]

Following the Apia Convention, the next regional environmental treaty developed in the Pacific was the Convention for the Protection of the Natural Resources and the Environment of the South Pacific Region (Noumea Convention).[16] The genesis of the Noumea Convention was the Conference on the Human Environment in the South Pacific, held in Rarotonga in 1982. At that conference participants agreed that a treaty should be developed to protect the Pacific environment from all forms of pollution and particularly from nuclear contamination. Future negotiations to this end resulted in the adoption of the text of the Noumea Convention in November 1986, which entered into force in 1990.

The Noumea Convention deals with a broad range of environmental and natural resource management issues, including marine pollution from vessels (Article 6), land-based sources (Article 7) and sea-bed activities (Article 8), as well as air pollution (Article 9), waste disposal and storage (Articles 10 and 11), nuclear testing (Article 12), coastal erosion (Article 13) and environmental impact assessment (Article 16). The Noumea Convention also duplicates the Apia Convention's requirements for Parties to establish protected areas (Article 14).

Article 4(1) of the Convention provides in part that: 'Parties shall endeavour to conclude bilateral or multilateral agreements, including regional or sub-regional agreements, for the protection, development and management of the marine and coastal environment of the Convention Area.' Two agreements of this kind were adopted at the same time as the Convention: the Protocol Concerning Co-operation in Combating Pollution Emergencies in the South Pacific Region,[17] and the Protocol for the Prevention of Pollution of the South Pacific Region by Dumping.[18] These three texts were opened for signature simultaneously.

Despite attracting membership from more PICs than the Apia

---

15 Rose (2008). Vierros *et al.* (2010).

16 *Convention for the Protection of the Natural Resources and the Environment of the South Pacific Region* (adopted 24 November 1986, entered into force 22 August 1990) [1990] ATS 31.

17 *Protocol Concerning Co-operation in Combating Pollution Emergencies in the South Pacific Region* (adopted 25 November 1986, entered into force 22 August 1990) [1990] ATS 32.

18 *Protocol for the Prevention of Pollution of the South Pacific Region by Dumping* (adopted 25 November 1986) [1990] ATS 32.

Convention, and having been developed in a manner that was more responsive to the priorities of the island nations, the Noumea Convention has not been particularly influential as a focus of environmental protection in the region. The SPREP Director made the following comments at the Ninth Meeting of the Conference of the Parties to the Noumea Convention in 2008:

> The Noumea Convention faces similar headwinds [to the Apia Convention]. The focus of the Noumea Convention – the preservation of coastal and marine areas from pollution and resource degradation – is the subject of numerous plans, strategies and international agreements, many of which have financial mechanisms. Work relevant to the implementation of the Noumea Convention is therefore being carried out under these other arrangements. This greatly reduces the need for a separate work programme under the Noumea Convention and consequently the Parties are spared from incurring costs. The downside is that the Convention risks becoming a dead letter.[19]

The Director's comments point to one of the key ironies of Pacific regional environmental law – the primary deficit relating to environmental regulation in this region of isolated island nations is availability of financial and technical resources, rather than additional transboundary cooperation or agreement. Regional cooperation and coordination is important, but meeting this goal is not typically reliant upon legal agreements being in place. Moreover, while regional treaties may have the advantage of being better tailored to the needs of a smaller group of parties with more similar sets of social, economic and ecological characteristics, it is membership of the global treaties which trigger the availability of funding mechanisms such as the Global Environment Facility (GEF).

The above is not intended to suggest that the Noumea Convention is without import or consequence. In proceedings commenced in the International Court of Justice by New Zealand in August 1995 seeking to prevent France from testing nuclear weapons in French Polynesia, the obligations accepted by France in ratifying the Noumea Convention were central to the arguments presented.[20] While New Zealand failed to convince the court that there was sufficient legal basis to reopen the case that it had commenced in opposition to French atmospheric nuclear testing in 1974 (a procedure made necessary by the fact that France had denounced the Court's compulsory jurisdiction in 1975) the Court specifically stated that its Order was 'without prejudice to the obligations of States to respect and protect the natural environment, obligations to which both

[19] SPREP (2008) 11.

[20] *New Zealand v France (Jurisdiction)* (1974) ICJ Reports, 457.

New Zealand and France have in the present instance reaffirmed their commitment'.[21] Australia, Samoa, Solomon Islands, Marshall Islands and FSM all sought permission to intervene in the proceedings, each citing provisions of the Noumea Convention among the bases for their claims.

The development and deployment in the Pacific island region in the coming decade of technology capable of bringing to fruition the long-anticipated goal of extracting valuable minerals from the seabed may well catalyse renewed interest in the Noumea Convention, particularly Article 8 requiring Parties to prevent and control pollution from seabed mineral exploration and exploitation. At the time of writing SOPAC was coordinating a project throughout the region assisting national governments to develop policy and legal frameworks in preparation for the inevitable onset of seabed mineral exploration and extraction.[22]

The most recent environmental treaty negotiated by PICs is the Convention to Ban the Importation into Forum Island Countries of Hazardous and Radioactive Waste and to Control the Transboundary Movement and Management of Hazardous Waste within the South Pacific Region (Waigani Convention).[23] This instrument largely mirrors the Convention on the Control of Transboundary Movements of Hazardous Waste and Their Disposal (Basel Convention),[24] with the exceptions that it specifically prohibits any importation of hazardous waste into PICs and its scope includes radioactive wastes.[25] The text of the Waigani Convention was finalised in 1995 and it entered into force in 2001. All parties to the Waigani Convention are also members of the Basel Convention, and despite each of these conventions requiring parties to enact specific legislative regimes to regulate transboundary movements of hazardous waste, at the time of writing Tonga and FSM were the only PICs to have done so.

An achievement more significant in the development of international environmental governance in the Pacific island region than the creation

---

[21] Ibid, 463.

[22] Secretariat of the Pacific Community Applied Geoscience and Technology Division (2012).

[23] *Convention to Ban the Importation into Forum Island Countries of Hazardous and Radioactive Waste and to Control the Transboundary Movement and Management of Hazardous Waste within the South Pacific Region* (adopted 16 September 1995, entered into force 21 October 2001) [2001] ATS 17 (Waigani Convention).

[24] *Convention on the Control of Transboundary Movements of Hazardous Waste and Their Disposal* (adopted 22 March 1989, entered into force 5 May 1992) 1673 UNTS 67.

[25] Waigani Convention, art 4.

of the Apia, Noumea and Waigani Conventions was the establishment of SPREP, initially as a division within SPC in 1981. In 1993 SPREP became a separate regional intergovernmental organisation. All PICs, as well as the countries responsible for administering territories in the region (Australia, New Zealand, the United States and France) are parties to the Agreement Establishing the South Pacific Regional Environment Program.[26] Article 2 of the agreement states that SPREP's purposes are:

> 1. To promote co-operation in the South Pacific region and to provide assistance in order to protect and improve its environment and to ensure sustainable development for present and future generations. SPREP shall achieve these purposes through the Action Plan adopted from time to time by the SPREP Meeting, setting the strategies and objectives of SPREP.
> 2. The Action Plan shall include:
>   (a) coordinating regional activities addressing the environment;
>   (b) monitoring and assessing the state of the environment in the region including the impacts of human activities on the ecosystems of the region and encouraging development undertaken to be directed towards maintaining or enhancing environmental qualities;
>   (c) promoting and developing programmes, including research programmes, to protect the atmosphere and terrestrial, freshwater, coastal and marine ecosystems and species, while ensuring ecologically sustainable utilisation of resources;
>   (d) reducing, through prevention and management, atmospheric, land based, fresh water and marine pollution)
>   (e) strengthening national and regional capabilities and institutional arrangements;
>   (f) increasing and improving training, educational and public awareness activities; and
>   (g) promoting integrated legal, planning and management mechanisms.

SPREP now has 83 staff working at its offices in Apia, Samoa, on a wide variety of environmental issues and programs with a total budget of US$13.4 million in 2012.[27] The annual SPREP meetings bring together senior officials from each member country where they discuss, comment upon and (typically) endorse the plans and programs of the Secretariat. These include assisting PICs to prepare for international environmental meetings such as multilateral treaty negotiations, the conferences of the parties of the various MEAs, as well as major intergovernmental meetings on sustainable development such as the World Summit on Sustainable

---

[26] *Agreement Establishing the South Pacific Regional Environment Program* (adopted 16 June 1993, entered into force 31 August 1995) 1982 UNTS 3.

[27] SPREP (2013) 73 and 67.

Development and the 1992 and 2012 iterations of the United Nations Conference on Sustainable Development.[28] Regarding the 2012 meeting, the SPREP Annual Report notes the following:

> Our regional efforts resulted in the inclusion of the Pacific region's key issues in the Rio+20 Outcomes Document. These issues were: highlighting the role of oceans; applying the green economy in a blue world; and maintaining the special case for Small Island Developing States (SIDS). Our efforts were rewarded with 19 paragraphs in the outcomes document focusing solely on oceans, making it the biggest thematic area in the document.[29]

While there are no substantial conflicts or inconsistencies between the SPREP Action Plan, the Apia Convention and the Noumea Convention, for practical and financial reasons the former is more influential in guiding regional cooperation and joint action on issues of environmental protection and management.

PACIFIC ISLAND PARTICIPATION IN MULTILATERAL ENVIRONMENTAL AGREEMENTS

PICs participate actively in many international law regimes including MEAs and various program-oriented soft law initiatives such as the World Summit on Sustainable Development and the island specific Barbados Programme of Action on Small Island States. This participation is not without difficulties and contradictions however, and these have led to calls for reform in the manner in which PICs engage with international environmental governance frameworks. It is beyond the scope of this chapter to review in detail the participation of PICs in all MEAs. Instead, observations of a general nature are presented.

In 2003 Tuiloma Neroni Slade, former International Criminal Court Judge, former Chair of the Alliance of Small Island States (AOSIS) and current Secretary General of the Pacific Islands Forum Secretariat, noted that '[s]mallness, geography, environmental fragility, and a general state of vulnerability are key determinants in the international policy and positions of the small island states. The ocean and its resources in particular, as well as the environment, have become areas of major policy concentration. Their importance is quite simply fundamental.'[30] Slade proceeded to note the irony of the fact that while the Pacific Ocean unites PICs and nourishes

---

28 Ibid, 28–31.

29 Ibid, 28.

30 Slade (2003) 534.

Pacific islanders, it is also the ocean and the prospect of rising seas caused by anthropogenic climate change that represents an acute threat to PICs.[31]

In considering PICs engagement in MEAs, it is helpful to consider three categories of treaty. The first are those addressing issues which impact directly upon critical national interests of countries in the region. Prominent examples in this category are the United Nations Law of the Sea Convention[32] and the United Nations Framework Convention on Climate Change (UNFCCC).[33] All PICs are parties to these MEAs and their participation reflects the fact that the rules and processes embodied in these agreements represent the most effective mechanisms by which PICs can influence global cooperation and norm-creation on these critical matters. PIC participation in the UNFCCC is discussed more fully below.

The second category are those MEAs addressing issues that, while not irrelevant to PICs national interests, may not be a focus of priority for PIC governments to invest their scarce financial and technical resources if not for the funding provided to them as a result of joining these MEAs. Examples of MEA in this category are the Montreal Protocol on Ozone Depleting Substances,[34] the Convention to Combat Desertification (CCD)[35] and the Stockholm Convention on Persistent Organic Pollutants.[36] All PICs are members of each of these treaties despite the fact that no PIC generates or uses significant quantities of ozone depleting substances, desertification is not a concern in any PIC (although other forms of land degradation are common and this is where CCD funding support is directed), and persistent organic pollutants are typically a peripheral concern for PICs relative to more pressing environmental priorities. The reason for comprehensive PIC membership of such agreements as these is related directly to the fact that PIC governments have a severe deficit of financial and technical resources and joining these MEAs opens new avenues of international assistance. Chasek sets this out in plain terms, but overstates the universal importance of financial

---

31 Ibid.

32 *United Nations Convention on the Law of the Sea* (adopted 10 December 1982, entered into force 16 November 1994) 1833 UNTS 3.

33 *United Nations Convention on Climate Change* (adopted 9 May 1992, entered into force 21 March 1994) 1771 UNTS 107.

34 *Montreal Protocol on Ozone Depleting Substances* (adopted 16 September 1987, entered into force 1 January 1989) 1522 UNTS 3.

35 *United Nations Convention to Combat Desertification in Countries Experiencing Serious Drought and/or Desertification, Particularly in Africa* (adopted 17 June 1994, entered into force 26 December 1996) 1954 UNTS 3.

36 *Stockholm Convention on Persistent Organic Pollutants* (adopted 22 May 2001, entered into force 17 May 2004) 2256 UNTS 119.

incentives: '[I]n the early 1990s, many developing countries, including the PICs, saw a new way to attract foreign aid – becoming parties to MEAs linked to external sources of funding. In fact . . . the driving factor behind MEAs ratification is the funding opportunities.'[37]

The third and final category of MEA is residual; those that neither address issues critical to the national interests of PICs nor provide substantial funding to developing country parties by virtue of their membership. Examples in this category are the Convention on Migratory Species,[38] the Ramsar Convention and the Rotterdam Convention on Prior Informed Consent Procedure for Certain Hazardous Chemicals and Pesticides.[39] While PIC governments are in no way opposed to the objectives of these MEAs, patterns of ratification and accession indicate that the majority of them have weighed the costs and benefits of joining and have decided that their scarce resources are better spent on other issues and priorities.

These considerations apply equally to regional environmental treaties, even though the regional instruments are negotiated among a smaller group of countries and reflect more directly PIC concerns and priorities. This may be illustrated by comparing PIC membership of the regional Apia Convention and the multilateral CBD. While the texts of the two treaties reflect the language of the different historical periods in which they were negotiated, many of their core objectives and obligations are shared, especially that of in-situ conservation of biological diversity. Nevertheless, the Apia Convention has only three PICs as members whereas all PICs are members of the CBD. The discrepancy is related primarily to the fact that membership of the CBD attracts substantial amounts of GEF funding whereas participation in the Apia Convention provided no financial benefits but instead required an annual fee to be paid to the secretariat.[40]

PIC participation in the international negotiations and instruments relating to climate change are sufficiently important to justify more specific discussion. Small island developing states, and specifically the lowest lying atoll states such as Tuvalu, Kiribati and the Marshall Islands, are among the countries that are most vulnerable to the impacts of climate change such as sea level rise, increasing sea surface temperatures, ocean acidification, more frequent severe weather events and changes in

---

37 Chasek (2010), 9.

38 *Convention on Migratory Species of Wild Animals* (adopted 23 June 1979, entered into force 1 November 1983) 1651 UNTS 333.

39 *Rotterdam Convention on Prior Informed Consent Procedure for Certain Hazardous Chemicals and Pesticides in International Trade* (adopted 10 September 1998, entered into force 24 February 2004) 2244 UNTS 337.

40 SPREP (2008).

precipitation patterns.[41] While the oft-reported prospect of atoll inundation is unlikely to occur during the current century, impacts such as those mentioned above may well render some atolls uninhabitable within the next 50 years. Even for PICs that are predominantly comprised of islands with higher elevations the prospect of widespread coral bleaching, acidified oceans and an increase in severe weather events means that food security is under severe threat in a region wherein most people rely upon subsistence activities for a large proportion of their calorific intake.[42]

Accordingly, to the extent they are able given their small size and consequent lack of geopolitical influence, PICs have been 'a consistent and strong presence' in climate change negotiations since the 1980s.[43] PICs were central players in forming AOSIS, an organisation of island nations with shared concerns and priorities, in the lead-up to the Second World Climate Conference in 1990.[44] 'AOSIS has since worked as a negotiating group to ensure that the position of small island states was fully represented and reflected in the provisions of the Climate Change Convention and the Kyoto Protocol' as well as other international processes of relevance to PICs and SIDS.[45] It was an AOSIS proposal at the UNFCCC COP 1 that first raised the prospect of a legally binding commitment to cut emissions of greenhouse gases. At that meeting AOSIS proposed a protocol that would require Annex I Parties to reduce their CO_2 emissions by 2005 to a level at least 20 per cent below that of 1990, and to establish timetables for controlling emissions of other gases.[46] At the same meeting Samoa intervened in strong and direct terms that have since typified PIC and AOSIS contributions to UNFCCC processes:

> AOSIS will not allow the world to barter the islands' future for short-term interests. The island States will continue to play the role of the earth's early warning system to put the heat on this process, to close the commitment gap and to reach out for new partnerships. The upcoming negotiations should use the AOSIS protocol as their basis.[47]

PICs continue to make strong representations within UNFCCC processes, such as the uncompromising stance taken by Tuvalu at the COP 15 in Copenhagen in 2009. While there is some evidence that AOSIS was

---

41 Chape (2006) 19–20.
42 Food and Agriculture Organization of the United Nations (2008).
43 Slade (2003) 540.
44 Ashe, Van Lierop and Cherian (1999) 209–20.
45 Slade (2003) 540.
46 Davis (1996) 217–19.
47 Anon (1995) 12.

influential in the drafting of the UNFCCC, after the treaty entered into force AOSIS was less successful in advancing the commitments accepted by the global community in relation to mitigating climate change, which continue to reflect a lowest common denominator position manifestly inadequate to reverse or slow the current dire trajectory of anthropogenic climate change.[48] Despite the PICs inability to shift global international environmental legal positions, commentators and political actors both within and outside the Pacific island region continue to use the plight of PICs in relation to climate change to illustrate the need for cooperative global action to mitigate climate change.[49] While PIC governments will continue to put strong positions to UNFCCC climate negotiations, their priority in relation to international climate governance can be seen to have shifted towards securing financial resources to enable them to take action to effectively adapt to the impacts of climate change that have already commenced and are predicted to become acutely severe in the future.[50]

CRITICAL ANALYSIS OF PACIFIC PARTICIPATION IN INTERNATIONAL ENVIRONMENTAL LAW

Activities directed towards participating in MEAs represent a substantial proportion of the total effort directed towards environmental protection and management in PICs, and far exceeds (as a percentage of total effort measured by staff time, resource allocation etc) the equivalent MEA-related activities in developed countries or large developing countries. This can be problematic because the issues addressed by the MEAs, with the exception of climate change, are not always among the most acute environmental issues faced by PICs. There is thus a risk that PICs reliance on MEA-related funding skews national environmental planning and management resulting in suboptimal outcomes.

The CBD is an interesting case in point – in some cases – even where the issues addressed by the treaty in question are of universal importance, such as conservation and sustainable use of biodiversity – the unique social, economic and ecological contexts of PICs renders the provisions and processes of the relevant international convention peripheral and superfluous to the actual activities taken by Pacific peoples and their governments towards achieving that end. That is, grass-roots actors and their

48 Ashe *et al.* (1999) outline AOSIS influence on UNFCCC negotiations.

49 For a discussion of this see Barnett and Campbell (2010) 155–74.

50 Maclellan (2011a). Maclellan (2011b).

civil society and governmental collaborators most concerned with sustainably managing Pacific island biodiversity are inspired to do so because their island environments support their livelihoods and cultures. In many cases they are only concerned to identify links between their activities and the CBD because their national status as a CBD Party enables access to GEF project funds for biodiversity-related activities.

PIC governments are thus strategic actors engaging in a technocratic game wherein a disproportionate amount of their environmental protection efforts are responsive not to national concerns and priorities, but instead are directed towards participating in and fulfilling national obligations under MEAs. If played successfully, the outcomes of this game increase national capacity to address all environmental concerns, whether or not these are treaty-related. If played unsuccessfully the outcome is that MEA negotiations, meetings, processes and priorities receive scarce PIC human, financial and technical resources the opportunity cost of which is a reduced emphasis upon acutely problematic national environmental concerns, such as unsustainable use of inshore marine resources.[51]

To illustrate the above discussion one need only consider the small size of PIC environment departments and the number of international meetings at which MEA Parties are expected to send representatives. For example, the Vanuatu Environment Unit employed only three officers until an expansion in 2009. At the time of writing the Environment Division of the Office of Environment and Emergency Management of the Federated States of Micronesia has three permanent professional staff and three temporary 'project' staff whose salaries are supported under donor-funded projects related to MEAs. The two senior permanent staff are required to attend both technical and high-level meetings relating to the UNFCCC, Stockholm Convention, the Basel Convention, the Convention on Desertification and the Vienna Convention and Montreal Protocol. In addition to these are regular regional meetings and ad-hoc meetings such as those relating to GEF finance planning. These travel commitments drain the staff time available to address national priorities to an extent that is rarely outweighed by the benefits accrued from participation.

These issues are recognised as being problematic by key stakeholders in the region. For example, the 2011 Pacific Environment Forum, held in Samoa in conjunction with the annual SPREP Meeting reported that participants

---

[51] Chasek (2010) 13.

> noted the disconnect between the international level discourse and implementation on the ground, and drew attention to the challenges of meeting the obligations of the many Conventions and Agreement processes, decisions, etc. that are required to be implemented at the local levels at different scales. In this context participants supported reform of international environmental governance, in particular better synergies and coherence in the UN system and between MEAs. In this context the participants saw value in support for action addressing environmental issues, including climate change in the Pacific, to be driven more strongly by national needs.[52]

Some commentators point to the SIDS-specific soft law processes and declarations, most notably the Barbados Program of Action for the Sustainable Development of Small Island Developing States and its follow up +5 and +10 meetings as evidence that the international community is responding effectively to the needs of SIDS both within and outside of the Pacific island region.[53] These observations are typically made by those who have little actual first-hand experience of Pacific environmental management activities, whereas there are few if any within the region who would claim that these processes have delivered real benefits to PICs, as opposed to mere rhetorical recognition of the vulnerability and special circumstances of Pacific SIDS. Some are deeply critical, such as Ian Fry who argues that SIDS have in fact become 'becalmed in a sea of soft law' that offers little in terms of concrete or measurable improvements.[54] Fry reports that in the ten years following the 1994 Barbados Program of Action official development assistance to SIDS in fact declined by an average of 50 per cent.[55]

The critical assessment presented above does not suggest that a radical withdrawal of PICs from MEAs would benefit the region's people or environment but rather that the manner in which PICs engage with international environmental legal processes and institutions, both as individual nations and as a region, be reconsidered. At the regional level a 2005 Asian Development Bank research project made a useful contribution. Drawing upon economic club theory, the ADB authors suggest carefully revaluating the costs and benefits of Pacific regionalism. '[C]osts effectively limit the size and scope of a club. In the Pacific, adding more remote countries entails higher diseconomies of isolation—the high cost of shipping goods, services, information, and people to increasingly remote countries across the region. From this tension between scale benefits and distance costs of

---

52 SPREP (2011a) 43.
53 Techera (2010).
54 Fry (2005).
55 Ibid, 90.

collective action, the "optimal club" (in this case, a group of countries), can be derived.'[56] The report ultimately suggests a more frequent adoption of subregional approaches:

> The composition of the 'optimal club' may vary significantly according to the issue or service under consideration. *The diseconomies of isolation are particularly high in the Pacific. Only regional initiatives with large-scale benefits will be sustainable. Often subregional initiatives will produce more viable 'clubs'*.[57]

When applied to Pacific engagement with international legal processes the club theory analysis leads to two conclusions. The first is that environmental regionalism in the Pacific could transform from the current objective of regional cooperation to a situation where regional bodies deliver actual services. The second is closely linked to the first and comprises strong support for proposals such as SPREP following the lead of SPC in opening sub-regional offices with the result that there are SPREP offices in Micronesia and Melanesia, as well as the existing office in Samoa (Polynesia).[58] In practice this would mean that the three groupings of culturally and environmentally similar countries would be better served by their regional environmental organisation, and that the outcomes of this enhanced regionalism would go beyond facilitating discussing and coordinating donor-funded projects, but would extend into actual delivery of certain environmental governance services. This might involve limited concessions of sovereign control over some matters, but in general these would be technical in nature and any costs of this kind would be outweighed by the consequent benefits. Examples of environmental governance services that might be delivered on a sub-regional scale could include the administrative and technical tasks relating to compliance with MEAs such as the Basel, Waigani, Rotterdam and Stockholm Conventions, as well as the Montreal and Cartagena Protocols. Subregional representation at international environmental forums could also deliver substantial efficiency gains while freeing up national staff to work more directly on national priority issues. Resistance to suggestions of this kind can be expected from PIC government agencies whose budgets and travel allowances might be reduced if they were adopted.[59]

Another focus of reform is the nature of delivery of international

---

56 Asian Development Bank (2005) xv.

57 Ibid. Emphasis in original.

58 SPREP (2011b).

59 For importance of travel allowances in this context see Chasek (2010) 29–30.

environmental law-related funding assistance. At present this is delivered in a manner that is disaggregated and very much project-based. That is, a large number of bilateral and multilateral donors offer funding assistance linked to specific objectives relating to MEA-derived outcomes or other donor determined priorities and objectives. In order to receive the necessary funds to supplement the meagre allocations given by national governments, PIC environment sectors actors are forced to organise their activities based around an increasingly complex array of donor-funded 'projects'. The result is that staff turnover is high and career paths are difficult to plan due to the limited time horizons of these projects, typically one to three years. More importantly, coherent national environmental management planning is inhibited by the uncertainty of long-term funding levels and availability. While all relevant donor partners are notionally supportive of the principles enunciated in the Paris Declaration on Aid Effectiveness, 'larger geopolitical interests continue to be the primary motivation among bilateral donors and hold much more sway than the goals of the Paris Declaration'.[60]

A more productive mechanism than the complex array of environmental project funding, and one that is gaining traction in the field of climate change adaptation, is for PICs to undertake comprehensive and robust national priority-setting and action planning, including setting out timetables for implementation and identifying performance indicators. Donors would then provide funds to support the implementation of these national programs of action, rather than developing their own projects to be offered to PICs.[61] The benefits of such an approach are numerous and include greater certainty enabling long-term planning, enhanced ability to develop and build the skills of staff at all levels, efficiency gains flowing from reduced reporting-related administrative burdens, and an end to the game of fitting various 'round' national environmental priorities into 'square' pre-determined international donor project criteria.

CONCLUSION

PICs have since independence been active players in international and regional environmental governance. In the interests of international environmental justice it is important for them to continue doing so.

---

[60] Ibid, 24.

[61] For a discussion of the 'budget support' approach to aid delivery in the context of the European Commission see European Commission (2011).

Participating in global environmental governance processes maximises PICs ability to influence action and commitments on issues of great importance to them such as climate change and oceans management. PICs, in forming an effective negotiating bloc with a wider group of like-minded countries in AOSIS, have successfully influenced the climate change treaty negotiations and in this way SIDS were in the vanguard of a new type of regionalism in international governance. But influence has not always translated into just or sustainable outcomes; this deficit being felt most acutely in the form of unmitigated and worsening climate change. Moreover for small, in some cases micro, governments, the burdens and restrictions that MEA implementation and compliance imposes are substantial. There is also an identified disconnect between international and national environmental governance; in essence this means that effort spent administering international environmental law is in some situations hindering optimal implementation of effective national environmental governance. Ultimately, regardless of any perceived shortcomings in international processes, PICs and AOSIS will continue to engage with MEAs as they are fora in which small nations are comparatively advantaged in bringing some influence to bear on global agreements.

REFERENCES

Treaties

Agreement Establishing the South Pacific Commission (adopted 6 February 1947, entered into force 29 July 1948) 97 UNTS 227.

Agreement Establishing the South Pacific Regional Environment Program (adopted 16 June 1993, entered into force 31 August 1995) 1982 UNTS 3.

Convention to Ban the Importation into Forum Island Countries of Hazardous and Radioactive Waste and to Control the Transboundary Movement and Management of Hazardous Waste within the South Pacific Region (adopted 16 September 1995, entered into force 21 October 2001) [2001] ATS 17.

Convention on the Conservation of Nature in the South Pacific (adopted 12 June 1976, entered into force 26 June 1990) [1990] ATS 41.

Convention on the Control of Transboundary Movements of Hazardous Waste and Their Disposal (adopted 22 March 1989, entered into force 5 May 1992) 1673 UNTS 67.

Convention on Migratory Species of Wild Animals (adopted 23 June 1979, entered into force 1 November 1983) 1651 UNTS 333.

Convention for the Protection of the Natural Resources and the Environment of the South Pacific Region (adopted 24 November 1986, entered into force 22 August 1990) [1990] ATS 31.

Montreal Protocol on Ozone Depleting Substances (adopted 16 September 1987, entered into force 1 January 1989) 1522 UNTS 3.

Protocol Concerning Co-operation in Combating Pollution Emergencies in the South Pacific Region (adopted 25 November 1986, entered into force 22 August 1990) [1990] ATS 32.
Protocol for the Prevention of Pollution of the South Pacific Region by Dumping (adopted 25 November 1986) [1990] ATS 32.
Rotterdam Convention on Prior Informed Consent Procedure for Certain Hazardous Chemicals and Pesticides in International Trade (adopted 10 September 1998, entered into force 24 February 2004) 2244 UNTS 337.
Stockholm Convention on Persistent Organic Pollutants (adopted 22 May 2001, entered into force 17 May 2004) 2256 UNTS 119.
United Nations Convention on Climate Change (adopted 9 May 1992, entered into force 21 March 1994) 1771 UNTS 107.
United Nations Convention on the Law of the Sea (adopted 10 December 1982, entered into force 16 November 1994) 1833 UNTS 3.
United Nations Convention to Combat Desertification in Countries Experiencing Serious Drought and/or Desertification, Particularly in Africa (adopted 17 June 1994, entered into force 26 December 1996) 1954 UNTS 3.

Other

Anon (1995), 'A Summary Report on the First Conference of the Parties to the United Nations Framework Convention on Climate Change' 21 *Earth Negotiations Bulletin* 9.
Ashe, J., R. Van Lierop and A. Cherian (1999), 'The Role of the Alliance of Small Island States in the Negotiation of the United Nations Framework Convention on Climate Change' (1999) 23 *Natural Resources Forum* 209.
Asian Development Bank (2005), *Toward a New Pacific Regionalism* (Manila: Asian Development Bank).
Barnett, J. and J. Campbell (2010), *Climate Change and Small Island States: Power, Knowledge and the South Pacific* (London: Earthscan).
Chape, S. (2006), 'Review of Environmental Issues in the Pacific Region and the Role of the Pacific Regional Environment Programme' (Paper presented to *Colloquium on Collaboration for sustainable development of the Pacific Islands: Towards effective e-learning systems on environment*, Okinawa, Japan, 27–28 February 2006).
Chasek, P. (2010), *Confronting Environmental Treaty Implementation Challenges in the Pacific Islands* (Honolulu: East West Center).
Davis, J. (1996), 'The Alliance of Small Island States: The International Conscience' *Asia-Pacific Magazine* 217.
European Commission (2011), *How the Commission provides budget support*, accessed 28 March 2015 at http://ec.europa.eu/europeaid/policies/budget-support-and-dialogue-partner-countries_en.
Food and Agriculture Organization of the United Nations (2008), *Climate Change and Food Security in Pacific island Countries* (Rome: Food and Agriculture Organization of the United Nations).
Fry, I. (2005), 'Small Island Developing States: Becalmed in a Sea of Soft Law' 14 RECIEL 89.
Maclellan, N. (2011a), *Improving Access to Climate Financing* (Sydney: Lowy Institute).

Maclellan, N. (2011b), 'Show Me The Money: Pacific Governments Lobby for Climate Finance' *Island Business*, June issue, 13.

New Zealand v France (Jurisdiction) (1974) ICJ Reports 457.

Pulea, M. (2002), *Working Paper on the Convention on the Conservation of Nature in the South Pacific* (SPREP Working Paper).

Rose, J. (2008), 'Community-Based Biodiversity Conservation in the Pacific: Cautionary Lessons in Regionalizing Environmental Governance', in M. Jeffery, J. Firestone and K. Bubna-Litic (eds), *Biodiversity Conservation, Law and Livelihoods: Bridging the North–South Divide* (Cambridge: Cambridge University Press).

Slade, T. (2003), 'The Making of International Law: The Role of Small Island States' 17 *Temple International and Comparative Law Journal* 531.

Secretariat of the Pacific Community Applied Geoscience and Technology Division (2012), *Pacific-ACP States Regional Legislative and Regulatory Framework for Deep Sea Minerals Exploration and Exploitation* (Suva: SOPAC).

Secretariat of the Regional Environment Program (SPREP 2013), *2012 Annual Report of the Secretariat of the Regional Environment Programme* (Apia: SPREP).

SPREP (2008), *Report of the Ninth Meeting of the Conference of the Parties to the Noumea Convention* (SPREP Meeting Report).

SPREP (2011a), *Report of the Pacific Environment Forum 2011: Building Resilience for a Sustainable Future* (Apia: SPREP).

SPREP (2011b), *22nd SPREP Meeting Documents Agenda Paper 6.1: Study on Options for Establishing a Subregional Presence for SPREP* (Apia: SPREP).

Techera, E. (2010), 'Legal Pluralism, Indigenous People and Small Island Developing States: Good Environmental Governance in the South Pacific' 61 *Journal of Legal Pluralism* 171.

Vierros M., A. Tawake F. Hickey, A. Tiraa and R. Noa (2010) *Traditional Marine Management Areas of the Pacific in the Context of National and International Law and Policy* (United Nations University).

12. Safe harbours, closed borders? New Zealand legal and policy responses to climate displacement in the South Pacific

Vernon Rive

INTRODUCTION

Amid recurrent media depictions of 'sinking islands' and scenarios of mass relocation of island communities from low lying atolls, three consistent messages from Pacific peoples can be heard. The first is that for most, their wish and intention is to continue to live in their home countries despite the mounting effects of climate change with dignity, in safety and prosperity.[1] Secondly, Pacific communities have no wish to relieve the international community of its obligations and commitments to reduce greenhouse gas emissions by offering large-scale migration from low-lying islands as 'the' solution to climate change within the region. Thirdly, migration should, if it is ultimately necessary, be undertaken in a planned, coordinated way, respecting and reflecting the resilience of people who are no strangers to re-establishing themselves in new environments in response to changing environmental conditions. This is what they have done for centuries.

For over 150 years, New Zealand has played a significant role in the South Pacific. Vibrant cultural, political, economic, and sporting interchanges reflect recognition amongst a broad cross-section of New Zealand society that its spiritual as well as geographic home is within the southern waters of the Pacific, rather than cities or fields of Europe. New Zealand hosts significant expatriate populations of Samoan, Tongan, Tuvaluan and others of Pacific origin. The ancestors of its indigenous Maori population traversed the Pacific Ocean to establish their home there.

[1] For a recent discussion of the tension between the desire of residents of low-lying Pacific islands to remain in their home locations and the potential for migration see, for example Smith and McNamara (2013).

Given its strong ties with other South Pacific nations, it would be natural to expect New Zealand's support role to flow into proactive planning and legal and policy provision for responding to the effects of climate change in the Pacific. To an extent, it has. New Zealand is a significant donor to many Pacific countries. It has committed to ongoing financial and technical support on climate change adaptation projects in a number of low-lying island states, including a recently announced five-year partnership to improve water security in Tuvalu, Tokelau, Kiribati, the Cook Islands and the Republic of the Marshall Islands.[2]

New Zealand's support for *in situ* adaptation measures amongst its Pacific neighbours is not in real doubt. Its position on the more contentious aspect of climate change adaptation within the Pacific: whether, and to what extent, New Zealand would be willing to open its borders to climate change-displaced persons in the region is less clear.[3] This chapter examines legal and policy issues arising out of the latter issue.

SCALE AND PATTERN OF CLIMATE CHANGE MIGRATION IN THE SOUTH PACIFIC

An informed assessment of legal and policy issues associated with climate displacement in the South Pacific would logically build upon robust assessments of the scale and pattern of existing and predicted future climate-influenced migration and displacement in the region. However, despite sustained interest in this area by academics, non-governmental organisations (NGOs) and regional inter-governmental organisations for over ten years, there remains a dearth of information on, and considerable debate over, likely future migration and displacement flows which can be directly or indirectly attributed to the effects of climate change.[4]

---

[2] New Zealand Prime Minister John Key news release 4 September 2013.

[3] It is noted at the outset that migration to 'developed' South Pacific countries such as New Zealand or Australia is by no means the only, or likely even to be the preferred option, in the event that citizens of low-lying Pacific countries are not able to remain in their home nations as a result of climate change impacts. As noted by Elliott and Fagan, 'Some people have raised the possibility of expanded systems of migration to Australia and New Zealand, but Pacific leaders have suggested it might be more appropriate to call for support from Australia and New Zealand to help people resettle to other Pacific islands. These islands may provide a more suitable cultural context for displaced rural communities.' Elliot and Fagan (2009) 75.

[4] A leading New Zealand commentator on climate change related displacement and migration, Bruce Burson, recently observed, "The lack of accurate infor-

In 2009, Waikato University geographer John Campbell estimated that there would be between 665,000 and 1.7m climate-displaced people in the Pacific by 2050.[5] A major 2012 study on existing and predicted future population movement in the Pacific commissioned by New Zealand's Department of Labour reached the conclusion that climate change represented a 'threat to the livelihoods, security and well-being of Pacific people . . . which may force mass migrations'; however, it did not include any quantification of the potential numbers involved.[6]

In May 2013, conveners of the *Nansen Initiative* published a background report in preparation for consultative meetings involving representatives of Pacific nations and other stakeholders with an interest in displacement and migration implications of climate change in the region. In a similar vein to the 2012 New Zealand Department of Labour report, the authors of the Nansen background report noted that (for a range of reasons, including demographic, population, economic and environmental) 'human mobility in the Pacific region is expected to significantly increase in the coming decades and beyond'.[7] No attempt was made, however, to arrive at quantitative estimates of numbers.

For the purpose of this chapter, a related (and obvious) question is: what proportion of the number of climate-displaced persons within the South Pacific region may seek to be resettled within New Zealand? Attempted answers to that question are, at this stage, likely to be speculative. As far as the author is aware, no specific empirical investigations have taken place. What is known, however, is that: New Zealand has significant expatriate communities of people of South Pacific origin whose members retain ongoing and strong links with relatives in their countries of historic origin;[8] empirical studies within South Pacific countries and in New Zealand indicate that New Zealand is seen as a natural and desirable

---

mation on the possible migratory consequences of climate change impedes our ability to adequately prepare for and comprehensively respond to the humanitarian and protection needs of environmental migrants. Understanding more clearly the potential scale and patterns of climate change related migration is therefore *the* most pressing issue.' Burson in Leckie, Simperingham and Bakker (2012) 159.

[5] Campbell cited in Campbell in Burson (ed.) (2010), 12, 38.

[6] Bedford and Hugo (2012) vi.

[7] Background Paper: 'Human Mobility, Natural Disasters and Climate Change in the Pacific' (2013) 2.

[8] See: Shen and Gemenne (2011) (3,000 Tuvaluans estimated to reside in New Zealand). In January 2013, New Zealand's Ministry of Foreign Affairs and Trade recorded on its website 'There is a vibrant I-Kiribati community of over 2,000 people in New Zealand' http://www.mfat.govt.nz/Countries/Pacific/Kiribati.php (accessed 20 March 2015). 2006 census statistics for other Pacific populations in

destination for migration by some;[9] and a number of leaders of Pacific countries have identified New Zealand as a country whose assistance is sought to facilitate planned migration as one of a number of adaptive responses to the effects of climate change.[10]

PROTECTION OF DEFICIT IN INTERNATIONAL LAW

International Conventions and Documents

There are a number of conventions and documents with potential relevance to the legal status and protection of persons displaced as a result of climate change, analysed extensively in the academic and NGO literature. They include: the 1951 Convention Relating to the Status of Refugees;[11] the 1966 International Covenant on Civil and Political Rights;[12] the 1966 International Covenant on Economic, Social and Cultural Rights;[13] the 1954 Convention relating to the Status of Stateless Persons (not yet ratified by New Zealand); the 1961 Convention on the Reduction of Statelessness (ratified by New Zealand in 2006); the 1998 United Nations Guiding Principles on Internal Displacement; the 1992 United Nations Framework Convention on Climate Change (UNFCCC) and subsidiary instruments.

A detailed account of the arguments for and against the relevance and application of these instruments or documents to climate-displaced persons is beyond the scope of this chapter. In summary however, none provide unequivocal binding direction on countries such as New Zealand

---

New Zealand include: Samoan (131,103); Cook Islands Maori (58,008); Tongan (50,481); Niuean (22,476), Fijian (9,864); Tokelauan (6,819).

9 See, for example, Fedor (2012) I; Shen and Gemenne (2011) 1.

10 President Anote Tong of Kiribati has, to date, been the most vocal of Pacific leaders in this regard. For a statement of his office's position on relocation as one of a number of responses to the effects of climate change in Kiribati see http://www.climate.gov.ki/category/action/relocation/ (accessed 20 March 2015). For a useful recent analysis of contrasting views, see Smith (2013).

11 Convention relating to the Status of Refugees (1951) (189 UNTS 137), in conjunction with the Protocol relating to the Status of Refugees (1967) 606 UNTS 267. New Zealand acceded to the 1951 Convention on 30 June 1960 and to the 1967 Protocol on 6 August 1973.

12 International Covenant on Civil and Political Rights (1966) 999 UNTS 171.

13 International Covenant on Economic, Social and Cultural Rights (adopted 16 December 1966, entered into force 3 January 1976) 993 UNTS 3.

concerning domestic obligations to assist the citizens of other states displaced as a result of climate change.[14]

Regional Instruments

There are no existing legally binding regional conventions or treaties which address obligations of developed countries with the South Pacific region such as New Zealand towards their Pacific counterparts in the climate change context.

In 2008, members of the Pacific Islands Forum (PIF) signed what is known as the 'Niue Declaration', described at the time as 'the first ever climate change declaration for the region'.[15] The document records (non-binding) commitments of signatories to ongoing advocacy and support on regional and international climate change mitigation measures.

Notably (for the issues discussed in this chapter), under the Niue Declaration, leaders of the PIF undertook to:

> ENCOURAGE the Pacific's Development Partners to increase their technical and financial support for climate change action on adaptation, mitigation and, if necessary, relocation, while welcoming the pledged increases in resources to address the climate change challenge . . . (emphasis added)

Responding to threats from climate change on Pacific states was a central topic for discussion at the September 2013 meeting of the PIF in the Marshall Islands capital Majuro in September 2013. The widely publicised 'Majuro Declaration' was a key output of that meeting – a document which develops, with greater urgency, themes addressed five years earlier in Niue.[16] Unsurprisingly, provisions of the Majuro Declaration highlight

---

14 In Cancun in 2010, parties to the United Nations Framework Convention on Climate Change agreed to take 'measures to enhance understanding, coordination and cooperation with regard to climate-change induced displacement, migration and planned relocation, where appropriate, at the national, regional and international levels'. Notably, this has explicitly brought the issue of climate migration onto the UNFCCC agenda. However the agreement imposes no binding obligations on nations. It can be regarded as no more than a start to what may be a long process of negotiation within that forum. Conference of the Parties to the United Nations Framework Convention on Climate Change, Action Taken by the Conference of the Parties at its Sixteenth Session (Addendum Pt 2 to the Report of the Conference of the Parties on its sixteenth session, held in Cancun from 29 November to 10 December 2010) FCCC/CP/2010/7/ Add.1, (15 March 2011) 5 ('COP16').

15 Niue Declaration on Climate Change, 39th Pacific Islands Forum, Forum Communiqué Annex B (19–20 August 2008).

16 Majuro Declaration for Climate Leadership, 44th Pacific Islands Forum, Majuro, Marshall Islands (5 September 2013).

the need for, and commitment to, measures to 'urgently reduce and phase down greenhouse gas pollution in order to avert a climate crisis for present and future generations'. The need for support for adaptive measures is addressed, but the document omits the reference to 'relocation' made in the Niue Declaration:

> In addition, we commit to accelerate and intensify our efforts to prepare for and adapt to the intensifying impacts of climate change, and to further develop and implement policies, strategies and legislative frameworks, with support where necessary, to climate-proof our essential physical infrastructure, adapt our key economic sectors and ensure climate-resilient sustainable development for present and future generations.

NEW ZEALAND LEGAL AND POLICY FRAMEWORK

Contrary to the (mis)understandings of an intriguing number of international commentators,[17] New Zealand has no specific immigration policies which, explicitly at least, are intended to address hardship and deprivation experienced in South Pacific nations as a result of climate change.

New Zealand does have a number of targeted immigration schemes which include capped quotas allowing defined groups from defined Pacific nations to participate in an annual ballot, and if successful, to have the opportunity to then be considered against a number of other criteria (including language, income and work offer requirements). Most notably, they include the Pacific Access Category (PAC), the Samoan Quota and the Recognised Seasonal Employment (RSE) Scheme. Each of these schemes is well known by citizens of most Pacific nations, and the policies appear to be regarded as important practical and symbolic reflections of ties between New Zealand and Pacific nations. It is understood that all of the targeted schemes are fully subscribed. There are no indications however that the government is planning to increase target/quota numbers, whether in response to increased demand by an ever-growing South Pacific population, or in light of existing and predicted future drivers for migration and displacement associated with deteriorating environmental conditions because of climate change.

---

[17] Jane McAdam lists a number of academic publications which perpetuate the error, noting that it appears that the misunderstanding was perpetuated by Al Gore's film, *An Inconvenient Truth*, in McAdam, in Piguet, Pecoud and de Guchtenieree (eds) (2011) 18.

Refugee Status in New Zealand for Climate-displaced Persons

A number of cases have come before the New Zealand Immigration and Protection Tribunal (formerly the Refugee Appeals Authority) involving applicants seeking refugee status relying at least in part on hardship and deprivation in their home countries caused or contributed to by climate change. Consistent on this point with similar cases in Australia,[18] the appeals have, without exception been unsuccessful.

In 2000, a group of appeals was heard by the New Zealand Refugee Appeals Authority (as it was then named) involving applications for refugee status from related appellants from Tuvalu.[19] In similar terms, the Tuvaluan family members advanced grounds for refugee status in New Zealand, citing concern at rising sea levels which would exacerbate existing issues of inundation of the family home, together with poor medical facilities and the scarcity of employment opportunities within their home country. It was also submitted that 'the Tuvalu government failed in its duty of protecting the civil political, social, cultural and economic rights of the appellant for reasons of race (Tuvaluan), as nationals of Tuvalu (citizens) and as a member of a particular social group (defined as having no means to sustain themselves and survive)'.

The RAA dismissed the appeals, holding:[20]

> Clearly, none of the fears articulated by the appellant vis-à-vis his return to Tuvalu, can be said to be for reason of any one of the five Convention grounds in terms of the Refugee Convention, namely race, religion, nationality, membership of a particular group and political opinion. This is not a case where the appellant can be said to be differentially at risk of harm amounting to persecution due to any one of these five grounds. All Tuvalu citizens face the same environmental problems and economic difficulties living in Tuvalu.

In 2013, an appeal was brought to the successor of the RAA, the New Zealand Immigration and Protection Tribunal by a resident of Kiribati, also seeking asylum in New Zealand in large part due to deprivation resulting from adverse environmental conditions caused by climate change in his home country.

---

18 See n 21.

19 *Refugee Appeal No 72185* (10 August 2000); *Refugee Appeal No 72186* (10 August 2000); *Refugee Appeal Nos 72189–72195* (17 August 2000); *Refugee Appeal Nos 72179–72181* (31 August 2000); *Refugee Appeal No 72313* (19 October 2000); *Refugee Appeal No 72314* (19 October 2000); *Refugee Appeal No 72315* (19 October 2000); *Refugee Appeal No 72316* (19 October 2000).

20 *Refugee Appeal No 72185* (10 August 2000) at para [16].

The decision of BL Burson, Member of the IPT, in the 2013 *AF (Kiribati)*[21] case may well represent the most detailed legal analysis of an application for asylum on behalf of a climate-displaced person anywhere in the international refugee jurisprudence to date.

On behalf of the IPT, Burson accepted in its entirety the evidence adduced on behalf of the i-Kiribati appellant relating to the physical and geographical vulnerability of Kiribati to existing and future effects of climate change, including rising sea levels, 'risks to the land resource based livelihood of the people . . . from droughts, inundation of land from storm surges, salt water intrusion to water lenses, and excessive rainfall creating runoff into drinking groundwater wells', coastal erosion and deterioration of marine resources including coral reefs and fish stocks.[22] In combination with growing population and general economic conditions, the IPT accepted without demur the significant hardships already being experienced by residents of the low-lying atolls, as well as predicted future difficulties that will arise as the range of effects of climate change make themselves known with increasing intensity in Kiribati.

Consistent with previous New Zealand[23] and Australian decisions,[24] the IPT dismissed the appeal. On the central claim for refugee status under the 1951 Convention, the IPT held:[25]

> . . . the appellant's claim under the Refugee Convention must necessarily fail because the effects of environmental degradation on his standard of living were, by his own admission, faced by the population generally. The sad reality is that the environmental degradation caused by both slow and sudden onset natural disasters is one which is faced by the Kiribati population generally.

A parallel submission that denying the appellant's asylum in New Zealand (thus requiring him to return to Kiribati) would contravene Article 6 of the ICCPR (the 'right to life') was also rejected:[26]

---

21 *AF (Kiribati)* [2013] NZIPT 800413.

22 At para [38], it is recorded: 'The Tribunal finds the appellant to be credible. His account was told candidly and openly. It is accepted in its entirety.'

23 *Refugee Appeal No 72185* (10 August 2000); *Refugee Appeal No 72186* (10 August 2000); *Refugee Appeal Nos 72189–72195* (17 August 2000); *Refugee Appeal Nos 72179–72181* (31 August 2000); *Refugee Appeal No 72313* (19 October 2000); *Refugee Appeal No 72314* (19 October 2000); *Refugee Appeal No 72315* (19 October 2000); *Refugee Appeal No 72316* (19 October 2000); *BG (Fiji)* [2012] NZIPT 800091.

24 For example, *0907346* [2009] RRTA 1168 (10 December 2009).

25 *AF (Kiribati)* [2013] NZIPT 800413, at [75].

26 *AF (Kiribati)* [2013] NZIPT 800413, at [91].

> . . . the risk to the appellant and his family still falls well short of the threshold required to establish substantial grounds for believing that they would be in danger of arbitrary deprivation of life within the scope of Article 6. It remains firmly in the realm of conjecture or surmise.

In dismissing the appeal, the IPT took care to make it clear that the decision should not be regarded as definitively rejecting the potential for refugee or protection status under New Zealand or international law in all instances where displacement has or will occur in circumstances involving the effect of climate change. The decision contains an impressive analysis of climate change-influenced displacement under international refugee and human rights law, and careful qualification of its findings.[27]

Nevertheless the decision confirms the position already taken in previous New Zealand refugee appeals, international case law and academic commentary, namely that under New Zealand's existing legal regime for refugees and immigrants (itself built upon the existing international law in this area), only in the most exceptional circumstances will persons displaced as a result of climate change be entitled to legal recognition as refugees or protected persons.

New Zealand Government Policy Development

In summary, under the existing international and domestic legal and policy framework, persons seeking refuge in New Zealand from the worst impacts of climate change in the South Pacific have no clear legal avenues available to them. Existing immigration schemes such as the PAC, Samoan Quota and RSE may provide opportunities for some seeking temporary or permanent residence in New Zealand. However, those schemes require pre-arranged employment with minimum obligations for financial support. They are also tightly controlled in terms of annual quotas.

There is no obvious sign of any existing or imminent 'wave' of would-be migrants to New Zealand from the South Pacific. However despite the lack of empirical analysis on the likely future migration flows within the South Pacific as a result of climate change-related effects, it is not especially controversial that by 2050, large numbers of South Pacific residents will have been displaced as a result of a combination of population and environmental factors. It would be naïve, given New Zealand's existing strong ties with its South Pacific neighbours, to expect anything other than

[27] See, in particular, paras [56]–[65].

a significant increase in the numbers of Pacific residents seeking refuge in the relatively climate-change buffered environment of New Zealand.[28]

One might expect that the New Zealand government would be actively considering the implications from a legal, policy and practical perspective of future migration and displacement scenarios within the region.[29] Is it happening?

In a 2011 article, Australian academic Jane McAdam cited a 2008 New Zealand Ministry of Foreign Affairs and Trade (MFAT) document as evidence of a 'revised' approach towards the issue of 'environmental migrants' in the South Pacific.[30] According to the MFAT document, New Zealand's new focus would be to:

> a) acknowledge the concerns of Pacific Island countries in relation to this issue;
> b) stress that current climate change efforts in the Pacific should continue to focus on adaptation, and should be underpinned by the desire of Pacific peoples to continue to live in their own countries; and
> c) reaffirm that New Zealand has a proven history of providing assistance where needed in the Pacific, and that our approach to environmentally displaced persons would be consistent with this.
> . . . This includes a commitment to 'respond to climatic disasters in the Pacific and manage changes as they arise.

In March 2013, the author lodged a request under the Official Information Act 1982 (OIA) seeking a formal response as to whether there had been any further consideration given to New Zealand's legal and policy response to issues of climate-contributed displacement or migration within the South Pacific. Officials from MFAT and Ministry of Pacific Affairs were also interviewed.

In response to the March 2013 OIA, a number of internal briefing and policy documents were provided. They confirm, in summary, that New Zealand's domestic policy (and international positioning) on the issue

---

28 For a summary of anticipated climate change impacts on New Zealand, see Rive and Weeks in Cameron (2011) ch 9, section 6.4.

29 In 1990, the authors of a report representing the outcome of a six-month, prime ministerial-initiated study of New Zealand's relationship with Pacific nations noted 'There is widespread concern in the region about the potentially profound effects of climate change, and especially a sea level rise would have on Pacific Island countries . . . the region faces a major potential problem of environmental refugees.' Amongst its recommendations were: 'That early consultations be held with the Governments of Kiribati and Tuvalu about the means by which their people might make up a greater proportion of Pacific Island immigrants.' South Pacific Policy Review Group (1990).

30 McAdam (2011).

of climate-displaced persons within the South Pacific has not advanced in any meaningful sense from the 'revised approach' adopted in 2008, reported by McAdam. In a 2009 policy paper, MFAT and Department of Labour officials advised their Ministers:[31]

> . . . New Zealand's existing immigration policy settings are sufficiently flexible that they may be able to form one response to this issue, should it become a reality in future. Pacific migrants can currently enter New Zealand through general immigration policies, such as those for skilled migrants, temporary workers or family sponsorship. There are also immigration policies specifically for Pacific countries, such as the Pacific Access Category (for migrants from Tuvalu, Kiribati and Tonga); the Samoan Quota and Recognised Seasonal Employer (RSE) Scheme.
>
> None of these policies were developed in response to climate change or climate induced migration although they could potentially be helpful in responding to it as part of a broader toolkit of policy options in which adaptation and mitigation options are given priority . . .

A January 2013 MFAT briefing paper to the Associate Climate Change Minister expanded on the theme:[32]

> New Zealand's policy on the issue of 'environmental refugees' remains under review. Such 'refugees' have no current status under international law . . . New Zealand has indicated that it will continue to respond to climatic disasters in the Pacific and manage changes as they arise . . .
>
> Media reporting that New Zealand has agreed to take 'environmental refugees' from Tuvalu . . . is incorrect. There is no such policy. However New Zealand will continue to monitor the situation and provide climate change assistance and disaster relief as it has always done.

Queried on the reference to New Zealand's policy remaining 'under review', in a telephone interview on 28 May 2013, an MFAT official advised:[33]

> I think that in that context, I wouldn't want to imply that we have a grand process . . . it's more like, we are keeping a watch on it . . . that if things change or we judge that we may need to refer to ministers for more guidance, or

---

[31] Joint Ministry of Foreign Affairs and Trade and Department of Labour submission to the Ministers of Foreign and Immigration 22 July 2009, released to the author under the Official Information Act 1982 in May 2013.

[32] Ministry of Foreign Affairs and Trade briefing to the Associate Minister of Climate Change, January 2013 released to the author under the Official Information Act 1982 in May 2013.

[33] Telephone interview by the author of Mr Roger Dungan, Senior Policy Officer Climate Change Environment Division, New Zealand Ministry of Foreign Affairs & Trade, 28 May 2013.

> whatever, then we will. To say it is 'under review' doesn't mean that it is 'under active review'. But it is not like the case is closed, and our policy is done and dusted. It is certainly a living thing, and we keep our eye on developments, that if something did come up that we needed to get some guidance or make recommendations to ministers on, then we would certainly do so.

It is apparent that the government agency with responsibility for policy development on New Zealand's response to climate-displacement in the South Pacific – MFAT – has not updated its policy since 2008, has no active working groups looking at the issue, and as recently as May 2013 has explicitly reconfirmed its position not to reassess its policy settings.[34] This is despite:

- An open call for New Zealand (as one of the 'Pacific's Development Partners') to 'increase [its] technical and financial support for climate change action on adaptation, mitigation and, if necessary, relocation' in the 2008 Niue Declaration;[35]
- The issue of responses to climate displacement having been openly placed on the agenda for international consideration in a decision of the conference of parties to the UNFCCC in Cancun in 2010;[36]
- Direct calls by Pacific leaders for engagement by New Zealand and Australia in consideration of a framework and process for planned migration-as-adaptation as part of a wider package of measures to address the impact of climate change on low-lying island states within the South Pacific.[37]

OPTIONS AND OPPORTUNITIES

Over the past 10 years as issues of the potential magnitude and distribution of climate-displaced people have begun to enter public consciousness through media reports and NGO awareness-raising, there has been an

---

[34] Compare the observations in Hausler and McCorquodale (2011) 617–27; McAdam (2011) 102–37 which indicate that the New Zealand government is in the process of developing a specific policy on Pacific climate migrants. It is not apparent to the author that this is the case.

[35] Niue Declaration on Climate Change, 39th Pacific Islands Forum, Forum Communiqué Annex B (19–20 August 2008).

[36] See n 14.

[37] See, for example (in relation to Kiribati President Anote Tong), McAdam (2011) n 76.

exponential growth in academic analysis and public policy consideration of various legal and policy responses to the issue.

New or Modified Existing Multi-lateral Instruments?

A range of possible solutions or responses to the 'protection deficit' at international law for climate-displaced persons has been developed and discussed in the literature, including:

- Amending the 1951 Refugee Convention to specifically cover cross-border displacement as a result of environmental/climate change-caused degradation;
- Developing a new, stand-alone multilateral treaty or convention on climate change/environmental displacement;[38]
- Developing a new protocol to the UNFCCC which specifically addresses climate change displacement.

A detailed assessment of the merits of the multilateral instrument options listed above is beyond the scope of this chapter. Briefly, the author:

- Shares the strong reservations expressed by a number of commentators concerning suggested redrafting or supplementing of the 1951 Refugee Convention in order to confer refugee or protected person status on persons displaced for environmental or climate change-related reasons;[39]
- Concurs with the views expressed by McAdam and others regarding the short-medium-term practical and political impediments to negotiation of an effective stand-alone multilateral treaty or convention addressing climate change/environmental displacement, while not ruling out entirely the possibility of such an international instrument being developed in the fullness of time;
- Sees potential for some sort of multilateral framework for coordinating state and regional arrangements and responses for climate change-related displacement to be included in future UNFCCC instruments or decisions; however, doubts that in the short-medium-term, a full-blown dedicated protocol is likely to be politically or practically feasible.

---

[38] See, for example, Docherty and Giannini (2009); Hodkinson *et al.* (2009).

[39] See, for example McAdam (2011) 13–14; Burson (2012) in Leckie, Simperingham and Bakker (eds) 167.

Regional Solutions?

Coordinated regional arrangements, whether recorded in 'hard law' instruments or 'soft law' declarations or statements offer a number of distinct advantages over fully multilateral negotiated outcomes. In the climate displacement context, this is particularly the case for a number of reasons. First, there is the pragmatic issue of reaching a meaningful agreement which contains sufficient specificity and relevance to usefully guide the development of domestic emigration/immigration, protection and other support processes. As has been rightly noted by a number of commentators, for an issue likely to be as politically contentious and sensitive as immigration and refugee policy, the prospects of achieving consensus on the large number of issues that would need to be addressed in such a document within a workable timeframe can only be regarded as wildly optimistic.

On the other hand, documented agreed regional arrangements (while still likely to be challenging politically for the same reasons as those noted above) would appear to have better prospects of success, especially if negotiated through existing regional fora and if they build upon existing regional arrangements, including institutional as well as legal and political affirmations of shared policy objectives.

In the South Pacific context, the Pacific Islands Forum has the question of regional responses to climate displacement already on its agenda and, no doubt, would be central to the development of a coordinated regional response.

The Swiss and Norwegian-led *Nansen Initiative*, a 'state-led, bottom-up consultative process . . . intended to build consensus on the development of a protection agenda addressing the needs of people displaced across international borders by natural disasters, including the effects of climate change' held the first of a planned series of five regional consultations in Rarotonga in May 2013.[40] The New Zealand government was represented at the event.

The outcome document from that consultation exercise records agreement amongst participants that:[41]

- 'As a consequence of sea level rise, acidification and more extreme weather patterns, voluntary migration, planned relocation and

---

[40] For a thoughtful assessment of the potential for the Nansen Initiative to facilitate solutions in relation to climate displacement, see Kälin (2012) 48.

[41] Nansen Initiative (2013).

forced displacement are expected to rise significantly in the next decades and beyond';
- 'In the context of natural disasters and climate change these developments require action and resource mobilization to be taken at community, national, regional and international levels'.

Regional actions agreed as necessary included:

- 'Continue the regional dialogue on voluntary migration, forced displacement and planned relocation';
- 'Develop appropriate normative frameworks to address the protection needs of displaced or relocated populations, including temporary protection schemes or template agreements, which take into account lessons from past experience and incorporate existing good practices from the Pacific Island countries'.

It will be interesting to observe the New Zealand government's response, in particular to the second action point noted above.

CONCLUSIONS

For compelling historical, cultural and social reasons, most residents of Pacific nations at risk from the effects of climate change regard remaining where they are, and developing adaptive solutions to issues such as rising sea level and increased exposure to weather events, as their first priority.

However, it is clearly the case that migration – whether that is to other, closer, Pacific neighbours such as Fiji, or to countries such as Australia and New Zealand where more favourable employment and other opportunities are likely to exist – is not only under contemplation, but is also a predictable and rational response as part of a wider set of potential adaptive responses to the effects of climate change in the region.

To date, despite rhetorical support for its Pacific neighbours, the New Zealand government has not actively engaged with legal, policy or practical implications of likely significant future flows of climate change-related migration to its shores. Its current policy, if it can be described as such, is not substantively more than a vague commitment to 'wait and see'. No doubt this is convenient in terms of existing domestic politics. But a failure to plan now will have lasting adverse consequences which, it is suggested, New Zealand, as well as its Pacific neighbours, will come to regret.

REFERENCES

Cases

New Zealand

AF (Kiribati) [2013] NZIPT 800413.
BG (Fiji) [2012] NZIPT 800091.
Refugee Appeal No 72185 (10 August 2000).
Refugee Appeal No 72186 (10 August 2000).
Refugee Appeal Nos 72189–72195 (17 August 2000).
Refugee Appeal Nos 72179–72181 (31 August 2000).
Refugee Appeal No 72313 (19 October 2000).
Refugee Appeal No 72314 (19 October 2000).
Refugee Appeal No 72315 (19 October 2000).
Refugee Appeal No 72316 (19 October 2000).

Australia

0907346 [2009] RRTA 1168 (10 December 2009).

International Instruments

Conference of the Parties to the United Nations Framework Convention on Climate Change, Action Taken by the Conference of the Parties at its Sixteenth Session, (Addendum Pt 2 to the Report of the Conference of the Parties on its sixteenth session, held in Cancun from 29 November to 10 December 2010) FCCC/CP/2010/7/ Add.1 (15 March 2011) 5 ('COP16').

Convention relating to the Status of Refugees (1951) 189 UNTS 137.

International Covenant on Civil and Political Rights (1966) 999 UNTS 171.

International Covenant on Economic, Social and Cultural Rights 993 UNTS 3.

Majuro Declaration for Climate Leadership, 44th Pacific Islands Forum, Majuro, Marshall Islands (5 September 2013).

Niue Declaration on Climate Change, 39th Pacific Islands Forum, Forum Communiqué Annex B (19–20 August 2008).

Protocol relating to the Status of Refugees (1967) 606 UNTS 267.

Books and Chapters in Books

Burson, B. (2012), 'Securing Meaningful International Agreement on Climate Change Related Displacement and Migration: The Refugee Convention as a Window on International Burden (Responsibility) – Sharing in an Involuntary Movement Context' in S. Leckie, E. Simperingham and J. Bakker (eds), *Climate Change and Displacement Reader* (Abingdon: Taylor & Francis, Routledge/Earthscan) 159.

Campbell, J. (2010), 'Pacific Island Populations 2009', Secretariat of the Pacific Community, Noumea, cited in J. Campbell, 'Climate Change and Population Movement in Pacific Island Countries' in B. Burson (ed.), *Climate Change and Migration: South Pacific Perspectives* (Wellington: Institute of Policy Studies) 12, 38.

Elliot, M. and D. Fagan (2009), 'From Community to Copenhagen: Civil Society Action on Climate Change in the Pacific' in B. Burson (ed.) *Climate Change and Migration: South Pacific Perspectives* (Wellington: Institute of Policy Studies) at 75.
McAdam, J. (2011), 'Refusing "Refuge" in the Pacific: (De)Constructing Climate-Induced Displacement in International Law', in E. Piguet, A. Pecoud and P. de Guchtenieree (eds) *Migration and Climate Change* (Cambridge: Cambridge University Press/UNESCO).
Rive, V. and T. Weeks (2011), 'Adaptation to Climate Change in New Zealand' in A. Cameron (ed.) *Climate Change Law and Policy in New Zealand* (Wellington: LexisNexis) ch 9.

Journal Articles

Docherty, B. and T. Giannini (2009), 'Confronting a Rising Tide: A Proposal for a Convention on Climate Change Refugees' 33 Harv. Envtl. L. Rev. 349.
Hausler, K. and R. McCorquodale (2011), 'Climate change and its impact on security and survival' 37 *Commonwealth Law Bulletin* 4, 617.
Kälin, W. (2012), 'From the Nansen Principles to the Nansen Initiative' 41 FMR December 2012, 48.
Shen, S. and F. Gemenne (2011), 'Contrasted Views on Environmental Change and Migration: the Case of Tuvaluan Migration to New Zealand' 49 *International Migration*, 19 May 2011, e224–e242.
Smith, R. (2013), 'Should They Stay or Should They Go? A Discourse Analysis of Factors Influencing Relocation Decisions Among the Outer Islands of Tuvalu and Kiribati' 1 *Journal of New Zealand & Pacific Studies* 1, 1 April 2013, 23.

Parliamentary and Government Materials

Joint Ministry of Foreign Affairs and Trade and Department of Labour submission to the Ministers of Foreign and Immigration 22 July 2009, released to the author under the Official Information Act 1982 in May 2013.
Ministry of Foreign Affairs and Trade briefing to the Associate Minister of Climate Change, January 2013 released to the author under the Official Information Act 1982 in May 2013.

Reports

Background Paper: 'Human Mobility, Natural Disasters and Climate Change in the Pacific', May 2013, Nansen Initiative Secretariat, Geneva.
Bedford, R. and G.J. Hugo (2012) *Population Movement in the Pacific: A Perspective on Future Prospects* (Department of Labour, New Zealand).
Nansen Initiative, 'Conclusions: Nansen Initiative Pacific Regional Consultation', Undated (recording outcome of meetings in Rarotonga from 21 to 24 May 2013), Nansen Initiative Secretariat, Geneva.
South Pacific Policy Review Group (1990) 'Towards a Pacific Island Community' Victoria University of Wellington.

Theses

Fedor, I. (2012), 'Cultural and National Identity in the Face of Climate Change: A Case Study of I-Kiribati Migrants in New Zealand' (Thesis, Master of Arts). University of Otago.

Internet Resources

Hodkinson, D. *et al.* (2009), 'Hour When the Ship Comes in: A Convention for Persons Displaced by Climate-change' accessed 20 March 2015 at www.ccdpconvention.com.

New Zealand Ministry of Foreign Affairs and Trade Country Profile – Kiribati accessed 20 March 2015 at www.mfat.govt.nz/Countries/Pacific/Kiribati.php.

New Zealand Prime Minister John Key news release 4 September 2013 'Clean water initiative for low-lying Pacific islands' accessed 20 March 2015 at www.johnkey.co.nz.

President Anote Tong statement of position on relocation as response to the effects of climate change in Kiribati, accessed 29 March 2015 at http://www.climate.gov.ki/category/action/relocation/.

Smith, R. and K. McNamara, 'Government Discourses of Climate Change Migration in Tuvalu and Kiribati', (8 July 2013), editorial on the website of the Asia-Pacific Migration and Environment Network accessed 20 March 2015 at www.apmen.iom.int.

Other Resources

Telephone interview by the author of Mr Roger Dungan, Senior Policy Officer Climate Change Environment Division, New Zealand Ministry of Foreign Affairs & Trade, 28 May 2013.

13. Overcoming climate inertia with unilateral action on black carbon

Anastasia Telesetsky

International climate policy is embedded in inertia. After the initial promising adoption of the 1992 United Nations Framework Convention on Climate Change and the 1997 Kyoto Protocol, there have been a series of false starts and non-starts. Key greenhouse gas producers from existing industrialised States have balked at cutting emissions as long as States in the process of industrialising refuse to curb carbon emissions. The targets set by developed and developing countries in the Copenhagen Accord and Cancun Agreements have been decidedly unambitious. It is not hard to become cynical about the promise of multilateral negotiations. Collectively, States do not expect much from the process and so they do not invest much in the process. While in principle States agree that two degrees Celsius of average global warming should not be exceeded and that climate change is posing irreversible risks, the 2009 Copenhagen Accords could be relabeled the 'Hopenhagen' Accords as little fundamental change has resulted from agreements in principle.

Commenting on the 2012 Durban meetings, a brief published by the Harvard Center for Climate Agreements noted that for progress to be made in decelerating climate change that 'Governments around the world now need fresh, outside-of-the-box ideas, and they need those ideas over the next two to three years. This is a time for fundamentally new proposals for future international climate-policy architecture, not for incremental adjustments to the old pathway.'[1] This chapter accepts this challenge by suggesting negotiators should walk temporarily away from the existing stalemate that has categorised the carbon dioxide negotiations and instead focus attention on developing effective national policies to combat short-lived climate forcers through technology transfer and financing greener technology.

While short-lived climate forcers have been of great interest to

---

[1] Aldy and Stavins (2012) 8.

scientists,[2] there has been insufficient attention in the policy realm regarding how States can implement immediate black carbon reduction schemes.[3] This reluctance to give concerted attention to revising pollution policies may be because elimination of the short-lived climate forcers alone will not be enough to avoid climate change impacts. Reductions of short-lived climate forcers such as black carbon, at best, will decelerate the speed at which climate change is currently happening and, at worst, would have little impact on climate change but use resources that might have been used to address carbon dioxide. Even though reducing black carbon may not be a panacea for global climate woes, there are additional reasons to continue focusing public international attention on black carbon in order to improve human health and quality of life.

This chapter argues for unilateral adoption by each State of a black carbon reduction strategy which will improve air quality while simultaneously alleviating one climate forcer. After describing the phenomenon of black carbon, this chapter starts by suggesting that the current efforts to internationalise the issue of black carbon may be counterproductive since ultimately any international decision must be domesticated. Instead, a strategy for the reduction of black carbon should be negotiated by each State. Other States should support domestic black carbon reduction strategies particularly for States that generate either the largest percentages of global black carbon or produce black carbon outputs in areas that are already geographically sensitive to climate change. Where large particulate producing States are reluctant to create national black carbon reduction policies, civil society may want to seek domestic injunctive relief to protect their health and their livelihoods or relief from regional tribunals.

WHY FOCUS LEGAL POLICYMAKING ON BLACK CARBON?

The short-lived climate forcers include black carbon, methane and tropospheric ozone.[4] Tropospheric ozone is a byproduct of sunlight interacting with carbon monoxide, non-methane volatile organic compounds, and nitrogen oxides. Reducing tropospheric ozone depends on reducing carbon monoxide and methane. In turn, methane reduction depends on

---

2 See e.g. Hu *at al.* (2013); Shindell *et al.* (2012).
3 UNEP (2011).
4 UNEP (2011) 3–4.

regulating certain human activities such as agriculture, including both livestock and rice cultivation, fossil fuel energy production and landfills. Some efforts are currently underway to reduce methane by capturing methane gas and using it for energy. These capture efforts are currently hampered by technological challenges.[5]

While there are direct efforts to reduce methane that indirectly leads to ozone reductions, black carbon has, until recently, received significantly less attention from innovators than the other short-lived climate forcers. Black carbon is known as a 'heating aerosol' that combines both elemental carbon and various organic acids.[6] As the major component of soot produced by incomplete combustion of fossil fuels, woods, and other biomass, black carbon may be easily identified without specific scientific instrumentation. Smoke plumes and exhaust from diesel machinery frequently contain black carbon and can be visually identified. Unlike methane, black carbon is not a greenhouse gas but it still has a strong capacity for warming by (1) creating conditions for surface dimming by absorbing solar radiation that would have reached the earth's surface and (2) absorbing solar radiation from the earth's surface and then radiating energy back into the atmosphere rather than reflecting energy back into the atmosphere. Black carbon can also be deposited on ice and snow surfaces leading to increased absorption of heat which causes melting. One aspect that makes eliminating black carbon challenging is that black carbon is often co-emitted with sulphates and nitrates which are 'cooling aerosols'.[7] While the black carbon warms the environment, the sulphates and nitrates act as cooling agents. Therefore law and policy interventions need to comprehend the correlation between cooling aerosols and warming aerosols and understand that the effect of aerosols can vary depending on region and season.[8] Certain targets such as diesel vehicles and engines have a particularly high rate of 'warming' black carbon as compared to 'cooling' organic carbons and other substances.[9]

Taking into consideration that a State needs to be strategic in terms of which short-lived emissions it may want to eliminate in order to avoid unintentionally removing the cooling aspects of some aerosols, black carbon is still a prime candidate for action for two reasons. First, black carbon-laden aerosols are highly localised so that efforts to eliminate black carbon should theoretically have measurable regional impacts on

---

5 Ifran (2013).
6 UNEP (2008).
7 See e.g. Bauer *et al.* (2007).
8 UNEP (2008).
9 Ibid.

warming.[10] Secondly, black carbon is a major component of particulates that contribute to premature deaths across the globe by lodging in individuals' respiratory systems.[11]

Black carbon reductions present a climate deceleration opportunity that has not yet been embraced systematically by States even though black carbon is allegedly responsible for 18 per cent of the existing warming.[12] While it may not amount to a long-term mitigation opportunity for reducing carbon dioxide stocks, reducing known sources of black carbon could in the long-term lower rates of warming and reduce the extent of expected sea level rise.[13] There are two advantages to tackling black carbon now rather than continuing to delay action until there is a multilateral agreement: a directly correlated public health benefit and, to the extent that black carbon has been linked to precipitation patterns, food security benefits.[14]

WHY FOCUS LEGAL POLICYMAKING AT A NATIONAL LEVEL RATHER THAN AN INTERNATIONAL LEVEL?

As suggested above, a new climate strategy needs to reorient its focus to a different more tractable political level.[15] UNEP in its 2011 report suggested that while national activities might be given a special focus because the benefits of improving local air quality are tangible, there must also remain a regional and international focus since black carbon may be a transboundary pollutant.[16] While black carbon does cross borders, the UNEP conclusion of an international strategy does not necessarily lead to a more efficient outcome to achieve what is necessary at a national level.

While black carbon has been familiar to the international policymaking community for at least half a decade, there has been remarkably little action in curbing its production. Discussions in conjunction with revisions to the

---

10 Ramanathan (2005).

11 Rosenthal (2009).

12 Ibid.

13 Hu *et al.* (2013).

14 UNEP (2008) (Describing how surface dimming caused by black carbon may lead to reduced evaporation of water vapor from the surface with impacts on precipitation patterns.)

15 Otherwise, one risks the potential of being accused of the observation attributed to Albert Einstein: 'Insanity is doing the same thing over and over again and expecting different results.'

16 UNEP (2011), 36.

post-2012 Kyoto Protocol could theoretically engage black carbon and other short-lived climate forcers, but it is unclear how the new obligations would be distributed. If the Protocol continues to provide for 'common but differentiated responsibilities', it is possible that any restrictions on black carbon emissions would be delayed for an unknown amount of time. If this is the case, a multilateral agreement would provide a barrier rather than a bridge to black carbon reductions. Black carbon is not an appropriate subject for trading since it is emitted from so many dispersed sources that the costs required to monitor and verify emissions would be cost prohibitive.

Others have suggested including black carbon in a renegotiated text of the Montreal Protocol because the agreement has already proven effective in reducing chlorofluorcarbons through global caps on ozone-depleting substances.[17] While this approach might prove more successful than a revision of the Kyoto Protocol, such a negotiation would carry with it substantial transaction costs and lead to delays in State response. Likewise proposals to regulate State behaviour under the Gothenburg Protocol to the Convention on Long-range Transboundary Air Pollution (CLRTAP) face similar transactional costs and delays. While there has been an agreement among the CLRTAP parties to issue the first standard guidelines for estimating and reporting black carbon emissions in order to create a black carbon international inventory,[18] it is unclear what the value of having an international inventory is when it is well-established that every country already has a strong health incentive to unilaterally reduce black carbon rather than engage possibly in future black carbon trading.

The International Maritime Organization has directly addressed 'black carbon' but there appears to be limited urgency in harmonising standards for members. The Sub-Committee on Pollution Prevention and Response in 2014 discussed two technical definitions for black carbon and various methods for measurement but ended up deciding to refer the issue to the Marine Environment Protection Committee for further discussions on the definitions, measurement methods, and possible control measures.[19] Given the concerns by scientists to take action immediately on black carbon in order to offset additional warming, the IMO's responses seem dilatory given that the parties to MARPOL, which can be amended through the IMO, already agreed as of January 2013 to greenhouse gas reductions through ship efficiency measures.[20]

---

17 Molina *et al.* (2009).

18 United Nations Economic Commission for Europe (UNECE 2013).

19 Sub-committee on Pollution Prevention and Response, 1st Session (2014).

20 *See generally* MARPOL Annex VI, Chapter 4.

Each of the multilateral efforts is laudable but the resources being placed into international and regional negotiations should be reallocated to developing national plans that may include substantial subsidisation of black carbon reducing technologies for industry or other financial incentives not to engage in black carbon generating activities. The remainder of this chapter examines one region and two States who have the potential to contribute the most to meaningful black carbon reduction that may have critical regional impacts on decelerating climate impact. Specifically, each of these areas needs to have a legal strategy to shift practices related to diesel engines, certain industrial processes, and residential heating and cooking fuels. To the extent that this is a public governance problem where governments will be the leaders, the legal strategies need to be composed nationally to reflect the challenges in each region. The long-term financial strategies to finance some of the shifts away from black carbon generating sources may be an appropriate subject for multilateral negotiations.

Urgent Need for National Responses by Arctic States

As noted above, black carbon accelerates climate change when it is deposited on ice and snow. Imagine a sheet of ice peppered with dark particulate matter. Like a blacktop driveway, the ice and snow melt preferentially in the dark areas leading to ice and snowfields pocked with small pits that melt into basins. Eventually, in some areas of the Arctic, the preferential melting of the ice leading to the melting of permafrost, the usually permanently frozen subsoil, has the added impact of releasing methane, another short-lived climate forcer, and carbon dioxide. Keeping the permafrost frozen is an urgent regional need with global implications. Some studies predict that release of greenhouse gases from the Arctic due to melting could negate 42–88 per cent of the planet's ability to store and sequester carbon within vegetation and soils.[21] The challenge with the Arctic are the multiple sources of black carbon that originate largely but not exclusively from the Arctic States, including emissions from oil and gas flaring, coal burning for energy,and diesel operations, including shipping emissions.

The direct radiative forcing problem of black carbon in the Arctic is well understood. Multilaterally, there has been no agreement about how to regulate black carbon and it is unclear when such an agreement might be negotiated and more importantly implemented. The Arctic Council, an intergovernmental organisation, was created under the Ottawa Declaration, provided that States would cooperate, coordinate

---

21 Hayes *et al.* (2013) 13.

and interact with each other and with Arctic indigenous organisations to support sustainable development and environmental protection in the Arctic region. It is the obvious forum for regionally coordinated policies on black carbon. In May 2013 at the Arctic Council ministerial meeting, there were some expectations from civil society that the States would agree on coordinated action to reduce black carbon and other short-lived climate forcers.[22] Yet, nothing concrete was decided in terms of how each of the States would reduce its contributions to black carbon generation. The States merely agreed to continue working on options to reduce black carbon.[23] Norway and Finland, under the auspices of the Arctic Council, have undertaken workshops targeting black carbon reductions specifically for wood combustion.[24] While this effort is laudable, it does not address the more daunting issue of nationally regulating diesel engines since poor fuel-combustion within diesel engines poses more of a long-term warming threat than wood combustion.[25] In December 2013, a task force on Black Carbon and Methane was established by the Arctic Council with the intent of creating deliverables by 2015. All of these cooperative actions reflect good faith efforts, but ultimately, individual States will still need to do more if there is to be a region-wide reduction.

Individual member States do have some policies that are addressing black carbon from mobile and stationary diesel emissions but it is not apparent that these programs are being fast-tracked for emission reduction results. For example, the United States has set emissions standards for new engines and has a retrofit program for in-use mobile diesel engines.[26] The expectation is that by 2030, the new emission standards coupled with the industry phasing in new fleets will reduce black carbon emissions by 90 per cent from a 1990 baseline.[27] This is a positive development that

---

22 World Wildlife Fund (2013) (noting that Russia blocked progress on a black carbon agreement).

23 Arctic Council (2013as

24 Arctic Council (2013b) (June 2013 workshop organised through the Arctic Contaminants Action Program was designed to share findings and suggestions on how to calculate black carbon emissions, share information about such emissions, and explore emission reducing technologies focused on wood combustion).

25 US Environmental Protection Agency, accessed 20 March 2015 at http://www.epa.gov/blackcarbon/mitigation.html (observing that mobile diesel engines produce about 75% black carbon, while wood burning is largely dominated by organic carbon which also has the capacity to heat the environment but less so than black carbon).

26 Current retrofit programs such as the National Clean Diesel Campaign providing loans and grants for retrofits are voluntary and not well funded.

27 US Environmental Protection Agency (see n 25).

should not be discounted, but it is essential to realise that this predicted reduction relies on the assumption that mobile diesel engine industries will phase in new fleets. There is no legal requirement for industry to do so. These hoped for reductions by 2030 may not be achievable without additional regulation that seeks immediate black carbon reductions. Presently, the United States has no specific cross-cutting black carbon reduction policy in spite of investing some attention in reducing black carbon in other parts of the world.[28] The United States does regulate for particulates but as observed earlier the term 'particulate matter' is not synonymous with black carbon for purposes of climate strategy since not all reductions of particulate matter will reduce black carbon.

While the US Environmental Protection Agency (EPA) has reported to Congress on black carbon, there has yet to be any legislative action. In 2009, a bill entitled the Black Carbon Emissions Reduction Act failed to leave the committee process for a vote. The Act, if passed, would have required the EPA to propose regulations under the existing authorities of the Clean Air Act to reduce emissions of black carbon, the Secretary of State to create an international black carbon mitigation program, and Congress to appropriate money for these programs.[29] The 'Super Pollutant Emissions Reduction Act of 2013' was introduced but failed to leave the committee. The Act called only generically for reductions in 'short-lived climate pollutants' including black carbon but does not provide any specific congressional oversight for the issue. Instead, the bill proposed formation of a multi-stakeholder task force to review existing and potential policies and measures that promote reduction of short-lived climate pollutants, to identify gaps where program do not exist 'with an emphasis on industry standards and public-private partnerships where possible', and finally, to develop best practices for reductions of short-lived climate pollutants.[30]

Other Arctic States also seem to lack coherent national black carbon reduction policies particularly addressing diesel engines. The European

---

[28] United States Environmental Protection Agency, Office of International and Tribal Affairs (2011b); see also US Environmental Protection Agency (2011a).

[29] H.R. 1760, A bill to mitigate the effects of black carbon emissions in the United States and throughout the world (6 March 2009) 111th Congress (2009–2010).

[30] H.R. 1943, A bill to establish a task force to review policies and measures to promote, and to develop best practices for, reduction of short-lived climate pollutants, and for other purposes, 113th Congress (2013–2015) accessed 20 March 2015 at http://www.gpo.gov/fdsys/pkg/BILLS-113hr1943ih/pdf/BILLS-113hr1943ih.pdf.

Union of which Denmark, Sweden and Finland are both members has partially addressed the issue of improving diesel standards with the introduction in 2013 of the EURO VI standards for heavy-duty diesel engines.[31] Neither Denmark, Sweden or Finland have black carbon specific emission reduction strategies although all of these States have particulate reduction legislation.[32] Russia does not appear to have any specific black carbon legislation. Local efforts in Russia to reduce sources of black carbon, such as agricultural burning, lack adequate enforcement measures.[33] Finally, Canada has no specific black carbon reduction laws although like the European States and the US has particulate emission laws.

What is necessary at this point is greater attention by each of the Arctic States to rapidly reducing its black carbon footprint. The key for any legal intervention in the Arctic is that it must have immediate possibilities for reductions, unlike the current US legislative proposals for task forces to meet and generate reports. There is no clear indication that any of the Arctic States are pursuing bold regulatory programs for reducing black carbon. While many of the States support black carbon reductions, few have created legal frameworks to achieve these reductions. As the Arctic melts, States fiddle with policies, programs, projects and reports.

While litigation rarely provides for a speedy resolution for environmental problems, there may be opportunities for civil society groups and organisations to use litigation tools to push for immediate legislative action on short-term climate forcers. Within Canada, there have been interesting developments with Arctic communities using the multilateral dispute resolution system to seek action from the State of Canada. The Arctic Athabaskan Council (AAC), an indigenous peoples rights group, recently filed a petition with the Inter-American Commission on Human Rights ('the Commission') for physical harm caused by Canada's release of 98,000 tons of black carbon annually into the Arctic environment where the Athabaskan reside and hunt for subsistence.[34] The AAC did not file in Canada because it alleged that the legal remedies available under federal law are inadequate or ineffective.[35] Instead, they filed with the

[31] See generally Euro VI standard-emissions from heavy duty vehicles, accessed 20 March 2015 at http://ec.europa.eu/enterprise/sectors/automotive/environment/eurovi/.

[32] Arctic Council (2011).

[33] Schevchenko (2013).

[34] Artic Athabaskan Council (2013).

[35] Ibid, 81–4.

Commission to request that Canada adopt 'mandatory measures to limit emissions of black carbon from key Canadian emissions sectors'.[36]

It is unclear how the Commission will handle the Athabaskan human rights petition given its rejection of the Inuit's petition that United States greenhouse gas emissions were contributing to Arctic melting. The Commission indicated on the Inuit petition that it was unable to provide relief because the petition failed to establish 'whether the alleged facts would tend to characterize a violation of rights protected by the American Declaration'.[37] The petitioners in the Athabaskan suit have taken pains to create a chain of causation between black carbon and its impacts on indigenous property, subsistence options, culture and health. Assuming for purposes of this discussion that the Commission is willing to find the petition admissible, it will be interesting to see (1) how quickly the Commission will hear the petition given the time-sensitive nature of the petition; (2) whether they will issue precautionary measures; and (3) whether any report from the Commission would reflect a recommendation for the petitioner's request for mandatory black carbon reduction measures for key Canadian sectors. The Petitioners recommend a variety of potential regulatory interventions including retrofitting the existing fleet of on-road diesel vehicles with participle traps, removing high-emitting vehicles, improving efficiency for residential heating, eliminating most gas flaring and banning agricultural biomass burning.[38] It is possible that a Commission inclined to support the petitioner's arguments might agree to forward the petitioner's regulatory proposals to the Canadian government as recommendations. The Canadian federal government may use such a report to boost efforts to achieve otherwise politically difficult emission reductions. The challenge for the Athabaskan case, as pointed out in the petition, is that there is a need for numerous interventions at the provincial level (where many environmental regulatory powers reside) and not just at the federal level.

In parallel with its application to the Commission, the AAC could attempt to either seek precautionary measures from Canada to better manage those industrial sectors which contribute the majority of emissions to Canada's overall black carbon emission registry. Precautionary measures serve an injunctive relief role and may be granted under the Commission's rules of procedure. Specifically, the Commission may either at the request of the petitioners or on its initiative seek

---

36 Ibid, 86.
37 Letter from Inter-American Commission on Human Rights (2006).
38 Ibid, 6.

precautionary measures when it has been demonstrated that the situation may have a 'grave impact' on a protected right, 'grave impact' on the eventual effect of a pending decision, or the situation poses a 'risk or threat that is imminent and can materialize'.[39] One might argue that the current situation, with the melting of the sea ice in the Arctic region over the course of the past decade, poses an 'urgent situation'. This would be a novel argument for the Commission to consider since most of its previous precautionary measures have been directed at situations created by human conditions, not environmental conditions. Albeit, the petition describing the flooding, erosion and changes in ice and snow cover in the region suggest that the conditions facing the Athabaskan people represent an 'urgent situation' where there may be irreparable harm. No one understands how to restore the Arctic and there is no compensation for loss of traditions, food sources and livelihoods that define the Arctic Athabaskan peoples as groups tied to the life of the tundra. Relocation or compensation payments are insufficient to address the harms. While the Arctic Athabaskan Council's petition did not request precautionary measures, the AAC might want to subsequently request such measures, or the Commission on its own might consider a decision that might ask Canada to consider specifically its black carbon policies while the petition is being considered by the Commission, in order to prevent further controllable environmental deterioration. Whether the AAC can succeed in generating change in Canadian national black carbon policy remains to be seen, yet their effort represents an important mitigation push by citizen action to generate national actions.

Urgent Need for National Response in Rapidly Industrialising States

As the primarily industrial Arctic States create long-term national policies to reduce black carbon or contemplate adopting regional policies through the Arctic Council, there remains an equally pressing need for India and China to address black carbon intensive activities within their territories. While there has been a concerted effort through multi-stakeholder initiatives such as the Global Alliance for Clean Cookstoves to reduce black carbon which constitutes almost 40 per cent of India's black carbon inventory,[40] there has been inadequate national attention given to the

---

[39] Rules of Procedures of the Inter-American Commission for Human Rights (entry into force August 1, 2013), Rule 25 (2)(a) and (2)(b) accessed 20 March 2015 at https://www.oas.org/en/iachr/mandate/Basics/rulesiachr.asp.

[40] United States Environmental Protection Agency (2011) 10.

transport and industrial sectors that produce approximately 36 per cent of the remaining black carbon.[41]

Researchers estimates that 40 per cent of the world's current black carbon is generated by China and India.[42] This raises questions about whether these regions' smaller per capita carbon dioxide footprint is now being offset by this substantially higher sooty footprint. Presently China meets much of its electricity demand from coal-fired plants and was responsible for about 47 per cent of the world's coal consumption in 2011.[43] China is home to a number of black carbon intensive industries. Since 2000, China has been the world's largest coking coal producer[44] and is responsible for 54 per cent of global brick production.[45] India produces about 10 per cent of global brick production.[46] Both States continue to house highly polluting production kilns.

In neither State has there been a concerted effort to tackle black carbon directly even though the impacts are regionally cognisable. For example, high levels of black carbon in Himalayan valleys of India may be contributing to glacial melt[47] and may be leading to increased cardiovascular mortality.[48] The largest climate forcing as a result of black carbon is occurring in regions such as Southeast China with significant forcing in areas such as Northern India.[49] There have been indirect efforts to remove black carbon as a health threat by controlling industries. In China, there is a transition to new models of less polluting brick kilns.[50] Likewise in India, the government is now requiring Environmental Impact Assessments for industries that engage in more than five hectares of soil mining including brick manufacturing.[51]

Far less effort has been tailored to address the transportation sector. In China and India, around 40 and 66 per cent respectively of transport fuel is diesel fuel.[52] Diesel engines, including engines for construction equipment,

---

41 Ibid.

42 Bond *et al.* (2004).

43 US Energy Information Agency (2013).

44 World Coal Association (2011) (producing as much coking coal as the remaining top nine producers combined).

45 Sarraf and Croitoru (2012).

46 Shakti Sustainable Energy Foundation and Climate Works Foundation (April 2012), vi.

47 UNEP and WMO (2011) 13–15.

48 Geng *et al.* (2013) 27–32.

49 Bond *et al.* (2013) 5434.

50 UNEP (2011) 29.

51 Chakravartty (2012).

52 Natural Resources Defense Council (2013).

agricultural machinery and railway locomotives, are one of the largest emitters of black carbon due to a lack of diesel particulate filters.[53] Advanced filter technology is not readily available in China or India. Retrofitting diesel particulate filters or requiring such filters on new vehicles could reduce particulate emissions which include black carbon by as much as 95 per cent.[54] Effort has been made through international collaborations such as the Partnership for Clean Fuels and Vehicles to transition to lead-free, low-sulphur fuels.[55] Typically, low-sulphur fuels are needed for optimal performance of the more popular diesel particulate filters. There are potential unintended consequences, however, in attempting to innovate through fuel mixes, since low-sulphur fuels are energy-intensive to produce leading to additional carbon dioxide releases, and may also end up causing additional warming by reducing the formation of cooling sulphate particles, which are currently offsetting some of the impacts of global warming.[56]

Focusing only on industry and transport, there is a need for greater integration between reducing black carbon intensive activities and long-term planning. As with the Arctic States described above, there is a need for national plans that include some regulatory framework directly addressing black carbon production. Because time is of the essence and we know that globally we will collectively be experiencing the residual warming effects of climate change for decades to come, the national plans cannot rely on the voluntary impulses of industry. Instead, there must be reliable regulatory frameworks focused on the rebuilding of existing polluting industries such as the brick industry or retrofitting of both public and private vehicles. The challenge for China and India is to create these programs as incentive programs in order to be able to continue regional development efforts while reducing black carbon.

A first step for both States would be to create national black carbon action plans that address black carbon explicitly in air pollution rules. In 2009, India revised its air quality standards but did not set any air quality standards specifically for black carbon although it did limit other air pollutants that are often found with black carbon.[57] Beijing, China's

---

[53] US Environmental Protection Agency (see n 25) (particles emitted by mobile diesel engines are about 75% black carbon).

[54] US Environmental Protection Agency (2011b) 27.

[55] Partnership for Clean Fuels and Vehicles accessed 20 March 2015 at www.unep.org/transport/pcfv.

[56] Chemistry World, (2012).

[57] India National Ambient Air Quality Standards, 2009, 826 Gen. S.R.&O, 3 accessed 20 March 2015 at http://moef.nic.in/downloads/rules-and-regulations/Latest_48_FINAL_AIR_STANDARD.pdf.

second largest municipality, agreed in 2013 to implement vehicle emission controls for particulate matter.[58] Yet neither of these legal frameworks explicitly addresses the use of diesel or industrial coal which contribute substantially to the black carbon inventories of both States.

A second step for both States is to invest nationally or seek global financing to support regulatory efforts to rebuild industries to reduce black carbon intensive emissions or to retrofit of 'dirty diesel' vehicle fleets. Already, in these regions, there have been efforts to support financing to combat short-lived climate forcers including work by the Global Alliance for Clean Cookstoves to create development loan guarantees for cookstove manufacturers.[59] Similar projects might be possible in the diesel engine sector for diesel filter manufacturers particularly for high-sulphur fuel blends such as those in China.[60]

What if there is continued government inertia on this issue because government leaders prioritise gross domestic product over public health? Concerned citizens have limited legal options though it may be possible for a group in India to bring a public interest action or a group in China to bring a case before the existing environmental courts. In India, M.C. Metha, an environmental lawyer and activist brought an air pollution case against the Government of India and prevailed. The Supreme Court agreed that India must adopt low emission public transportation and required all of the city buses in Delhi to adopt compressed natural gas technology to replace polluting diesel buses.[61] While there was some delay in implementation due to the fact that Ministry of Petroleum and Natural Gas did not provide adequate supplies of compressed natural gas to New Delhi, the program is now fully operational.[62] This transition to CNG buses alone has not been sufficient to reduce black carbon production; New Delhi continues to have poor air quality because of other diesel sources.[63] It may be possible for citizens to bring a case similar to Metha's earlier case to require diesel particulate filters to be installed nationally across both public and private fleets. Such a case may have traction before the Indian judiciary since the Supreme Court has already proven

---

58 English News, Xinhua (2013).

59 UNEP (2011) 47.

60 Companies exist with the technology to provide diesel particulate filters for high sulphur fuel. See e.g. Innospec, accessed 20 March 2015 at http://www.innospecinc.com/market/fuel-borne-catalysts.

61 *M.C. Metha v Union of India*, Supreme Court of India, AIR 2002 SC 1696.

62 Clean Air Portal, Case Study of Delhi CNG Buses (October 28, 2010) accessed 20 March 2015 at http://cleanairinitiative.org/portal/node/6582.

63 Mandhana (2012)

that it will take on complex public environmental policy cases and offer rulings.

In China, there are limited options for public interest litigation. Recently, environmental courts have emerged in China to address environmental harms. In Yunnan Province, for example, the court may permit injunctive relief in cases where an enterprise causes harm to the environment.[64] In Guizhou province, the court in a case against the Tianfeng Chemical Factory was willing to give injunctive relief to the plaintiffs against a polluting industry.[65] Both of these developments bode well for the rise of public interest litigation in China. Yet environmental courts only exist in particular provinces; black carbon is present in every province. It may still prove a fruitful legal strategy for parties to bring black carbon injunction claims in those provinces where there are environmental courts. The greatest hurdle to bringing and succeeding in such claims will be avoiding local protectionism and concerns by government leaders that imposing requirements to install filters will substantially impact gross domestic product.

CONCLUSION

Black carbon offers an unusual opportunity for States to act unilaterally since the impacts of black carbon have immediate local impacts on health and the environment. While it may be theoretically possible for Canada to identify where each black carbon particle originated that has settled on the Canadian ice shelf and allocate responsibility among States, this approach does not address Canada's immediate contribution to its own environmental degradation. The same is true for every other State.

While black carbon may have transboundary impacts, it has localised impacts. These types of impacts may be increasing as fuel suppliers such as Exxon Mobil predict an increase in transportation demand from traditional diesel sectors such as heavy duty transport, rail vehicles and marine vessels leading to a 65 per cent increase in diesel in North America and a 40 per cent increase in Asia-Pacific countries.[66] For global diesel use to increase without addressing black carbon emissions would be catastrophic.

Black carbon reduction, particularly for diesel and coal emissions, has the added benefit of being something that can be done immediately. The

---

64 Wang and Gao (2010) 47.
65 Ibid, 43.
66 ExxonMobil (2013) The Outlook for Energy: A View to 2040: 20.

emission reduction technology is largely understood and is not economically disruptive. Where States have become trapped in endless multilateral meetings on creating a global strategy for climate policy, black carbon offers a different model: start national programs now and then proceed to regional or global strategies as appropriate. Many of the benefits of any black carbon intensive activity reduction are immediately captured at the national level with improved air quality and health metrics. There are few political leaders who do not want to rally around outcomes that result in visibly cleaner skies. This does not mean that we do not need a multi-emission transboundary approach, because we do. But we need to start with the politically possible and buy time to reach consensus on more difficult subjects such as transitioning from a carbon dioxide excessive world to a carbon dioxide neutral world. Because we know that we need to start somewhere, reducing black carbon is the perfect stepping stone for future cooperation on emissions.

REFERENCES

Aldy, J. and R. Stavins (2012), *Climate Negotiations Open a Window: Key Implications of the Durban Platform for Enhanced Action* (Cambridge, MA: Harvard Project on Climate Agreements).

Arctic Athabaskan Council (2013), *Petition to the Inter-American Commission on Human Rights Seeking Relief from the Violation of the Rights of Athabaskan Peoples Resulting from Rapid Arctic Warming and Melting Caused by Emissions of Black Carbon by Canada*, accessed 31 March 2015 at http://earthjustice.org/sites/default/files/AAC_PETITION_13-04-23a.pdf.

Arctic Council (2013a), Press Release: 'Arctic Council Presents Vision for Future Cooperation in the Arctic' (15 May), accessed 20 March 2015 at http://www.arctic-council.org/index.php/en/resources/news-and-press/news-archive/732-press-release-15-may-kiruna.

Arctic Council (2013b), Press Release: 'Arctic Contaminants Action Program' (4 June), accessed 20 March 2015 at http://www.arctic-council.org/index.php/en/acap-home/acap-psgs/slcfc/179-short-lived-climate-forcers-and-contaminants-info/745-black-carbon-workshop-oslo-norway-18-and-19-june-2013.

Arctic Council Task Force on Short-Lived Climate Forcer (2011), *An Assessment of Emissions and Mitigation Options for Black Carbon for the Arctic Council* (Tromso, Norway: Arctic Council).

Bauer, S. *et al.* (2007), 'Nitrate Aerosols Today and in 2030: a global simulation including aerosols and tropospheric ozone' 19 *Atmospheric Chemistry and Physics* 7, 5043.

Bond, T. *et al.* (2004), 'A Technology-Based Global Inventory of Black and Organic Carbon Emissions from Combustion' 109 *Journal of Geophysical Research* D14.

Bond, T. *et al.* (2013), 'Bounding the Role of Black Carbon in the Climate System: A Scientific Assessment' 118 *Journal of Geophysical Research* 11, 5380–5552.

Chakravartty, A. (2012), 'Ban Paves the Way', *Down To Earth: Science and Environment Online* (15 December), accessed 20 March 2015 at http://www.downtoearth.org.in/content/ban-paves-way.

Chemistry World (2012), 'Ultra-low sulfur jet fuel on the radar' (17 May), *Chemistry World News: Research* accessed 20 March 2015 at http://www.rsc.org/chemistryworld/2012/05/ultra-low-sulfur-jet-fuel-radar.

English News, Xinhua (2013), 'Beijing tightens vehicle emission controls against PM 2.5' (2 September), accessed 20 March 2015 at http://news.xinhuanet.com/english/china/2013-09/02/c_132684853.htm.

Geng, F. *et al.* (2013), 'Differentiating the Associations of Black Carbon and Fine Particle with Daily Mortality in a Chinese City' 120 *Environmental Research* 27.

Hayes, D. *et al.* (2013), 'Managing for the Future in a Rapidly Changing Arctic: A Report to the President' (Interagency Working Group on Coordination of Domestic Energy Development and Permitting in Alaska), accessed 20 March 2015 at http://www.afsc.noaa.gov/Publications/misc_pdf/IAMreport.pdf.

Hu, A. *et al.* (2013), 'Mitigation of Short-Lived Climate Pollutants Slows Sea-Level Rise' 3 *Nature Climate Change* 730.

Irfan, U. (2013), 'Methane Gas Proves Hard to Capture', *Scientific American* (23 April).

Inter-American Commission on Human Rights (2006), *Letter from Inter-American Commission on Human Rights* (16 November), accessed 20 March 2015 at http://graphics8.nytimes.com/packages/pdf/science/16commissionletter.pdf.

International Maritime Organisation (IMO 2014), *Sub-committee on Pollution Prevention and Response, 1st Session (February 2014)*, accessed 20 March 2015 at http://www.imo.org/MediaCentre/MeetingSummaries/PPR/Pages/PPR-1st-Session.aspx.

Mandhana, N. (2012), '"Untamed Motorization" Wraps an Indian City in Smog', *New York Times* (26 December), accessed 20 March 2015 at http://www.nytimes.com/2012/12/27/world/asia/indian-city-overwhelmed-by-air-pollution-new-delhi-journal.html?_r=0.

Marine Environment Protection Committee (MEPC 2011), Annex VI, Ch. 4 (International Maritime Organisation), accessed 20 March 2015 at http://www.imo.org/MediaCentre/HotTopics/GHG/Documents/eedi%20amendments%20RESOLUTION%20MEPC203%2062.pdf.

Molina, M. *et al.* (2009), 'Reducing Abrupt Climate Change Risk Using the Montreal Protocol and other Regulatory Actions to Complement Cuts in CO_2' 106 PNAS 49.

Natural Resources Defense Council, (2013), 'Black Carbon More Powerful Contributor to Climate Change than Previously Thought: New Study' (17 January), accessed 31 March 2015 at switchboard.nrdc.org/blogs/jschmidt/black_carbon_more_powerful_con.html.

Ramanathan, V. *et al.* (2005), 'Atmospheric brown clouds: Impacts on South Asian climate and hydrological cycle' 102 PNAS 15, 5326.

Rosenthal, E. (2009), 'Soot from Third-World Stoves is Target in Climate Fight' *New York Times* (16 April 2009).

Sarraf, M. and L. Croitoru (2012), 'Cleaner Bricks for Better Air Quality in Dhaka' *World Bank Blog* (8 February), accessed 20 March 2015 at http://blogs.worldbank.org/endpovertyinsouthasia/cleaner-bricks-better-air-quality-dhaka.

Schevchenko, D. (2013), 'Future success of new agricultural burning ban in Russia's Kuban region hampered by scant enforcement options' *Bellona*

(2 September 2013), accessed 20 March 2015 http://bellona.org/news/climate-change/2013-09-feature-future-success-new-agricultural-burning-ban-russias-kuban-region-hampered-scant-enforcement-options.

Schmidt, J. (2013), 'Black Carbon More Powerful Contributor to Climate Change than Previously Thought: New Study', *Natural Resources Defense Council Staff Blog* (17 January), accessed 20 March 2015 at http://switchboard.nrdc.org/blogs/jschmidt/black_carbon_more_powerful_con.html.

Shakti Sustainable Energy Foundation and Climate Works Foundation (2012), *A Roadmap for Cleaner Brick Production in India* (United Nations Environment Program (UNEP)), accessed 20 March 2015 at http://www.unep.org/ccac/portals/50162/docs/brick_kilns_performance_assessment.pdf.

Shindell, D. *et al.* (2012), 'Simultaneously Mitigating Near-Term Climate Change and Improving Human Health and Food Security' 335 *Science* 183.

United Nations Economic Commission for Europe (UNECE 2013), *Guidance document on control techniques for emissions of sulphur, NOx, VOC, and particulate matter (including PM10, PM2.5 and black carbon) from stationary sources*, accessed 20 March 2015 at http://www.unece.org/fileadmin/DAM/env/documents/2012/EB/ECE.EB.AIR.117_AV.pdf.

United Nations Environmental Programme (UNEP 2008), *Atmospheric Brown Clouds: Regional Assessment Report with Focus on Asia*, accessed 20 March 2015 at http://www.unep.org/pdf/ABCSummaryFinal.pdf.

United Nations Environment Programme (UNEP 2011), *Near-Term Climate Protection and Clean Air Benefits: Actions for Controlling Short-Lived Climate Forcers*, accessed 20 March 2015 at http://www.unep.org/pdf/Near_Term_Climate_Protection_&_Air_Benefits.pdf.

United Nations Environmental Program and World Meterological Organization (UNEP and WMO 2011), *Integrated Assessment of Black Carbon and Tropospheric Ozone: Summary for Decision Makers*, accessed 20 March 2015 at http://www.unep.org/dewa/Portals/67/pdf/Black_Carbon.pdf.

United States Energy Information Agency (2013), 'China Consumes Nearly as Much as Coal as the rest of the World Combined' (29 January), accessed 20 March 2015 at http://www.eia.gov/todayinenergy/detail.cfm?id=9751.

United States Environmental Protection Agency (USEPA 2011a) *Initiative to Reduce Black Carbon from Diesel Sources in the Russian Arctic*, accessed 20 March 2015 at http://www.arctic-council.org/index.php/en/document-archive/category/389-psg-slcfc-documents?download=1404:final-report-diesel-black-carbon-workshops-russia-oct-2011.

United States Environmental Protection Agency, Office of International and Tribal Affairs, (USEPA 2011b), *Reducing Black Carbon Emission in South Asia: Low Cost Opportunities*, accessed 20 March 2015 at http://www.unep.org/ccac/Portals/50162/docs/BlackCarbonSAsiaFinalReport5.22.12.pdf.

Wang, A. and J. Gao (2010), 'Environmental Courts and the Development of Environmental Public Interest Litigation in China', 3 J Court Innovation 1.

World Coal Association (2011), 'Coal Statistics', accessed 20 March 2015 at http://www.worldcoal.org/resources/coal-statistics/.

World Wildlife Fund (WWF 2013), 'Arctic Council on Right Track – But Slow Track' (15 May 2013), accessed 20 March 2015 at http://wwf.panda.org/what_we_do/where_we_work/arctic/news/?208621.

14. Is there relief for transnational harm?

Christopher Chaulk

As multinational corporations expand, so too does the potential for transnational harm.[1] When foreign plaintiffs seek relief in American courts for transnational harm implicating such corporations, these courts have repeatedly dismissed claims under the doctrine of *forum non conveniens*.[2] Foreign plaintiffs have also turned to a centuries-old statute, the Alien Tort Statute ('ATS'), to try to bring their claims against multinational corporations under the jurisdiction of American courts.[3] In 2013, however, the Supreme Court of the United States in *Kiobel v Royal Dutch Petroleum Co.* severely limited the application of the ATS to corporations for acts of harm occurring outside of the United States.[4] Writing for the majority in *Kiobel*, Chief Justice John Roberts explained: '[c]orporations are often present in many countries, and it would reach too far to say that mere corporate presence suffices' to bring a corporation within the scope of the Alien Tort Statute.[5] Admittedly, the defendant corporations in *Kiobel* were not American;[6] however, Chief Justice Roberts' majority opinion focused on the presumption of extraterritoriality, not the state of incorporation of the defendants.[7]

---

1 Multinational refers to, among other things, 'a company or corporation operating in more than two countries.' 'Multinational.' http://www.thefreedictionary.com/multinational. Transnational means, among other things, '[r]elating to or involving several nations or nationalities.' 'Transnational.' http://www.thefreedictionary.com/transnational (both accessed 20 March 2015).

2 See, e.g., *Dow Chemical Co. v Castro Alfaro*, 786 S.W.2d 674, 675 (Tex. 1990); *Aguinda v Texaco*, 303 F.3d 470, 473 (2d Cir. 2002).

3 See, e.g., *Filartiga v Pena-Irala*, 630 F.2d 876 (2d Cir. 1980).

4 *Kiobel v Royal Dutch Petroleum Co.*, 133 S. Ct. 1659, 1662, 1669 (2013).

5 *Kiobel*, 133 S. Ct. at 1669.

6 *Kiobel*, 133 S. Ct. at 1662. The corporate defendants were incorporated in the Netherlands, England, and Nigeria. See ibid.

7 *Kiobel*,133 S. Ct. at 1659–9. Chief Justice Roberts, in fact, only mentions the word 'corporations' in his majority opinion to state the following: 'Corporations

Against the backdrop of expanding multinational corporations, incorporated both in the United States and abroad, as well as an increasingly restrained American judiciary, is there relief for foreign plaintiffs who have suffered transnational harm facilitated or perpetrated by such corporations? To answer this question, I begin by explaining the position of restraint that the American judiciary has historically adopted in cases involving foreign plaintiffs. I then consider this restraint in prominent transnational cases involving Union Carbide Corporation and the Royal Dutch Petroleum Company. I proceed to analyse several alternate forms of relief or strategies that foreign plaintiffs could adopt in light of the American judiciary's restraint and assess their effectiveness. I conclude that the use of the Alien Tort Statute presents a more promising avenue to secure a verdict of corporate wrongdoing when targeted at the applicable corporate officers, yet I also conclude that foreign plaintiffs may more likely secure compensation by leveraging litigation or its potential to settle a dispute.

THE AMERICAN JUDICIARY AND THE FOREIGN PLAINTIFF: A CONSISTENT POSITION OF RESTRAINT

American courts approached foreign litigants availing themselves of American courts with scepticism, if not outright hostility, as early as 1906.[8] Yet throughout the 20th century, American courts have continuously drawn foreign plaintiffs. British lawyer and judge Lord Denning captured this phenomenon most succinctly: 'As a moth is drawn to the light, so is a litigant drawn to the U.S.'[9] Russell Weintraub has noted that 'compared with foreign courts, United States forums offer a plaintiff both lower costs and higher recovery'; thus, it has served as 'a magnet forum for the afflicted of the world'.[10] Relevant factors include the availability and extent of compensatory and punitive damages, a contingent fee system, the availability of discovery, and access to 'class action litigation'.[11] However, these factors alone may not drive a foreign plaintiff's decision

---

are often present in many countries, and it would reach too far to say that mere corporate presence suffices.' See *Kiobel*, 133 S. Ct. at 1669.

8 *Disconto Gesellschaft v Terlinden*, 127 Wis. 651, 662 (Wis. 1906); see Blair (1929) 26.

9 Weintraub (1994) 322.

10 Weintraub (1994) 323.

11 Robertson (2010) 1087–8.

to seek a remedy in an American court. For example, Cassandra Burke Robertson has written of the 'socio-legal expectation' in some countries that a 'defendant can reliably be sued in its home forum'.[12] Ronald Brand and Scott Jablonski go further, identifying this expectation as 'a basic rule of jurisdiction in Latin America'.[13]

Notwithstanding differing expectations, American courts have drawn a line to 'increasingly resist' transnational suits.[14] Indeed, the overarching goals of fairness, convenience and an efficient use of judicial resources are legitimate bases to support a doctrine like *forum non conveniens*. William Reynolds raises cogent policy questions about the United States imposing its views and standards on other countries. Where another country is faced 'with different needs, problems and resources', that country may 'give different weight to factors than would our society'.[15] Thus, American courts possess a power that 'brings with it the need to exercise responsibility in its use'.[16] Otherwise, the United States may adopt an imperialistic, paternalistic attitude by insisting that 'operations conducted by U.S. corporations outside the U.S. adhere to U.S. standards whether or not, as a legal matter, they apply or whether other governments may be involved'.[17] The cases discussed below represent a consistent emphasis over the past 30 years that American courts will not resolve controversies arising on foreign soil and involving multinational corporations, incorporated in the United States or abroad.

CORPORATE LIABILITY FOR TRANSNATIONAL HARM: ANALYSIS DEFERRED

Union Carbide Corporation

Union Carbide Corporation ('UCC'), incorporated in New York, was the parent company of Union Carbide India Limited ('UCIL'), incorporated in India.[18] UCIL operated a chemical plant in Bhopal, India in the 1980s.[19] On 2 and 3 December 1984, a chemical named methyl isocyanate

---

12 Robertson (2010) 1088.

13 Brand and Jablonski (2007) 128.

14 Robertson (2010) 1088.

15 Reynolds (1992) 1708–9.

16 Reynolds (1992) 1710.

17 Seward III (1987) 705.

18 *In re Union Carbide Corp. Gas Plant Disaster at Bhopal, India in December 1984*, 809 F.2d 195, 197 & n.3 (2d Cir. 1987).

19 *In re Union Carbide Corp.*, 809 F.2d at 197–8.

escaped and covered 'densely occupied parts' of Bhopal.[20] The 'world's greatest "chemical catastrophe"' killed at least 3,000 and injured more than 200,000 Indians.[21] More than 100 claims against UCC came before the District Court for the Southern District of New York in 1985, but UCC prevailed after the district court dismissed on *forum non conveniens* grounds shortly thereafter.[22]

Under the doctrine of *forum non conveniens*, a court has the discretion to 'decline to exercise jurisdiction' if it determines that parties may litigate 'in a more appropriate forum in another state'.[23] In *Gulf Oil Corp. v Gilbert*, the Supreme Court supported a district court's use of *forum non conveniens* if litigation could proceed in more than one forum.[24] As the Supreme Court in *Gulf Oil* explained, a court 'may resist imposition upon its jurisdiction even when jurisdiction is authorized' after balancing 'the combination and weight of [public and private] factors'.[25] Private factors include access to evidence, cost of witnesses, 'and all other practical problems that make trial of a case easy, expeditious and inexpensive'.[26] Public factors include the potential burdens of piling too many cases on one forum and requiring members of a community not affected by the dispute to participate in jury duty.[27] In 1981, the Supreme Court then altered the doctrine of *forum non conveniens* in *Piper Aircraft Co. v Reyno*, a suit brought by a foreign plaintiff.[28] The Court explained that, though 'there is ordinarily a strong presumption in favor of the plaintiff's choice of forum . . . [T]he presumption applies with less force when the plaintiff or real parties in interest are foreign'.[29] Consequently, a court need not defer to the plaintiff in the plaintiff's choice of forum if the plaintiff is foreign.[30]

Upon review, the United States Court of Appeals for the Second Circuit affirmed the district court's *forum non conveniens* dismissal of the claims against UCC.[31] The Second Circuit explained that 'all but a few of the 200,000 plaintiffs are Indian citizens located in India who, according to the UOI [the Union of India, the party who represented the claimants

---

20 Ibid.
21 Ibid; Pillay (2006) 483
22 *In re Union Carbide Corp.*, 809 F.2d 195 at 197–8.
23 Brand and Jablonski (2007) Xiii.
24 330 U.S. 501, 506–9 (1947).
25 *Gulf Oil*, 330 U.S. at 507, 508–9; see Childress III, D. (2013) 165–6.
26 *Gulf Oil*, 330 U.S. at 508.
27 *Gulf Oil*, 330 U.S. at 508–9.
28 454 U.S. 235 (981); see Brand and Jablonski (2007) 52.
29 *Piper Aircraft*, 454 U.S. at 255.
30 *Piper Aircraft*, 454 U.S. at 256
31 *In re Union Carbide Corp.*, 809 F.2d at 202–6.

on appeal], have revoked the authorizations of American counsel to represent them here and have substituted the UOI, which now prefers Indian courts';[32] 'the proof bearing on the issues to be tried is almost entirely located in India [including witnesses and documents]';[33] additionally, the UOI was 'firmly opposed' to a previously proposed settlement.[34] In 1989, the Indian government reached a settlement with UCC and UCIL for $470 million '[w]ithout any consultation with the victims' it represented.[35] All charges against the defendants 'were quashed, and no further suits [were] permitted'.[36] While 'the Supreme Court of India approved [this] settlement of all claims as "just and reasonable"', a 'public outcry' ensued.[37] India's Supreme Court, however, 'did not address the liability of Union Carbide', even though the Indian government had complained during the U.S. litigation that a multinational corporation 'must be held to a standard of absolute liability for foreign harms'.[38] The Supreme Court of India argued that the 'interests of providing relief to the victims' mattered most.[39]

The dismissal based on *forum non conveniens* facilitated UCC's subsequent, speedy departure from a site of unparalleled chemical disaster without an acknowledgment of culpability or a genuine commitment to the restitution of a devastated community. Many have undertaken enormous efforts to hold those responsible – such as former UCC chairman Warren Anderson – and to compensate those afflicted by reopening the 1989 settlement; yet those efforts continue to fall short.[40] In 2011, the Indian Supreme Court rejected a petition by the country's Central Bureau of Investigation to impose harsher penalties upon the accused.[41] Dow, the current owner of UCC, was issued a summons in 2013 to appear before a

---

32 *In re Union Carbide Corp.*, 809 F.2d at 199, 202. After passing a statute, the Indian government had assumed the 'exclusive right to represent the victims in India.' Ibid at 197. The statute was the Bhopal Gas Leak Disaster (Processing of Claims) Act; see Hosein (1993) 292.

33 *In re Union Carbide Corp.*, 809 F.2d at 203.

34 *In re Union Carbide Corp.*, 809 F.2d at 203.

35 Pillay (2006) 489. The Indian Government assumed 'parens patriae control over the Bhopal case' under the Bhopal Act and introduced an 'administrative framework' to handle claims in place of the 'disbursement of any compensation monies.' Cassels (1991) 13.

36 Cassels (1991) 13.

37 Weintraub (1994) 335; Pillay (2006) 490.

38 Pillay (2006) 485, 490.

39 Pillay (2006) 490.

40 Pillay (2006) 491.

41 *Environmental Defender Law Center* (accessed 27 March 2014); India Today (accessed 27 March 2014).

court in India in July, 2014, 'to present its stand with regard to [the Bhopal disaster]'.[42]

Royal Dutch Petroleum Company

Nigerian nationals sued, among others, the Royal Dutch Petroleum Company, incorporated in the Netherlands,[43] under the theory that it '"aided and abetted" . . . government actors or government activity in violation of international law'.[44] A joint subsidiary incorporated in Nigeria, Shell Petroleum Development Company, had been searching for oil in Ogoniland, 'located in the Niger delta area of Nigeria'.[45] When Ogoniland residents learned of the 'environmental effects' of the subsidiary's oil practices, they protested but were resisted and attacked.[46] Though the assailants were members of the 'Nigerian military and police', the victims claimed the oil companies used these forces to quash the local resistance movement.[47] Before the District Court for the Southern District of New York, the plaintiffs relied on the Alien Tort Statute ('ATS'), which states that 'district courts shall have original jurisdiction of any civil action by an alien for a tort only, committed in violation of the law of nations or a treaty of the United States'.[48] The district court dismissed four of seven claims alleging these companies were aiding and abetting the assailants;[49] moreover, the United States Court of Appeals for the Second Circuit later dismissed the entire complaint, holding that '[corporate liability] is not a rule of customary international law that we may apply under the ATS'.[50]

The Supreme Court affirmed the Second Circuit's dismissal of the Nigerian nationals' complaint, holding that a 'presumption against extraterritoriality' extended to the ATS.[51] The Supreme Court's analysis focused on the applicability of this statute to harm 'occurring in the territory of a

---

42 *The Economic Times* (2014).
43 *Kiobel v Royal Dutch Petroleum*, 133 S. Ct. 1659, 1662 (2013).
44 *Kiobel v Royal Dutch Petroleum*, 456 F.Supp.2d 457, 463 (2006); see *Kiobel*, 133 S. Ct. at 1662.
45 *Kiobel*, 133 S. Ct. at 1662. The Supreme Court articulates the facts more clearly and specifically than the district court; thus, I cite the Supreme Court's opinion in describing the facts.
46 Ibid.
47 Ibid.
48 *Kiobel*, 456 F.Supp.2d at 459; see 28 U.S.C. 1350.
49 *Kiobel*, 456 F.Supp.2d at 468.
50 *Kiobel v Royal Dutch Petroleum Co.*, 621 F.3d 111, 145 (2010).
51 *Kiobel*, 133 S. Ct. at 1669.

foreign sovereign'.[52] The Court examined the 'text, history, and purposes' of this statute and concluded that 'nothing . . . rebuts' the presumption against extraterritoriality such that the plaintiffs could have a sufficient claim under the ATS.[53] This presumption encompasses the notion that 'United States law governs domestically but does not rule the world' and such law will not apply extraterritorially without a 'clear indication'.[54] The *Kiobel* opinion, however, seemed to indicate that a foreign plaintiff could prevail on a claim under the ATS if the harm were caused in the United States, but only if evidence sufficiently 'touch[ed] and concern[ed]' American territory 'with sufficient force to displace the presumption against extraterritorial[ity]'.[55] Justice Breyer concurred to explain that the Court need not have relied on the presumption against extraterritoriality to reject the plaintiffs' claim; instead, he advanced a three-part test for a court to use to determine whether to exercise jurisdiction over a claim under the ATS, a test which the plaintiffs did not meet given the facts.[56]

A FOREIGN PLAINTIFF'S SEARCH FOR RELIEF IN A POST-*KIOBEL* WORLD

These cases demonstrate that American courts have exercised restraint when confronting a controversy involving harm by a multinational corporation on foreign soil. In applying *forum non conveniens* or the presumption against extraterritoriality, American courts have used tools that multinational corporations, whether incorporated in the United States or another country, can rely on to foreclose future cases of transnational harm so that courts do not analyse the merits of the victims' claims. This analysis prompts the following question: how can foreign plaintiffs seek relief against a multinational corporation for harm caused outside the United States? Upon reviewing various ideas raised among scholars on this issue, I examine two promising alternate strategies: (1) using the Alien Tort Statute to sue corporate officers; and (2) leveraging legitimate litigation and consequent public embarrassment to settle the dispute.

---

52 *Kiobel*, 133 S. Ct. at 1664.

53 *Kiobel*, 133 S. Ct. at 1665–9.

54 *Kiobel*, 133 S. Ct. at 1664.

55 *Kiobel*, 133 S. Ct. at 1669.

56 Ibid at 1671 (Breyer, J., concurring). Justice Breyer advanced the following test: (1) Did the alleged tort occur 'on American soil'? (2) Is the defendant an 'American national'? (3) Have the defendant's actions 'substantially and adversely affect[ed] an important American national interest'? Ibid.

As an initial matter, before weighing these alternate forms of relief, it is worth emphasising the importance of the courtroom, and the American courtroom in particular, as a means of redressing the kind of harm the victims in Bhopal and Nigeria suffered. A corporation that polices itself is still susceptible to engage in bad actions. The corporate codes of ethics ('CCOEs') designed to eliminate or limit such conduct are 'voluntary, self-regulatory mechanisms'.[57] While CCOEs are 'well established' for corporations to regulate the conduct of their employees, and are not necessarily just 'window dressing' to establish credibility in the public eye, the courtroom is the arena where bad actors remain accountable, where the law applies equally to everyone, and where the judge and jury serve as independent arbiters to resolve complex disputes.[58] Also, notwithstanding the policy reasons underpinning the American courts' decisions to dismiss cases of transnational harm, not every host government and judiciary can handle such a complex task. 'From the date of the catastrophe [in Bhopal] to the settlement [directed by the Indian government], four years elapsed.'[59] In tracking the history of the fallout of Bhopal, Hanson Hosein states that '[t]he delay, in and of itself, was a disaster'.[60] Nevertheless, pessimism in other countries' legal systems, *ex ante* or *ex post*, does not justify an unshakable or 'untroubled faith in the United States legal system'.[61] If the foreign plaintiff wishes to sue a corporate defendant on the defendant's home turf, however, as the plaintiffs first attempted after the Bhopal disaster, then that is a permissible strategy for the plaintiff to pursue as long as the corporate defendant has 'continuous and systematic' connections with the forum state.[62] In light of American courts' use of *forum non conveniens* and the Supreme Court's recent decision in *Kiobel*, however, foreign plaintiffs need to pursue alternate routes to seek justice and secure compensation.

USING THE ALIEN TORT STATUTE TO SUE CORPORATE OFFICERS

Zaid Haider explains that the United States Court of Appeals for the Second Circuit in *Kiobel* stated that 'nothing in this opinion limits or

---

57 Newberg (2005) 264–6.
58 Newberg (2005) 264–5.
59 Hosein (1993) 296–7.
60 Hosein (1993) 297.
61 Galanter (1985) 287.
62 *Goodyear Dunlop Tires Operations v Brown*, 131 S. Ct. 2846, 2851 (2011).

forecloses suits [under the Alien Tort Statute] against a corporation's employees, managers, officers, directors, or any other person who commits, or purposefully aids and abets violations of international law'.[63] Even after the Supreme Court's decision in 2013, the Second Circuit's dictum instils confidence that this measure could prove a fruitful alternate strategy for foreign plaintiffs. The Supreme Court focused its analysis on the application of the Alien Tort Statute to corporations, not corporate officers. The Court explained, for example, that '[c]orporations are often present in many countries, and it would reach too far to say that mere corporate presence suffices'.[64] By targeting corporate officers, plaintiffs would not trigger this concern of the Supreme Court's in *Kiobel.* A Colombian labour union adopted this approach in *Romero v Drummond Co., Inc.* in 2008, where the plaintiff union sued, among other things, executives under the Alien Tort Statute under a claim of aiding and abetting extrajudicial killings.[65] The union did not prevail at trial, but the District Court for the Northern District of Alabama did find sufficient evidence for the claim to proceed to trial.[66] Admittedly, the standard for liability under a charge of aiding and abetting is high. In *Presbyterian Church of Sudan v Talisman Energy, Inc.*, the Second Circuit held that 'the *mens rea* standard . . . is purpose rather than knowledge alone'.[67] While this evidentiary bar is high, this avenue of targeting individual officers or directors of a corporation legitimately permits foreign plaintiffs to bring their claims before a judge or jury.

LEVERAGING LITIGATION, ITS POTENTIAL AND PUBLIC EMBARRASSMENT TO SETTLE THE DISPUTE

Successful prosecution of individual officers, however challenging, leaves unanswered the question of compensation, of making the plaintiff whole. This challenge remains significant even if foreign plaintiffs rely on the ATS: '[n]o ATS suit has resulted in a monetary judgment against a major multinational corporation'.[68] Nevertheless, American courts'

---

63 Haider (2012) 1383 (quoting *Kiobel v Royal Dutch Petroleum Co.*, 621 F.3d 111, 122 (2d Cir. 2010)).

64 *Kiobel*, 133 S. Ct. at 1669.

65 *Romero v Drummond Co., Inc.*, 552 F.3d 1303, 1312 (11th Cir. 2008).

66 *Romero*, 552 F.3d at 1309, 1312.

67 582 F.3d 244, 259 (2d Cir. 2009), cert denied, 131 S. Ct. 122, No. 09-1418 (2010); see Bellinger III (2010) 34.

68 Bellinger, III (2010) 34.

resistance to hear the cases of foreign plaintiffs may, at first blush, have begun to shift legal systems globally so that foreign fora are strengthening their institutions in a manner that better ensures relief for their own citizens. Christopher Whytock states that 'foreign legal systems appear to be developing some of the plaintiff-favoring qualities of the U.S. legal system, and they appear more likely to grant relief to plaintiffs and to do so in larger amounts than they previously were'.[69] For example, a $9.5 billion judgment issued in Ecuador against Chevron for acts of pollution was a marked improvement on the $470 million judgment issued by the Indian Supreme Court for the disaster in Bhopal.[70] However, a protracted and still unresolved struggle to enforce the Ecuadorian judgment signals that plaintiffs may not actually recover damages if a corporate defendant can, among other things, point to evidence that the trial was not fair.[71] Indeed, in March 2014, a New York federal judge declared that the judgment against Chevron was a product of 'coercion, bribery, money laundering, and other misconduct'.[72] More is at stake than simply the amount of damages awarded.

Foreign plaintiffs may be more likely to secure consideration, then, by bringing their story of corporate harm into the public eye. Companies such as Unocal, Yahoo, and Shell have recently settled disputes, thereby avoiding not only 'lengthy' but 'embarrassing litigation'.[73] In contrast to the protracted fallout from Bhopal, avoiding litigation also facilitates a more expedited process of securing compensation for the plaintiffs.

Burmese peasants first brought Unocal to court in 1997 for abuses perpetrated by the Burmese military in connection with a Unocal pipeline project.[74] While Unocal 'consistently' defended its claim that it did not support the military's action, including 'forced relocation, forced labor, rape, torture, and murder', Unocal eventually agreed to settle in late 2004.[75] Several years before the settlement, the United States Court of Appeals for the Ninth Circuit held that 'the standard for aiding and abetting under the ATCA [Alien Tort Claims Act] is . . . knowing practical assistance or encouragement that has a substantial effect on the

---

69 Whytock and Robertson (2011) 1448–9.

70 The Ecuadorian 'high court' nearly slashed the judgment in half, from $18 billion to $9.5. Ax, J. (2014).

71 Gilbert and Gonzalez (2013).

72 Smith and Gilbert (2014); see *Chevron Corp. v Donziger*, 11 Civ. 0691 / 1:11-cv-00691-LAK-JCF (2014).

73 Bellinger, III, (2010) 34.

74 Earthrights International.

75 'Unocal Settles Rights Suit in Myanmar' (2004); see Earthrights International.

perpetration of the crime'.[76] That is, the Ninth Circuit imposed a lower evidentiary bar than the Second Circuit in *Talisman Energy*.[77] Because the Supreme Court in *Kiobel* addressed the applicability of the Alien Tort Statute to a corporation in its 2013 decision, it did not analyse the *mens rea* for culpability of corporate officers.[78] This conflict between the federal courts of appeals remains unresolved. Nevertheless, if a foreign plaintiff has sufficient evidence to bring a suit against corporate officers or to embroil the officers and the corporation in a lengthy, public trial, the consequent shame or embarrassment may push the corporation to settle, whether the plaintiff's burden of proof requires a showing of intent or knowledge.

In 2009, Shell settled a lawsuit for the 'striking sum' of $15.5 million, notwithstanding its denial of 'any wrongdoing' surrounding the death of Ken Saro-Wiwa, a Nigerian activist, in the mid-1990s.[79] Shell settled just days before it was to begin a trial that would have purportedly revealed 'extensive details' of its conduct in the Niger Delta.[80] The *New York Times* explained that '[c]ompanies are increasingly being called to account for their environmental record as well as collusion with repressive governments'.[81] While this statement may indeed be accurate, companies like Shell are distinguishing the act of settling from the act of acknowledging wrongdoing. In describing the settlement, Shell explained that it 'will provide funding for [a] trust and a compassionate payment to the plaintiffs and the estates they represent in recognition of the tragic turn of events in Ogoni land [where Mr. Saro-Wiwa protested Shell's environmental practices], even though Shell had no part in the violence that took place'.[82]

Yahoo's settlement with the families of imprisoned Chinese dissidents represents another example of compensation designed to avoid a public relations mess. In 2007, Yahoo provided an undisclosed settlement to the families of two Chinese dissidents after the company 'gave their e-mail records' to the Chinese government, thereby helping the government to imprison the two men 'for crimes against the state' involving, among other things, 'writing pro-democracy articles'.[83] Thereafter, 'the case brought

---

76 *Doe I v Unocal Corp.*, 395 F.3d 932, 947 (9th Cir. 2002).

77 Compare *Unocal*, 395, F.3d at 947, with *Talisman Energy*, 582 F.3d at 259.

78 Nor did the Supreme Court have to analyse this evidentiary standard. The defendants were corporations, not officers of corporations.

79 Mouawad (2009).

80 Ibid.

81 Ibid.

82 Ibid.

83 Rampell (2007).

widespread negative publicity to Yahoo . . .'.[84] While a translator for the families stated that 'Yahoo "admitted this is wrong and would not happen again"', an attorney for the families stated that 'Yahoo is not admitting fault'.[85] Like Shell, Yahoo declared in writing that it would 'provide humanitarian and legal aid to dissidents who have been imprisoned for expressing their views online'.[86] The Yahoo example demonstrates that foreign plaintiffs may be more successful in pressuring a corporation to settle if they can muster support from influential actors. A representative for the two Chinese families explained that '[t]he pressures by Congress on [Yahoo chief executive] Jerry Yang were of tremendous importance to making this settlement happen'.[87] By turning to powerful American actors in the government or the human rights field, foreign plaintiffs may be able to compel a corporation that its reputation and business relationships are at stake, not just a factual inquiry into acts of transnational harm.

The stories of Unocal, Shell, and Yahoo offer a glimmer of hope to future foreign plaintiffs. These stories do not demonstrate, however, that corporations are simply willing to admit wrongdoing to resolve a matter involving transnational harm. Rather, when portrayed in an unflattering or unpleasant light in the public eye, corporations have allocated nominal sums to eliminate the risk of an extensive trial or of revelations of damning evidence involving their knowledge of or intent to harm. For example, in 2009, when Shell issued the sum of $15.5 million to settle its Nigerian dispute, the company generated over $21 billion in net cash from operating activities alone.[88] The settlement constituted 0.07 per cent of its profits for 2009. While the unfortunate reality is that these nominal sums hardly impact these multinational corporations in the short or the long term, millions of dollars to victims of real harm are a legitimate form of compensation, even if these corporations neither receive a verdict nor acknowledge their own guilt or the guilt of their officers in the process.

CONCLUSION

In cases of transnational harm, American courts have adopted the position that the American judiciary must restrain itself where it might otherwise intrude on foreign policy and matters better left to the foreign fora to

---

84 Hopkins (2007).
85 Rampell (2007).
86 Ibid.
87 Ibid.
88 Shell, Annual Reports (2013).

resolve.[89] Even as American and other multinational corporations extend their networks across continents, the American judiciary's resistance may not foreclose all opportunities for foreign plaintiffs to have their day in court or to receive compensation. The application of the ATS to corporate officers or the emphasis on leveraging the prospects of litigation to settle may still bring justice and compensation to those aggrieved by transnational harm.

REFERENCES

Ax, J. (2014), 'Ecuador $9.5 billion ruling against Chevron was corrupt; U.S. judge,' *Reuters* (London, 4 March).

Bellinger III, J. (2010), 'Will Federal Court's Kiobel Ruling End Second Wave of Alien Tort Statute Suits?' 25 *Legal Backgrounder* 34, accessed 21 March 2015 at http://www.wlf.org/Upload/legalstudies/legalbackgrounder/11-12-10Bellinger_LegalBackgrounder.pdf.

Blair, P. (1929), 'The Doctrine of Forum non conveniens in Anglo-American Law,' 29 Colum. L. Rev. 1.

Brand, R. and S. Jablonski (2007), *Forum Non Conveniens: History, Global Practice, and Future Under the Hague Convention on Choice of Court Agreements* (New York: Oxford University Press).

Cassels, J. (1991), 'The Uncertain Promise of Law: Lessons from Bhopal,' 29 Osgoode Hall LJ 1.

Childress III, D. (2013), 'Forum Conveniens: The Search for a Convenient Forum in Transnational Cases,' 53 Va. J. Int'l L. Digest, No. 1, 157.

Earthrights International, 'Doe v. Unocal Case History', accessed 20 March 2015 at http://www.earthrights.org/legal/doe-v-unocal-case-history.

The Economic Times (2014) 'Bhopal court summons Dow Chemicals in gas tragedy case,' (Mumbai, 1 March), accessed 21 March 2015 at http://articles.economictimes.indiatimes.com/2014-03-01/news/47799438_1_dow-chemicals-gas-tragedy-case-bhopal-gas-leak-disaster.

Environmental Defender Law Center, 'Bhopal case back before the Indian Supreme Court', accessed 21 March 2015 at http://www.edlc.org/cases/grants/bhopal-indian-court-case/.

Galanter, M. (1985), 'Legal Torpor: Why So Little Has Happened in India after the Bhopal Tragedy,' 20 Tex. Int'l L.J. 273.

Gilbert, D. and A. Gonzalez (2013), 'Court Deals Blow to Ecuador Plaintiffs in Chevron Case,' *Wall Street Journal* (New York City, 1 May).

Haider, Z. (2012), 'Corporate Liability for Human Rights Abuses: Analyzing *Kiobel* & Alternatives to the Alien Tort Statute,' 43 Geo. J. Int'l L. 1361.

Hopkins, J. (2007), 'Yahoo Settles Lawsuit with Chinese Dissidents,' *USA Today* (Fairfax County, 14 November), accessed 21 March 2015 at http://usatoday30.usatoday.com/tech/world/2007-11-13-yahoo-chinese-journalists_N.htm.

Hosein, H. (1993), 'Unsettling: Bhopal and the Resolution of International

---

89 See Short (2007) 1063–4; *Sinochem Int'l Co. Ltd. v Malaysia Int'l Shipping Corp.*, 549 U.S. 422, 435–6 (2007).

Disputes Involving An Environmental Disaster,' 16 B.C. Int'l & Comp. L.Rev. 285.

India Today (2011), 'Bhopal gas tragedy: SC dismisses CBI's curative petition for harsher charges,' (11 May), accessed 20 March 2015 at http://indiatoday.intoday.in/story/bhopal-gas-tragedy-sc-dismisses-cbis-curative-petition/1/137747.html.

Mouawad, J. (2009), 'Shell to Pay $15.5 Million to Settle Nigerian Case,' *New York Times* (New York City, 8 June).

Newberg, J. (2005), 'Corporate Codes of Ethics, Mandatory Disclosure, and the Market for Ethical Conduct,' 29 Vt. L. Rev. 253.

Pillay, S. (2006), 'Absence of Justice: Lessons from the Bhopal Union Carbide Disaster for Latin America,' 14 Mich. St. J. Int'l. L. 479.

Rampell, C. (2007), 'Yahoo Settles with Chinese Families,' *Washington Post* (Washington, D.C., 14 November).

Reynolds, W. (1992), 'The Proper Forum for a Suit: Transnational Forum Non Conveniens and Counter-suit Injunctions in the Federal Courts,' 70 Tex. L. Rev. 1663.

Robertson, C. (2010), 'Transnational Litigation and Institutional Choice,' 51 B. C. L. Rev. 1081.

Seward III, A. (1987), 'After Bhopal: Implications for Parent Company Liability,' 21 Int'l L. 695.

Shell, Annual Reports (2013), accessed 21 March 2015 at http://reports.shell.com/annual-report/2013/strategic-report/results/selected-financial-data.php?cat=b.

Short, A. (2007), 'Is the Alien Tort Statute Sacrosanct? Retaining Forum Non Conveniens in Human Rights Litigation,' 33 N.Y.U. J. Int'l. L. & Pol. 1001.

Smith, J. and D. Gilbert (2014), 'U.S. Judge Hands Win to Chevron, Slams Lawyer,' *Wall Street Journal* (New York City, 4 March).

'Unocal Settles Rights Suit in Myanmar', (2004) *New York Times* (New York City, 14 December).

Weintraub, R. (1994), 'International Litigation and Forum Non Conveniens,' 29 Tex. Int'l. L.J. 321.

Whytock, C. and C. Robertson (2011), 'Forum Non Conveniens and the Enforcement of Foreign Judgments,' 111 Colum. L. Rev. 1444.

15. The Australian biotechnology regulatory framework: issues concerning adventitious presence (AP), co-existence, liability and coherence

Ramesh Karky and Mark Perry

INTRODUCTION

One of the issues facing the sustainable supply of food, particularly when imported products are included in the supply-chain, is quality that is the content and the provenance of the product. It is internationally contentious as to the purity levels required for a crop to be admitted to the market, and with some crops the presence of genetically modified organisms (GMOs) is becoming a common stumbling block. There is a divergence between perceptions of what constitutes an organic crop, a traditional crop and a biotechnology enhanced GM crop and their potential interactions. Concepts of environmental justice, discussed from many perspectives in this volume, get traction neither at the macro level of international trade talks on crops nor at local level in conflicts between neighbouring farmers.

Unlike the United States of America and Canada, Australia has dedicated biotechnology legislation. The Gene Technology Act 2000[1] and the Gene Technology Regulations 2001[2] regulate gene technology at the federal level in Australia. Despite the regulatory framework, currently Australian agricultural biotechnology is facing many issues: for example coherence and co-existence with 'legacy' crops; the Adventitious Presence (AP) of genes and plants; liability for economic loss and impact on international trade. AP and liability are highly contentious issues.

[1] Act No 169 of 2000 as amended. The Gene Technology Act 2000 took effect on 21 June 2001. This Commonwealth's Act was enacted after consultation with all states and territories.

[2] Statutory Rules 2001 No 106 as amended.

As discussed below, even very low levels[3] of AP of GMOs can affect the price and market access for conventional and organic crops, causing economic loss to growers and dealers of such crops. In literature, there is some confusion over differentiating Low Level Presence (LLP) and AP: essentially LLP is looking at levels of GM that are detected typically at the sub-5 per cent of a total shipment as a GM that has arrived in a crop product adventitiously. AP has raised multiple issues relating to coexistence of GM crops and other crops, liability, and some claim even the protection of health (both human and animal),[4] protection of the environment[5] and market access.[6]

The recent FAO background paper for the Technical Consultation provides definitions for LLP and AP:[7]

> Low Level Presence (LLP): LLP refers to the detection of low levels of GM crops that have been approved in at least one country on the basis of a food safety assessment according to the relevant Codex guidelines. Readers should note that low level presence (LLP) is not specifically defined by Codex, however in the context of the Codex guidelines it is referred to as LLP.
>
> Adventitious Presence (AP): AP refers to detection of the unintentional presence of GM crops that have not been approved in any countries on the basis of a food safety assessment according to the relevant Codex guidelines.

The FAO Technical Background Paper 2,[8] which focuses on production, trade and regulation of GM crops, for example, makes no mention of compensation where a regulation has been breached but rather focuses on the negative impact on trade of restrictive regulation, such as zero tolerance for any amount of non-approved GM.

In Australia, as in many countries, AP has become a central issue for the co-existence between conventional, organic and genetically modified crops. As can be seen below, in Australia:

---

3 With a zero tolerance policy, 0.01% is set as the threshold: this number is determined by the current sensitivity and reliability of testing methods. This equates, in a single test, to around one seed in 10,000, or for corn, one kernel in around 3.8 kg.

4 Mgbeoji (2007); Lichtman (1997); Demeke, Perry and Scowcroft (2006); Phillipson (2008).

5 Tsui and Chu (2003); Rogers (2003); Glenn (2003).

6 Kershen and McHughen (2005). Gonzalez (2004); Repp (2000) 593; Ellstrand, Prentice and Hancock (1999) 541; See also Bullock and Desquilbet (2002) 83; Black and Wishart (2008).

7 Food and Agricultural Organisation of the United Nations (FAO) (2014a).

8 FAO (2014b).

(1) there is lack of coherence of policy and regulation between the Commonwealth and states and territories;
(2) there is provision for co-existence between non-GM and GM farming;
(3) there is no provision for specific liability for damages or losses caused by unintended contamination.[9] Due to lack of specific liability for damage or losses, there is a perceived crisis of confidence among conventional, organic farmers and crop processors, in the face of opposition to GM crops; and
(4) as a solution, the provision of specific liability for damage or losses caused by drifting genes and plants will increase confidence and tolerance among conventional and organic farmers, and it will increase the level of acceptance of GM crops in Australian soil.

This chapter examines the issue of AP at international level, and then the Australian regulatory framework on agricultural biotechnology focusing AP in non-GM plants, covering the issues of coexistence, liability and trade disruption.

ADVENTITIOUS PRESENCE AS AN ISSUE AT INTERNATIONAL LEVEL

AP has become the international issue as the cultivation of genetically modified crops has been growing in many countries.[10] Recently Australia has shown concern on this issue by signing the International Statement on Low Level Presence (LLP).[11] Literally, LLP is a term used to describe low levels of material that is not described as the main product, but recent international level discussions have focused on the LLP of GMOs in crop products. Some argue that because of the unintentional and unavoidable nature of low levels of AP, conventional and organic agriculture is said to be struggling for survival.[12] Under the laws of many countries,

---

[9] The recent decision in Western Australia of *Marsh v Baxter* [2014] WASC 187 [hereafter *Marsh*] illustrates the difficulties facing organic farmers. In this case the plaintiff lost organic certification for his crops (not canola) due to the unintended transfer of GM canola seeds from his neighbour. He failed in his attempt to recover his losses under the tort of nuisance from the defendant. See also 5.4 infra.

[10] See Perry and Karky (2013) for lengthy discussion of the North American situation and upon which this chapter is founded.

[11] Department of Agriculture (2012), *International Statement on Low Level Presence* (LLP 2012).

[12] For a description of situation regarding Canadian non-genetically modified farming, see Oguamanam (2007).

conventional and organically grown crops are not protected from the effects that genetically modified organisms (GMO)[13] may have on their marketability.[14] Due to the lacuna in regulation, the effects and concerns caused by genetically modified crops are being addressed outside any specific regulatory framework.[15] Furthermore, stakeholders such as biotechnology companies, conventional and organic farmers and the public at large are being excluded from policy-making processes.[16]

Following the Triffid flax issue, where non-approved GM in flax was exported from Canada and reached 35 countries,[17] the Canadian Government lurched into action in pursuing international standards, at least for AP[18] that can be classified as an LLP.[19] Some 13 countries, including Australia, the U.S. and Canada signed the International Statement on Low Level Presence in Vancouver, Canada on 22 March 2012.[20] The alteration of conventional[21] or organic[22] crops by transfer of genes from genetically modified (GM) crops through cross-pollination is now not uncommon.[23] Indeed, one argument being made at international level

---

[13] Despite being mis-descriptive, 'genetically modified organisms' has become the term that is generally accepted for organisms that have been created using recombinant DNA and generated by molecular cloning. Such plants transformed through this type of genetic engineering are under discussion herein.

[14] See *Marsh v Baxter* [2014] WASC 187.

[15] Glenn (2010) 255.

[16] Glenn (2010) 255–6.

[17] Mr Alex Atamanenko during the Second Reading and Referral to Committee on 14 April 2010 of Bill C-474 'An Act respecting the Seeds Regulations (analysis of potential harm)' which was defeated at report stage on 9 February 2011.

[18] Herein the term adventitious presence (AP) is used to refer to both genes that have entered conventional and organic crops, as well as mixture of GMO product with conventional/organic product, for example crop being mixed in a grain conveyor.

[19] Although the term LLP is being used a lot in the current discussions on 'low levels' of AP, one of the key arguments is over what is meant by 'low'.

[20] LLP (2012) 8.

[21] The issue of the make up of conventional crops is discussed in Perry (forthcoming).

[22] Organic production in Canada has a GM exclusion as detailed in the 'National Standards of Canada *Organic Production Systems General Principles and Management Standards*' CAN/CGSB-32.310-2006 as amended in June 2011 at s 1.4.1: 'it is forbidden to use any of the following substances or techniques: All materials and products produced from genetic engineering as these are not compatible with the general principles of organic production and therefore are not accepted under this standard.'

[23] Over 15 years ago, in Timmons, Charters, Crawford, Burn, *et al.* (1996), it was predicted that in a region where only 10% of the fields were sown as transgenic, genetic 'contamination' would reach 0.1% at a distance of over 2 km.

today is that due to the wide adoption of GM crops in many exporting countries, it is becoming impossible to maintain a zero tolerance policy without serious trade disruption.

CODEX ALIMENTARIUS CONSIDERATIONS

The Codex Alimentarius Commission is a joint commission of the World Health Organisation and the Food and Agricultural Organisation (FAO), both United Nations Specialised Agencies.[24] It has been tasked with establishing health and safety standards and regulating international food trade, and is a powerful influence on international food regulation developments. The Sixth Session of the Codex Alimentarius Ad Hoc Intergovernmental Task Force on Foods Derived from Biotechnology set up a working group on LLP, chaired by the U.S.A. and co-chaired by Germany and Thailand, in 2006. The Task Force put a proposed draft forward, and had it considered at the Seventh Session at the Task Force's September 2007 meeting in Chiba, Japan.[25]

Although the Task Force on LLP did not address the meaning or quantitative measurements for determining LLP, it provided an annex to the Codex Alimentarius Commission's Plant Guidelines addressing LLP and discussed two 'dietary exposure' situations. The first being from commodities, which tend to be mixed and 'diluted', such as grain, beans and oils, and second, from foods consumed whole, such as fruits and vegetables. The former is the more likely scenario.[26]

The Task Force proposal allows jurisdictions to adopt a short food safety assessment for imported products with LLP, should they wish to so do. The key advance made by the Task Force was the recommendation for there to be a database available on recombinant DNA plants that have

---

[24] The Commission has a long history of over a century. It was formally established as part of the joint World Health Organisation and Food and Agricultural Organisation in 1963. See Shubber (1972).

[25] Codex Alimentarius CX/FBT 07/7/1, Agenda Item 1 May 2007 for the Joint FAO/WHO Food Standards Program, Codex Ad Hoc Intergovernmental Task Force on Foods Derived from Biotechnology Seventh Session Chiba, Japan, 24–28 September 2007 (FAO 2007). The United States had made a similar proposal to form an ad hoc task force on LLP at the Fifth Session in 2005, but it was not accepted at that time.

[26] Report of The Seventh Session of The Codex Ad Hoc Intergovernmental Task Force on Foods Derived From Biotechnology Chiba, Japan, 24–28 September 2007, ALINORM 08/31/34 (FAO 2008), Appendix IV at para 4.

been authorised under Codex guidelines,[27] to allow for the Annex to be applied. In addition to details on the authorisation country and type, the important requirement is that information on where protocols for detection can be obtained. This allows an importing country of, say, canola, to request testing data to see if imports contain recombinant DNA approved in the exporting country, or growing country.[28]

The Codex Alimentarius Commission accepted the Annex on LLP and it is now part of the Guideline for the conduct of Food Safety Assessment of Foods Derived from Recombinant-DNA Plants.[29] There are some limitations on the abbreviated assessment that may be adopted: for example, if a country has already rejected authorisation of a recombinant-DNA instance it would not be likely that it would approve any AP, even LLP.

In March 2014, following requests from 'several countries' the FAO held a Technical Consultation on LLP.[30] Although the meeting was not intended to provide any policy directives or agreements, it served as a platform for participating nations to better understand the trade and food supply issues involved.

The key issue yet to be adopted at an international level is the meaning of LLP in terms of thresholds, that is the maximum AP that can be considered as LLP, the number of tests required, and how testing is conducted. The current status of evaluation continues to lead to uncertainty for trading crops. Most countries to date have had a zero tolerance policy. In addition to Triffid and other Canadian product incidents, problems have also arisen inside the European Union. For example, in *Bablock*,[31] a German honey producer found that his honey contained MON810 Maize pollen (likely from a nearby field where the test MON810 crop had been grown). The European Court of Justice decided that as MON810 was not

---

[27] Section 3 of Guideline for the Conduct of Food Safety Assessment of Foods Derived from Recombinant-DNA Plants (FAO 2003).

[28] This is under European Union Commission Regulation No 619/2011, 24 June 2011.

[29] Codex Alimentarius Commission Thirty-first Session International Conference Centre, Geneva (Switzerland), 30 June–4 July 2008.

[30] Food and Agricultural Organisation (2014). The FAO Technical Consultation on Low Levels of Genetically Modified (GM) Crops in International Food and Feed Trade, Rome, Italy, 20–21 March 2014. It received feedback from 75 countries to their questionnaire on the issue.

[31] EC, *Court of Justice Decision 2011/EC Karl Heinz Bablok and Others v Freistaat Bayern*, [2011] (*Bablock*). In addition to the honey, pollen and Triffid Flax cases, there have been many other occurrences of crops and foods being removed from markets due to AP.

approved for consumption in the EU, the honey and pollen could not be sold.[32]

AUSTRALIAN REGULATORY FRAMEWORK ON AGRICULTURAL BIOTECHNOLOGY

In Australia, the Gene Technology Act 2000[33] and the Gene Technology Regulations 2001[34] regulate gene technology. The main objective of the Gene Technology Act 2000 is 'to protect the health and safety of people, and the environment, by identifying risks posed by or as a result of gene technology, and by managing those risks through regulating certain dealings with genetically modified organisms (GMOs)'.[35] The Gene Technology Act 2000 covers any technique for the modification of genes or other genetic material but it does not include sexual reproduction or homologous recombination or any other technique specified in the Gene Technology Regulations 2001.

The Gene Technology Act 2000 defines GMOs as: (a) an organism that has been modified by gene technology; or (b) an organism that has inherited particular traits from an organism (the initial organism), being traits that occurred in the initial organism because of gene technology; or (c) anything declared by the regulations to be a GMO, or that belongs to a class of things declared by the regulations to be GMOs; but the Act does not include: (d) a human being, if the human being is covered by paragraph (a) only because the human being has undergone somatic cell gene therapy; or (e) an organism declared by the regulation not to be a genetically modified organism, or that belongs to a class of organisms declared by the regulations not to be GMOs.[36] The Gene Technology Agreement (2001) sets out an understanding by all state and territory Governments of the need for a nationally consistent approach to the regulation of gene technology and GMOs.[37] Accordingly, the states and territories have their own legislation reflecting the Gene Technology Act 2000.[38]

---

32 *Bablock*.

33 Act No 169 of 2000 as amended. The Gene Technology Act 2000 took effect on 21 June 2001. This Commonwealth Act was enacted after consultation with all states and territories.

34 Statutory Rules 2001 No 106 as amended.

35 Gene Technology Act 2000, s 3.

36 Gene Technology Act 2000, s 10.

37 Biotechnology and Australian Agriculture (2008) 38.

38 Biotechnology and Australian Agriculture (2008).

In Australia, the regulatory framework requires risk assessment before releasing GM crops into the environment and marketing, and it requires authorisation by the Gene Technology Regulator. Canola and cotton are the only GM food crops produced in Australia. In Australia, GM cotton has been growing commercially since 1996, and now makes up over 99 per cent of the crop. GM canola was approved for commercial production in 2003. However, GM canola has been banned from cultivation at the state level except in NSW, Victoria and Western Australia.[39] Currently there are no GM fruit and vegetables.[40] Labelling on GM products is mandatory.[41] But labelling is not required if it contains less than one per cent GMOs.[42] Meat, milk and eggs derived from animals consuming GM products are not required to be labelled.[43] The Australian New Zealand Food Standard Code[44] regulates issues such as labelling. There is no provision for testing for LLP in seeds or other crops, but rather a reliance on a strategy of 'industry co-regulation; isolation of risks offshore, and; government monitoring to focus on highest risk imports'.[45]

The Gene Technology Act 2000 prescribes a process to assess risks to human health and the environment associated with various dealings with GMOs.[46] It has established an office of the Gene Technology Regulator and also the Gene Technology Technical Advisory Committee (GTTAC) and the Gene Technology Ethics and Community Consultative Committee (GTECCC). The Act also provides for a centralised database of all GMOs and GM products approved in Australia.

The Ministry of Health and Ageing is responsible for the regulation of the GMOs and GM foods and crops. The Gene Technology Regulator is responsible for administering and implementing the Gene Technology Act 2000.[47]

---

[39] Small commercial trials of Roundup Ready® canola on 20 sites are underway in Western Australia as exempted by the Genetically Modified Crops Free Areas Act 2003, accessed 21 March 2015 at http://www.agric.wa.gov.au/PC_93324.html?s=0.

[40] Pazzano (2013).

[41] Food Standard 1.5.2 of the Australian New Zealand Food Standard Code requires GM labelling on any foods that contain more than 1 percent GMOs. Food Standard 1.5.2 is explained on Labelling Genetically Modified Food: A User Guide to Standard A18/1.5.2.

[42] Pazzano (2013).

[43] Ryan (2011).

[44] Established by Food Standards Australia New Zealand Act 1991.

[45] Office of the Gene Technology Regulator (2014).

[46] Gene Technology Act 2000, s 47(1).

[47] Ryan (2011) 45.

The Gene Technology Act 2000 bans any 'dealing' with a GMO including research, manufacture, production, marketing and importation without authorisation/license from the Regulator.[48] The Regulator will issue such a license once the result of the risk assessment is positive. The Act also does not cover products that are produced from a GMO but which themselves are not GMOs.

AUSTRALIAN REGULATORY FRAMEWORK ON AP

On Non-coherence

The Statutory Review of the Gene Technology Act 2000 and the Gene Technology Agreement 2006 recommended 'the Commonwealth and States and Territories should together develop a national framework for co-existence of both non-GM and GM crops and to address market considerations'.[49] Several flowers in addition to cotton and canola have been approved for commercial use, including carnations, as well as field trials for other crops.[50] However, the States and Territories have authority to decide whether to allow GM crops or not in their territory. Issues of co-existence also fall within State jurisdiction.[51] There are various bans on the commercial cultivation of GM crops despite approvals being given for GM crops by the Gene Technology Regulator (OGTR). For example, South Australia banned all commercial GM crops until 2014. Tasmania's moratoria on the release of GMOs continued until 2014.[52] Western Australia has banned commercial GE planting, except in limited, designated areas. Some communities, for example, Bondi/Sydney, West Wimmera Shire declared themselves GE free.[53] Victoria and New South Wales ended moratoria on the release of GMOs in February 2008. Northern Territory and Queensland have no moratorium.[54] 'Clearly,

---

[48] Gene Technology Act 2000 (Cth) part IV; Standard 1.5.2 of the Food Standard Australia and New Zealand (FSANZ).

[49] Biotechnology and Australian Agriculture (2008) 40.

[50] Ryan (2011) 45.

[51] Ibid.

[52] GMO-free Europe 2012, accessed 21 March 2015 at http://www.gmo-free-regions.org/gmo-free-regions/australia-nz.html.

[53] Countries & Regions with GE Foods/Crops Bans, Organic Consumers, accessed 21 March 2015 at http://www.organicconsumers.org/gefood/countries withbans.cfm.

[54] Lilith (2008).

the current regulation of GM crops has created a great deal of uncertainty in the minds of farmers, the biotechnology companies and consumers.'[55]

On Co-existence

In Australia, the Gene Technology Act 2000[56] empowers the Gene Technology Ministerial Council the authority to issue policy principles on:

- ethical issues in dealings with GMOs; recognising areas, if any, designated under State law for the purpose of preserving the identity of GM and/or non-GM crops for marketing purposes.
- matters relating to dealings with GMOs that are prescribed by regulation. These regulations may involve matters other than the health and safety of people or the environment, but must not derogate from the health and safety of people or the environment.[57]

Based on this provision, the Gene Technology Ministerial Council issued a policy principle in 2003. This policy principle recognises areas designated under state and territories law to preserve the identity of GM-crops and non-GM crops for marketing purpose. Thus the Gene Technology Regulator is prevented from issuing GM licences inconsistent with the principle.[58] 'As a result of this policy principle, State and Territory Governments have the power to legislate to declare areas in their states to be "GM crop" areas or non-GM crop areas for marketing purposes.'[59]

ADVENTITIOUS PRESENCE

As stated before, there is a threshold of 1 per cent of AP of genes to determine when the presence in products will cause them to be considered as GM crops or foods. However, given any prescribed testing regime, finding such AP would be unlikely. In the European Union, if there is more than 0.9 per cent of the AP of genetically modified genes in a product then it is considered genetically modified and will require labelling to that effect. Furthermore, it has to be an approved GM. There is no minimum threshold point for seeds. By signing an Agreement on International Standard

---

55 Biotechnology and Australian Agriculture (2008) 43.

56 Gene Technology Act 2000, s 21(1).

57 Biotechnology and Australian Agriculture (2008) 39.

58 Biotechnology and Australian Agriculture (2008) 39. See Gene Technology (Recognition of Designated Areas) (2003).

59 Biotechnology and Australian Agriculture (2008) 40.

of LLP, the Australian Government has recognised that the LLP has been an issue since the introduction of GMOs is increasingly a source of trade disruption internationally. While Australia has laws over gene technology, the issue of AP of GM genes in non-GM crops/plants has not been specifically addressed by policy or law. AP, through pollen from GM crops for example, is unintended and unavoidable. Similarly, for some crops such as canola, it is very difficult to ensure absolute separation between GM and non-GM seeds when they share the same equipment at any stage in their processing.

AP is a complex issue that has direct implications on regulations, marketing approaches, importing and exporting, and health and safety. This issue must be addressed in order to build public confidence in a science-based regulatory regime.

AP can affect price and market access for conventional and organic crops. Where AP becomes part of non-GM harvests, farmers may find themselves in breach of their contractual obligations and/or without markets for their goods.[60] The scale of loss can be enormous. In 1999 and 2000, American farmers lost access to almost the entire US $200 million European Union corn export market due to the contamination of food corn stocks across the United States of America by the StarLink gene, a modification approved for feed corn only.[61] Also, when StarLink corn, which is also banned in Japan, was found to be mixed with non-GM corn shipments from the U.S.A., the result was 'trade disruption and considerable political turmoil'.[62] The economic harm caused by GMO contamination was not only limited to farmers who grew organic or conventional analogues of GM crops. In 1999, European Union authorities discovered a small percentage of transgenic pollen in Canadian honey shipments from Western Canada, much of which was produced amongst GM canola fields. The authorities responded by banning Canadian honey from the European Union, seriously damaging a ten million dollar market.[63]

Measures aimed at minimising AP levels and issues of compensating for the loss of conventional or organic crop status due to AP require policy direction. Currently, there are no laws or governmental policies to regulate

60 Black and Wishart (2008) para 10.

61 Black and Wishart (2008) para 11; see also Repp (2000) 593.

62 Black and Wishart (2008) para 11; see also Repp (2000) 593. See also Ellstrand, Prentice and Hancock (2006) 541; See also Bullock and Desquillet (2002) 83.

63 Black and Wishart (2008) para 11; see also Repp (2000) 593. See also Ellstrand, Prentice and Hancock (2006) 541; See also Bullock and Desquillet (2002) 83.

this issue. There are also no provisions to determine compensation for any economic losses that may result from such contamination.

ADVENTITIOUS PRESENCE AND LIABILITY IN AUSTRALIA

In Australia, there has been ongoing debate over whether strict liability for 'damage' caused by GMOs is an appropriate approach. Those who believe that GMOs pose no risks argue that commonly used liability regimes are available and those who believe that GMOs have a different nature argue that special legal liability regimes are required because of its different nature.[64] In Australia, the Gene Technology Act 2000 neither addresses the economic impact of GMOs crops nor provides a remedy for losses caused by GMOs.[65] The Constitution of Australia does not give constitutional power to the federal government in this area. Only state and territory legislation can impose a specific liability for the losses caused by GMOs.[66]

The Organic Federation of Australia (OFA) claims that the right to be 'GM-free' is a fundamental right.[67] The OFA is in favour of strict liability for damage caused by GMOs, an establishment of compensation fund and mandatory insurance.[68] The National Standard for Organic and Biodynamic Production bans GMOs use and its presence in organic farming.[69] The Australian Competition & Consumer Commission states that 'GM-free' crops must not contain any GMO's trace.[70] Under state and territory 'Sale of Goods' legislation,[71] non-GM, organic and GM-free farmers are under an obligation to meet contractual warranties regarding the GM status of their crops.[72] In 2005, a Statutory Review of the Gene Technology Act 2000 was conducted and it concluded that strict liability,

---

64 Department of Agriculture (2003) 2 (Liability Issues).

65 Liability Issues (2003) 5.

66 Liability Issues (2003) 6.

67 Liability Issues (2003) 3. See Submission No 54 to the Senate Community Affairs Reference Committee Organic Federation of Australia (2000).

68 Liability Issues (2003) 4.

69 Liability Issues (2003) 6. See Organic Produce Export Committee (2002), standard 3.1.8(b) and 3.6.3.

70 Liability Issues (2003) 6. See Fair trading legislation (misleading and deceptive conduct regarding GM status). See Australian Competition & Consumer Commission, 'Genetically Modified Organisms and Foods' (2001).

71 See Sale of Goods Act 1923 (NSW) s 18.

72 Liability Issues (2003) 11.

compensation funds, mandatory insurance and third party appeals should not be introduced. However, at the state level, the reviews of GM crop moratorium legislation concluded that there is no need for additional liability measures as this issue can be dealt with through common law and consumer protection legislation.[73]

The recent decision in *Marsh*[74] shows the difficulties that are faced when fundamentally different approaches to farming are coexisting in close proximity, and perhaps demonstrates an unmet need for legislation to address environmental justice surrounding GM crop production. In this case, GM canola of the defendant entered the farmland of the plaintiff resulting in the cancellation of the latter's organic certification for much of his farm. However the court found that the defendant was not liable for the plaintiff's loss; part of the reasoning considered that the certification should not have been removed. The court notes, in the 150 page judgement that:[75]

> A failure by NASAA/NCO [National Association of Sustainable Agriculture (Australia) Ltd / NASAA Certified Organic] to recognise and then apply the distinction between a case of the deliberate or negligent presence of GMOs in an organic operator's system, as opposed to an adventitious presence of GMOs, would be, in my view, a serious misapplication of the language of the standards – which clearly mandate this necessary differentiation be respected.

Here the court is applying a knowledge-based negligence standard for liability for perceived contamination of organic crops by AP. The main issue facing organic and conventional farmers in attempts to achieve compensation for AP is that GM crops are generally accepted as harmless by countries that permit their use in production. In *Marsh* the court accepted expert evidence supporting the benign character of Round up Ready (RR) GM canola, noting that it poses neither food safety nor environmental risks, even when grazed by livestock. Furthermore it accepted that there was no evidence of harmful or toxic substances in RR canola seeds.[76]

Other nations such as the U.S.A., Canada,[77] the U.K. and New Zealand also have no specific laws regarding 'contamination', whereas countries

---

[73] Ryan (2003) 48.

[74] See also note 8.

[75] [528]. As a long and complex tort decision, there are many issues in this case worthy of lengthy discussion, but they are outside the scope of the current chapter.

[76] *Marsh* [657].

[77] Despite some efforts in Canada to sue GM producers, such as the class action in *Monsanto Canada v Hoffman* (2005), 264 Sask R 1 (QB), aff'd (2007), 227 Sask R 63 (CA) (*Hoffman*) organic farmers have had little success.

like Austria and Germany have specific liability legislation to address this issue.[78] The Law Commission of New Zealand reviewed the existing legal regime in 2002.[79] The New Zealand Government also issued a discussion paper.[80] The New Zealand Government has proposed to amend the Hazardous Substances and New Organisms Act 1996 (HSNO Act) to include the provision of strict civil liability.[81] It was introduced to Parliament on 29 April 2003.[82] The HSNO Act was amended in October 2003 and provided civil liability for the damage caused by a new organism if the developing, field testing, importing or releasing of a new organism was done in contravention of the HSNO Act; possessing or disposing of any new organism imported, manufactured, developed or released in contravention of the HSNO Act; or failing to comply with any controls relating to a new organism imposed by an approval under the Act or specified in any regulations under the HSNO Act.[83] The European Commission issued Guidelines for the development of national strategies to ensure the co-existence of GM, organic and conventional crops. In this context, the Guidelines encourage Member States to examine their civil liability laws.[84]

Furthermore, the Fair Trading Act 1987 (NSW) and the Trade Practices Act 1974 (Cth)[85] prohibits misleading or deceptive conducts. The Australian Competition and Consumer Commission (ACCC) has indicated that a failure to disclose GMOs may be a violation of the fair trading legislation.[86] Organic and GM-free farmers need to make sure that their products are not misleading. In Australia, a GM-free status gives no room for ambiguity.[87]

In Europe, when DNA of GM maize was found in honey, the European

---

78 In the UK, Genetically Modified Food and Producer Liability Bill 2000 (UK) could not pass through Parliament. See Liability Issues (2003) 2, 3. See Endres (2000) 474–8.

79 New Zealand Law Commission (2002).

80 Ministry for the Environment (2002).

81 The proposed Bill was named as the 'New Organisms and other Matters Bill' (2003). In the UK, Genetically Modified Food and Producer Liability Bill 2000 (UK) could not pass through Parliament.

82 Liability Issues (2003) 2.

83 Lunney and Burrell (2006) 32, 33. See S. 124G, 124H of the Hazardous Substances and New Organisms Act, 1996 (HSNO Act).

84 Commission Recommendation (2010/C 200/01) on guidelines for the development of national co-existence measures to avoid the unintended presence of GMOs in conventional and organic crops ('2010 Coexistence Recommendation') [2010] OJ C200/1.

85 Sections 52, 52(a), 53(c), 53(d) or 55.

86 Liability Issues (2003) 12.

87 Liability Issues (2003) 12.

Court of Justice (ECJ) decided that honey and food supplements containing pollen derived from a GMO are considered foodstuffs produced from GMOs,[88] and cannot be marketed without prior authorisation for the sale of the product from which the pollen came.[89] The ECJ set out that the Directive on genetically modified organisms (GMOs)[90] provides that GMOs may be released deliberately into the environment or placed on the market only when prior authorisation has been given.[91] It stipulated the regulation on genetically modified food[92] provided that GMOs for food use, foodstuffs containing or consisting of GMOs, or foodstuffs produced from ingredients produced using or containing GMOs must be authorised before being placed on the market.[93]

In Canada, in May 2004, in *Monsanto Canada v Hoffman*,[94] the Saskatchewan Court of Queen's Bench dismissed a certification application filed by a group of organic farmers to initiate a class action against Monsanto and Bayer Cropscience for revenue lost due to contamination of their organic canola crops. The plaintiffs were certified organic farmers who wanted certification to sue for financial losses suffered as a result of the introduction of Roundup Ready and Liberty Link Canola. The Court simply dismissed the class action suit and stated that organic farmers could still sue on an individual basis.[95]

Seed purity and identity are also linked to AP, and can also cause trade disruption.[96] As an exporter, Australia cannot ignore the influence of the demands made by its customer countries. Customers' perception of Australia's inability to limit AP may result in the loss of Australian export markets.

---

[88] *Bablock*.

[89] *Bablock* [109].

[90] Commission Directive 2001/18/EC of the European Parliament and of the Council of 12 March 2001 on the deliberate release into the environment of genetically modified organisms [2003] OJ L268 at 24.

[91] Muller (2006) para 92.

[92] Commission Regulation (EC) No 1829/2003 of the European Parliament and of the Council of 22 September 2003 on genetically modified food and feed [2003] OJ L268 at 1.

[93] Muller (2006) para 109.

[94] (2005), 264 Sask R 1 (QB), aff'd (2002), 227 Sask R 63 (CA) (*Hoffman*).

[95] Hierlmeier (2005).

[96] The Canadian Seed Trade Association: 'the international trade of seed is threatened by the lack of international standards surrounding the adventitious presence of non-approved genetic events in seed.'

ADVENTITIOUS PRESENCE AND INTELLECTUAL PROPERTY

As illustrated in the Canadian case *Monsanto Canada v Schmeiser*,[97] some may argue that AP of a gene is an intellectual property issue and is protected by patent law. In general, a patented gene will be protected by patent law, but such protection has limitations. One of the requirements of patentability is usefulness. When GM plants or crops start to be an AP in non-GM counterparts, a different issue arises. 'Concerns about adventitious presence are economic concern: market access, contract specifications, and consumer preferences. The worry is that the mere presence of the transgenic materials decreases the value of the conventional or organic crop, especially in export market.'[98]

Although Germany gives a similar kind of patent protection to patented genes, Germany has also passed the Genetic Engineering Act,[99] which guarantees the freedom of choice between transgenic, conventional and organic crops. If GMO contamination is found on neighbouring conventional or organic crops, the law requires the GM farmer to compensate any loss to conventional or organic farmers. The law also requires the GM cultivator to maintain certain measures, such as isolation distance from other crops. The Supreme Court of Germany has upheld the constitutionality of the Genetic Engineering Act.[100] In 2005, the German Federal State of Saxony-Anhalt had brought an action against the Genetic Engineering Act before the Federal Constitutional Court of Germany. On 25 November 2010, the Federal Constitutional Court of Germany dismissed the action and upheld the restrictive provisions for the cultivation of genetic modified plants and liability. This law is also known as the Coexistence Law. Sixteen European countries including France,[101] Belgium,[102] the Netherlands[103] and others, have a similar 'coexistence

97 [2004] 1 SCR 902 (*Schmeiser*).

98 Kershen and McHughen (2005) 4.

99 *Gentechnikgesetz* BGB1 1990 1 G 2121-60-1 1080.

100 German Federal Constitutional Court, Press Release (24 November 2010) online: *Das Bundesverfassungsgericht*.

101 *Prévention des pollutions et des risques Loin° 2008-595 du 25 juin 2008 relative aux organismes génétiquement modifiés* JO 26 June 2008. See also *Code de l'Environnement* art L531-1ff.

102 *Arrêté royal du 21 février 2005 réglementant la dissémination volontaire dans l'environnement ainsi que la mise sur le marché d'organismes génétiquement modifiés ou de produits en contenant*, 24 February 2005, (2005) Belgian Official Journal 7129–7165. See also Lavrysen (2006).

103 *Coexistence Decree* 2005.

law', guaranteeing freedom of choice and provisions of compensation to non-GM farmers in case of AP of GM crops. These types of laws provide opportunities for the coexistence between transgenic, conventional and organic farmers, and a requirement of standards for GM farmers to ensure a minimal impact of AP. Nonetheless, these European countries have also provided patent protection to GM genes in such crops and remedies in case of infringement. This example demonstrates that the issues raised by the AP of GMOs on conventional or organic crops are different from the issue of gene patent protection.

CONCLUSION

The propensity for genes to spread, by whatever means, leads to AP. This leads to the heart of the problem of coexistence between transgenic, organic and conventional crops, particularly for trade. It is undeniable, and accepted by the FAO, that there will be more instances at the international trade level for AP being found in product shipments. At the local level, the concern is that if the AP issue is not addressed immediately, the organic and conventional (traditional) farming industry will simply be unable to continue their current business models unless there is a redefinition of what is acceptable. A loss of GM-free status caused by AP is a reality, and one that can only become more common as testing becomes more sensitive and more GM crops are produced, and it will become a barrier to organic product production despite a growing demand for organic foods. Organic farming is a steadily growing industry in industrialised countries.

In Australia, there is no provision for specific liability for losses caused by unintended genetic contamination. There is provision for co-existence between non-GM and GM farming but due to the lack of specific liability for damage or losses, there is a crisis of confidence among conventional and organic farmers and deep divides on attitudes to GM crops. The justice of ensuring an environmental balance, and one that meets the needs of stakeholders in crop production of whatever kind, is simply not present in the Australian regulation of GM crops, nor the definitions of 'organic'. Provision of specific liability for damage or losses caused by drifted genes would bring a partial solution by increasing confidence and tolerance among conventional and organic farmers, and perversely also has the potential to increase the level of acceptance of GM crops being grown in Australian soil. Uncertainty is a prime barrier to investment.

AP is a relatively novel issue created by biotechnology, but one that has found neither satisfaction in government regulation nor the courts. The issue of liability associated to the damage caused by AP has not been addressed, other than the rejection of the claims in *Marsh*. Biotechnology has an important role to play in the improvement of crop productivity and to provide some solutions to the changing environments for farming at a global level. With rising population density, loss of cultivatable land and increasing weather extremes, it can be argued that it is an essential contributor to continued food security. However, due to its unique nature, there is a need for legislation and regulation to address the issue of liability at this point, as the courts have neither the tools, nor the will, to tackle this thorny issue. It is a time for policy makers to both analyse the Australian stance on such issues, adopt some form of regulation to establish measures for minimising AP, and to address the potential liability and damages due to the use of products based on genetically modified crops. Furthermore, the lack of coherence of policy and regulation between the Commonwealth and states and territories needs to be addressed. Whether they arrive in a shipment on a boat, or blow across a paddock, genes know no borders.

REFERENCES

Biotechnology and Australian Agriculture, (2008) 'Towards the development of a vision and strategy for the application of biotechnology to Australian Agriculture', Report prepared for Biotechnology Australia and the Department of Agriculture Fisheries and Forestry, ACIL Tasman Pty Ltd.

Black, K. and J. Wishart (2008), 'Containing the GMO genie: Cattle trespass and the rights and responsibilities of biotechnology owners', 46 Osgoode Hall LJ 397.

Bullock, D. and M. Desquilbet (2002), 'The Economics of Non-GMO Segregation and Identity Preservation', 27 *Food Policy* 81.

Canadian General Standards Board (2006), *Organic Production Systems General Principles and Management Standards: National Standard of Canada*, CAN/CGSB-32.310-2006.

Demeke, T., D. Perry and W. Scowcroft (2006), 'Adventitious Presence of GMOs: Scientific Overview for Canadian Grains', 86 *Canadian Journal of Plant Science* 1.

Department of Agriculture (2003), *Liability Issues Associated with GM Crops in Australia* (Canberra: Australian Government).

Department of Agriculture (2008), *Towards a vision and strategy for agricultural biotechnology* (Canberra: Australian Government).

Department of Agriculture (2012), *International Statement on Low Level Presence* (Canberra: Australian Government).

Ellstrand, N., H. Prentice and J. Hancock (1999), 'Gene Flow and Introgression from Domesticated Plants into their Wild Relatives', 30 *Ann Rev Ecology & Systematics* 539.

Endres, B. (2000), '"GMO": Genetically Modified Organism or Gigantic Monetary Obligation? The Liability for GMO Damage in the United States and the European Union', 22 *Loyola of Los Angeles International & Comparative Law Review* 453.

Food and Agriculture Organisation of the United Nations (2003), Guideline for the Conduct of Food Safety Assessment of Foods Derived from Recombinant-DNA Plants CAC/GL 45-2003.

Food and Agriculture Organisation of the United Nations (2007), Joint FAO/WHO Food Standards Programme: Codex Ad Hoc Intergovernmental Task Force on Foods Derived From Biotechnology (Seventh Session), CX/FBT 07/7/1.

Food and Agriculture Organisation of the United Nations (2008), Report of the Seventh Session of the Codex Ad Hoc Intergovernmental Task Force on Foods Derived from Biotechnology ALINORM 08/31/34.

Food and Agriculture Organisation of the United Nations (2014a), Low levels of GM crops in food and feed: Regulatory issues (Technical Background Paper 1), TC-LLP/2014/2.

Food and Agriculture Organisation of the United Nations (2014b), Low levels of GM crops in international food and feed trade: FAO international survey and economic analysis (Technical Background Paper 2), TC-LLP/2014/3.

Glenn, J. (2003), 'Genetically Modified Crops in Canada: Rights and Wrongs', 12 *Journal of Environmental Law and Practice* 281.

Glenn, J. (2010), 'The Coexistence of Genetically Modified and Non-Genetically Modified Agriculture in Canada: A Courtroom Drama', in L. Bodiguel and M. Cardwell (eds) (2010) *The Regulation of Genetically Modified Organisms: Comparative Approaches* (Oxford: Oxford University Press).

Gonzalez, C. (2004), 'Trade Liberalisation, Food Security, and the Environment: The Neoliberal Threat to Sustainable Rural Development', 14 *Transnational Law & Contemporary Problems* 419.

Hierlmeier, J. (2005), 'Under the Microscope: Litigation, Law Reform and Genetically Modified Crops', 30 *Law Now* 32.

Kershen, D. and A. McHughen (2005), 'Adventitious Presence: Inadvertent Commingling and Coexistence and Farming Methods', QTA2005-1 The Council for Agricultural Science and Technology (CAST) Commentary.

Lavrysen, L. (2006), *Belgian Report*, accessed 27 March 2015 at http://hdl.handle.net/1854/LU-611574.

Lichtman, G. (1997), 'The Economics of Innovation: Protecting Unpatentable Goods', 81 *Minnesota Law Review* 693.

Lilith, M. (2008) 'GMO Situation in Australia', Conservative Council of Western Australia, presentation, accessed 21 March 2015 at http://www.planet-diversity.org/fileadmin/files/planet_diversity/Programme/Workshops/GMO_in_Australo-Pacific/GMOs_in_australia_overview.pdf.

Lunney, M. and R. Burrell (2006), *A Farmer's Choice? Legal Liability of Farmers Growing Crops* (Australian Centre for Intellectual Property in Agriculture).

Mgbeoji, I. (2007), 'Adventitious Presence of Patented Genetically Modified Organisms on Private Premises: Is Intent Necessary for Actions in Infringement against the Property Owner?', 27 *Bulletin of Science, Technology and Society* 314.

Ministry for the Environment (2002), *New Zealand, Public Discussion Paper: Improving the Operation of the HSNO Act for New Organisms.*

Muller, B. (2006), 'Infringing and Trespassing Plants: Patented Seeds at Dispute in Canada's Courts', 48 *Focaal: European Journal of Anthropology* 83.

New Zealand Law Commission (2002), *Liability for Loss Resulting from the Development, Supply or Use of Genetically Modified Organisms*, accessed

21 March 2015 at http://www.lawcom.govt.nz/sites/default/files/publications/2002/08/Publication_104_263_SP14.pdf.

Office of the Gene Technology Regulator (2014), *Unintended Presence Strategy (Unapproved GMOs in seed for sowing)*. accessed 21 March 2015 at http://www.ogtr.gov.au/internet/ogtr/publishing.nsf/Content/mon-unintended-1.

Oguamanam, C. (2007), 'Tension on the Farm Fields: The Death of Traditional Agriculture?', 27 *Bulletin of Science, Technology & Society* 260.

Pazzano, C. (2012), 'Genetically Modified Crops in Australia' (SBS News: Australia), accessed 21 March 2015 at http://www.sbs.com.au/news/article/2012/11/15/factbox-gm-foods-australia.

Perry, M. (forthcoming), 'What's So Conventional about Conventional Crops: Non-Recombinant DNA Techniques for Genetically Modified Organisms', in *Conventional*, working title.

Perry, M. and R. Karky (July 2013), 'Agriculture under Threat – A Crisis of Confidence? The Solution: Redefine Adventitious Presence Maximum Levels from Zero to Zero++', 11 *Canadian Journal of Law and Technology* 25.

Phillipson, M. (2008), 'Are Genetically Modified Crops in Canada Under-Regulated?', 18 *Journal of Environmental Law and Practices* 195.

Repp, R. (2000), 'Biotech Pollution: Assessing Liability For Genetically Modified Crop Production and Genetic Drift', 36 *Idaho L. Review* 585.

Rogers, C. (2003), 'Liability for the Release of GMOs into the Environment: Exploring the Boundaries of Nuisance', 62(2) *Cambridge Law Journal* 371.

Ryan, M. (2011), 'Genetically Modified Crops in Australia: Current Issues' (Department of Agriculture, Fisheries and Forestry), accessed 28 March 2015 at http://www.agriculture.gov.au/SiteCollectionDocuments/about/foi/201112/foi-201112-25/Doc_12.pdf.

Shubber, S. (1972), 'The Codex Alimentarius Commission under International Law', 21(1) *The International and Comparative Law Quarterly* 631.

The Canadian Seed Trade Association, *CSTA Position Statement on Adventitious Presence*, accessed 21 March 2015 at http://cdnseed.org/archive/pdfs/press/Position%20on%20Adventitious%20Presence.pdf.

Timmons, A., Y. Charters, J. Crawford, D. Burns, S. Scott, S. Dubbels, N. Wilson, A. Robertson, E. O'Brien, G. Squire and M. Wilkinson (1996), 'Risks from Transgenic Crops', 380 *Nature* 487.

Tsui, M. and L. Chu (2003), 'Aquatic Toxicity of Glyphosate-Based Formulation: Comparison between Different Organisms and the Effects of Environmental Factors', 52 *Chemosphere* 1189.

PART IV

Recognition of indigenous peoples' interests

The final section is focused upon indigenous peoples' issues and approaches. The questions raised in this Part bring into sharp focus the ambiguities and complexities of implementing environmental justice, either from the perspective of vulnerability, or from the perspective of human rights. The three chapters all suggest that the most challenging frontier of environment and justice is the issue of indigenous peoples' interests, and that responding effectively to these challenges is a fundamental concern both for environmental and social justice advocates.

16. Customary law systems for water governance in Kenya

Elizabeth Gachenga

In many jurisdictions including Kenya, the term 'law' is generally assumed to refer to enacted rules emanating from the state. Consequently, legal systems for water resource governance are considered largely as consisting of statutory law – rules enacted by state organs. Nonetheless, in many countries aspects of water resource management, particularly at the local level, include systems of rules that are beyond the scope of statutory frameworks, with local users developing informal norms and institutions to govern their water resources. This chapter uses the term 'customary law' to refer to these informal/ non-statutory normative and institutional frameworks. Customary law systems for natural resource governance continue to exist in many countries.[1]

The resilience of customary water governance regimes has led water law practitioners and researchers in the last two decades to acknowledge that these regimes constitute a factor to be reckoned with when preparing 'modern' legislation for water resource governance.[2] Research has demonstrated that in some cases, their resilience is the result of an inherent adaptive capacity that makes customary law systems more sustainable than state developed systems.[3] Further, as these customary governance forms are self-developed, they represent a more democratic process of development of law and thus are more likely to be successful at achieving sustainability.[4]

Despite the growing appreciation for their potential role, most water legal frameworks are primarily statute based and state-centric, with

[1] See New Zealand Law Commission (2006); Australian Law Reform Commission (1986); Bilal, Haque and Moore (2003).

[2] Eastern and Central Africa Programme for Agricultural Policy Analysis (ECAPAPA 2007).

[3] Ostrom and Gardner (1993).

[4] Ørebech (2006).

minimal provisions for recognition of customary governance systems.[5] This limited space for recognition of customary systems in statutory water law is reflective of the status of customary law in state legal systems. While various models for recognition of customary law have been adopted, their effectiveness in articulating and protecting customary rights is disputable.

Using a case study of the Marakwet of Kenya, this chapter explores the features of a resilient customary water resource governance system and the extent to which such a system is recognised or integrated into the statutory legal framework for water governance. Further, the possibility of extending the human right to water and the human rights-based approach to the realm of customary rights to water is explored, as a legal strategy for remedying the disconnect between customary and statutory frameworks for water resources.

CUSTOMARY LAW SYSTEMS FOR WATER GOVERNANCE: THE CASE OF THE MARAKWET

Most of the inhabitants living along the Marakwet Escarpment of the Kerio Valley, in Kenya belong to the Marakwet ethnic community, who have the oldest irrigation system in Kenya.[6] Irrigation occurs along more than 40km of the Escarpment from south of Arror to north of Tot.[7] The irrigation furrows of the Marakwet are the main source of freshwater resources for the community both for agriculture and domestic use.

The Marakwet community have been governed by a customary normative system that predates colonial rule.[8] The customary system extends to water resource governance and is effective to date as confirmed by data collected during field work undertaken in Sambalat, from November 2010 to February 2011.[9] Data was gathered using semi-structured interviews conducted with: a cross section of water users in the community; government officials; and a representative from a non-governmental organisation. Further insight was gained through three focus group discussions

---

5 This is evident from the analysis of modern legal and institutional frameworks of water governance across jurisdictions. See for example Hodgson and FAO (2006) and Caponera (2007).

6 Ssenyonga (1983) 96.

7 Watson, Adams and Mutiso (1996).

8 Beech (2008).

9 The data collected corroborated other studies on the customary water governance system of the Marakwet. See Adams, Watson and Mutiso (1997); Cheserek (2005).

with; clan elders – the custodians of customary law; a group of senior women in the community and another group of younger women. The researcher also used observation.[10] Although there is no written record of the customary law on water, the respondents explained that its existence is not disputable as, since its inception, it has been passed on orally from one generation to the next. While the existence of an informal normative and institutional framework for governing water resources among the Marakwet is undisputable, its recognition as a form of customary law in a legal positivist context, is dependent on the extent of recognition of customary law in Kenya's statutory law.

CUSTOMARY LAW IN KENYA'S LEGAL FRAMEWORK

Kenya's statutory framework for water governance is hinged on the Water Act 2002,[11] supporting legislation and national policies on water. The Water Act makes no explicit recognition of customary rights or law. However, Kenya's Constitution recognises the existence of customary law, while the Judicature Act confirms its limited application by the courts.[12]

The application of customary law in Kenya is subject to certain conditions. First, it must not be inconsistent with the provisions of the Constitution.[13] Second, its application is limited to civil cases in which one or more parties are subject to or affected by it and its application is not repugnant to justice and morality or inconsistent with any written law.[14] The above provisions confirm the recognition by the State of customary law. Arguably, Article 11 of the Constitution, by recognising the importance of protecting and fostering the culture of Kenyan people, also implicitly envisages the legitimacy of customary normative systems.

Kenyan law recognises the unwritten nature of customary law and for purposes of application requires its proof as a question of fact.[15] In Kenyan courts, evidence on customary law is provided by witnesses who often consist of elders regarded as knowledgeable in customary laws. It

---

[10] Gachenga (2012).

[11] Water Act 2003 (Kenya). The Act is currently under review to align it with the 2010 Constitution. See Water Bill (2013).

[12] Constitution 2010 (Kenya), art 2(4) and *Judicature Act 1967* (Kenya) s 3(2).

[13] Constitution 2010 (Kenya), art 2(4). This condition extends to all other written laws and serves to confirm the supremacy of the Constitution.

[14] Judicature Act 1967 (Kenya), s 3(2).

[15] *Kinyanjui Kimani v Muiru Gikanga and Another* East African Law Reports.

may thus be argued that Kenyan law potentially recognises the existence of Marakwet's customary law on water governance provided such law can be proved as a question of fact.

FEATURES OF MARAKWET'S CUSTOMARY LAW WATER GOVERNANCE SYSTEM

The Marakwet's furrow system does not include the infrastructure necessary to measure the volumetric quantities of water supplied to each individual or family per day. Nevertheless, most of the water users interviewed confirmed that the water supply system catered for their basic domestic and agricultural needs. Although there is a very limited supply of state-supplied water, respondents did not complain of lack of physical or economic access to water. Most of the respondents though agreed that the quality of water supplied from the furrow system was inadequate. Subject to these problems of quality, the community members interviewed all evaluated the performance of their customary water resource governance system favourably.

An analysis of the data collected and a review of literature on the Marakwet's customary law systems for water governance demonstrated some of the salient features of this normative and institutional framework.

OWNERSHIP AND INTEGRATION OF WATER WITH OTHER RESOURCES

According to the community, water is sacred and thus water resources are not owned but are a naturally occurring God-given resource. Every member of the community has a right to use the waters of the Embobut River given its proximity to their land. Water use is governed by customary law, comprising of rules on allocation, management of furrows, preservation of quantity and quality, and so on.

The Marakwet customary water governance system does not consider water resources independently of land in terms of governance. As a result, customary laws on water include norms governing land access and use. According to the community, land in the area is subject to customary tenure which recognises community land as well as privately held land.[16]

[16] Focus Group Discussion with Clan Elders and Representatives of Furrows Council (Marakwet District- Kenya, 10 February 2010).

In relation to privately owned land, no beacons or clear fences demarcating boundaries were evident but the respondents explained that each clan is aware of the respective owners of land.

HOME-GROWN

All the community members interviewed referred to the water law as their law and associated its origin with their ancestors.[17] The water rules have since evolved with subsequent changes being effected through a consultative process that is all-inclusive, as all clans are represented in the council of elders in charge of furrow issues. Although government administrative officials, such as the Chief, may be co-opted in the council, their role is merely advisory. The autonomy in design of the rules is considered sacrosanct as is evident from a remark from one of the respondents: 'there is no law that will come to tell us who will or how we will use the water. The water is for us and for our children from our elders. No one will tell us how to use it'.[18]

A further feature of the Marakwet customary governance systems is that it is not only user-developed but is also implemented and enforced by its users. Water governance is the responsibility of the council charged with furrow issues. The council allocates water to the various clans, ensures compliance with rules on allocation, and imposes sanctions for non-compliance. Implementation of rules and imposition of sanctions is discussed in community meetings. Sanctions imposed range from social sanctions such as peer remonstration to monetary fines, curses and in severe cases destruction of the offender's property and that of their sub-clan members.[19]

The rules on allocation of water for instance require community

---

[17] Focus Group Discussion with Clan Elders and Representatives of Furrows Council (Marakwet District- Kenya, 10 February 2010); Focus Group Discussion with a group of younger women on the customary water governance system (Marakwet District- Kenya, 10 February 2010); Focus Group Discussion with a group of older women on the customary water governance system (Marakwet District-Kenya, 10 February 2010); Interviews with water users from Kaben location, (Marakwet District-Kenya, November–February 2010).

[18] Focus Group Discussion with Clan Elders and Representatives of Furrows Council (Marakwet District- Kenya, 10 February 2010).

[19] One of the water users interviewed, explained that in the past, incorrigible offenders would be punished by a form of 'death penalty' and it was the responsibility of the offender's relatives particularly his uncles to implement the punishment. He clarified that this form of punishment is no longer prevalent.

members to contribute to the management and repair of furrow infrastructure. The furrow system is designed in such a way that the managers can start or stop the flow of water, thus controlling access. All households are expected to send male representatives to help with the management and repair of furrows. Those failing to contribute to furrow maintenance and repair are not entitled to irrigation water and may be subject to other sanctions imposed by their peers, including public humiliation. However, the clan elders explained that no restriction is placed on water for domestic use.[20]

The statutory framework established under the Water Act is premised on principles which are fundamentally distinct from those underlying the Marakwet customary water governance system resulting in a disconnect between law and the practice of water governance in the community.

Some of the main features of the statutory legal framework for water resource governance under the Act are highlighted below and contrasted with the main features of Marakwet's customary system.

TOP-DOWN DEVELOPMENT OF LAW AND POLICY

Unlike with the customary law system, the policy and law formulation process leading to the Water Act was largely a top-down exercise. Respondents indicated that they were neither aware nor involved in the process. Most of those interviewed had not heard of the Water Act. The council members interviewed were of the view that there ought to have been more consultation in the water law reform process, particularly where reforms had implications on their water resources. In the absence of such consultation, they believe it unlikely that the laws developed would cater for their interests.[21]

The Constitution of Kenya 2010 includes provisions regulating water resources in the country.[22] The process of drafting the new Constitution took approximately ten years, with great efforts taken to make the process consultative. During the field work the author sought to establish the extent to which the community members were aware of the Constitutional provisions relating to water resources. Respondents indicated that they were aware of the promulgation of the Constitution and had been involved

---

[20] Focus Group Discussion with Clan Elders and Representatives of Furrows Council (Marakwet District- Kenya, 10 February 2010).

[21] Focus Group Discussion with Clan Elders and Representatives of Furrows Council (Marakwet District- Kenya, 10 February 2010).

[22] Constitution 2010 (Kenya).

in the civic education programmes but argued that these sessions did not deal with issues of water resource governance in great depth.[23]

OWNERSHIP AND WATER RIGHTS

As noted, the Marakwet regard water as a God-given resource and thus not subject to ownership in the strict sense. The Water Act vests all water resources in the State. Under the Act, the primary right of use is granted to the Minister except where such right is alienated by the Act or by any other law.[24] In the absence of an 'Act' or 'any other law' granting customary rights to water resources, the right of control over all water resources including user rights lies with the State or with those to whom such rights are granted by the Minister.[25] The effect of these provisions is to extinguish any pre-existing rights including customary rights to water. This raises a fundamental issue regarding the basis of the customary water law of the Marakwet, given that the Water Act contains no provision recognising customary water rights.

Arguably the problem of finding a legal basis for customary rights to water for the Marakwet stands a chance of being redressed in the new Constitutional dispensation. The Constitution of Kenya 2010 and Sessional Paper No 3 of 2009 provide for the recognition of community rights to land.[26] Provisions on community land under the recently promulgated Constitution, could arguably serve as a basis for customary rights to land and by extension to water resources. Under the Constitution, all rivers, lakes, and other water bodies are defined as public land.[27] It could be argued that the rivers, lakes and other water bodies on community land can be defined as part of community land. However, the country is still in the process of enacting the supporting community land legislation and thus the extent to which this law can support customary rights to water is yet to be seen.

While community or customary rights over land may form a basis for the recognition of a customary law water governance system such as that of the Marakwet, the effectiveness of such a model is disputable. Experience from other jurisdictions demonstrates the challenges faced by similar

---

23 Focus Group Discussion with Clan Elders and Representatives of Furrows Council (Marakwet District- Kenya, 10 February 2010).

24 Water Act 2003 (Kenya) s 3.

25 Water Act 2003 (Kenya) ss 4–6.

26 Constitution 2010 (Kenya) arts 61 and 63.

27 Constitution 2010 (Kenya) art 63.

models of recognition of indigenous rights to water. For instance, in many settler colonies, a basis for indigenous rights to water resources has been sought in treaties or other laws recognising indigenous rights over land. In Australia, Canada, the United States and New Zealand for instance, indigenous water rights often accompany native title.[28] Under such models, the definition and scope of the indigenous water rights is delimited by the nature and content of rights granted by the respective treaties or land rights law. For example, customary law in most of these models is associated with antiquity and long usage with the effect of restricting the content and scope of customary rights to non-economic rights of use.[29]

Further, the distinction of customary or indigenous rights from other statutory rights over land and water in these models, results in the subordination of the former to the latter. These statutory frameworks consider indigenous rights as 'second-order rights to be assessed through broad policy objectives after others have been guaranteed or assigned their more concrete rights'.[30] Indigenous peoples seeking to use customary water governance systems are thus faced with the challenge of how to give meaning to their rights in such a narrowly defined rights-based discourse.[31] The experience with these models of Land Rights or Native Title as bases for indigenous water rights demonstrates some of the challenges likely to be faced in the attempt to use community land provisions to guarantee customary rights over water in Kenya.

INSTITUTIONAL FRAMEWORKS

The institutional framework established by the Water Act does not explicitly recognise customary law institutions such as Marakwet's council of elders in charge of furrow issues.

Arguably, the provisions in the Water Act allowing for stakeholder participation and particularly for community participation at the local level provide an opportunity for the Marakwet community to get involved in water governance. For instance, the Act establishes Catchment Area Advisory Committees (CAACs) to assist the Water Resources Management Authority with management functions at the catchment or regional level.[32] Membership of the CAACs is drawn from a wide variety

---

28 Durette (2010).
29 Ibid, 297.
30 Craig and Gachenga (2009).
31 Craig and Jeffery (2011) 535.
32 Water Act 2003 (Kenya) s 16.

of stakeholders including farmers, pastoralists, business communities, NGOs and other competent persons from the area.[33] However, none of those interviewed were members of the relevant CAAC nor were they aware of the existence of such an opportunity.

The Water Act also includes provisions on Water Resources User Associations (WRUAs), another potential vehicle of community participation.[34] WRUAs are defined as 'an association of water users, riparian land owners, or other stakeholders who have formally and voluntarily associated for the purposes of cooperatively sharing, managing and conserving a common water resource'.[35] The complexities associated with registration of WRUAs present challenges to community members.[36] Further, the separation in the statutory institutional framework, of water resource management from water service provision, limits the scope of the functions of the WRUAs to water resource management. Consequently, they are inadequate vehicles for integrating the institution of councils of elders in charge of furrows into the statutory legal framework.[37]

There is thus a disconnect between the statutory framework and the customary normative and institutional frameworks for water governance. The resilience of these systems demonstrates their effectiveness and the need to integrate them within the statutory framework. The next section explores the possibility of using the human rights-based approach to safeguard customary rights and institutions of water governance and thus remedy the disconnect between custom and statute.

HRBA AND RECOGNITION OF CUSTOMARY LAW SYSTEMS FOR WATER GOVERNANCE

The human rights-based approach (HRBA) is a conceptual framework for human development based on international human rights and standards, which in practice seeks to ensure the primacy of human well-being in the determination of development goals.[38] In the context of water resource governance, the HRBA attempts to direct all water resource governance systems towards a guarantee of the basic human need for water and to

33 Water Act 2003 (Kenya) s 16(3).
34 Water Act 2003 (Kenya) s 15(5).
35 Water Resource Management Authority (2007) r 2.
36 Mumma (2008).
37 Gachenga (2011).
38 Nyamu-Musembi and Cornwal (2004).

provide individual users with the instruments to enforce this need for water.[39]

This chapter argues that the HRBA, specifically the human right to water and sanitation and the recognition of the rights of indigenous peoples, provide a possible basis for a new model for seeking the recognition of customary rights to water and the right to use customary law systems for water governance.

THE HUMAN RIGHT TO WATER AND INDIGENOUS PEOPLES' RIGHTS

The Declaration of the Human Right to Water and Sanitation has contributed to the growing interest in the extension of the HRBA to water governance issues.[40] Although, not explicitly contained in any international human rights instrument, the right is enshrined in the national legal frameworks of water governance of most countries. Article 43 of the Constitution of Kenya includes among the economic and social rights, the right of all Kenyans to clean and safe water in adequate quantities.[41] The Constitution further requires the government to take affirmative action to ensure that minorities and marginalised groups have reasonable access to water.[42] Apart from these explicit provisions relating to the right to water, other Constitutional provisions related to the environment and natural resources may have implications on the right to water.[43]

The potential of using the HRBA to safeguard customary rights to water is further strengthened by the right of indigenous peoples' to self-governance. The adoption of the United Nations Declaration on the Rights of Indigenous Peoples (UNDRIP) in 2007 provides a significant elaboration of the rights of indigenous peoples.[44] As is the case with other

---

39 Bourquain (2008) 12.

40 *The Human Right to Water and Sanitation*, GA Res 64/292, UN GAOR, 64th sess, 108th mtg, Agenda Item 48, Supp No 49, UN Doc A/64/L.63/Rev.1 (26 July 2010).

41 Constitution 2010 (Kenya) art 43(1)(d).

42 Constitution 2010 (Kenya) art 56(e).

43 See for example Constitution 2010 (Kenya) arts 43. 69, 70 and 71.

44 *United Nations Declaration on the Rights of Indigenous Peoples*, GA Res 61/295, UN GAOR, 61st sess, 107th plen mtg, Supp No 49, UN Doc A/RES/61/295 (13 September 2007). At its adoption, 144 states voted in favour, four voted against (Australia, Canada, the United States and New Zealand) and 11 states, including Kenya, abstained from voting. The four countries that had voted against the Declaration have since endorsed it.

declarations in international law, UNDRIP does not bind states in the same way as conventions and treaties would. Nevertheless, it reflects the commitment of states towards the principles set out and to that extent represents the direction in which international law relating to indigenous peoples' rights is likely to develop in future.

Under the declaration, the right to self-determination is recognised as the basis for all other indigenous peoples' rights.[45] UNDRIP provides that, by virtue of this right, indigenous peoples 'freely determine their political status and freely pursue their economic, social and cultural development'.[46] Other provisions in the Declaration connect the right to self-determination of indigenous peoples with the right to maintain their own institutional structures and legal systems in accordance with their customs and traditions.[47] UNDRIP thus provides a basis for indigenous communities to defend their right to water.

The attempt to seek a legal basis for the customary right to water in UNDRIP has a basis in law, as demonstrated by the experience in the Philippines. Although, their Country's Water Code does not recognise the customary right to water, the 1997 Indigenous Peoples Right Act grants customary water rights to indigenous communities.[48]

HRBA AND THE LEGAL BASIS FOR CUSTOMARY RIGHTS FOR WATER GOVERNANCE

The constitutional recognition of the human right to water, coupled with the recognition of the rights of indigenous peoples, provide a basis for the use of the HRBA to safeguard customary rights to water resource governance in jurisdictions where models of recognition of customary law are lacking or ineffective. Customary systems of water governance, as demonstrated by the Marakwet, often focus on the protection of local water needs and so are prevalent among marginalised or under-serviced communities emphasising further the connection between these systems and the HRBA. Where customary water governance systems constitute the sole regime governing the provision of water to communities, it may be argued that the human right to water includes the right of individuals or communities to safeguard their customary governance system for water resources.

45 Ibid, art 3.
46 Ibid, art 3.
47 Ibid, arts 20, 33–5.
48 UNESCO (2009).

The elaboration of the content of the human right to water justifies this argument, as the right to water contains the right to maintain access to existing supplies and freedom from interference.[49] As the furrows of the Marakwet constitute their primary source of water supply, they provide the means for their realisation of the human right to water and this arguably grants the Marakwet a basis for maintaining that their customary law system of water governance is crucial for maintaining their access to water. Such an argument could be further strengthened through recourse to laws recognising the rights of indigenous peoples. A similar argument was upheld before the African Commission on Human and Peoples' Rights in the Endorois case, where it was argued that the community's loss of their ancestral land severely undermined their access to clean drinking water.[50]

The HRBA thus provides a promising avenue for the defence of customary rights to water in jurisdictions such as Kenya, in which the legal framework surrounding human rights is more established than that of customary rights to natural resources. This is evidenced by the budding case law relating to HRBA since the promulgation of progressive Constitutions enshrining social, economic and cultural rights in their Bill of Rights.[51] Although the potential effectiveness of HRBA in specifically securing a right to safeguard a customary law system for water governance remains untested in Kenya, some challenges can already be gleaned from the experience of litigating the provisions of Article 43 of the Constitution.

There are limited precedents on the enforcement of the human right to water. An attempt to enforce the right to water in a case of forceful evictions proved unsuccessful with the court pointing out that in spite of the Constitutional recognition of the right, the present Water Act does not explicitly provide for the right as in s 43 of the Water Services Act of South Africa.[52]

---

[49] Committee on Economic, Social and Cultural Rights, General Comment 15: The Right to Water, 29th sess, Agenda Item 3, UN Doc E/C.12/2002/11 (29 November 2002) 4.

[50] *Centre for Minority Rights Development (Kenya) and Minority Group International on Behalf of Endorois Welfare Council v Kenya*, 276/2003 African Commission on Human and Peoples' Rights.

[51] See for example in Kenya: *Satrose Ayuma and 11 Others v Registered Trustees of the Kenya Railways Staff Recruitment Benefits Scheme & 3 Others* Kenya Law Report Constitutional and Human Rights Division of the High Court (Muthurwa Case); *Mitubell Welfare Society v Attorney General and 2 Others* Kenya Law Reports High Court; In South Africa, *Government of the Republic of South Africa v Grootboom* South Africa Law Reports Constitutional Court, *Mazibuko v City of Johannesburg* [2009] ZA 28 (Constitutional Court).

[52] Muthurwa Case.

A further challenge for the Marakwet would be to prove that the failure to recognise or integrate their customary law system of water governance would severely undermine their access to water and so constitute derogation from their human right to water. Such an argument would be difficult to sustain unless it can be proved that the existing customary law system provides an effective means for the realisation of the right to water in terms of quantity, quality and accessibility of water for basic needs. While not strictly restricted to volumetric standards, a quantity of 20–25 litres per person, per day is proposed as a standard for adequacy. The content of the right with respect to the quality of water must also be met.[53] As observed in the fieldwork, Marakwet's furrow system does not include a means of measuring the quantities of water abstracted or allocated to each individual or household. Further, the quality of the water obtained from the furrows is not satisfactory for domestic use.

In relation to enforcing UNDRIP rights, the Marakwet face the challenge of demonstrating that they fall within the definition of the term 'indigenous' as anticipated by the African Commission on Human and Peoples' Rights. The Commission has in a case before it acknowledged the Endorois community as indigenous in so far as 'they consider themselves to be a distinct people, sharing a common history, culture and religion'.[54] However, a local recent case has held that such a definition would not only grant the Endorois the status of indigenous but would also grant all other 42 sub-nations of Kenya a right to claim rights under UNDRIP.[55] The use of UNDRIP to grant a particular community exclusive rights has thus been disputed on the basis that this would set an untenable precedent for all other communities.[56] Attempts by the Marakwet to seek rights under the UNDRIP are thus likely to be opposed on the basis of Article 46 of the Declaration which subordinates indigenous rights to the good of the state in terms of political unity and sovereignty.

There are thus opportunities and challenges in relation to the potential use of the HRBA as a basis for customary rights and customary law governance of water resources. However, as it has not been directly tested in

---

53 Committee on Economic, Social and Cultural Rights, General Comment 15: The Right to Water, 29th sess, Agenda Item 3, UN Doc E/C.12/2002/11 (29 November 2002) 5.

54 Centre for Minority Rights Development (Kenya) and Minority Group International on Behalf of Endorois Welfare Council v Kenya, 276/2003 para 162.

55 *Simion Swakey Ole Kaapei & 89 others v Commissioner of Lands & 7 others* eKLR High Court, para 29.07.

56 Ibid, 34.01.

Kenya, the jury is still out on how courts would in practice deal with such claims.

CONCLUSION

Customary law, defined in the sense of a living reality that emerges and evolves from social practices of a community and which the community eventually accepts as obligatory, continues to exist in the case of the Marakwet. For the Marakwet, customary law constitutes the primary regulatory framework for governance of their water resources. An analysis of the features of their customary law system distinguishes it from the statutory law system of water governance. The lack of integration of these plural normative systems adversely affects sustainable water governance. Existing models for recognition of customary rights on the basis of treaties or laws recognising indigenous rights over land are limited by the nature and scope of the rights granted under these treaties or laws. The inadequacy and in some cases lack of such models for recognition of customary water rights has led to the search for alternative legal strategies for recognition and integration of customary rights and law systems for water governance.

The HRBA provides a potential avenue for upholding customary rights to water. The basis for the HRBA in this case would be the human right to water and the recognition of rights of indigenous peoples. The successful application of the HRBA would depend on various factors and would not be without challenges as discussed in this chapter. Despite the challenges, the HRBA provides a novel legal avenue for gaining recognition of customary water and the right to use a customary law system of water governance.

REFERENCES

Adams W., E. Watson and S. Mutiso S. (1997), 'Water, Rules and Gender: Water Rights in an Indigenous Irrigation System, Marakwet, Kenya' 28 *Development and Change* 707.

Australian Law Reform Commission (1986), *The Recognition of Aboriginal Customary Laws, Report No 31*.

Beech M. (1921), 'Sketch of Elgeyo Law and Custom' 20(79) *Journal of the Royal African Society* 195.

Bilal A., H. Haque and P. Moore. (2003), *Customary Laws Governing Natural Resource Management in the Northern Areas* (IUCN, Environmental Law Programme).

Bourquain K. (2008), *Freshwater Access from a Human Rights Perspective: A Challenge to International Water and Human Rights Law* (Leiden: Martinus Nijhoff).
Caponera D. (2007), (M. Nanni (ed.)) *Principles of Water Law and Administration: National and International* (Abingdon: Taylor & Francis).
Centre for Minority Rights Development (Kenya) and Minority Group International on Behalf of Endorois Welfare Council v Kenya, 276/2003 African Commission on Human and Peoples' Rights.
Cheserek G. (2005), 'Indigenous Knowledge in Water and Watershed Management: 'Marakwet' Conservation Strategies and Techniques' FWU, Topics of Integrated Watershed Management – Proceedings 3.
Committee on Economic, Social and Cultural Rights, *General Comment 15: The Right to Water, 29th sess, Agenda Item 3, UN Doc E/C.12/2002/11 (29 November 2002).*
Constitution (2010) (Kenya)
Craig D. and E. Gachenga (2009), 'The Recognition of Indigenous Customary Law in Water Resource Management' 20 *Water Law* 278.
Craig D. and M. Jeffery M. (2011), 'Recognition and Enforcement of Indigenous Customary Law in Environmental Regimes and Natural Resource Management' in L. Paddock *et al.* (eds), *Compliance and Enforcement in Environmental Law* (Cheltenham, UK and Northampton, MA, USA: Edward Elgar).
Durette M. (2010), 'A Comparative Approach to Indigenous Legal Rights to Freshwater: Key Lessons for Australia from the United States, Canada and New Zealand' 27 *Environmental and Planning Law Journal* 296.
Eastern and Central Africa Programme for Agricultural Policy Analysis (2007), *Accommodating Customary Water Management Arrangements to Consolidate Poverty-focused Water Reform: A Policy Brief* (Project Title: Managing Conflicts over Natural Resources Management (ECAPAPA) – Phase II).
Gachenga E. (2011), 'Kenya's Water Act: Opportunities for Integration of Customary Institutions of Water Governance Through Water Resources Users Asssociations and Water Service Providers' 22 *The Journal of Water Law* 2–3.
Gachenga E. (2012), 'Integrating Customary and Statutory Law Systems of Water Governance for Sustainable Development. The Case of the Marakwet of Kenya' (University of Western Sydney).
Government of the Republic of South Africa v Grootboom South Africa Law Reports (Constitutional Court).
Hodgson S. and FAO (2006), *Modern Water Rights: Theory and Practice* (FAO).
Judicature Act 1967 (Kenya).
Kinyanjui Kimani v. Muiru Gikanga and Another East African Law Reports
Mazibuko v City of Johannesburg [2009] ZA 28 (Constitutional Court)
Mitubell Welfare Society vs Attorney General and 2 Others Kenya Law Reports (High Court)
Mumma A. (2008), 'Kenya's New Water Law: An Analysis of the Implications for the Rural Poor' in M. Giordano, B.V. Koppen and J. Butterworth (eds), *Community-Based Water Law and Water Resource Management Reform in Developing Countries* (Wallingford: CABI).
New Zealand Law Commission (2006), *Converging Currents. Custom and Human Rights in the Pacific* (New Zealand Law Commission).
Nyamu-Musembi C. and A. Cornwall (2004), 'What is the "Rights-Based

Approach" All About? Perspectives from International Development Agencies' IDS Working Paper 234.
Ørebech P. *et al.* (2006), *The Role of Customary Law in Sustainable Development* (Cambridge: Cambridge University Press).
Ostrom E. and R. Gardner (1993), 'Coping with Asymmetries in the Commons: Self-Governing Irrigation Systems Can Work' [American Economic Association] 7 *The Journal of Economic Perspectives* 4.
Satrose Ayuma and 11 Others v Registered Trustees of the Kenya Railways Staff Recruitment Benefits Scheme & 3 Others Kenya Law Report (Constitutional and Human Rights Division of the High Court)
Simion Swakey Ole Kaapei & 89 others v Commissioner of Lands & 7 others eKLR (High Court)
Ssennyonga, J. (1983), 'The Marakwet Irrigation System as a Model of a Systems Approach to Water Management' in B. Kipkorir, R. Soper and J. Ssennyonga (eds), *Kerio Valley: Past, Present and Future* (Nairobi: University of Nairobi, Institute of African Studies).
UNESCO (2009), 'Outcome of the International Expert's Meeting on the Right to Water' accessed 22 March 2015 at http://unesdoc.unesco.org/images/0018/001854/185432E.pdf.
United Nations Declaration on the Rights of Indigenous Peoples, GA Res 61/295, UN GAOR, 61st sess, 107th plen mtg, Supp No 49, UN Doc A/RES/61/295 (13 September 2007).
Water Act 2003 (Kenya)
Water Bill (Kenya 2013)
Water Resource Management Authority (WRMA 2007), *Water Resource Management Rules, Legal Notice No. 171.*
Watson E., W. Adams and S. Mutiso (1998), 'Indigenous Irrigation, Agriculture and Development, Marakwet, Kenya' [Blackwell Publishing on behalf of The Royal Geographical Society (with the Institute of British Geographers)] 164 *The Geographical Journal* 1.

17. Legal strategies to expand indigenous governance in climate change adaptation

Donna Craig

Concerns about the impact of climate change are triggering adaptation and mitigation responses. These responses implement concepts of governance that, among other issues and interests, reflect world-views about the function of law in governance. Notably absent from these developing governance frameworks – and, thus, the responses to climate change – is respect for indigenous rights in spite of the affirmation of such rights in international and domestic law.

Indigenous people are involved in climate change governance because of three distinct roles: they are citizens within the general population; many are vulnerable citizens; and their indigenous status gives them additional interests and rights. Indigenous rights can exist within the domestic legal order of nation-states or be independent of (and to some degree supervene) nation-state sovereignty.

This chapter considers literature from a range of disciplines, identifying the opportunities and barriers to empowering indigenous governance in the context of climate change. It begins with a critique of the concepts of adaptation and resilience relating to climate variability and climate change and the implications for sustainability governance. These themes are further explored through an analysis of international indigenous rights-based approaches, and the evolving approaches to indigenous self-determination. The current climate regime development of REDD+ (reducing emissions from deforestation, degradation and enhanced conservation of forests in developing countries) provides an example of their implications for future sustainable management of climate change impacts and adaptation options.

This aim of the chapter is to highlight the issue of indigenous rights as an important – and currently undermanaged – legal aspect to consider in climate change governance responses. New measures to adapt to climate change offer an opportunity to characterise contemporary natural resource governance with respect for indigenous rights in line with international law and strengthening legal principles. Should this opportunity be lost, it will represent a backward step for both environmental law and indigenous justice.

INTRODUCTION

The impacts of climate change, and actions taken to mitigate and adapt to climate change will fall heavily on vulnerable communities, states and regions (very often developing countries and Indigenous Peoples). UNEP suggests that, to continue to secure the United Nations Millennium Development Goals (MDGs), it will be necessary to respond to vulnerability by changing policies and practices[1] because climate change poses risk to each of the MDGs.[2]

Adger *et al.*[3] argue that the challenge is to use climate adaptation to 'find opportunities to transform social-ecological systems into development pathways that may improve human conditions'. Such an argument links climate adaptation to an older debate on the right to development. Article 1 of the United Nations Declaration on the Rights to Development, 1986[4] reads:

> The right to development is an inalienable human right by virtue of which every human person and all Peoples are entitled to participate in, contribute to and enjoy economic, social, cultural and political development, in which all human rights and fundamental freedom can be fully realised.[5]

Notably, this statement concerning 'right to development' gives little attention to the specific rights, needs, values, knowledge, know-how and practices of Indigenous Peoples. Indeed, the incorporation of a human rights dimension in development thinking has been slow to evolve and is incomplete. More than a decade elapsed between the point of recognition that development was a legal right to the point of recognising that respect for these rights is not only a legal and moral necessity, it is also important for achieving economic goals of development. The narrow paradigm of defining 'development' as 'economic development' was not seriously chal-

---

1 United Nations Millennium Declaration (2000), A/res/55/2, Taillant, J.D., *Human Rights, Development and Climate Change*, CEDHA, 2007, 3.

2 Ibid,12.

3 Adger *et al.* (2011) 765.

4 United Nations Declaration on the Right to Development, GA. Res 128, UN GAOR (41st mtg), UN Doc. A/Res/41/128 (1986).

5 Ibid.

lenged until the birth of the concept of 'sustainable development' in the Brundtland Report,[6] the Rio Declaration,[7] Agenda 21[8] and the MDGs.

In *Gabčíkovo-Nagymaros (Hungary v Slovakia)*,[9] Judge Weeramantry referred to 'sustainable development' as a 'principle of normative value'. Thus, though the value of rights is theoretically clear, the work of Grieber and his colleagues[10] shows there are significant difficulties in operationalising human rights-based approaches to sustainable development. In particular, there is a weak understanding of how to give recognition and effect to specific indigenous rights. In effect, the elaboration and implementation of legal frameworks based on sustainable development principles is an ongoing project;[11] operationalisation of indigenous rights is a component of that project.

In some jurisdictions, such rights are understood as the 'right to participate'; thus addressing the issue of disempowerment by giving indigenous people a voice in development and resource governance.

The Aarhus Convention,[12] takes this approach, albeit at a basic level. Some participatory approaches have adopted the language of democracy, decentralisation and accountable institutions.[13] However, 'participation' and 'partnership'[14] rights are not always effective because of inherent unequal power relationships, failures at the local levels and a lack resources and institutions for long-term change. Ineffective participation rights can exacerbate the marginalisation of groups (such as women), communities and peoples (such as Indigenous and tribal peoples).[15]

Addressing the issue of power imbalance Grieber *et al.* propose sophisticated rights-based approaches to 'conservation with justice' that include conflict resolution mechanisms.[16]

---

6 Brundtland, 1987.

7 *Report of the United Nations Conference on Environment and Development*, Rio de Janiero, 3–14 June 1992, United Nations Publication, Sales No. E.93.1.8, Vol. 1: Resolutions adopted by the Conference, resolution 1, Annex 11.

8 Ibid.

9 1997 I.C.J. 97, 98 (Sept. 1997) (separate opinion of Judge Weeramantry).

10 Grieber, Janki, Orellana, Savaresi and Shelton (2002).

11 See Dernbach (2011).

12 Convention on Access to Information, Public Participation in Decision-making and Access to Justice in Environmental Matters (hereinafter Aarhus Convention), 25 June 1998, 38 I.L.M. 517.

13 Bosselman, Engel and Taylor (2008); Brown (2009) 41–2.

14 Craig (2002).

15 Cooke and Kothari; Ribot, Agrawal and Larson (2006); Craig and Gachenga (2010); Craig and Jeffery (2010).

16 Grieber, Janki, Orellana, Savaresi, and Shelton (2009) 37–61. For further discussion on conflict and legal approaches see: Craig and Jeffery (2011a);

However, even now, mechanisms to ensure participation (let alone significant transfers of governance power) are only just emerging and are as yet far from fully effective. The same pattern of retarded recognition of the needs of vulnerable and of indigenous people is being repeated in climate change management. Environmental human rights jurisprudence has been mostly concerned with pollution claims. Shelton argues that 'issues such as resource management and nature conservation or biodiversity are more difficult to bring under the human rights rubric, absent a right to a safe and ecologically-balanced environment'.[17] Issues of indigenous interests identifying Indigenous Peoples as those to whom compensation is justified are distinct from indigenous rights-based arguments to participate in governance decisions and to have indigenous interests fully accounted for in those decisions.

CLIMATE VULNERABILITY OF INDIGENOUS PEOPLES

Macchi[18] identifies regions that are likely to experience certain types of environmental change:

> Areas of high risk with regard to changes in precipitation and surface temperature include: the Arctic region, the Caribbean and the Mediterranean region, the very south of Latin America and the Amazon, southern Africa, the Arabian Peninsula and large parts of Australia. Concerning sea level rise, areas at greatest risk include island states in general but especially small islands states, the Arctic region as well as low lying Asian coastal areas.

The Stern Review[19] provided evidence that the impacts of climate change are inequitably borne by developing countries, and vulnerable and indigenous communities. The IPCC *Fourth Assessment Report*[20] further reveals that Indigenous Peoples' livelihoods, especially of those living in the Arctic, have already been altered;[21] the *Report* suggests indigenous people be specifically considered in climate change research and policy-making processes because they will be disproportionately affected by climate

Glasbergen, Bierman and Mol (2007); Borrini-Feyerabend,. Pimbert, Farvar, Kothari and Renard (2004).

17 Shelton (2002) 230. See also Hannum, Anaya, and Shelton (2011).

18 Macchi *et al.* (2008) 27–8. See also, Abate and Kronk (2013).

19 Stern (2007).

20 IPCC (2007).

21 Quoted in Macchi (2008) 11. See also, UNPFIIS (2007).

change, predicted to impact health (increased prevalence of diseases), sea level rise and other environmental hazards.[22] Macchi, likewise, argues that global issues relating to equity must be addressed.[23]

Social vulnerability has several dimensions for Indigenous Peoples:

- Equity and justice, including participation in policy making as well as ethical and legal responsibility to address climate change;[24]
- Culture and knowledge concerning current and future generations, traditional ecological knowledge, sense of place, treaty rights and ownership and access to traditional resources;[25]
- Adaptive capacity, including political empowerment ability and resources to address climate impacts;[26]
- The role of race, ethnicity, gender and indigenous sovereignty and self-determination.[27]

Though vulnerable, indigenous and local communities have coping strategies and adaptive capacity; a factor that very few international policy documents acknowledge,[28] though the *IPCC Report Fourth Assessment Report* calls for further study of indigenous knowledge systems which could prove to be valuable sources of information for climate change impact, adaptation and vulnerability (CCIAV) assessments.[29] The magnitude of the impacts of climate change and adaptation responses was dramatically illustrated in the Inuit Circumpolar Conference Petition to the Inter-American Human Rights Commission.[30]

Future indigenous claims may draw on domestic law approaches to environmental harm, and approaches to sovereignty, responsibility and liability in international law. However, current international law is insufficient to support a specific right to an environment of a particular quality, although some national constitutions embody such a right.[31]

---

22 Macchi (2008) 12.

23 Macchi (2008) 28. See also, Dow, Kasperson, (2007); IWGIA (2008); ACIA (2004); Lynn, MacKendrick and Donoghue (2011).

24 Lynn, MacKendrick and Donoghue (2011) 6–7.

25 Ibid.

26 Ibid.

27 Krakoff (2008). See also, Limon (2009).

28 Macchi (2008) 28; See also Nakashima *et al.* (2012).

29 See IISD (2012).

30 Organisation of American States, *Inuit Petition* (2005).

31 HREOC, 2008.

INDIGENOUS RIGHTS AND CLIMATE JUSTICE

In most research and policy-making, Indigenous Peoples are equated with vulnerable and local communities in adaptation strategies. This characterisation overlooks Indigenous Peoples' distinct interests as right-holders. Note, however, a link between interests as vulnerable people and interests as rights-holders:

> Climate change threatens Indigenous land, which is often uniquely connected to Indigenous identity and cultural and natural resources. As a result, climate change potentially affects the very ability of some Indigenous communities to self-determine their identity and culture.[32]

There is a distinction between the two interest positions. Tsosie[33] argues that the first generation of the environmental justice movement in the 1980s and 1990s was a grass roots response to the disproportionate effect of environmental impacts and hazards on low income communities and minorities:

> The legal theories used to respond to such injustices were heavily premised on the intersection of environmental law and civil rights law.[34]

Native Americans, along with other racial minorities, were perceived to be victims of 'environmental racism'.[35] Native Americans disputed this characterisation as victims or a 'minority'. They concentrated on claims for sovereignty and regulatory control over reservation lands.[36] Tsosie considers that the second generation of climate justice involves the assertion that the global impacts of climate change will fall disproportionately on poor, vulnerable and minority communities.[37] However Indigenous Peoples again assert that:

> they have unique interests and ought to be represented as rights holders in national and international decision-making that impacts their communities. These claims for 'environmental self-determination' rest upon the unique cultural and political status of Indigenous Peoples throughout the world and evoke a human rights based set of norms, rather than a domestic sovereignty model.[38]

---

32 Abate and Kronk (2013) 14. See also, Krakoff (2008).
33 Tsosie (2007) 1629.
34 Ibid.
35 Ibid.
36 Ibid.
37 Ibid, 1633.
38 Ibid, 1628.

International law is evolving, particularly in the human rights and indigenous rights sphere,[39] and this needs to be fully reflected in climate change responses.

INTERNATIONAL DEVELOPMENT OF INDIGENOUS RIGHTS

James Anaya (UN Special Rapporteur on the Rights of Indigenous Peoples)[40] and Robert Coulter (Director of the Indian Law Resource Centre in the United States)[41] argue that international law can be effective in facilitating improved recognition of indigenous rights at all levels (local, regional, national and international). The United Nations Declaration on the Rights of Indigenous Peoples (UNDRIP)[42] highlights many human rights standards that are legally binding. It is important to recognise that international norms and their application change over time – as does indigenous customary law.[43] Anaya[44] advocates a realist approach to indigenous rights and rejects formalist and positivist jurisprudential positions. Many inappropriate laws, institutions and jurisprudence continue in post-colonial societies and sovereignty and self-determination have evolving meanings.[45]

The modern human rights system is based upon the Universal Declaration of Human Rights (UDHR), further articulated in the International Covenant on Civil and Political Rights (ICCPR)[46] and the International Covenant on Economic, Social and Cultural Rights (ICESCR).[47] The major human rights treaties were developed before climate change was understood as a threat.[48]

Even without a specific right to environmental qualities, there are broad rights recognised in the UDHR, ICCPR, ICESCR and the Convention Concerning Indigenous and Tribal Peoples in Independent

---

39 Anaya (2004).

40 Ibid; see also Anaya and Williams (2001).

41 Coulter (2006–2007); Coulter (2008–2009).

42 UN Declaration on the Rights of Indigenous Peoples, Adopted by GA Res. 61/295 (13 September 2007).

43 Craig and Jeffery (2011b); Young (2008).

44 Anaya (2005). See also, Griffiths (2002); Benda-Beckmann (2002); Nettheim, Meyers, and Craig (2006); Richardson and Craig (2006).

45 Richardson, Mgbeoji, and Botchway (2007); Barsch (1994); Allott (2002).

46 6 ILM 386 (1967).

47 Ibid.

48 Brundtland (1987).

Countries (known as ILO 169)[49] relevant to people whose way of life comes under threat from climate change. How these instruments should be implemented has been well argued by the Australian Human Rights and Equal Opportunity Commission (HREOC), United Nations Office of the High Commissioner for Human Rights and by Grieber *et al.*[50]

The basis for Indigenous Peoples' claims of right are still evolving. Falk[51] notes that five conceptual structures have been used in indigenous claims:

(1) Human rights and non-discrimination claims;
(2) Minority claims;
(3) Self-determination claims;
(4) Historic sovereignty claims;
(5) Claims as Indigenous Peoples, including claims based on treaties or other agreements between indigenous peoples and states.

He argues that the first four categories are well established in law (largely unrelated to Indigenous Peoples) and questions how well they can be integrated with the specific indigenous features in the fifth category.[52] Falk shows how the first four categories may assist indigenous claims to a limited extent, but concludes that:

> The construction and affirmation of a distinct programme of 'rights of Indigenous Peoples', going beyond universal human rights and existing regimes of minority rights, has been one of the objectives of the international indigenous movement. It has received support from some states prepared to recognise the validity of many claims by Indigenous Peoples but anxious not simply to endorse the extension of existing self-determination and historic sovereignty programmes to Indigenous Peoples without modification.[53]

The task of formulating relevant legal rules has largely fallen to the International Labour Organisation (ILO). Explicit references to the environment and natural resources can be found in Articles 2, 4, 7 and 15 of

---

49 June 27, 1989, 28 ILM 1382 (hereinafter ILO 169).

50 HREOC (2008); Grieber *et al.* (2009), 37–61; United Nations Office of the High Commissioner for Human Rights, *Report on the Relationship Between Climate Change and Human Rights*, UN Doc A/HRC/10/61D (Jan. 15, 2009). See also, Kravchenko (2008).

51 Falk, R (cited in Anton and Shelton (2011)) 546.

52 Ibid.

53 Ibid, See also, Grieber *et al.* (2009), 37–61.

ILO 169.[54] ILO 169 provides for a range of rights relevant to a comprehensive approach to climate adaptation. However, even ILO 169 falls short of the formulation of self-determination in UNDRIP Article 3.[55] Most ratifications have been by developing nations.

Indigenous Peoples should have universally applicable civil, political, social, cultural and economic rights as well as national constitutional and domestic legal rights. Indigenous Peoples have demonstrated leadership in international law, particularly in human rights.[56]

The critical reference point for Indigenous People's rights has become the UNDRIP. This re-statement significantly expands the rights to self-determination, intellectual and cultural property and free prior-informed consent. The UNDRIP formulation is critical to the approach taken by Anaya,[57] although he recognises that ILO 169 contains crucial normative standards. UNDRIP does not define Indigenous Peoples (this would be inconsistent with many of the Articles) but the Working Group on Indigenous Peoples considers indigenous peoples as culturally distinct groups, traditionally regarded, and self-defined, as descendants of the original inhabitants of areas to which they share a strong, often spiritual, attachment.[58] The cultural distinctiveness of Indigenous Peoples includes language, social organisation, religion and spiritual values, modes of

---

[54] ILO 169: art 4(1): 'Special measures shall be adopted as appropriate for safeguarding the persons, institutions, property, labour, cultures and environment of the peoples concerned'; art 7(3): 'Governments shall ensure that, whenever appropriate, studies are carried out, in co-operation with the peoples concerned, to assess the social, spiritual, cultural and environmental impact on them of planned development activities. The results of these studies shall be considered as fundamental criteria for the implementation of these activities'; art 15(1): 'The rights of the peoples concerned to the natural resources pertaining to their lands shall be specially safeguarded. These rights include the right of these peoples to participate in the use, management and conservation of these resources.'

[55] United Nations Declaration on the Rights of Indigenous Peoples (UNDRIP) adopted by General Assembly Resolution 61/295 on 13 September 2007. See also art 33: '1. Indigenous Peoples have the right to determine their own identity or membership in accordance with their customs and traditions. This does not impair the right of Indigenous individuals to obtain citizenship in the states in which they live. 2. Indigenous Peoples have the right to determine the structure and to select the membership of their institutions in accordance with their own procedures.'

[56] Anaya (2006).

[57] Anaya (2009a) 133.

[58] See further, United Nation's Working Group on Indigenous Peoples, *Preliminary Report on the Study of the Problem of Discrimination Against Indigenous Populations*, UN Doc E/CN.4/Sub.2/L.566 (1982).

production, laws and institutions.[59] They generally share an experience of subjugation, dispossession, exclusion or discrimination.[60]

The negotiation of self-determination in the UNDRIP was bitterly contested by some states. Kronk and Charles-Newton[61] make the point that:

> In the era of climate change, it is necessary to evaluate Indigenous claims to 'sovereignty' in relation to self-determination that belongs to all Peoples. The two concepts are not co-extensive . . . Despite their political differences, the right to self-determination for the Pacific Island Nations, as well as the Indigenous People in the US and elsewhere, is closely tied to their ancestral land base. This suggests that there is at least a moral right to 'environmental self-determination' that should entail the right to survive as a distinctive land-based People.

Anaya sees two major limits of sovereignty (for Indigenous Peoples).[62] Sovereignty upholds the status quo protective of state territorial integrity and political unity and it limits the capacity of the international system to regulate the matters within the sphere of authority claimed by states (recognised by the international system).[63] There can be overlapping claims for sovereignty and self-determination, but most contemporary indigenous claims use the language and norms of self-determination.[64] Daes[65] considers this to involve 'belated state building' through negotiation and other peaceful procedures involving meaningful participation by Indigenous Peoples:

> Through which Indigenous Peoples are able to join with all the other peoples that make up the state on mutually agreed terms, after many years of isolation and exclusion. This process does not require the assimilation of individuals, as citizens like all others, but the recognition and incorporation of distinct peoples in the fabric of the state, on agreed terms.

Anaya maintains that internationally recognised human rights advance a multicultural model of political ordering and incorporation of Indigenous Peoples into the fabric of the state on the basis of equality in cultural identity and not just individual citizenship.[66] Anaya specifically advocates

---

59 Daes (1996) 69.
60 Ibid.
61 Charles-Newton and Kronk (2013).
62 Anaya (2004), 109.
63 Ibid, 109.
64 Ibid, 110.
65 Daes (1993)
66 Anaya (2009b) 15.

a human rights-based approach to indigenous self-determination rather than a states rights-based framework.[67] He considers that the international human rights norms, particularly relating to non-discrimination and cultural integrity,[68] support this model and that cultural integrity is at the core of UNDRIP and ILO 169.[69] It is also expressed in the UNESCO Universal Declaration on Cultural Diversity:

> The defence of cultural diversity is an ethical imperative, inseparable from respect for human dignity. It implies a commitment to human rights and fundamental freedoms, in particular the rights of persons belonging to minorities and those of indigenous peoples.[70]

Indigenous peoples are increasingly adopting a role that goes beyond that of 'stakeholders' or 'participants'. The role of indigenous participants in negotiating UNDRIP, over 31 years, the UN Permanent Forum on Indigenous Issues (UNFIP)[71] and their role in the Arctic Council and under the Arctic Environmental Protection Strategy (AEPS)[72] demonstrate their distinct status.

---

67 Anaya (2006).

68 For example, *Apirana Mahuika v New Zealand* was a complaint to the UN Human Rights Committee (art 5, para 4), brought under the Optional Protocol to the ICCPR (San Salvador Protocol). Although the outcome was not favourable to the complainants, the Committee observed that, under art 27 of the ICCPR, according to which (especially Indigenous Peoples) the enjoyment of the right to one's own culture may require positive legal measures of protection by the state party and measures to ensure the effective participation by members of the communities in decisions that affect them (at para 9.4).

69 Anaya (2009b) 9. See also Tsosie (2013); Krakoff (2008).

70 Universal Declaration on Cultural Diversity, Gen. Conf. of UNESCO, 31st Sess., art 4, 2 November 2000.

71 The Permanent Forum on Indigenous Issues is the only body in the UN having indigenous persons as members. It is made up of eight indigenous individuals appointed by the President of the Economic and Social Council and eight members nominated by governments and elected by the Economic and Social Council. The Permanent Forum has a mandate to discuss indigenous issues relating to economic and social development, culture, the environment, education, health, and human rights. The Permanent Forum provides expert advice and recommendations on indigenous issues to the Economic and Social Council and to the various programs, funds, and agencies of the United Nations.

72 The Council is composed of Members (Canada, Denmark, Finland, Iceland, Norway, The Russian Federation, Sweden and the US), Permanent Participants (Inuit Circumpolar Conference and the Association of Indigenous Members of the North, Saami Council, Siberia and the Far East of the Russian Federation) and Observers (e.g. non-Arctic governments, NGOs). See also: Union of Concerned Scientists (2004).

> Indigenous peoples appear to be gaining recognition as having a unique or sui generis status among non-state actors within the international arena. Associated with this unique status is an enhanced level of participation . . . Indigenous Peoples are by definition longstanding communities with historically rooted cultures and distinct political and social institutions.[73]

Anaya[74] identifies four key changes in international human rights law promoted by indigenous peoples:

- The move towards collective rights;
- The softening of state sovereignty;
- Evolution of the norm of self-determination;
- The role of non-state actors.

The application of a rights-based approach in indigenous governance to climate adaptation is complex. Some impetus may come from international regimes, but most legal responses, necessarily, will be domestic.[75] The changing nature of domestic law is evidenced by the increasing recognition of constitutional indigenous rights and rights to environmental quality, common law rights (such as native title), treaty and statutory rights as well as gradual recognition of self-determination (often through negotiated self-governance and Comprehensive Land Claims Agreements as illustrated by Canadian experience).[76] Given the fluidity of international, regional[77] and national legal systems, it is important to develop normative standards that are not subject to erosion through litigation and negotiation with states and the private sector.

INTER-AMERICAN COURT OF HUMAN RIGHTS

Some key legal principles in UNDRIP have been developed by the Inter-American Court of Human Rights, established under the Organization

---

73 Anaya (2006), 119.

74 Ibid, 111–19.

75 Charles-Newton and Kronk (2013).

76 Firestone, Lily and Torres de Noronha (2005). See also, Nettheim, Meyers, and Craig, (2002).

77 African Charter on Human and People's Rights, 27 June 1981, 21 I.L.M. 58 (African Charter) includes provisions relating to environmental and Indigenous rights. See also Organization of American States, *Human Rights and Climate Change in the Americas*, Resolution 2429, AG/RES. 2429 (XXXVIII-O/08) (3 June 2008).

of American States (OAS).[78] Key cases include *Saramaka People v Suriname*,[79] *Indigenous Cmty. Yakye Axa v Para.*,[80] and *Maya Indigenous Cmty. of the Toledo Dist. v Belize*,[81] and *Indigenous Community of Awas Tingni v Nicaragua*.[82] Recent case law illustrates the judicial notice taken of UNDRIP in resolving conflicts.[83]

Awas Tingni Mayagna (Sumo) Indigenous Community v Nicaragua[84] was a decision by the Inter-American Court of Human Rights. It involved the protection of Nicaraguan forests in lands traditionally owned by the Awas Tingni. In 2001, the Court decided that the state violated the right to judicial protection and the right to property[85] (Articles 21 and 25 of the American Convention on Human Rights (American Convention)).[86] The Court unanimously declared that the state must adopt domestic laws, administrative regulations, and other necessary means to create effective title mechanisms for the properties of the indigenous communities, reflecting customary law and indigenous values, uses and customs. Pending demarcation the state must abstain

---

78 All American states that have ratified the Charter of the OAS accept the competence of the Inter-American Commission on Human Rights to consider individual human rights violations (includes the US). Those American states that have also ratified or acceded to the American Convention on Human Rights (American Convention on Human Rights, 22 November 1969, 9 ILM 673 (American Convention) are subject to the jurisdiction of the Inter-American Court (does not include the US).

79 Inter-Am. Ct. H.R. (ser. C) No. 172, para. 95 (28 November 2007).

80 Inter-Am. Ct. H.R. (ser. C) No. 146, para. 143 (17 June 2005).

81 Case 12.053, Inter-Am.C.H.R., Report No.40/04, OEA/Ser.L/V/II.122 doc. 5 rev., para 113 (2004).

82 Inter-Am. Ct. H.R. (Ser. C) No. 79, para. 148 (31 August 2001).

83 Pascqualucchi (2009–2010) 51. See also *Report on the situation of Human Rights in Equador* OEA/Ser.L/V/11.96,Doc.10 rev.1, 24 April 1997.

84 The Awas Tingi filed a case at the Inter-American Commission, alleging that the government of Nicaragua violated their rights to cultural integrity, religion, equal protection and participation in government. The Commission found in 1998 that the government had violated the human rights of the Awas Tingni and brought the case before the Court alleging violation by the state of Nicaragua of Articles 1, 2, 21 and 15 of the American Convention, through the state's failure to demarcate and to grant official recognition to the territory of that community. The Commission requested that the Court determine compensation for the consequences of the violation of rights. *The Mayagna (Sumo) Awas Tingni Community v Nicaragua*, Judgment of 31 August 2001, Inter-Am. Ct. H.R., (Ser. C) No. 79 (2001), para 167.

85 Ibid.

86 American Convention on Human Rights, 22 November 1969, 9 I.L.M. 673.

from acts by itself or third parties that could affect indigenous interests in those properties.[87]

In the case of *Maya Indigenous Communities*,[88] Belize violated Article 23 of the American Declaration on the Rights and Duties of Man (American Declaration)[89] by failing to effectively recognise the communal property rights of the lands traditionally occupied by the Maya, by granting concessions to third parties without effective consultation. The Commission recognised Maya property rights:

> Accordingly, the organs of the Inter-American human rights system have recognized that the property rights protected by the system are not limited to those property interests that are already recognized by states or that are defined by domestic law, but rather that the right to property has an autonomous meaning in international human rights law. In this sense, the jurisprudence of the system has acknowledged that the property rights of Indigenous peoples are not defined exclusively by entitlements within a state's formal legal regime, but also include that indigenous communal property that arises from and is grounded in indigenous custom and tradition.[90]

In the *Mary and Carrie Dann v United States*[91] case, the Commission extended the right to property under the American Convention to the property rights provision of the American Declaration.[92] They recognised due process and equal protections attaching to indigenous property interests. They determined that the proceedings under which the Western Shoshone lost their land interests did not afford them adequate opportunity to be heard and that the proceedings denied these groups the

---

[87] The Court also declared that the state must invest US$50,000 in public works and services of collective benefit to the Awas Tingni as a form of reparations for non-material injury and US$30,000 for legal fees and expenses.

[88] *Maya Indigenous Cmty. of the Toledo Dist. v Belize*, Case 12.053, Inter-Am.C.H.R., Report No.40/04, OEA/Ser.L/V/II.122 doc. 5 rev., para 113 (2004).

[89] American Declaration on the Rights and Duties of Man (American Declaration), April 1948, OAS Resolution XXX, OEA/Ser.L.V/II.82 doc.6 rev.1.

[90] *Maya Indigenous Cmty. of the Toledo Dist. v Belize*, Case 12.053, Inter-Am.C.H.R., Report No.40/04, OEA/Ser.L/V/II.122 doc. 5 rev., para 113 (2004) at paras 167–69.

[91] The Western Shoshone sisters, Mary and Carrie Dann, refused to submit to the permit system imposed by the US for grazing on large parts of Western Shoshone traditional lands. The US government tried to stop them from grazing cattle without a permit. The Danns argued that the permit system contravened Western Shoshone land rights. The US argued that Western Shoshone rights in the land had been 'extinguished' (*Mary and Carrie Dann v United States*, Inter-Am.C.H.R. Report NO.75/02, Dec.27,2002, OEA/Ser.L/V/11.117 Doc.5 rev., at 960 (2003)).

[92] Ibid.

protections generally available to property holders under U.S. law.[93] The Commission found that the U.S. had 'failed to ensure the Danns' right to property under conditions of equality contrary to Articles II (right to equal protection), XVIII (right to fair trial) and XXIII (right to property) of the American Declaration in connection with their claims to property rights in the Western Shoshone ancestral lands'.[94]

The Commission relied on developments that are applicable inside and outside the inter-American system, particularly focusing on ILO 169. They considered that the 'basic principles' in the Proposed American Declaration on the Rights of Indigenous Peoples reflect general international principles applicable to the U.S. (even without their ratification of ILO 169).[95]

The Inter-American Court of Human Rights has concluded that the inextricable connection that indigenous and tribal peoples have with territory (a property right) is necessary to guarantee their survival:

> Accordingly, the right to use and enjoy their territory would be meaningless in the context of indigenous and tribal communities if said right were not connected to the natural resources that lie on and within the land. (Saramaka People v Suriname).[96]

Thus special measures are required for the protection of their property and in relation to development that impacts on their resources. The requirements of free, prior and informed consent and benefit-sharing were also highlighted in *Saramaka*.[97]

INDIGENOUS PARTICIPATION IN REDD+

Unlike the UN Convention on Biological Diversity (CBD), the United Nations Framework Convention on Climate Change (UNFCCC) includes no formal recognition of Indigenous Peoples or their interests. Nor does

---

93 Ibid. The Commission noted the inadequacy of the historical rationale for the presumed taking of Western Shoshone group's adequate opportunity to be heard and that the proceedings otherwise denied these groups the same procedural and substantive protections generally available to property holders under US law.

94 *Mary and Carrie Dann v United States*, Inter-Am.C.H.R. Report NO.75/02, Dec.27,2002, OEA/Ser.L/V/11.117 Doc.5 rev., at 960 (2003).

95 Ibid.

96 Inter-Am. Ct. H.R. (ser. C) No. 172, para. 95 (Nov. 28, 2007) at para 121. The Court also quoted UNDRIP, art 32, with approval (para 131).

97 Ibid, paras 134, 147 and 153.

the Kyoto Protocol. They do prescribe remedies for individuals or communities for harm. There is some consideration of indigenous peoples by UNFCCC work on the impacts of climate change and the adaptation of communities. Local indigenous interests may also be considered when examining the 'sustainable development' component of CDM projects. Growing concern by indigenous peoples about the direction of UNFCC regime negotiations[98] has led to a series of Indigenous Declarations (such as the 'Anchorage Declaration', 'Cancun Declaration' and the 'Oaxaca Action Plan of Indigenous Peoples: From Cancun to Durban and Beyond'). A particular concern is the failure of the UNFCC to give true recognition to UNDRIP.

In December 2007, Parties to the UNFCCC and to the Kyoto Protocol adopted a process for agreeing future revisions to the UNFCCC and the Kyoto Protocol known as the 'Bali Roadmap' and the 'Bali Action Plan'.[99] This established an Ad Hoc Working Group on Long-term Cooperative Action (AWGLCA) with a view to reaching agreement by the 2009 Copenhagen COP meeting.[100] At COP17, in Durban, it was decided to terminate the AWGLCA at the end of 2012. A new body was formed, the Ad Hoc Working Group on the 'Durban Platform for Enhanced Action'.[101]

International discussions about REDD+ (reducing emissions from deforestation, degradation and enhanced conservation of forests in developing countries) have had a greater focus on Indigenous Peoples than other mitigation policy tools considered under the UNFCCC. In 2008[102] the Parties recognised that 'the needs of local and indigenous communities should be addressed when action is taken to address REDD+'.[103] An Annex provides guidance on conducting REDD+ demonstration activities consistent with sustainable forest management with the approval of the host country. UNFCCC also requested SBSTA to work on methodological issues concerning policies and incentives for REDD+ and invited parties to the UNFCCC to submit views on a range of outstanding methodological issues. The guidance makes no mention of Indigenous Peoples. The subsequent considerations of SBSTA 28 (June 2008) only identified one cross-cutting issue specifically mentioning indigenous peoples.

---

[98] IWGIA (2010).

[99] Para 1(b)(iii), UN Doc FCCC/CP/2007/L.7/Rev.1.

[100] UN Doc FCCC/CP/2007/L.7/Rev.1.

[101] See *Establishment of an Ad Hoc Working Group on the Durban Platform for Enhanced Action*, accessed 22 March 2015 at http://unfccc.int/files/meetings/durban_nov_2011/decisions/application/pdf/cop17_durbanplatform.pdf.

[102] UNFCCC, 2008a, Decision 2/CP.13.

[103] Ibid.

Indigenous Peoples' rights have gradually been given attention at Copenhagen (COP 15, 2009), Cancun (COP 16, 2010) and in Durban (COP 17, 2011). Lyster[104] notes that:

> Crucially, with regard to the legitimacy of REDD+ programmes, the safeguards emanating from COP16 include that: actions must complement or be consistent with the objectives of national forest programmes and relevant international conventions and agreements; transparent and effective national forest governance structures must be promoted and supported in accordance with national legislation and sovereignty, while respecting the knowledge and rights of Indigenous Peoples and members of local communities. The Appendix I notes that the United Nations General Assembly has adopted the United Nations Declaration on the Rights of Indigenous Peoples and that the full and effective participation of relevant stakeholders, in particular Indigenous Peoples and local communities, must be promoted and supported.

The current focus is on national strategies for REDD+, but the issues at the local scale are still under discussion.[105] The purely state-centred style of the negotiations is a matter of serious concern in terms of indigenous rights.

Other multilateral institutions have REDD+ proposals, activities or programmes. At the CBD COP 9 (2008), parties invited the UNFCCC to consider opportunities for its REDD+ work to benefit biodiversity. They also established an Ad Hoc Technical Expert Group on biodiversity and climate change. This included representatives from indigenous and local communities and small island developing states.[106]

Various funding initiatives have been launched to pilot REDD+ activities. The Strategic Climate Fund (2008) created a forest investment programme to mobilise funds for reducing deforestation and forest degradation and to promote sustainable forest management. The Forest Carbon Partnership Facility (FCPC) was launched in 2007 to assist developing countries with building capacity to undertake REDD+ activities

---

104 Lyster (2013), 7 referring to Decision 1/CP.16. See The Cancun Agreements: 2010 Outcome of the work of the Ad Hoc Working Group on Long-term Cooperative Action under the Convention, Decision 1/CP.16t, accessed 22 March 2015 at http://unfccc.int/resource/docs/2010/cop16/eng/07a01.pdf#page=2; The Cancun Agreements: Outcome of the work of the Ad Hoc Working Group on Further Commitments for Annex I Parties under the Kyoto Protocol at its fifteenth session, Decision 1/CMP.6 accessed 22 March 2015 at http://unfccc.int/resource/docs/2010/cmp6/eng/12a01.pdf#page=3; The Cancun Agreements: Land use, land-use change and forestry, Decision 2/CMP.6, accessed 22 March 2015 at <http://unfccc.int/resource/docs/2010/cmp6/eng/12a01.pdf#page=5.

105 Daviet (2010).

106 UNEP/CBD/COP/9/L.36.

and to test 'performance based incentive projects'. The FCPF and the UN-REDD Programme assist developing countries by building national capacity for REDD+ activities, and testing performance-based incentive payments. The two programs are contributing to the REDD+ readiness mechanisms for measurement, reporting and verification system; reference scenarios; REDD+ strategy and national management arrangements for REDD+.

It is anticipated that, if successful, a larger system of incentive-based activities will be developed in the future. While these World Bank initiatives could provide much-needed funds to developing countries, Indigenous Peoples have voiced grave concerns about adequacy of the consultation on these programmes.

DOES REDD+ RESPECT INDIGENOUS RIGHTS?

Aspects of REDD+ could be positive or destructive for Indigenous Peoples. The Indian law Resource Centre (ILRC) powerfully articulates International Law Principles which should be observed by the key actors in the design and implementation of REDD+:

> The REDD+ Principles are intended to govern the actions of both States and international implementing agencies. This includes States hosting REDD+ initiatives, as well as States funding them, either bilaterally or through multilateral institutions. The REDD+ Principles also govern the actions of international agencies implementing REDD+, including the UN-REDD Programme (UN-REDD), the World Bank's Forest Carbon Partnership Facility (FCPF), the Carbon Fund, and Forest Investment Program (FIP), the Global Environment Facility (GEF), regional development banks such as the Inter-American Development Bank (IDB), as well as activities of the UNFCCC Green Climate Fund.[107]

The *Principles* are presented as a Working Paper, to be refined following comments. Each principle is followed by a discussion and proposed implementation measures.[108] The Principles to which they refer are the legal obligations for states and international agencies engaged in REDD+ to: respect human rights; adopt domestic measures; prevent human rights violations and to redress human rights violations. This should

---

[107] Cripps, L. and G. Gordon (2013), *International Law Principles for REDD: The Rights of Indigenous Peoples and the Obligations of REDD Actors* (Montana: Indian Law Resource Centre).

[108] Ibid.

also include recognition of the rights of Indigenous Peoples in relation to self-determination and self-government; land, territories and natural resources; participation in decision-making, free, prior and informed consent; benefit sharing and to effective remedy for harms.[109]

CONCLUSIONS

Many Indigenous Peoples are (and will be) harmed disproportionately by climate change. In part this is because of continuing historical disadvantage, vulnerability and discrimination under national legal systems. Many have insufficient resources to deal with these risks to their survival as custodians of their own lands. These factors suggest the need for a coherent strategy for responding to inequities in terms of climate impact and the economic and political power to respond.

Overlaid on this, it is essential to incorporate into climate change management respect for the legal rights and social justice norms that relate particularly to Indigenous Peoples. Existing approaches through initiatives such as UNFCCC and Kyoto reflect state-based governance models and so fail to respect indigenous rights, which are frequently not reliant upon state sovereignty. Indigenous peoples' rights have advanced under international environmental regimes such as the CBD and the Desertification Convention. This has made the tension between state-based and human rights-based approaches acute. The discourse on governance for sustainable development has not fully comprehended the extent of the conflict in these approaches, and the divergence in contemporary environmental law between sovereignty and self-determination.

Indigenous Peoples' *sui generis* status and right to self-determination is expressed through UNDRIP and through other forums and applies to domestic law and policy. Effective implementation of UNDRIP in relation to climate change initiatives (such as REDD+) is in its early stages. It requires much more understanding of indigenous law, practices and knowledge. State-based national initiatives that do not purposefully address these international developments threaten indigenous rights.

Initiatives such as REDD+ are exceptionally complex and difficult. Effective sustainable forest management, like CDM and biodiversity projects, will need strategies and implementation at the local level that respect indigenous rights. Ideally these ought actively to strengthen social justice. Umbrella funding (such as GEF), micro-finance and payment for

---

[109] Ibid.

ecosystem services should strengthen prospects for indigenous livelihoods and poverty alleviation but this requires active prioritisation of this goal.

Adaptive management approaches should support flexible locally adapted strategies. However, in the absence of institutionalised indigenous rights there is a risk that privileged experts will exercise disproportionate power. Sustainability governance is difficult in any context but it can no longer be assumed that Indigenous Peoples are mere 'stakeholders' or 'participants'. They have rights that must be respected in law and in policy.

Indigenous Peoples have courageously contributed to the evolution of international norms that support their self-determination. They possess crucial knowledge acquired through past experience with climate variability and climate change. The urgent challenge for environmental lawyers is to engage with indigenous jurisprudence and indigenous peoples to give meaning to rights-based approaches to governance. The IUCN Academy of Environmental Law is in a unique position to lead this scholarship, teaching and advocacy as leaders who have pioneered environmental law and related human rights-based approaches.

REFERENCES

Abate, R. and E. Kronk (2013), 'Commonality among Unique Indigenous Communities: An Introduction to Climate Change and its impacts on Indigenous Peoples' in R. Abate and E. Kronk (eds), *Climate Change and Indigenous Peoples: The Search for Legal Remedies* (Cheltenham, UK and Northampton, MA, USA: Edward Elgar).

Adger, N., K. Brown, D. Nelson, F. Berkes, H. Eakin, C. Folke, K. Galvin, L. Gunderson, M. Goulden, K. O'Brien, J. Ruitenbeek and E. Tompkins (2011), 'Resilience Implications of Policy Responses to Climate Change' 2 *WIREs Climate Change* 757.

Allott, P. (2002), *The Health of Nations: Society and Law Beyond the State* (Cambridge: Cambridge University Press).

Anaya, J. (2004), *Indigenous Peoples in International Law* (2nd edn, Oxford: Oxford University Press)

Anaya, J. (2005), 'Divergent Discourse about International Law, Indigenous Peoples and Rights Over Lands and Natural Resources: Towards a realist Trend' 16(2) [Spring] *Colorado Journal of International Environmental Law* 237–58.

Anaya, J. (2006), 'Indian Givers: What Indigenous Peoples Have Contributed to International Human Rights Law' 22 *Washington University Journal of Law & Policy* 107.

Anaya, J. (2009a), *International Human Rights and Indigenous Peoples* (New York: Aspen Publishers).

Anaya, J. (2009b), 'International Human Rights and Indigenous Peoples; The

Move Toward the Multicultural State' 09–34 *Arizona Legal Studies Discussion Paper*.

Anaya, J. and R. Williams (2001), 'The Protection of Indigenous Peoples Rights Over Land and Resources Under the Inter-American Human Rights System' 14 *Harvard Human Rights Journal* 33.

Anton, D. and D. Shelton (2011), *Environmental Protection and Human Rights* (Cambridge: Cambridge University Press).

Arctic Climate Impact Assessment (ACIA 2004), *Impacts of a Warming Climate: Arctic Climate Impact Assessment* (Cambridge: Cambridge University Press).

Barsch, R. (1994), 'Indigenous Peoples in the 1990s: From Object to Subject of International Law' 7 *Harvard Human Rights Journal* 33.

Benda-Beckmann, F. (2002), 'Who's Afraid of Legal Pluralism?' 47 *Journal of Legal Pluralism and Unofficial Law* 3.

Borrini-Feyerabend, G., M. Pimbert, M. Farvar, A. Kothari and Y. Renard (2004), *Sharing Power: Learning by Doing in Co-management of Natural Resources throughout the World* (IIED and IUCN/CEESP/CMWG).

Bosselman, K., R. Engel and P. Taylor (2008), *Governance for Sustainability – Issues, Challenges and Successes* (IUCN).

Brown, K. (2009), 'Human Development and Environmental Governance' in W.N. Adger and A. Jordan, *Governing Sustainability* (Cambridge: Cambridge University Press).

Brundtland, G. (1987), *Our Common Future* (World Commission on Environment and Development).

Charles-Newton, E. and E. Kronk (2013), 'Introduction to Indigenous Sovereignty under International and Domestic Law' in R. Abate and E. Kronk (eds), *Climate Change and Indigenous Peoples: The Search for Legal Remedies* (Cheltenham, UK and Northampton, MA, USA: Edward Elgar).

Convention on Access to Information, Public Participation in Decision-making and Access to Justice in Environmental Matters (Aarhus Convention), 25 June 1998, 38 ILM 517.

Cooke, B. and U. Kothari (2001), *Participation: the New Tyranny* (London: Zed Books).

Coulter, R. (2006–2007), 'Using International Human Rights Mechanisms to Promote and Protect Rights of Indian Nations and Tribes in the United States' 31(2) *American Indian Review* 573.

Coulter, R. (2008–2009), 'The UN Declaration and the Rights of Indigenous Peoples: An Historic Change in International Law' 45 *Idaho Law Review* 539.

Craig, D. (2002), 'Recognising Indigenous Rights Through Co-Management Regimes: Canadian and Australian Experiences' 6 *New Zealand Journal of Environmental Law* 199.

Craig, D. and E. Gachenga (2010), 'The Recognition of Indigenous Customary Law in Water Resource Management' 20 *Water Law* 1.

Craig, D. and M. Jeffery (2010), 'Non-lawyers and Legal Regimes: Public Participation for Ecologically Sustainable Development' in D. Leary and B. Pisupati (eds), *The Future of International Environmental Law* (New York: United Nations University Press).

Craig, D., and M. Jeffery (2011a), 'Application of Environmental Conflict Resolution to Public Interest Issues in Water Disputes' Special Edition *International Journal of Rural Law and Policy*.

Craig, D. and M. Jeffery (2011b), 'The Recognition and Enforcement of Indigenous Customary Law in Environmental Regimes and Natural Resource Management' in L. Paddock, D. Qun, L. Kotze, D. Markell, K. Markowitz and D. Zaelke (eds), *Compliance and Enforcement in Environmental Law* (Cheltenham, UK and Northampton, MA, USA: Edward Elgar) 535.

Cripps, L. and G. Gordon (2013), *International Law Principles for REDD: The Rights of Indigenous Peoples and the Obligations of REDD Actors* (Montana: Indian Law Resource Centre).

Daes, E. (1993), 'Some Considerations on the Right of Indigenous Peoples to Self-determination' 3 *Transnational Law & Contemporary Problems* 1.

Daes, E. (1996), *Standard-Setting Activities: Evolution of Standards Concerning the Rights of Indigenous People* (UN ESCOR Sub-Comm'n on Prevention of Discrimination and Protection of Minorities, UN Doc E/CN.4/Sub.2/AC.4/1996/2, P 26).

Daviet, F. (2010), *From Copenhagen to Cancun Forests and REDD* (Washington, DC: World Resources Institute).

Dernbach, J. (2011), 'Creating the Law of Environmentally Sustainable Economic Development', 28 *Pace Environmental Law Review* 614, accessed 22 March 2015 at http://digitalcommons.pace.edu/pelr/vol28/iss3/1.

Dow, K., R. Kasperson and M. Bohn (2007), 'Exploring the Social Justice Implications of Adaptation and Vulnerability' in N. Adger, J. Paavola, S. Huq and M. Mace (eds) *Fairness in Adaptation to Climate Change* (Cambridge, MA: MIT Press).

Firestone, J., J. Lily and I.Torres de Noronha (2005), 'Cultural Diversity, Human Rights and the Emergence of Indigenous Peoples in International and Comparative Environmental Law' 20 *American Univesity International Law Review* 219.

Glasbergen, A., F. Bierman and P. Mol (eds) (2007), *Partnerships, Governance and Sustainable Development: Reflections on Theory and Practice* (Cheltenham, UK and Northampton, MA, USA: Edward Elgar).

Grieber, T., M. Janki, M. Orellana, A. Savaresi and D. Shelton (2009), *Conservation with Justice* (IUCN).

Griffiths, A. (2002), 'Legal Pluralism' in R. Banakar and M. Travers (eds), *An Introduction to Law and Social Theory* (Oxford: Hart Publishing).

Human Rights and Equal Opportunity Commission (HREOC 2008), *Human Rights and Climate Change* (HREOC, Background Paper).

Hannum, H., J. Anaya and D. Shelton (2006), *International Human Rights: Problems of Law, Policy and Practice* (New York: Aspen Publishing).

Intergovernmental Panel on Climate Change (IPCC 2007), *Climate Change 2007: Impacts, Adaptation and Vulnerability* (The Working Group II Contribution to the IPCC Fourth Assessment Report, Cambridge: Cambridge University Press).

International Institute for Sustainable Development (IISD 2012), *CRISTAL Users Manual: Community-based Risk Screening Tool – Adaptation and Livelihoods* (IISD), Version 5.

International Work Group for Indigenous Affairs (IWGIA), *Indigenous Affairs*, 08(1–2), accessed 22 March 2015 at http://www.iwgia.org/sw29009.asp.

IWGIA (2010), *REDD+ and Indigenous Peoples. A Briefing Paper for Policy Makers* (IWGIA).

Krakoff, S. (2008), 'American Indians, Climate Change and Ethics for a Warming World' 85(865) *Denver University Law Review*.
Kravchenko, S. (2008), 'Right to Carbon or Right to Life: Human Rights Approaches to Climate Change' 9 *Vermont Journal of Environmental Law* 513.
Limon, M. (2009), 'Human Rights and Climate Change: Constructing a Case for Political Action' *Harvard Environment Law Review* 33.
Lynn, K., K. MacKendrick and E. Donoghue (2011), *Social Vulnerabilty and Climate Change: Synthesis of Literature* (USDA).
Lyster, R. (2013), *International Legal programmes for REDD+: Ensuring Legitimacy* (University of Sydney Law School, Legal Studies Research Paper No.13/27).
Macchi, M. *et al.* (2008), *Indigenous and Traditional Peoples and Climate Change* (IUCN Issues Paper).
Nakashima, D., K. Galloway McLean, H. Thulstrup, A. Ramos Castillo, and J. Rubis (2012), *Weathering Uncertainty: Traditional Knowledge for Climate Change Assessment and Adaptation* (Darwin: United Nations University Press).
Nettheim, G., G. Meyers and D. Craig (2002), *Indigenous Peoples and Governance Structures: A Comparative Analysis of Land and Resource Management Rights* (Canberra: Aboriginal Studies Press).
Organization of American States, Inter-American Commission on Human Rights (2005), *Petition Seeking Relief from Violations Resulting from Global Warming Caused by Acts and Omissions of the United States* (*Inuit Petition*) accessed 30 March 2015 at http://www.inuitcircumpolar.com/uploads/3/0/5/4/30542564/finalpetitionicc.pdf.
Pascqualucchi, J. (2009–2010), 'International Indigenous Land Rights: A Critique of the Jurisprudence of the Inter-American Court of Human Rights in light of the United nations Declaration on the Rights of Indigenous Peoples' 27 *Wisconsin International Law Journal* 51.
Ribot, J., A. Agrawal and A. Larson (2006), 'Recentralising While Decentralising: How National Governments Re-appropriate Forest Resources' 34 *World Development* 1864.
Richardson, B. and D. Craig (2006), 'Indigenous Peoples, Law and the Environment' in B. Richardson and S. Wood (eds), *Environmental Law for Sustainability* (Oxford: Hart Publishing).
Richardson, B., I. Mgbeoji, and F. Botchway (2007), 'Environmental Law in Post-colonial Societies: Aspirations, Achievements and Limitations' in B. Richardson and S. Wood (eds), *Environmental Law for Sustainability* (Oxford: Hart Publishing).
Shelton, D. (2002), *Human Rights and the Environment: Jurisprudence of Human Rights Bodies* (UNEP-OHCHR Expert Seminar on Human Rights and the Environment, Background Paper 2) 230.
Stern, N. (2007), *The Economics of Climate Change; The Stern Review* (Cambridge: Cambridge University Press).
Tsosie, R. (2007), 'Indigenous Peoples and Environmental Justice: The Impacts of Climate Change' 78 *University of Colorado Law Review* 1625.
Tsosie, R. (2013), 'Climate Change and Indigenous Peoples: Comparative Models of Sovereignty' in R. Abate and E. Kronk, *Climate Change and Indigenous Peoples: The Search for Legal Remedies* (Cheltenham, UK and Northampton, MA, USA: Edward Elgar).

Union of Concerned Scientists (2004), *Impacts of a Warming Arctic: Arctic Climate Impact Assessment* (Cambridge: Cambridge University Press).

United Nations Permanent Forum on Indigenous Issues (UNPFIIS 2007), *Climate Change: An Overview*, Paper prepared by the UNPFIIS Secretariat, November 2007), accessed 22 March 2015 at http://www.un.org/esa/socdev/unpfii/documents/Climate_change_overview.doc.

Young, S. (2008), *The Trouble with Tradition: Native Title and Cultural Change* (Annandale: Federation Press).

18. Inclusive practices, innovative collaboration, governance and recognising cultural capital: environmental law through a cultural lens*

> I believe that to meet the challenge of our times, human beings will have to develop a greater sense of universal responsibility. Each of us must learn to work not for his or her self, family or nation, but for the benefit of all mankind. Universal responsibility is the real key to human survival. It is the best foundation for world peace, the equitable use of natural resources and through concern for the future generations, the proper care of the environment.[1]

SHARING EXPERIENCE: AUSTRALIA AND NORTH AMERICA

Australia and North America share highly urbanised characteristics: urban Australia comprises 87 per cent of population, urban USA 84 per cent, only 13 per cent of Australia's population and 16 per cent of US residents

* The authors' circular graphic represents the true nature and intent of this chapter, as well as our attempt for the inclusion of a cultural perspective in current NRM and Environmental Law Discourse. Further, it represents a non-linear application of our collaborative efforts that recognise all of the First Nation's perspectives, knowledge and contributions that made the collaborative efforts possible.

[1] Dalai Lama (1992).

live in the rural areas, which are 97 per cent of the landmass.[2] Rural agrarian communities, and more particularly First Nations, often feel that their natural resource knowledge, interests and their connections to land are depreciated by the politically dominant resource governance paradigm. This chapter will explore the disparity and marginalisation of these communities to conversations about resource management and environmental justice.

First Nations' traditional governance structures generally rest upon cultural relationships with nature. Distinct from First Nations, agrarian rural communities exhibit noticeable relationships with their environments, whereas policies that structure institutional governance arrangements arise from very different constructs. First Nations approaches might be expressed as 'holistic' compared to dominant 'linear' perspectives, with attempts to explore integration advanced as 'innovative' or 'collaborative' governance.[3] However, is such integration really possible? What common cultural ground exists for Indigenous and non-indigenous peoples to collaborate? What role might environmental law play in changing attitudes and methods for more genuine collaboration prospects?

Empirical evidence reveals the constraints of power structures in institutional governance, methodology and practice upon genuine collaborative governance.[4] Indigenous peoples' perspectives of cultural integrity, cultural practice and governance often do not translate nor conform to institutional parameters. New institutional structures (with the best of intentions) often lack a designated and recognisable 'space' for these perspectives to be heard and understood. Actual outcomes are too often the antithesis of expressed policy objectives espousing collaborative frameworks,[5] neglecting the collective knowledge of both groups. Such difficulties leave First Nations and agrarian rural communities without the place where participation in meaningful discussions can enrich concepts such as environmental justice and earth jurisprudence.

---

[2] World Bank 2014 Urban Population (% of total) for further information see ABARES (2010); Australian Bureau of Statistics (2012); *Public Land Statistics Volume 198* (U.S. Department of the Interior, Bureau of Land Management 2013).

[3] United Nations, *The Rio Declaration on Environment and Development* (1992); Davis (2008).

[4] United Nations (2009).

[5] Bohensky and Maru (2011); Das Gupta (2011).

CULTURAL PERSPECTIVES AND THE ANTHROPOCENE

Despite global commitments to ecological sustainable development (ESD),[6] since the 1980s human consumption of natural resources has exponentially outstripped the earth's regenerative capacity.[7] The resultant Anthropocene[8] (a human-dominated epoch) including climate change[9] threatens the earth's ability to sustain future human generations.[10] Natural Resource Management[11] (NRM), intended to manage towards sustainable use of the earth, remains ill-defined and refers to managing the natural resource base alone without sufficient recognition of indigenous peoples' interests, knowledge or potential contributions. Despite the rhetoric, Indigenous people and their cultural knowledge are excluded or segregated within NRM policies and programs.[12] Reflecting a 'way of life' conscious of harmony with nature, their knowledge systems offer resources for building social ecological resilience.[13] Indigenous peoples' environments (natural and cultural resources) have been displaced and manipulated since colonization. Reflecting North American and Australian experiences, Figure 18.1 proposes an interpretive model of the Anthropocene inclusive of First Contact (1492 and 1780 respectively).

Indigenous peoples and their knowledge systems can offer possible solutions to problems of unsustainable use, yet how can Western society use this knowledge in a manner that does not dominate, appropriate, misinterpret or abuse?[14] Agrarian communities, often marginalised in national

---

6 World Commission on Environment and Development, *Our Common Future* (WCED 1997) 1987; United Nations (1992); United Nations, *Report of the World Summit on Sustainable Development* (2002); United Nations (2012).

7 Brown (2003). See also WWF (2010).

8 Jones (2011) and Nature Editorial (2011).

9 Inter-Government Panel on Climate Change (2013); Climate Commission (2013).

10 Millenium Ecosystem Assessment Board (2005).

11 Natural Resource Management defined as 'Sustainable development strategy focusing on the natural resource base and the institutional arrangements required to maintain this base'. Williams *et al.* (2008).

12 For examples see Stoainoff (2012); May (2010); Markwell Consulting (2011); Altman *et al.* (2011); US National Park Service Mount Rushmore National Memorial www.nps.gov/moru/historyculture (accessed 22 March 2015); C White Eyes *et al.* (2012).

13 Indigenous People, when talking about 'looking after country' refers to both natural resources and cultural heritage in a holistic way. Bohensky and Maru (2011); Bavikatte and Robinson (2011).

14 Harry (2011) and Churchill (2011). See Davis (2008).

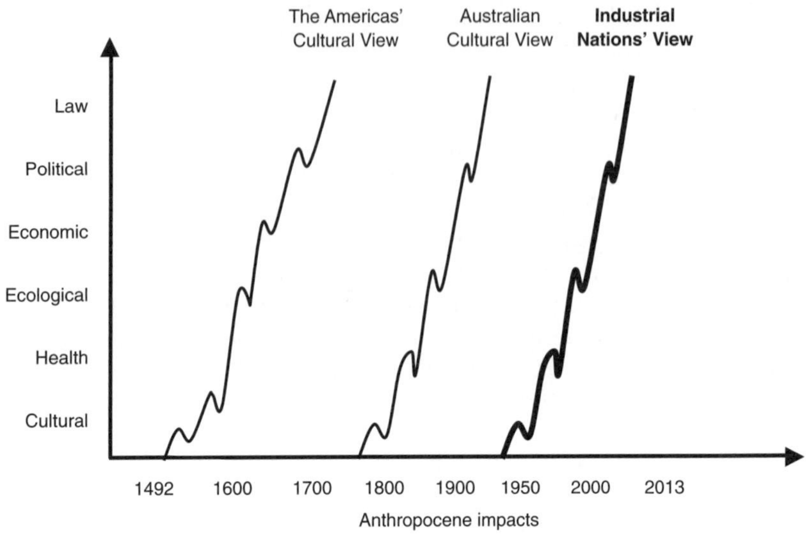

Figure 18.1 Interpretive model of Anthropocene inclusive of first contact

NRM,[15] may also lack a genuine safe place for collaboration and shared learning.

Since British and European settlement of Australia and North America, notions of NRM have evolved through attitudinal changes from pioneering exploitation and stewardship obligation, effectively advancing science and policy development, to the soil erosion crisis of the 1930s, which resulted in a conservation approach that continued until the 1980s. Eurocentric[16] sustainability strategies have used approaches such as decentralised NRM,[17] triple bottom or quadruple bottom line reporting,[18] ecological footprints[19] and other measures to facilitate ESD.[20] Such

---

15 La Via Campesina http://viacampesina.org/en; Land Workers Alliance: http://landworkersalliance.org.uk/ and International Fund for Agricultural Development (2013).

16 Reflecting the Western European philosophies and practices of the colonizing powers.

17 Williams (2007); Williams, Beeton and McDonald (2008).

18 For example the 'Global Reporting Initiative' (2013); Ban Ki-moon (2012); Environment Australia (2003).

19 WWF claims that Earth's people used about 50% more of the natural resources than the planet could regenerate in the year 2007 with Australians having the largest environmental footprint per capita.

20 'Ecologically Sustainable Development'. The first World Summit on Sustainable Development, Rio 1992 underpinned Australia's commitment to

systems can be narrow and reductionist, limiting the role for rural and First Nations Peoples' cultural knowledge. In Australia NRM governance has relied on command and control mechanisms[21] and 'quasi' community NRM approaches which have given rise to issues of social justice, market failure and unresolved science disputes.[22] North America shares similar problems as '. . . more interests than ever before are competing for use of and access to both renewable and nonrenewable resources'.[23]

First Nations and agrarian communities must compete with the concerns of large corporate and political interests,[24] and work across agencies and policies reflecting overlapping governance structures[25] often with conflicting interests. Figure 18.2 illustrates the current Australian NRM Governance structure, demonstrating the top down 'command and control' approach and raising the question, 'where is the space for Indigenous perspectives to help shape resource governance?'

In contrast, Figure 18.3 provides an interpretive First Nations Governance model from North America, illustrating the holistic approach that encompasses natural resources, cultural heritage and practice as indivisible parts of that whole.

Figure 18.4 visually represents the cultural and institutional challenge for inclusive practices, collaboration and the inclusion of First Nations Peoples' cultural perspectives.

Emerging concepts in environmental law, like 'Earth Jurisprudence',[26] and more broadly environmental justice, emphasise the need for governance that prioritises earth and nature, and the needs and interests of people with direct connections to the earth. While within academia there is discourse for indigenous peoples' interests and perspectives, the dialogue takes place and is framed by the colonizing paradigm of European legal research, using language and methods that are intrinsically disrespectful

---

ESD; subsequent UN Summit on Sustainable Development in 2002 and; recent Rio+20 UN Conference on Sustainable Development review.

[21] Robins and Kanowski (2011).

[22] Williams, 'Credit Makers and Credit Takers: Issues of Equity in Australian Government NRM programs'.

[23] Campbell (1996).

[24] Stapp and Burney (2002); Chaloux and Paguin (2013).

[25] For example the agencies responsible for wilderness management in the US consist of: The Bureau of Land Management; The Fish and Wildlife Service, The Forest Service and the National Park Service. Often all of the services intersect near or on Tribal Lands. For more information see www.blm.gov (accessed 22 March 2015).

[26] Earth Jurisprudence refers to earth-centred governance rather than human-centred governance.

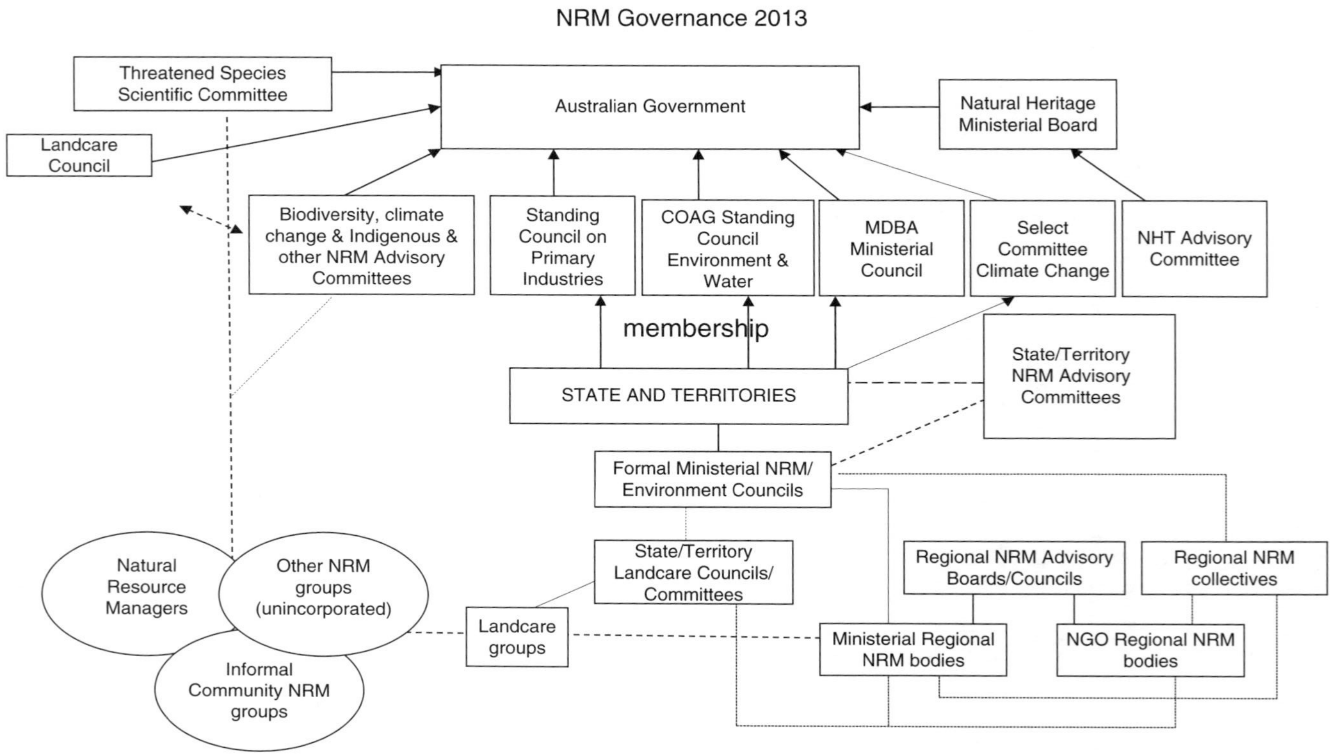

Figure 18.2 Natural resource governance in Australia

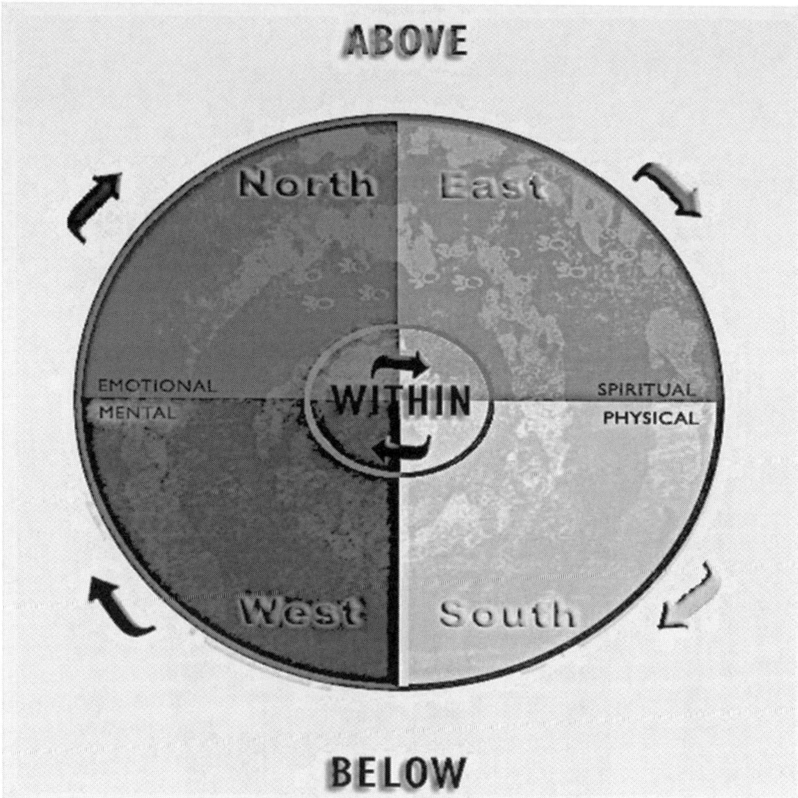

Source: Courtesy of Rediscovering the Seventh Direction © 2000.

Figure 18.3 Interpretive First Nations Governance model from North America

and disempowering of Indigenous peoples' cultural perspectives. If environmental law scholars are genuinely committed to an inclusive and holistic understanding, and in particular value First Nations' perspectives, should not the journey begin with a re-examination of our own understanding, methods and attitudes?

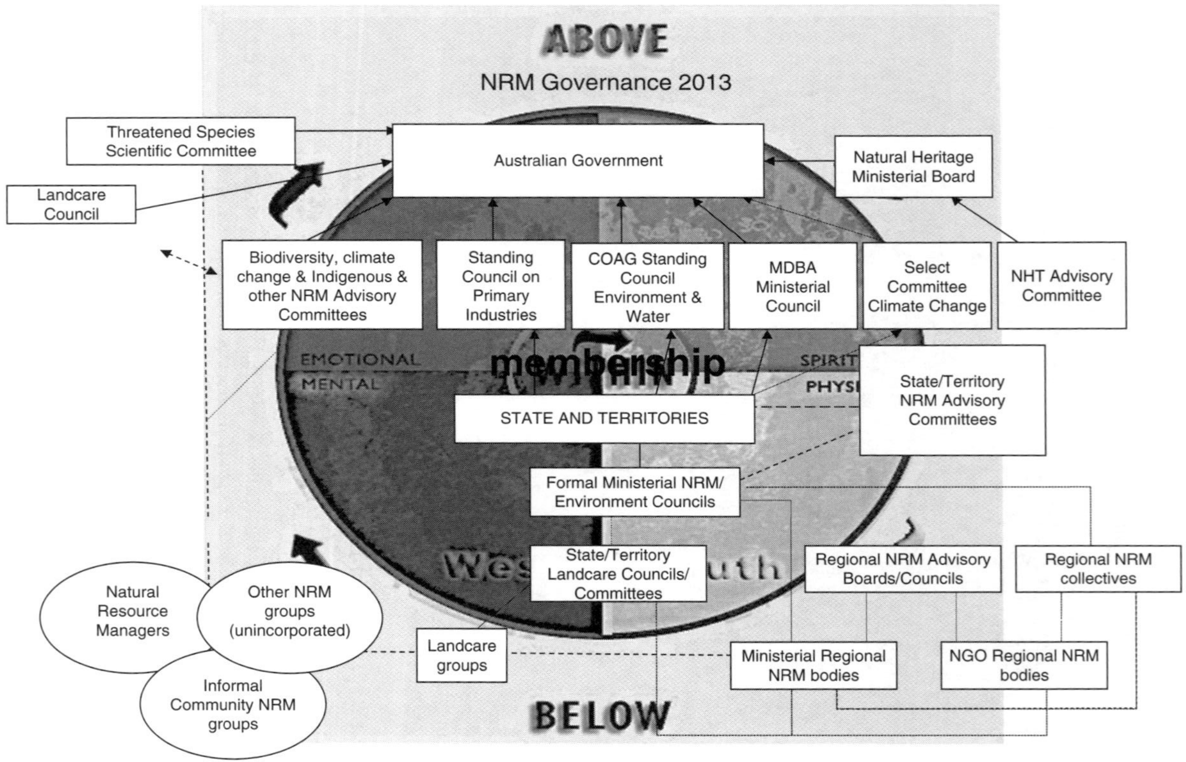

Figure 18.4 Visual interpretation of the cultural and institutional challenges of the two governance systems

COLLABORATION AND CULTURAL CONFLICTS: FUNDAMENTAL PROBLEMS FOR EUROCENTRIC RESEARCHERS

The challenge of shared knowledge and cultural compatibility is well highlighted in natural resources research.

> The white man does not understand the Indian for the reason that he does not understand America. He is too far removed from its formative processes. The roots of the tree of his life have not yet grasped the rock and soil. The white man is still troubled with primitive fears; he still has in his consciousness the perils of this frontier continent, some of its fastness not yet having yielded to his questing footsteps and inquiring eyes. He shudders still with the memory of the loss of his forefathers upon its scorching deserts and forbidding mountaintops. The man from Europe is still a foreigner and an alien. And he still hates the man who questioned his path across the continent. But in the Indian the spirit of the land is still vested; it will be until other men are able to divine and meet its rhythm. Men must be born and reborn to belong. Their bodies must be formed of the dust of their forefathers' bones.[27]

The problems of the absence of 'safe places' to share knowledge and address fundamental cultural differences, and the embedded challenges of power relationships, are pervasive. In *Doing Whitefella research in Blackfella Communities in Australia*[28] authors Rossi, Rynne, and Nelson acknowledge that: 'As "Whitefella" researchers we are presented both with a problem and as a problem', further concluding that within their project efforts they still:

> . . . tended to rely on western systems of knowledge even to challenge our original thinking.

Tuhiwai Smith recognised that:

> . . . researchers from different projects and different research teams can be in and out of the same community (much in the way many government social services are in and out of family homes) showing 'as a collective' little responsibility for the overall impact of their activities. At other levels criticism of individual researchers and their projects is deflected by the argument that those researchers are different in some really significant 'scientific way' from others. How indigenous (sic) communities are supposed to work this out is a mystery.[29]

---

27 Luther Standing Bear (1933).
28 Rossi, Rynne and Nelson (2013).
29 Tuhiwai Smith (2012) 71.

Such statements suggest a need for comprehensive rethinking of the manner of participation including consideration to, and the inclusion of, the following:

- collaborative governance;
- recognition of culture, cultural perspective, and the capital found therein;
- ideas and definitions for what comprises collaboration and the manner of participation that is, Participatory Action Research[30] (PAR) or Community Action Research (CAR); and
- Cultural safety and cultural safety practices.[31]

Often-inadvertent marginalisation and commodification of indigenous peoples' knowledge (including cultural practices and ways of expression) are symptoms of fundamental inconsistencies. Too often the implementation of collaborative governance or knowledge-sharing research requires the cultural governance and cultural practices of Indigenous participants to be altered, if not excluded (see Brown and Bishop, *Chasing our Tails*[32]).

Unspoken albeit important questions emerge. Could it be that accepted research paradigms, by their very nature, create fundamental impediments when aiming to 'empower' Indigenous peoples or rural agrarian communities? How can we create a platform for genuine and balanced participation? Some ideas can be drawn from the attempts of participatory action researchers to ensure equitable collaboration. Kemmis and McTaggart[33] describe the key features of participatory action research as:

> . . . a spiral of self-reflective cycles of the following: Planning a change, Acting and observing the process and consequence of the change, Reflecting on these processes and consequences, Replanning, Acting and observing again, Reflecting again, and so on . . .[34]

Explaining further:

> Participatory action research offers an opportunity to create forums in which people can join one another as coparticipants (sic) in the struggle to remake the

---

[30] Kemmis and McTaggart (2005); Minkler and Wallerstein (2008); Stokols (2006).

[31] Ramsden in Te Whaiti, McCarthy and Durie (eds) (1997). Brascoupe and Waters (2009); Lynam and Young (2000); Aseron *et al.* (2013).

[32] For a deeper understanding of these paradoxical practices see Browne and Bishop (2011).

[33] Kemmis and McTaggart (2005).

[34] Ibid.

> practices in which they interact—forums in which rationality and democracy can be pursued together without an artificial separation ultimately hostile to both.[35]

A community-oriented definition is found in Tuhiwai Smith's *Decolonizing Methodologies*:

> Social research at community level is often referred to as community action research or emancipatory research. Both approaches are models which seek to make a positive difference in the conditions or lives of people.[36]

In describing Stringer,[37] Smith explains that:

> Community action approaches assume that people know and can reflect on their own lives, have questions and priorities of their own, and have skills or sensitivities that can enhance (or undermine) any community based projects.

In the field of environmental law a Community in Action Research (CAR) approach may lead to a more genuine recognition of both First Nations peoples' contribution to earth jurisprudence and environmental justice and to new and fundamentally redefined collaboration efforts. As recognised by D. Smith:

> If we can have decisive action in Indigenous communities, presumably the same is possible within government . . . the case study evidence of the ICG Project[38] indicate that there are communities, organisations and leaders who want decisive action from government, but in partnership and with reform on both sides . . .[39]

Redefining collaboration is critical to sincere discussion about law, governance practice and First Nations peoples. This requires that we think more 'how' our thought processes are, as opposed to 'what' they are. The book *Protecting Indigenous Knowledge and Heritage*, describes:

> . . . the subtle effects of the linguistic and cognitive frameworks created and legitimized by imperialism have displaced the systemic discrimination against Indigenous Peoples during colonial times, and pose the most crucial cultural challenge facing humanity today. Meeting the responsibility of challenging

---

35 Ibid, 563.
36 L. Smith (2012).
37 Stringer (1996).
38 Indigenous Community Governance Project in D. Smith (2008).
39 Ibid.

these frameworks is not just a task for the colonized and the oppressed; it is the defining challenge and the path to a shared and sustainable future for all peoples.[40]

THE RADICAL SUBTLETIES OF DIFFERENCE

The following further examines aspects of the under-recognised complexity of indigenous peoples' language, governance, knowledge and practices. Through language, thought is shaped and transformed into collective actions such as ceremonies, alliances, cooperative events for hunting or planting, or acts that bring peace or cause war. The power of language can shape our perception of the world and indeed the world itself. In *Language, Culture and Personality* Edward Sapir noted it was illusory to think that people adjust to reality without the use of language, or that language was merely a means for solving specific problems of communication.

> The fact of the matter is that the 'real world' is . . . built up on the language habits of the group. . . (and those) worlds in which different societies live are distinct worlds, not merely the same world with different labels attached.[41]

In *Protecting Indigenous Knowledge and Heritage*, authors Sa'ke'j Henderson and Marie Battiste state:

> . . . to insist to analyse Indigenous thought from a Eurocentric point of view is cultural racism and cognitive imperialism.[42]

English is a language of conquest. Many Indigenous peoples' languages have been suppressed. Any claim that scholarship should be conducted in these suppressed languages would fall on deaf ears in academic or policy circles, but language has fundamental implications for the integrity of collaborative enquiry. Henderson states that:

> . . . since Eurocentric thought mediates the entire world through its theories, then there is little possibility for an independent comparison of Eurocentric and Indigenous theories about physical reality.

How can Indigenous peoples have confidence in dialogue that 'must' be conducted in European languages, which does not question the

---

40 Battiste and Henderson (2000).
41 Sapir (1956).
42 Battiste and Henderson (2000).

assumption that the Eurocentric worldview of knowledge is the only legitimate worldview? Under the Sapir/Whorf Hypothesis (the principle of linguistic-relativity: that language influences our thought), a respectful space at the academic table should not require that Indigenous peoples' thoughts be transformed into an English voice.

For First Nations peoples a foundational cultural feature that shapes action, respect and a balanced presence upon the Earth are ceremonial rituals. Rituals help forge an integrated and balanced lifestyle. Rituals aid Indigenous peoples to understand their position in the world as not one of dominance, but rather the realisation of one's responsibility in maintaining balance within the world. When imbalances occurred, cultural mechanisms, or rituals, were performed to restore balance. By living in this way the people stood in a blessed relationship within creation.

Richly encoded narratives of oral traditions served as a multidimensional vehicle of learning. Through ancient narratives the people's world had greater meaning, fostering worldviews and practices that engendered unique relationships to the environment. Thus in this way Indigenous peoples have come to understand the forces that bring *balance*, *change*, *order*, and *disorder*. From within encoded narratives people learn where they come from, how natural phenomena came to be and how cultural material items were acquired and should be used. Stories also taught the necessary tools to survive, teaching about healing ceremonies, prayer, dances, medicine plants and conflict resolution. Stories, like libraries, help form the foundation for what tribal people come to understand is their responsibility; for individuals, community and nature.

TRANS DISCIPLINE: COMMUNAL SYSTEMS OF GOVERNANCE.

Government systems tend to be rigid, governing through strict interpretation of written codes. Community systems of governance are more flexible, organic and work more holistically to maintain the well-being of the community and its individual members, seeking sustainability within the world. Indigenous peoples' forms of justice attempted to resolve problems, maintaining the values and integrity of the society. The ability to redefine relationships through authority enabled the reduction of conflicts and tensions, promoting individual well-being for the greater good of the community. When tribes came together primary principles were understood, ensuring that members followed protocols for proper conduct. It was understood that if people acted properly the tribe prospered, and if they acted inappropriately the tribe suffered. This taught that the tribe was greater than the sum of its individual members, who must not behave in any way that would disrupt balance with the world.[43] Among Plains Indians (and many Indigenous societies) justice was corrective, not vindictive, using measures equal to only what was necessary for individual reformation. Once this occurred the individual was reincorporated back into the community.

An example of the subtle and unique nature of Indigenous people's governance that involved war and peace dates back to the 1840s, long before any reservations existed on the Plains. A group of Cheyenne out on a horse raid against the Kiowa and Comanche had stopped for rest and provisions at a large encampment of their allies, the Arapaho. While there a group of Apache, who were allies of the Kiowa and Comanche, had gone to the lodge of an Arapaho leader called Buffalo Bull (Heneecee) to inform him that the Kiowa, Comanche and Apache desired peace with the Arapaho and Cheyenne. Heneecee called for eight Cheyenne to come to his lodge to speak on the matter. When all were assembled he filled his Pipe and offered it. Declining the Pipe, Seven Bulls, who led the Cheyenne war party, said:

> Friend, you know that we are not chiefs. We have no authority to smoke to make peace with these men. We can only carry your message and leave it with our chiefs to decide.[44]

As war leader, he called his warriors back and upon their return to camp he reported the request for peace. The following morning a big double-pitched lodge was set up, and when all was in order Seven Bulls and his warriors were sent for to officially present the matter.

Hesitant to make a ruling, the chiefs turned the decision over to the Dog Soldier society. High Backed Wolf, the presiding head chief, sent a runner to get White Antelope and Little Old Man, the bravest chiefs among the Dog Soldiers. After speaking to the two warriors High Backed Wolf ended with these words:

> Now my friends you go and assemble your Dog Soldiers. Tell them about this matter, and talk it over among them. Let us know what . . . you think is best to be done.[45]

---

43 Hoebel (1978) 18.
44 Llewellyn and Hoebel (1941).
45 Ibid.

White Antelope addressed the Dog Soldiers telling them the problem:

> The chiefs are leaving this matter to us, because we are the strongest of military groups. It is my own thought that our chiefs are in favor of making peace. What do you now think about this?[46]

One of the assembled chiefs proposed that the decision be left to White Antelope and Little Old Man, who both accepted. After discussion they returned to the Council Chiefs and told them it was decided to make peace. All the chiefs stood up, pleased with the decision, and said; Hoohou, hoohou; thank you, thank you.

The complexity of this event displays important aspects of tribal diplomacy that go beyond speeches and discussions. The horse, paramount on the Plains, was an object of status. The Kiowa and Comanche were rich with horses and for Cheyenne youth horses represented a path to glory, recognition, and cultural wealth. Ongoing hostilities (over 50 years) between the Kiowa and Comanche lent greater importance to this decision, which explains the Council Chiefs' hesitancy to resolve the matter on their own. Choosing to turn the decision-making over to the Dog Soldiers turned the seat of authority for decision-making on its head, but once a decision was reached, it was flipped back again without a contentious word. The responsibility of a decision moved from the hands of the Council of Chiefs to the Dog Soldiers, and from the Dog Soldiers to two of their most celebrated warriors, and bound the entire nation.

Throughout the process the authority of the Council of Chiefs was not in question. White Antelope and Little Old Man returned and dutifully handed their decision to the Council of Chiefs who then discharged them. Once in motion the process allowed the Council of Chiefs, as the seat of tribal governance, to neither lose face nor authority. Ultimately the decision for peace came from the Council of Chiefs who delivered it to the tribe through the highest authority, the Priest-Chief. Although no religious ceremony was involved, by having policy flow through the tribe's most sacred leader the decision became sacred law. Thus, in the 1840s, a peace between the Kiowa, Comanche, and Apache (made through the Cheyenne and Arapaho) became a sacred trust. This sophisticated decision-making process, without the need for written rules, was governed through cultural protocols that ensured cohesive decisions that bound all the tribes concerned, and should stand as a lesson of notable worth.

Further highlighting the depth and sophistication of Indigenous

---

46 Ibid.

people's knowledge and governance systems are descriptions from the Northern Territory of Australia. In their work with the Warlpiri Peoples, Holmes and Box, with the guidance of Warlpiri cultural practitioner Wanta Jampijinpa, demonstrate the depth of cultural knowledge and conceptualisation required for understanding and practice.

After giving the introduction to the Warlpiri word for law as *Kuruwarri*, the authors describe the meaning of this *kuruwarri* as:

> . . . the knowledge, beliefs, customs, practices, rules, and regulations of the Warlpiri way of life. It may include rules such as who can marry whom, or the principals of land tenure, as well as ethical and moral edicts such as 'don't be greedy or irresponsible' . . .[47]

In comparing this law to Eurocentric criminal and civil law, and of secular and religious institutions, Holmes and Box note that this law also has a comparable role to scientific knowledge, of explaining the proper functioning of the world:

> . . . the fact that a plant flowers at a particular time of year is said to be the Law for that plant. The reason why people should burn country is said to be the Law for looking after that land. For Warlpiri, the Law is the highest reference for direction about how to live in the world . . .[48]

Quoting Wanta Jampijinpa further:

> The Law is something to follow like a road guide. The Law is a serious thing and it needs to be followed. Wawirri [red kangaroo] is a symbol of the Law. Men cooking a kangaroo is a serious thing . . . even the dance and the ceremony for that one is serious.[49]

The distinctiveness from European approaches, and in particular the interweaving of concerns for culture, religion, resource uses and sustainability with ritual, deserves to be given special consideration. The fundamental differences between, and the sophistication of both the European and the First Nations approaches, suggest that finding the common ground where each can inform the other is not likely to be simple.

Holistic approaches to safeguarding the environment found in First Nations cultures are, by necessity, trans-disciplinary. This is largely

---

47 Jampijinpa, Holmes and Box (2008) 16.
48 Ibid.
49 Jampijinpa, Holmes and Box (2008).

incompatible with the dominant Eurocentric scientific paradigm. As noted in the *Wisdom of Elders*:[50]

> Science's basic strategy for making sense of the natural world is to break it up into conceptual fragments. Faced with the almost overwhelming complexity and size of nature, it prudently opts to engage it not all at once in its fearsome totality but in piecemeal fashion, one digestible morsel at a time . . . they carry out an ingenious and intellectually potent deceit . . .

The authors further state:

> Science's progressive mirroring of the universe in provisional models has paid handsome intellectual, material, and economic dividends, of course, over just a few brief centuries.[51]

WHERE LIES CULTURAL SAFETY?

The clash between a scientific and an Indigenous peoples' understanding of phenomena is often fundamental. First Nations peoples' cultural perspectives arise directly from their close interactions with the natural environment. However, European culture has long been largely removed from direct engagement with the natural world (other than as an exploitable resource), through industrialisation and cultural disassociation. First Nations peoples have suffered from the imposition of this fractured perspective through colonial and industrial practice, for many generations. As noted in *Progress can Kill*:

> . . . indigenous peoples (sic) have become a minority with little influence over policies that affect their lives. Their lands may be taken 'in the national interest' for dams, mines, conservation projects, and other schemes which 'promise development' but leave the lands true owners marginalized.[52]

The report further notes that without a strong voice in the political process or recognition for inalienable legal rights to their lands it is difficult, if not impossible, for First Nations to influence governance or protect their independence.

For First Nations and the descendants of the colonisers to engage with each other genuinely and productively requires an institutional and

---

50 Knudtson and Suzuki (1992) 63, 64.
51 Ibid.
52 Woodman and Grig (2007).

political 'space' where the Eurocentric dominance is reduced, so that First Nations' knowledge and perspectives can be understood. Without 'cultural safety',[53] those expert in traditional understandings of the natural world and man's relationship with it will have little reason, and very little opportunity, to inform non-Indigenous thinking. Non-Indigenous people will be deprived of the opportunity to learn how to sustain and respect the earth.

All of these considerations: political, religious, cultural and pragmatic, highlight the need for 'spaces' that are culturally safe within which to develop the knowledge and negotiate the agreements necessary to incorporate First Nations' vocabularies. Cultural safety is necessary to engender sincere engagement with First Nations peoples (and indeed all peoples) in environmental law and practice. In our work we conduct these important dialogues within "Cultural Safety Circles".[54]

Our research on First Nations' cultural perspectives has found divergent ideas for what comprises cultural safety:

> . . . after the focus group discussions about cultural safety ideas, respondents were potentially challenged on the notion that they initially felt (pre-discussion) that they were 'culturally aware'. . .[55]

Further:

> . . . following the focus group discussions about cultural safety and methodology, participants were more positive in agreement to the use and implementation of a cultural safety circle as a methodology to engender both greater understanding and confidence for feeling culturally safe . . .[56]

There is a continuing need for supportive mechanisms to allow holistic, cross–disciplinary and trans-institutional dialogue. Despite the attempts of environmental law scholars to 'consult' and to reflect indigenous people's perspectives, these efforts may still, albeit unintentionally, perpetuate the marginalisation of First Nations. There is a growing recognition in some disciplines of the need for cultural safety standards and practices within research, work with communities and collaboration.[57] The discourse of environmental law scholarship does not yet emphasise cultural safety as a concern for researchers or as an issue of environmental justice.

---

53 See 32.
54 Aseron *et al.* (2013).
55 Ibid.
56 Ibid.
57 See 32.

For First Nations people steeped in and respectful of First Nations law and lore, dialogue with non-Indigenous people about natural resource issues and governance carries risks that may not be recognised by others. These include the potential for accidental or intentional disrespect (which can trigger serious cultural, social or even physical penalties within Indigenous communities), the risk of being misunderstood or 'mis-translated', and the potential that the time and emotional investment will not yield any greater respect for, nor any application of, sensitive knowledge. Even a well-intended commitment by the European-cultured researcher to listen and try to understand is a trivial counterweight to these personally significant risks. If legal scholars are to be true to expressed values of environmental and social justice, their approach to their own work should treat cultural safety very seriously. Cultural safety practices for building, strengthening and maintaining relationships through environmental law pursuits might therefore be seen as integral to better collaborative outcomes.

> But the basic value of a sustainable society, the ecological equivalent of the Golden Rule, is simple: each generation should meet its needs without jeopardizing the prospects for future generations to meet their own needs.[58]

RECOGNISING ALLIES: A NEW MODEL FOR CONSIDERATON

When Europeans arrived to the shores of Australia and North America, seeking lands teeming with abundant water, plant, animal life and other resources no longer available or accessible in their own countries, the First Nations already had developed structures that allowed this abundance to prosper, as the people prospered. Where the colonizers usurped these Indigenous systems of resource governance, the negative consequences have been, and continue to be, borne by the First Nations' custodians of these bio-diverse 'Gardens of Eden' claimed by Europeans. Ironically, the descendants of European colonizers now grapple with ever-increasing concern to re-create stewardship of the natural environment within their legal, political, economic and social structures.

Time and time again First Nations representatives have petitioned Eurocentric North American and Australian political and legal representatives for acknowledgment of the custodianship embodied within

---

58 Durning (1992).

their cultural and law practices.[59] How much more evidence is needed for the descendants of the colonizers to recognize that the peoples they have disenfranchised hold an essential perspective on the unique environments of Australia and North America? How many statements of Elders, court cases and research will it take for Eurocentric practices to be informed by the knowledge of the First Nations, who have looked after that which is needed by all for millennia?

Most of this chapter has been concerned with 'unpacking' the challenges of achieving an effective discourse about natural resources between First Nations people and Western industrial society. There are many environmental lawyers and social justice activists (as well as First Nations peoples) who wish to bridge the yawning gap between our understandings of the world, and to share knowledge and about how to protect and sustain the Earth. Traditional knowledge and law in respect to how we govern our use of the Earth requires that we have more effective dialogues. Figure 18.5 proposes a new model for consideration, specific to environmental law.

In Australia and North America, First Nations have often suffered unclear or disingenuous environmental governance, environmental law and conflicting local, regional, state and federal arrangements. The living culture of these nations still incorporates a holistic understanding, practice (law) and interconnected 'kinship' structure encompassing the whole of the natural environment. Some environmental law and justice researchers are genuinely committed to learning from First Nations peoples how to manage man's relationship with the earth and how to respect and value First Nations culture and practical knowledge. As this chapter has attempted to explain, fulfilling this commitment requires far more than applying European traditional approaches with their inherent values and power imbalances. It requires even more than a commitment to consult in good faith.

The ideals of environmental justice are fundamentally important, but moving the ideals off the page and into the real world requires practical steps, including new methods for creating new paradigms. Where it may be uncomfortable for researchers or practitioners, it will be more equitable, and more useful, than approaches that perpetuate the largely unfair status quo.

---

59 See for example the history of land rights struggles for First Nations Peoples in Australia (http://www.nfsa.gov.au/digitallearning/mabo/lr.shtml) and the US (https://www.iltf.org/resources/land-tenure-history/court-cases) (both accessed 22 March 2015).

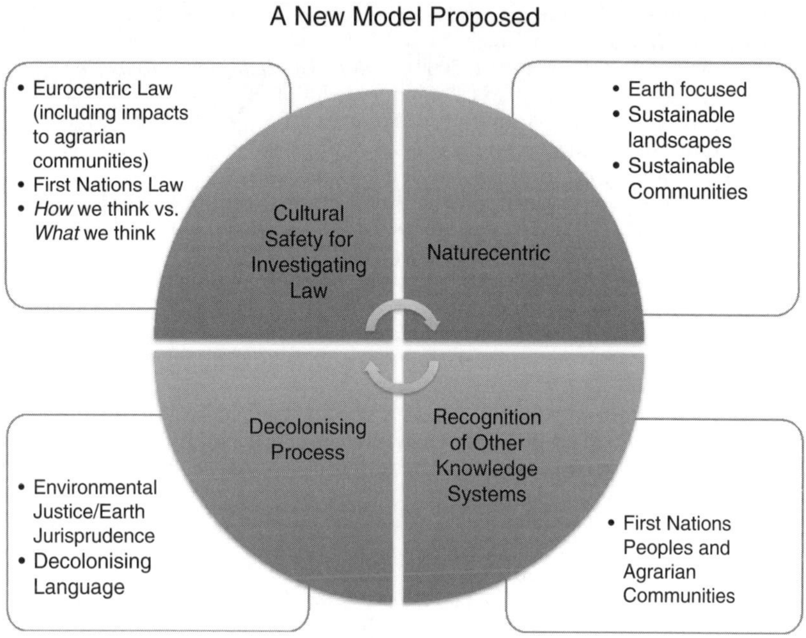

Figure 18.5 Proposed new environmental law model

ACKNOWLEDGEMENTS

For their interest, support and participation, we wish to recognise, with sincere thanks, the Gumbaynggirr, Dhunghutti, Bundjalung, Gomeroi, Haudenosaunee, Blackfeet, Arapaho, and Lakota Nations and the Tamar and Namoi Agrarian Communities.

We also gratefully acknowledge all of our Elders, past and present, for their wisdom, forbearance, maintenance and custodianship of our cultural ways and practices.

REFERENCES

ABARES (2010), *Land Use in Australia at a Glance 2006* (ABARES).

Altman, J. *et al.* (2011), *Indigenous Cultural and Natural Resource Management Futures* (Canberra: ANU).

Aseron, J. *et al.* (2013), 'Cultural Safety Circles And Indigenous Peoples' Perspectives: Inclusive Practices For Participation In Higher Education' 6(4) *Contemporary Issues In Education Research* 409.

Australian Bureau of Statistics (2012), *Regional Population Growth Australia 2011* (Australian Bureau of Statistics).

Battiste, M. and J. Henderson (2000), *Protecting Indigenous Knowledge and Heritage: A global challenge* (Saskatoon: Purich Publishing Ltd).

Bavikatte, K. and D. Robinson (2011), 'Towards a People's History of the Law: Biocultural Jurisprudence and the Nagoya Protocol on Access and Benefit Sharing' 7(1) *Law, Environment and Development Journal* 35.

Bohensky, E. and Y. Maru (2011), 'Indigenous Knowledge, Science, and Resilience: What Have We Learned from a Decade of International Literature on "Integration"' 16 *Ecology and Society* 6.

Brascoupe, S. and C. Waters (2009), 'Cultural Safety Exploring the Applicability of the Concept of Cultural Safety to Aboriginal Health and Community Wellness' 5 *International Journal of Indigenous Health* 6.

Brown, R. (2003), *Rescuing a Planet under Stress and a Civilisation in Trouble* (New York: W.W. Norton & Company).

Browne, A. and B. Bishop (2011), 'Chasing Our Tails: Psychological, Institutional and Societal Paradoxes in Natural Resource Management, Sustainability, and Climate Change in Australia' 47 *American Journal of Community Psychology* 354.

Campbell, T. (1996), 'Co-management of Aboriginal Resources' 22(1) *Information North*.

Chaloux, A. and S. Paguin (2013), *Working Paper: Water resource management and North American green paradiplomacy: the case of the Great Lakes–St. Lawrence River Basin* (The Canada Research Chair in International and Comparative Political Economy).

Churchill, W. (2011), 'A Travesty of a Mockery of a Sham: Colonialism as Self Determination in the UN Declaration on the Rights of Indigenous Peoples' 20 *Griffith Law Review* 526.

Climate Commission (2013), *The Critical Decade 2013 Climate Change Science, Risks and Responses* (Climate Commission Secretariat).

Dalai Lama (1992), 'Address to the Parliamentary Earth Summit (Global Forum) of the United Nations Conference on Environment and Development (UNCED)' (His Holiness the 14th Dalai Lama: The Office of His Holiness the Dalai Lama), accessed 22 March 2015 at http://www.dalailama.com/messages/environment/global-environment.

Das Gupta, A. (2011), 'Does Indigenous Knowledge have anything to deal with Sustainable Development?' 7 *Antrocom Online Journal of Anthropology* 57.

Davis, M. (2008), 'Bridging the Gap or Crossing a Bridge? Indigenous Knowledge and the Language of Law and Policy' in W. Reid *et al.* (eds), *Bridging Scales and Knowledge Systems: Concepts and Applications in Ecosystem Assessments* (Washington, DC: Island Press).

Durning, A. (1992), *How much is enough?* (New York: W.W. Norton & Company).

Environment Australia (2003), *Triple Bottom Line Reporting in Australia: A Guide to Reporting against Environmental Indicators* (Commonwealth of Australia).

Global Reporting Initiative (2013), 'Global Reporting Initiative' Accessed 22 March 2015 at http://www.globalreporting.org/Pages/default.aspx.

Harry, D. (2011), 'Biocolonialism and Indigenous Knowledge in United Nations Discourse' 20 *Griffith Law Review* 702.

Hoebel, E. (1978), *The Cheyenne, Indians of the Great Plains* (2nd edn, Belmont, CA: Wadsworth Publishing Company).

Inter-Government Panel on Climate Change (2013), 'Summary for Policymakers' in *Climate Change 2013: The Physical Science Basis. Contribution of Working Group I to the Fifth Assessment Report of the Intergovernmental Panel on Climate Change* (Cambridge: Cambridge University Press).

International Fund for Agricultural Development (2013), *Smallholders, Food Security and the Environment* (International Fund for Agricultural Development).

Jampijinpa, W., M. Holmes and A. Box. (2008), *Ngurra-kurlu: A Way of Working with Warlpiri People* (Desert Knowledge CRC Report).

Jones, N. (2011), 'Human Influence Comes of Age' 473 *Nature* 133.

Kemmis, S. and R. McTaggart (2005), 'Participatory Action Research: Communicative Action and the Public Sphere' in N. Denzin and Y. Lincoln (eds) (2005), *The Sage Handbook of Qualitative Research* (3rd edn, Thousand Oaks, CA: Sage Publications).

Ki-moon, B. (2012), *Secretary-General's remarks at United Nations Global Compact High-Level Luncheon* (United Nations).

Knudtson, P. and D. Suzuki (1992), *Wisdom of the Elders* (Sydney: Allen and Unwin Pty Ltd).

Llewellyn, K. and E. Hoebel (1941), *The Cheyenne Way, Conflict and Case Law in Jurisprudence* (Norman: University of Oklahoma Press).

Luther Standing Bear (1933), *Land of the Spotted Eagle* (Lincoln: University of Nebraska Press).

Lynam, M. and R. Young (2000), 'Towards the Creation of a Culturally Safe Research Environment' 4 *Health* 5.

Markwell Consulting (2011), *Summary Report – Caring for our Country Review Indigenous Forum* (Australian Government).

May, K. (2010), *Indigenous Cultural and Natural Resource Management and the Emerging Role of the Working on Country Program* (Centre for Aboriginal Economic Policy Research, Australian National University).

Millenium Ecosystem Assessment Board (2005), *Ecosystems and Human Well-being*. (Washington DC: Island Press)

Minkler, M. and N. Wallerstein (eds) (2008), *Community-based Participatory Research for Health: From Process to Outcomes* (San Francisco, CA: Wiley).

Nature Editorial (2011), 'The Human Epoch' (Nature Publishing Group, a division of Macmillan Publishers Limited. All Rights Reserved.) 473 *Nature* 254.

Ramsden, I. (1997), 'Cultural Safety: Implementing the Concept the Social Force of Nursing and Midwifery' in P, Te Whaiti, M. McCarthy and A. D. (eds), *Mai i Rangiatea: Maori wellbeing and development* (Auckland: Auckland University Press).

Robins, L. and P. Kanowski, (2011), '"Crying for our Country": eight ways in which "Caring for our Country" has undermined Australia's regional model for natural resource management' 18 *Australasian Journal of Environmental Management* 88.

Rossi, A., S. Rynne and A. Nelson (2013), 'Doing Whitefella Research in Blackfella Communities in Australia: Decolonizing Method in Sports Related Research' 65 *Quest* 116.

Sapir, E. (1956), *Culture, Language and Personality* (Los Angeles: University of California Press).

Smith, D. (2008), 'From Collaboration to Coercion: a Story of Governance Failure, Success and Opportunity in Australian Indigenous Affairs' in J. O'Flynn and

J. Wanna (eds), *Collaborative Governance: A new era of public policy in Australia* (Canberra: ANU ePress).
Smith, L. (2012), *Decolonizing Methodologies: Research and Indigenous Peoples* (2nd edn, London: Zed Books).
Stapp, D. and M. Burney (2002), *Tribal Cultural Resource Management: The Full Circle to Stewardship* (Lanham, MD: AltaMira Press).
State of the Environment 2011 Committee (2011), *Australian State of the Environment 2011* (Commonwealth of Australia).
Stoainoff, N. (2012), 'Navigating the Landscape of Indigenous Knowledge – A Legal Perspective Intellectual Property Forum' 90 *Intellectual Property Forum* 23.
Stokols, D. (2006), 'Towards a Science of Transdisciplinary Action Research' 38 *American Journal of Community Psychology* 63.
Stringer, E. (1996), *Action Research: A handbook for practitioners* (Sage, California).
Tuhiwai Smith, L. (2012), *Decolonizing Methodologies: Research and Indigenous Peoples* (2nd edn, London and New York: Zed Books Ltd).
United Nations (1992), *The Rio Declaration on Environment and Development* (United Nations Conference on Environment and Development).
United Nations (2002), *Report of the World Summit on Sustainable Development.*
United Nations (2009), *State of the World's Indigenous Peoples.*
United Nations (2012), *The Future We Want.*
White Eyes, C *et al.* (2012), 'The Black Hills are Not for Sale' *Indian Country Today* (13 December) Opinion available at http://indiancountrytodaymedianetwork.com/ (accessed 22 March 2015).
Williams, J. (2007), 'Success Attributes of Regional NRM systems in Australia' (Doctorate, University of Queensland).
Williams J. (2013), 'Credit Makers and Credit Takers: Issues of Equity in Australian Government NRM Programs' *He Tapuwae: The Search for Environmental Justice* 11th Annual Colloquium of the IUCN Academy of Environmental Law, Hamilton NZ 24–28 June, 2013.
Williams, J., R. Beeton and G. McDonald (2008), 'Success Attributes of Regional Natural Resource Management' 3 *International Journal of Sustainable Development and Planning* 203.
Woodman, J. and S. Grig (2007), *Progress Kills* (London: Survival International).
WWF (2010), *Living Planet Report 2010: Biodiversity, Biocapacity and Development.*

Index